Dada and
Surrealist Performance

UMETID

Annabelle Henkin Melzer

The Johns Hopkins University Press
Baltimore and London

Originally published in a hardcover edition by UMI Research Press, 1980
Johns Hopkins Paperbacks edition, 1994

The Johns Hopkins University Press
2715 North Charles Street
Baltimore, Maryland 21218-4319
The Johns Hopkins Press Ltd., London

Library of Congress Cataloging-in-Publication Data will be found at the end of this book.

A catalog record for this book is available from the British Library.

ISBN 0-8018-4845-8

To my parents
Judith and Eleazar Winograd

Contents

List of Illustrations

Acknowledgments

For permission to reproduce photographs from their books or collections I thank: Roger Cardinal and Robert Short for the photo of the group of Paris Dadas, reproduced from their book *Surrealism: Permanent Revelation;* Arthur A. Cohen for the Sonia Delaunay photos, which appeared in his book, *Sonia Delaunay;* the Dance Collection, Lincoln Center for the Performing Arts, for the Laban/Wigman photos: illustration 12; illustrations 13, from Hans Brandenburg, *Der Moderne Tanz* (Munich, Georg Muller, 1917) and 16 (from Brandenburg, 1921 ed.); illustration 19, from André Levinson, *La Danse d'Aujourd'hui* (Paris: Editions Ducherte et Van Buggenhundt, 1929); and illustration 20, from Rudolph von Laban, *Die Welt des Tanzers* (Stuttgart: Verlag von Walter Weifert, 1922). I thank Dr. and Mrs. Hans J. Kleinschmidt for permission to reproduce portraits of Emmy Hennings and Hugo Ball, the photograph of Ball's performance of "Karawane," posters from performances at the Galerie Dada, Maison de l'Oeuvre, Salle Gaveau, and St. Julien le Pauvre, and text from *L'amiral cherche une maison à louer* and from "Ursonate." I thank Timothy Baum for photographs of the Maurice Barrès trial and of Paris Dadaists playing games of chance.

In addition, I thank the Depero Museum, Rovereto, Italy, for permission to reproduce Depero's costumes for *Machine of 3000*, the Musée National d'Art Moderne for permission to reproduce Marcel Janco's *Mask* (1919), and SPADEM/VAGA and the Département des Arts du Spectacle, Bibliothèque de l'Arsenale, for photographs of characters and sets from Apollinaire's *Les Mamelles de Tirésias*, Jarry's *Ubu Roi*, Cocteau's *Le Boeuf sur le toît* and *Les Mariés de la Tour Eiffel*, and Tzara's *Le Coeur à Gaz*, and for Pierre Albert-Birot's design for a "théâtre nunique."

My thanks as well to *Theatre Quarterly* for permission to reproduce material of mine originally published with them ("The Premier of Apollinaire's *The Breasts of Tirésias* in Paris," *Theatre Quarterly*, Vol. VII, No. 27, 1977); as well as to ARTFORUM ("Dada Performance at the Cabaret Voltaire," November, 1973; "The Dada Actor and Performance Theory," December, 1973), and *Comparative Drama* ("Louis Aragon's *The Mirror Wardrobe One Fine Evening:* a play of the surrealist "époque de sommeil," Spring, 1977), for the same service.

I am indebted to Mme. M.F. Christout at the Bibliothèque de l'Arsenal, Paris, not only for permission to reproduce rare materials from the Bibliothèque Nationale, Département des Arts du Spectacle's distinguished theatre collection, but for her continuing warm and attentive concern with my work.

My special thanks to my teachers and friends Bernard Beckerman and Albert Bermel, under whose guidance I began this research and who, through the years, have always been available to listen, advise and encourage; to Savta Yehudit for the special care and caring she gave to two generations of her "daughters"; and for quiet rooms in borrowed houses, for lakes with slow sunsets, for festive meals to raise the spirits and hours of playing with Natalie, to Susan, David, Barbara, Alan, to Nurit and Anita. To Yehuda, my love, which is different than thank-you, for all the kinds of being there.

A.H.M.
Jerusalem 1980

Introduction

We feel the need of a dramatic art that will be
new . . . now it seems that a number of our
contemporaries are beginning to be weary of
always seeing plays divided into three or four
acts . . . Excess, even madness, is less boring
than banality . . . Those who want to break
the old rules always deserve the most respect-
full attention.

Nozière, *Le Temps,* June 23, 1918

The initial impetus for a look at the theatre of dada and surrealism came from the chance reading of Antonin Artaud's sketch *Le Jet de Sang.* The piece was barely four pages long but its impact was considerable. A hurricane separates a young girl and a young man who have been reciting to each other, "I love you and everything is beautiful," live pieces of body fall to the stage, and a nurse holds her swollen breasts in both hands. "Shit, what's the matter with you?" asks the knight who accompanies her. The nurse lets loose her breasts and releases an army of scorpions from under her dress. They swarm over the knight's penis until it swells up and bursts, becoming glassy and shining like the sun.

The play did not evoke a distinct emotional response. To call it "shocking" would be too strong; "confusing" is appropriate, and perhaps "disturbing." I could not readily understand the piece and yet was loath to let it go. A year later, after the subject of this essay had already shaped itself and I was in Paris researching, the librarian at the Bibliothèque de l'Arsenal said to me, "Votre sujet est séduisant." I still the find the material seductive and present this essay echoing Breton's statement, "criticism can exist only as a form of love."

The Artaud play was written in Paris in 1924. The search for its antecedents led back through the work of the group of young surrealists who, in the early 1920s, clustered around the magazine *Littérature,* past Picasso, Satie, and the erotic Diaghilev ballets with their new plastic sense of the stage, to Tristan Tzara and Hugo Ball who danced with masks and assaulted their audiences at the Cabaret Voltaire in Zurich in 1916. It brought into focus a period of theatrical history which has been almost completely neglected as critics and theatre historians have again and again jumped from Jarry to Artaud.

How to fill the gap? What I thought I was looking for was material that would substantiate my intuition that the surrealists had done "wild" things on the stage. I was looking for Dali on a platform. The first weeks of research in Paris were a nightmare: it was June, Aragon had refused to see me saying he was no longer interested in the subject, Hugnet was on vacation and unavailable, Jean Vilar died before he could keep our appointment. I was so indebted to Soupault for according me an interview, that I brought him roses. The tape recorder wouldn't work, he coughed a lot, remembered little and was the first of a series of people to tell me, "I've written it all down, read my letters and memoirs." I am, however, forever grateful to him, for he did sit with me and somehow made me feel that even if I began with only five particles of information, I might be able to put them together into a whole.

Within six weeks the project had clarified itself. What I had envisioned as surrealist performance was actually dada. The "wild" theatrics were theirs. The surrealists, more inhibited, wrote the texts, lived the disjuncted dream images on paper, but could not alone find the ways to actualize them in performance. I had expected surrealist performance to be surreal; instead, the surreal was in dada. There was no doubt that one had to begin with Tzara.

Historical periods do not come with labels. What began to emerge from the search for a theatre of dada and surrealism was a clear sequence of events whose outline framed an epoch of theatre: the founding of the Cabaret Voltaire in Zurich in 1916 and the experiments in performance done there and at the Dada Gallery by Tzara and Ball; the avant-garde theatre experiments conducted in Paris at the same time: *Les Mamelles de Tirésias* and *Parade;* Tzara's arrival in Paris to join Breton and Soupault (who had already written a play by the method of automatic writing); and the Paris-dada manifestations which erupted again and again from 1920-1922, forcing the young *Littérature* poets into performing roles which proved antithetical to their dispositions. Finally—the rupture between Tzara and Breton which effectively signaled the demise of dada and which freed surrealism to choose or not choose performing as its preferred mode of expression.

Tzara's emphasis on performance had been unrelenting. There is hardly a theatrical "innovation" perpetrated on our contemporary audiences by the environmental and psycho-physical theatres, the happening and the event, which had not been explored before 1924 by Tzara, his cohorts and disciples. The iconographic fantasy level of the dada plays and performances, the plastic quality of the staging, the innovations in costume and sound, the flow of energies between performer and audience were not equaled in the contemporary theatre until the 1960s. The emphasis on process and spontaneity in the creative act released a set of energies which blew the world of performance wide open.

To speak then of dada and surrealist performance is to describe the theatre of a particular idiom and not simply of a particular clique or school. It is to follow a type of performance which began in Zurich in 1916 and ended the first phase of its development in Paris by 1924: performance work which was highly innovative and experimental, and which was carried out within the framework of a closely knit and sympathetic group. This is true of Tzara and the Zurich dadas (despite the differences with Ball) and of Tzara and the young surrealists in Paris (despite their eventual altercations). It is artistic work done on the model of what Cocteau, in his preface to *Les Mariés de la Tour Eiffel,* called the "universal athlete":

> A theatrical piece ought to be written, presented, costumed, furnished with musical accompaniment, played and danced, by a single individual. This universal athlete does not exist. It is therefore important to replace the individual by what resembles an individual most: a friendly group.

By 1924, the friendly group had dissolved. Surrealism had clearly separated itself from dada and was entering the period of numerous arguments regarding philosophy and political action. By 1924, most of the plays that the members of the surrealist group were to write had been written, and the group had ceased to function as an acting-producing unit. After 1924, those surrealist plays produced were done by avant-garde theatres outside the periphery of the group, by professional actors, and often with the group's outspoken disapproval. Aragon's *Au pied du mur,* scheduled for production at the Vieux-Colombier in June of 1925, was successfully sabotaged by the surrealists, and the author's *L'Armoire à glace un beau soir,* was performed at the *Théâtre Art et Action* in March, 1926 after Aragon had denied permission for its presentation. Vitrac's *Les Mystères de l'Amour* opened the *Théâtre Alfred Jarry* in 1927 to the hoots and catcalls of the surrealists, while Vitrac himself, along with Artaud, had already been banished from the surrealist circle for yielding to what Breton considered commercial instincts in wanting to produce surrealist plays in the framework of a professional theatre. The attempts of both the *Théâtre Art et Action* and the *Théâtre Alfred Jarry* to produce surrealist texts merits a full study of its own. After 1924, however, the surrealist group was no longer performance oriented and the clique of young poets that had studied under Tzara fragmented and split. The *Bureau des Recherches Surréalistes* closed its doors, Soupault was expelled from the movement for engaging in "la stupide aventure littéraire," Breton became the sole editor of *La Revolution Surréaliste,* and the movement began to take a decidedly political turn. By 1925, then, the type of performance which had its beginnings with Tzara and the Cabaret Voltaire group in Zurich had stopped to catch its breath. During the next 40 years it would rear its head in the works of individual theatre-people of the avant-garde. Not until the 1960s, however, would it again find the soil in which it could grow most fertilely: that of performing groups such as the Living Theatre and the Open Theatre or the theatre of happenings made by an intimate group of artists and their friends.

Coming to the theatre of dada and the early surrealist sketches 50 years after their production poses some problems. The clearest one is technical: the difficulty in obtaining primary source material and of validating information largely gleaned from personal memoirs and recollective essays. Tzara's recollections of his participation at the *Premier vendredi de Littérature,* for example, are as follows:

> As for me, announced as "Dada," I read aloud a newspaper article while an electric bell kept ringing so that no one would hear what I said. That was very badly received by the public who had become exasperated and shouted: "Enough! Enough!"

Georges Ribemont-Dessaignes recalls that,

> . . . when Tzara, after announcing a manifesto, merely read a vulgar article taken out of some newspaper while the poet Paul Eluard and Theodore Fraenkel, a friend of Breton, hammered on bells, the public began to grow indignant and the matinée ended in an uproar.

and Georges Hugnet writes,

> Tzara read a newspaper story, which he called a poem, accompanied by an inferno of bells and rattles. Naturally, the audience was exasperated and began to whistle.

The slightly differing versions of the same event make any attempt to reconstruct the evenings of dada and surrealist theatre a difficult task. In my interview with Soupault, the then 75-year-old former surrealist was hard put to it to remember much specific information concerning the years of his 20s. What I have relied on in my descriptions of the many performance events were the numerous contemporary newspaper articles and reviews collected in files at the Bibliothèque de l'Arsenal. Labelled *Dada,* or *Guillaume Apollinaire,* or *Surrealism,* the small hand-sewn notebooks, filled with pasted, yellowed newsprint, yielded testimony: the balloons were "yellow" and the audience shouted "Chut, alors," well into the evening.

There is, however, no such thing as pure description. Any description is theory-laden and my own bias here is apparent if only in the choice of material and the structuring of it. I come to the material heavily influenced by the theatre of the 60s. I have participated in happenings, and am sensitive to assaults on the audience and to attempts to shock. Being a product of the 60s "indecent" exposure of the unconscious, I find the theatrical "tantrums" of dada and surrealism affirming rather than shocking. The passage of time since these events has played its part as well. Such shocks as the dada-surrealists attempted to perpetrate on a usually placid audience are no longer repeatable—the anti-artistic value the dadas used to possess has gone back to zero. However, the performance techniques, which Tzara brought to the founders of surrealism merit investigation on their own as part of a daring and innovative chapter in the history of theatre.

The first part of the essay therefore traces the development of certain performance techniques in Zurich through the work of Tzara, Arp, Ball, Janco, Huelsenbeck and Hennings at the Cabaret Voltaire and the Dada Gallery (1916-1919). It includes a discussion of the relationship between dada and futurist performance, for the techniques of the two movements are striking in their resemblances. The next chapters follow the meeting of dada performance (brought to Paris by Tzara in 1920) with the world of the Parisian artistic avant-garde and the young *Littérature* (later surrealist) poets: Breton, Soupault, Aragon, and their entourage. What is noteworthy at this point is that the theatre had erected such strong bastions that the avant-garde theatre person came to his work almost uniquely from the literary and art movements and not out of the theatre itself. Still within the theatre world proper, there were a number of shock-producing performances. Included among them were Jarry's *Ubu Roi*, Apollinaire's *Les Mamelles de Tirésias* and the Cocteau-Picasso-Satie *Parade*, (all of which antedated Tzara's arrival in the French capital); Picasso's *Mercure*, and Cocteau's *Le Boeuf sur le toît*. Almost all of these were seen by the surrealists and no doubt influenced their sense of theatre. I conclude with a look at some of the plays of Breton, Soupault and Aragon, which show that a strong surrealist sense of the stage existed even before the arrival of Tzara. Although his influence on the young *Littérature* poets was undeniable, the path that would be taken by the surrealist sketch was already evident in the writing of *Les Champs Magnétiques* (1919). Tzara himself could not sustain the scheme of the dada text and had moved by 1924 to write a pseudo-avant-garde play based on the models of boulevard dramaturgy.

A conceptual problem remains: just what is this "performance" that I set about describing? The problem of reconstructing performance is a serious one, and one that has hardly been dealt with. Performance is "event," not object; to dissect a text alone is not sufficient. The whole process of reconstruction, therefore, becomes more individual, more creative. Must I look at the text? Yes! Are the personalities of the performers important? Yes! Is the cultural history relevant? Absolutely! It would be misleading then, on the part of the reader, to expect after the treatment of what is deemed relevant in the text, on stage, in the audience, and in the personalities of the artists, a separate discussion entitled "performance." Instead he is called upon to regard the assembled material in a way not unlike the way one looks in science upon evidence for the confirmation of a hypothesis. For all one can fairly understand by performance is what the critic-researcher-author has proposed as a reconstruction of "It," the event.

Although Breton was undoubtedly right in his insistence on the connection between criticism and love, love is after all a necessary but not a sufficient condition for sound critical work (as Sartre clearly argued in his challenge—"Qu'est-ce que la littérature,"—to the surrealist philosophy). The danger in dancing in the ring of *l'amour fou* is that one may become too passionate. I have tried in this essay to love without being possessive and to offer criticism as a lover's service.

Le premier vendredi de *Littérature:*
Tzara's Arrival in Paris and a Look Backward

What's become of (if you please)
all the glory that or which was Greece
all the grandja
that was dada

e.e. cummings

Illustration 1   A group of Paris Dadas, ca. 1921. Paul Eluard is in the center of the second row with Tristan Tzara at his left and Georges Ribemont-Dessaignes at his right. In the front row Philippe Soupault stands on the left, Benjamin Peret is wearing the monocle, and the workman on the right is an authentic workman

Source: Roger Cardinal and Robert Short, *Surrealism, Permanent Revelation*

Although there was much excitement in anticipation of Tristan Tzara's arrival in Paris, no one was waiting for him at the station. Alone, on January 17, 1920, he made his way to the apartment of Germaine Everling and Francis Picabia, following an invitation of Picabia's made in Zurich a year before. André Breton, Paul Eluard, Louis Aragon and Philippe Soupault rushed there to see him a few hours later. The real Tzara did not quite live up to the vision of the "messiah" they had expected,

> He was small, slightly stooped, swinging two short arms at whose ends hung chubby hands. His skin was waxen, his myopic eyes seemed, from behind his monocle, to be seeking out a fixed point upon which to light. He was continually throwing back, with a mechanical gesture, a long lock of black hair which fell across his forehead.[1]

And he spoke a bad French. Even the word "dada" emerged through his thick Rumanian accent like the crackling of a machine-gun.

Despite the initial disappointment, no one was willing to dismiss Tzara out of hand. His experience with dada in Zurich was at that point indispensable to the young founders of *Littérature,* for the journal was in a rut and the decision had just been made to take the material of the publication more directly to the audience. Breton, Soupault, Eluard and Aragon had decided on some "action publique." It was to this end that they had planned the first of a series of *matinées* to be scheduled every other week, beginning January 23, 1920. To distinguish them from other such poetic afternoons, some avant-garde painting and sculpture would be shown, and musical selections would be played by the "Groupe des Six." The small room, set with a simple stage, which had been rented in the *Palais de Fêtes (rue Saint-Martin)* was quite suited to the ambiance desired for the program. The "Palais" was a well-known haunt of the young "Littérateurs" who packed its film auditoriums to see the episodes of "Fantômas" and "The Vampires," or the serials of Charlie Chaplin. The rent was cheap and the location, amidst cosmetic and jewelry stores, announced a decided rupture with the loftier recital halls of the Left Bank which usually accommodated the audiences of literary and artistic events.

The desire to include Tzara in this first public event was understandable. Since January 1919, Breton, then 23 years old, had been in correspondence with Tzara who was the same age. They had exchanged poems and photographs and Tzara had quickly assumed the role of demi-god for Breton, and through him, for Soupault and Aragon.

> It is to you today that I turn all my attention . . . We have dedicated two evenings to the rereading of your twenty-five poems. I gaze at your photograph at length.

With Philippe Soupault and Louis Aragon, the day does not pass when we do not speak of you: "Tristan Tzara would like this, or . . ." I wait for you, I wait for nothing more than you.[2]

Between January 6 and 8, 1920, the anticipated time of Tzara's arrival in Paris, Breton went to wait for his mentor five different times at the *Gare de Lyon.* He had by this time already written Tzara about the program proposed for January 23 and had added, "There will be a great need for you at that moment. . . ."[3] Tzara was not only the author of "les vingt-cinq poèmes," the editor of the revue *Dada,* and a founding father of the dada movement, but also the person who, in Zurich, had been experimenting since 1916 with a type of public manifestation which the *Littérature* group was beginning to find seductive. Writing to Picabia almost a year before his arrival in Paris, Tzara noted:

I write to you in a sort of fever because I've finally come upon an idea which will entertain me for a while: the "soirée." There are people who live from one day to the next, me, I live from one amusing idea to the next. . . . In secret I've kept an idea which might make you come to Zurich: a huge "soirée." Now it's becoming a reality. On April 9th in the largest auditorium here (1,000 people). It's the first time I regret not being able to ride a bicycle; I would like to go out on stage on a bicycle— get off, read, get on, exit. Curtain. Instead I'll hire someone who will parade about the stage while I read. Arp dreads excitement: We're constructing a big cone on stage, bearing the inscription: "Arp," and at the moment that he fires a shot, a red tongue emerges from an opening and the cone, that is to say the person inside, starts to read his poems.[4]

Picabia answered:

I would have loved to come see your "soirée" in Zurich: we'll do some in Paris, come very quickly.[5]

And so the *Littérature* group eagerly awaited the man who could make their new *matinées* a success. With his arrival, work on dada-surrealist performance in Paris had begun.

In addition to its particular importance for Picabia, Breton, and their entourage, Tzara's name on the program would alone have sufficed to fill the small hall. The *Littérature* group was not unaware of the financial implications of its ventures and of the value of "name attractions" on the playbill. Breton in his *Entretiens* relates that:

the costs of renting auditoriums were high, we were for the most part, very poor and the price of the tickets was adjusted so as just to cover the costs, that is if all the seats were sold.[6]

But Tzara agreed to participate only on condition that his appearance on the program remain secret until the last moment and that the program, which he considered naive and banal, undergo certain changes. Where in this anti-literary event was the unexpected "geste" which would surprise and jostle the audience and completely alter the mood of the program? Picabia suggested a bomb; Soupault, the washing of hands either alone or with the participation of the audience. Tzara finally declared that he himself would both effect and embody the shock element. Fearful of the impact of his heavy Roumanian accent on the audience,[7] he decided to read a fragment from a newspaper with bells sounded at the same time, to prevent the audience from clearly discerning his voice.

On Thursday, January 22, 1920, the newspaper *L'Intransigeant* carried an announcement of a lecture by André Salmon on "La Crise du Change" for the following day. The title of the lecture was ambiguous because of the recent devaluation of the franc, for though it could be interpreted as a lecture on economic questions, neither the "crise" nor the "change" had anything to do with economics. A precedent however had been set for later fallacious announcements which would precede other dada manifestations. The announcement had its desired effect. Neighborhood entrepreneurs flocked to hear Salmon speak on the franc while more knowledgeable journalists and members of the avant-garde came to witness the *première* of Paris dada.

The program, as it appears in print, is in no way irregular for a cultural afternoon: a brief lecture, the reading of some poems, musical selections, and the showing of the works of a number of young artists.

1. André Salmon will lecture on "the crisis of change."
2. Poems by MM. Max Jacob, André Salmon, Pierre Reverdy, Blaise Cendrars, Maurice Raynal, read by MM. Pierre Bertin, Marcel Herrand, Jean Cocteau and Pierre Drieu la Rochelle.
3. Presentation of works by Juan Gris, Georges Ribemont-Dessaignes, Georges de Chirico, Fernand Leger, Francis Picabia, Jacques Lipschitz.
4. Poems by MM. Francis Picabia, Louis Aragon, Tristan Tzara, André Breton, Jean Cocteau, read by MM. Pierre Bertin, Marcel Herrand, Théodore Fraenkel, Louis Aragon, Tristan Tzara, André Breton, Pierre Drieu la Rochelle.
5. Music. Works by MM. Erik Satie, Georges Auric, Darius Milhaud, Francis Poulenc, Henri Cliquet. At the piano Mlle. Marcelle Meyer and the composers.
6. Poems by MM. Georges Ribemont-Dessaignes, Philippe Soupault, Pierre Drieu la Rochelle, Paul Dermée, Pierre Albert-Birot, read by MM. Pierre Bertin, Marcel Herrand, Louis Aragon, André Breton, Jean Cocteau, Pierre Drieu la Rochelle and Théodore Fraenkel.[8]

The public, however, was in for a few surprises. The small stage at the *Palais des Fêtes* still bore the set pieces abandoned by an amateur performing group and Tzara and his friends, not at all unhappy with the eclectic setting, left it in its state of half-salon, half-forest. Completely unrelated to this environment, the program proceeded. André Salmon led off with his lecture "The crisis of change," speaking not on an economic question but on the reversal of values in literature since the Symbolist period. This first switch did not elicit the response that had been hoped for from the audience: "no one protested, one even heard some polite applause." The reading of the first group of poems proceeded in similar calm. Pierre Bertin and Marcel Herrand, two professional actors, had joined the dadas for the reading and perhaps unwittingly lent the program an unwanted air of dignity.[9] It was not until well into the "art" segment that the *Littérature* group confronted its first response to dada. After Breton read a piece about the works of Léger, Gris, and de Chirico, and several canvases and sculptures were shown, he introduced onto the stage Picabia's painting entitled "Le Double Monde." The painting appeared wrapped in a carton on which were painted a confusion of black enameled lines and the words "Top" (on the bottom), "Bottom" (across the top), "Fragile," "Destination: Home," and other such confusing and meaningless designations. Across the carton in bold red letters the obscene pun "L.H.O.O.Q." appeared in public for the first time.[10] The audience barely had time to respond to this effrontery when Breton wheeled out a blackboard on which there was a "painting" and several inscriptions in chalk, among them the painting's title "Riz au nez." The blackboard painting remained in its original form only long enough for the public to see it when Breton erased it—"the picture was valid for only two hours."[11] Such ephemeral validity brought the audience to further anger and through the next few events they were alternately calmed and goaded into fury. Musical selections by "les Six" were played to subdue the distressed crowd. People in masks then recited a disjointed poem by Breton. Further anger. The poems of Radiguet, Soupault, and Aragon were recited until the public subsided into a state of boredom. At this point Aragon announced that Tzara himself was present and would recite one of his works. The dada leader came on stage and began to read Léon Daudet's most recent speech to the French Parliament. No sooner had he begun than Breton and Aragon, off-stage, set to ringing a series of bells it had taken them all morning to set up. The surprise-shock element in Tzara's presentation, a secret to all but the bell-ringers, caught the audience (and most of the cast) unawares. The audienced reacted with outrage: whistles, shouts of "Enough, enough" and insulting invectives, "A Zurich, Au poteau." Even the "Littérateurs," who had wanted dada performance with its elements of grating annoyance and shock, were surprised at how unprepared they themselves were to accept it. André Salmon and Juan Gris, who had helped organize and had participated in the *matinée,* were stunned by Tzara's "act," which they interpreted as a direct attack on their reputations. Aragon, lacking any sense of theatre, attempted to continue the program with a matter-of-fact reading of the works of other poets. The audience filed out around him and he read the last poem, a work by Pierre Albert-Birot, to an empty hall (an inadvertent dada act).

Were we to look at this first Paris-dada evening through Tzara's eyes, "successful numbers" would be those in which the audience got what it didn't expect and reacted violently; "unsuccessful numbers," those in which the audience got what it didn't expect but still reacted politely. The *Littérature* group was not yet sure of what it wanted. Breton, who had been sick that evening but had participated nonetheless, wrote a letter to Picabia and Tzara the next morning, reflecting a deep disappointment with the evening's activities, and embarrassment at having involved Picabia (who was 17 years his senior) in such an event:

> I have such a need to see you again! Last night we got such a surprising reception; there were of course, also a few mistakes made due to lack of experience—I hope that it did not make you too unhappy? How correct Mme. Gabrielle Buffet was, concerning the reactions of the audience. What a lesson. Excuse me for writing so badly, but I just wanted to apologize. I was clearly mistaken in having involved Francis Picabia in this adventure.[12]

Picabia himself was not even present at the performance, beginning what would be his practice of not showing up at any of the dada events though he participated actively in their planning. Ribemont-Dessaignes explains it as a question of stage fright:

> He never physically participated in a manifestation. His nervous state, which he knew to put marvellously well to advantage, according to the circumstances, didn't fare so well being exhibited on stage. That is to say that though he had the courage to write and sign the most audacious proclamations (even against his friends), he had no physical courage.[13]

Tzara's own recollections of the evening conclude on a note of almost precious naiveté.

> An attempt was made to give a futuristic interpretation to my act, but all I wanted to convey was simply that my presence on stage, the sight of my face and my movements ought to satisfy people's curiosity and that anything I might have said really had no importance.[14]

It is difficult here to take Tzara at his word, for the master conferencier was nobody's fool when it came to eliciting the response he wanted from an audience. Writing of the grand Zurich soirée in the *Saal zur Kaufleuten* (9 April 1919) Hans Richter recalls:

> Tzara had organized the whole thing with the magnificent precision of a ring-master marshalling his menagerie of lions, elephants, snakes and crocodiles . . . at just the right point in the evening all hell broke loose. A simultaneous poem by Tristan Tzara, performed by twenty people who did not always keep in time with each other. This was what the audience . . . had been waiting for. Shouts, whistles, chanting in unison,

laughter . . . all of which mingled more or less antiharmoniously with the bellowing of the twenty on the platform. Tzara had skillfully arranged things so that this simultaneous poem closed the first half of the program. Otherwise there would have been a riot at this early stage in the proceedings and the balloon would have gone up too soon.[15]

In evaluating the "premier vendredi" of Paris dada, Ribemont-Dessaignes writes, "the effect produced by the presentation of the pictures and particularly of the manifesto by Tzara showed the group how useless it was by comparison to have Max Jacob's poems read by Jean Cocteau."[16] Everyone had to be "shown" but Tzara. If Aragon was inept, Picabia fearful, Breton disappointed, and Ribemont-Dessaignes a willing student, Tzara was fully aware of where the program had been poorly planned and was merely biding his time before taking over the complete running of the soirées and working them into the mold he had tried and tested in Zurich.

Dada Performance: the Beginnings

I have gone far back, farther back than the
horses of the Parthenon . . . as far back as the
Dada of my babyhood, the good rocking horse.

Paul Gauguin, *Intimate Journals*

Illustration 2   Marcel Janco, *Mask* (1919). Paper, cardboard, twine, gouache, and paste

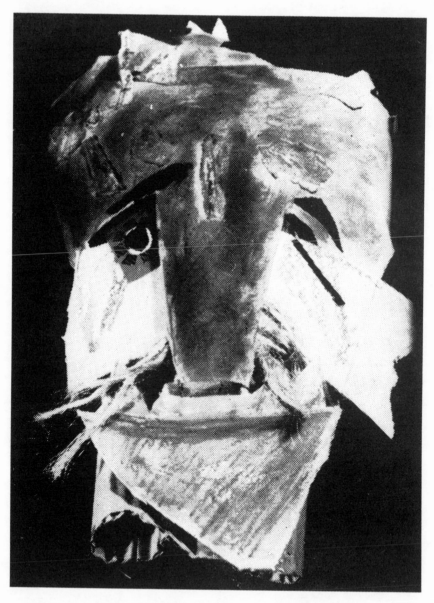

Collection: Musée National d'Art Moderne, Centre Georges Pompidou, Paris

The Cabaret Voltaire: Zurich, 1916

Zurich in 1916 was the "peaceful dead-center of the war."[1] Coming from walled-in and half-starved Germany was like stepping from a closely suffocating room into invigorating and sun-filled air. There were no ration stamps, no "ersatz" food; newspapers printed what they pleased, radical magazines were published and anti-war poems were recited. Seagulls flew in the middle of the city above the Limmatquai. People still had the time not to confuse business cycles with life. Switzerland was "a birdcage surrounded by roaring lions."[2]

And so it was to Zurich that many of the artists of war-torn Europe fled. While housing such established writers as James Joyce, Frank Wedekind and Romain Rolland, Zurich also received the Russian Socialist exiles Lenin and Zinoviev. It was the gathering spot for German expressionists like Ludwig Rubner and Leonard Frank who were pacifist socialists. From Germany as well came Hugo Ball—writer, theater manager, and pianist; Emmy Hennings—cabaret singer; and Richard Huelsenbeck—medical student, from Rumania came the architect and painter Marcel Janco and the young poet Tristan Tzara.[3] From Alsace-Lorraine came Hans Arp, artist, and Yvon Goll, poet. The world of these refugee artists and litterati was a fluid one. At the *Café de la Terrasse*, Lenin played chess; Hans Richter met with his friends, Albert Ehrenstein and the expressionist Ferdinand Hardekopf; and Tzara, Walter Serner and Arp composed their first simultaneous poem. One group, however, composed of the younger expatriates Ball, Hennings, Huelsenbeck, Tzara, Janco and Arp, did separate itself out, first by deeds, and then by the name "dada."[4] For Zurich, the old university town with under 200,000 inhabitants, was just enough at peace to allow the ideological conflicts of its residents to rage: freedom vs. system, spontaneity vs. order, imagination vs. calculation.

George Hugnet, himself a dadaist, claims that there was no contact between Lenin and the dada writers and artists: "They ignored each other, cordially."[5] But Lenin, who lived just opposite the center of dada activity, the Cabaret Voltaire, was conscious enough of their artistic goings-on to state:

> I will not admit that the creations of expressionism, futurism, cubism and all the other -isms are the highest revelations of artistic genius. I do not understand them and they do not give me pleasure.[6]

Lenin was not alone in his feelings. His feelings though were quite in line with dada's expectations of its audience. The dada performers at the Cabaret Voltaire had taken up a path of deliberate provocation and inevitable scandal was to accompany their venture in the theatre.

On February 2, 1916, a notice appeared in the local paper:

Cabaret Voltaire. Under this name a group of young artists and writers has been formed whose aim is to create a center for artistic entertainment. The idea of the cabaret will be that guest artists will come and give musical performances and readings at the daily meetings. The young artists of Zurich, whatever their orientation, are invited to come along with suggestions and contributions of all kinds.

2.II.1916

Given the diverse artistic preoccupations of the Zurich group—artists, poets, writers, theatre-people—the choice of a cabaret setting was most appropriate as a center for experimentation in the arts. It was Hugo Ball who undertook to seek out a location.

I went to Mr. Ephraim, the owner of the Meiri,[7] and said to him: "I beg you Mr. Ephraim, please let me use your place. I should like to start an artists' cabaret" .... I went to some of my acquaintances. "Please give me a picture, a drawing, an etching. I should like to have an exhibition in connection with my cabaret." To the friendly Zurich press, I said: "Help me, I want to start an international cabaret; we'll do some wonderful things." I was given the pictures, the press releases were published. So we had a cabaret.[8]

At six o'clock on the evening of Saturday, February 5, 1916, Ball was still busy hammering and putting up Futurist posters when

there appeared an oriental-looking deputation of four little men with portfolios and pictures under their arms, bowing politely many times. They introduced themselves: Marcel Janco the painter, Tristan Tzara, Georges Janco and a fourth whose name I did not catch. Arp was also there, and we came to an understanding without many words. Soon Janco's opulent "Archangels" hung alongside the other objects of beauty.

5.II.1916

The cabaret, with its 15 or 20 round tables, and a seating capacity of 35 to 50, boasted a stage of about 100 square feet. A piano stood on stage and as there was no dressing room, the performers changed behind a trestle over which a tattered canvas was stretched. The room was hung with the paintings of Kandinsky, Léger, Matisse and Klee, and with etchings by Picasso. That same evening, the place was full to bursting with "painters, students, revolutionaries, tourists, international crooks, psychiatrists, the demi-monde, sculptors, and polite spies on the lookout for information."[9] A caustic cindery smell wafted through the entrance corridor and everytime someone opened the door, thick clouds of smoke would pour out. The Zurich students had brought their long pipes with them. This was their way of irritating the bourgeois, and they would sit with their feet up on the tables drinking beer and shouting. The wooden benches that lined the walls were filled as well. The cabaret and its innovative program was an overnight success.[10]

The soirées that were held at the Cabaret Voltaire[11] between February and July 1916 were shaped in the main by Ball, the eldest at 30, Tzara and Janco, the youngest at 20 and 21, Arp, 29, and Huelsenbeck, 24. By the time of Huelsenbeck's arrival about a week after the opening, the cabaret had a personality of its own:

> Hugo was sitting at the piano, playing classical music, Brahms and Bach. Then he switched over to dance music. The drunken students pushed their chairs aside and began spinning around. There were almost no women in the cabaret. It was too wild, too way out.
> Hugo had written a poem against war and murderous insanity. Emmy recited it, Hugo accompanied her on the piano and the audience chimed in, with a growl, murdering the poem.[12]

Janco, tall and with an easy smile, had done most of the decoration of the Cabaret. His pictures hung on the walls. He had made exotic-looking masks and had even talked the hesitant proprietor into accepting the hanging of modern posters. He danced and recited as well. Arp was responsible for set and costume design, though he never performed. He wasn't interested in publicity, and his energies were, with a singleness of purpose, directed toward the revolutionary implications of art.

> I was in search of the personality, I had no interest in the uproar of the cabaret, although I don't deny the value of the noise.[13]

Huelsenbeck emphasized the work with language while Tzara, who had published poems and edited the avant-garde journal *Simbolul* in Rumania, at first played the circus barker and general factotum. But being a natural propagandist, he quickly assumed administrative control. He corresponded with Rome and Paris channeling into the cabaret news of Picasso, Braque and cubism, the Futurists Carra, Boccioni and Severini (Marinetti was already in correspondence with Ball), Picabia and Delaunay. He was the aesthete who collected antiques, African sculpture and primitive art. He was the *littérateur,* waiting to record on paper everything that was done, documenting the work at the cabaret, keeping an eye out for posterity.

Of the cabaret members at that time Ball wrote:

> There are five of us, and the remarkable thing is that we are never actually in complete or simultaneous agreement, although we agree on the main issues. The constellations change. Now Arp and Huelsenbeck agree and seem inseparable, now Arp and

Janco join forces against Huelsenbeck, then Huelsenbeck and Tzara against Arp, etc. There is a constantly changing attraction and repulsion. An idea, a gesture, some nervousness is enough to make the constellation change without seriously upsetting the little group.

24.V.1916

But this was written in May, 1916, when the dynamics of the group had only begun to evolve and the liaisons were largely those based on origin. Ball had met Huelsenbeck in Munich in 1912, Tzara and Janco knew each other from Bucharest, and just how little Arp was known to the others is evident in Ball's reply to Huelsenbeck's question "What does Arp do?" "I believe," answered Ball, "he paints."[14] What is clear is that it was Ball who largely initiated the group's theatrical experiments.

Hugo Ball: Dada Theaterperson

Hugo Ball, born in Pirmasens, Germany on February 22, 1886, was attracted to theatre in his youth, and by the age of 18 had written two plays: an imitation of Shakespeare's *Caesar and Cleopatra,* and an original script, *The Hangman of Brescia,* which remained uncompleted until he was 27. A third play, *Michael-angelo's Nose,* was written in 1908. In his plays, Ball resorted to grotesque caricatures to launch a strong polemical attack against the evils of the world as he saw them, but the works themselves bear no mark of the beginnings of a promising dramatist. They do, however, allude to a subject which would continue to preoccupy the young artist—the conflict between aesthetic nihilism and religious faith.[15]

During his studies at the University of Munich, Ball became heavily immersed in the works of Nietzsche, on whom he wrote his dissertation. Through Nietzsche, and through the philosopher's attraction to the work of Wagner, Ball was led to formulate his own dionysian theory of art based on the instinctive and unconscious elements in man. He became convinced that only through the theater could the saving power of the arts be demonstrated, and in 1910 he left Munich (without his degree), and enrolled in Max Reinhardt's School of Dramatic Art in Berlin.

From 1910-1914, life for Ball revolved around the theatre. His career at the school was a disappointment. He proved to be a poor actor ("It is tyranny that furthers the development of acting talents." 3.XII.1915), and so decided to take up critical writing and stage management. But at the *Stadttheater* in Plauen and later at the *Munich Kammerspiele,* his work as stage manager and dramaturg (a combination critic-playwright-artistic director), led to similar disappointments. Ball began to lead the after-theater-cafe life common to avant-garde artists and made friends with Frank Wedekind, Paul Klee, Wassily

Illustration 3   Richard Huelsenbeck

Portrait of Richard Huelsenbeck from the dust jacket of *Memoirs of a Dada Drummer* by Richard Huelsenbeck. English translation © 1974 by The Viking Press. Used by permission.

Kandinsky, and Oskar Kokoschka. In the work of Wedekind, Ball watched the struggle of the playwright to eliminate from his theatre the firm traditions of an established genre.[16]

Among the painters, Ball saw a breakthrough in the use of the creative and stimulating power of the unconscious—the type of work that he hoped to achieve in the theatre. Especially in the work of Kandinsky, he found inspiration for an art which, through the union of all artistic media and potentialities, would bring about the rebirth of society. Kandinsky, as organizer and propagandist of new ideas in the arts, was to be Ball's teacher, guide and colleague in the formative pre-war years. Much as Apollinaire served as the channel through which the Parisian avant-garde community learned of the dada work being done in Zurich and of the futurist experiments, so Kandinsky, moving between the art worlds of Munich, Moscow and Paris, served Ball, introducing him to the Russian futurists, the Russian composer Thomas von Hartmann and dancer Alexander Sacharoff, to Picasso, Gleizes, Metzinger and African art. "We must show," he had written, "that something is happening everywhere."[17]

Ball and Kandinsky

Ball first met Kandinsky in Munich in 1912 when the artist was in the midst of that period of intense creativity which was to last until 1914. In 1912, Paris was painting analytic cubism, a new presentation of the object derived from a series of direct visual images. Kandinsky, then a 45-year-old ex-professor of law, who played the piano and the cello, was painting "improvisations," in which dependence on the immediate visual image even as a point of departure had been abandoned. At the core of the creative process was the unaided imagination which functioned in terms of past assimilated experience. In that same year, Kandinsky and Franz Marc, a 30-year-old painter, had organized 2 "Blaue Reiter" exhibitions, and Kandinsky's essay *Concerning the Spiritual in Art* had just appeared in print.[18] This essay (which saw its second printing within the same year) and *The Blaue Reiter Almanac,* edited by Kandinsky and Marc in March, 1912, set forth an aesthetic philosophy which became the rallying point for modern artists and members of the avant-garde as diverse in their fields as Hans Arp, Arnold Schoenberg, and Ball. In a period of spiritual rebirth, they felt, the arts would move closer to each other with their common disposition to abstraction, their common concern for fundamentals, their common pursuit of inner nature.

The impact on Ball of both Kandinsky's essay and the material published in *The Blaue Reiter* was enormous. Here new thoughts and the new gods were forcefully presented: Schoenberg wrote of his experiments with sound "the artist creates not what others think is beautiful but what is necessary for him"; von Hartmann proposed "Suppose it is necessary for a composer to shock the audience" and August Macke, in his essay "Masks," intoned a litany of deities:

"the cymbales and their sound, masks and stages of the Japanese and the Greeks, the beauty spot stuck on the pretty cheek of a Parisian cocotte, and the mysterious hollow drumming of the Indian fakir." *The Blaue Reiter* illustrations offered figures from Egyptian shadow plays, naive folk prints, and children's drawings. In its pages, Ball encountered the theories of Robert Delaunay's "simultaneism," Scriabin's use of "synesthesia" in his performance of *Prometheus*, and of course Kandinsky's two texts for the theatre, written in 1909, "On Stage Composition—an essay on method,"[19] and *The Yellow Sound—a stage composition.*[20]

Ball saw Kandinsky as the "creator of a new theatrical style,"[21] as revolutionary as those of Ibsen and Maeterlinck. Violently attacking the dramatic arts of the nineteenth century (drama, opera, ballet), which had become so orthodox that any tiny change in them appeared revolutionary, Kandinsky had denounced Wagnerian "gesamtkunstwerk" to the extent that it only served to unify by external means—never really aiming at a true fusion: at times making the music prominent, at times the text, and never even considering color and pictorial form. He denounced the futurists for their palid transposition of Wagner's thesis: "We proclaim as an absolute necessity that the composer must be the author of a dramatic or tragic poem that he has set to music."

Hartmann, writing about Kandinsky at the time, said:

> This period for him was marked by an ever growing interest in music, the setting up of rapports perceived between painting and musical theory—and a permanent dissatisfaction with theatre and even more so with opera. The manner in which Wagner had given substance to these three forms of art in a musical-drama didn't satisfy him. He often said that what Wagner had achieved in that quarter consisted merely of babbling. He himself provided, in his most interesting theatre piece *The Yellow Sound* which probably will only be presented in the future, the result of his research and his ideas.[22]

In opposition to Wagner's ideal, Kandinsky proposed a symphonic composition in which every act is reduced to its essentials—a paring down which would result in a stage composition where blank spaces of time were an integral part of the work:

> I always find it advantageous in each work, to leave an empty space; it has to do with not imposing. Don't you think that in this there rests an eternal law—but it's a law for tomorrow.[23]

Kandinsky moved toward a total work based on "inner necessity." Art would function to express spiritual realities and a stage composition drawing on this source would be based on three elements:

1. The musical sound and its movement
2. The physical-psychial sound and its movement, expressed through people and objects
3. The colored tone and its movements (a special possibility for the stage)[24]

The union would take place with all three elements playing equally important roles, subordinate only to the inner goal. No mention is made of "characters." "Movement," is all important. Music, sound, voices, forms, and colored lights—all would move, assemble and decompose. They would work their effects sometimes simultaneously, sometimes separately. Forms would appear, develop and vanish, while colours changed through shifting lights. The color and light would not serve to illustrate the music more than the music served to comment on the drama—all would rest precisely on the action common among all the elements. The method allowed for numerous combinations of effect: collaboration, contrast, or the three "movements" running in entirely separate, externally independent directions. There was also the possibility of "synesthesia"—finding in the stimulation of a second sense, an echo or reverberation, an after-image translated from the original sense. Kandinsky himself underwent such an experience at a performance of Wagner's *Lohengrin* at the Moscow Court Theatre in the 1890s. There he suddenly saw the music as color and line:

> The violins, the deep bass notes and particularly the wind instruments embodied for me the intensity of the sunset hour. I saw all the colors in my mind; they stood before my eyes. Wild, almost mad lines drew themselves before me. . . . Wagner musically had painted "my lesson." . . . it became entirely clear to me that art is universally more powerful than it had seemed to me, that . . . a painting could develop the same strengths that music possesses.[25]

In his very close working relationship with von Hartmann and with the dancer Sacharoff (whom the two had met in 1909), Kandinsky attempted his own experiments in synesthesia:

> From among some of my water-colors, the musician picked that which seemed to him to produce the strongest musical impact. In the absence of the dancer he played his watercolor. Then the dancer joined us; the music was played to him, he danced to it and then he pointed out the watercolor that he had expressed in his dance.[26]

He witnessed other experiments as well at the Moscow Institute of Art Culture:

> The musicians will strike three bass chords: the painters are set the task of drawing them, first in pencil. Subsequently a diagram is made, and each painter is asked to depict each single chord in colours.[27]

The idea of the "inner sound" which the painter senses in each object and which he reproduces for the viewer, provided the easiest access to the idea of synesthesia. Much space is devoted in *The Blaue Reiter* to the relationship of painting and music, and although the idea of a relationship between these arts was not new,[28] still, only here was this thesis seriously documented.

Kandinsky's own text *The Yellow Sound* provides an interesting model for the artist's theories. Reading the theory is nowhere as startling as meeting the play which von Hartmann called "one of the greatest audacities in the theatre."[29]

The Yellow Sound goes beyond the anti-naturalistic experiments of Jarry, Appia, Strindberg, Craig, and Oskar Panizza in its almost complete elimination of dialogue, plot and sequential action, and its reliance on light, movement, and the abstract dances of figures to fill the space of the stage and the duration of the performance. A quick glance at the division into "Prelude" and six "pictures," sets up the musical and visual orientation of the piece, and von Hartmann actually did write the first draft of a musical score for the play.[30] "Characters," including five giants, "vague creatures," a (backstage) tenor, a child and man, people in flowing robes, people in tights, and a (backstage) chorus, are participants in a grotesque ballet and light show, in an opera of grunts and shrieks. The only comprehensible words spoken in the play are an eight-line choral prelude:

> Dreams hard as stones . . . And speaking rocks . . .
> Earth with riddles of fulfilling questions . . .
> The motion of the heavens . . . And melting . . . of stones . . .
> Invisible rampart . . . growing upward . . .
> Tears and laughter . . . Prayers while cursing . . .
> The joy of union and the blackest battles.
> Dark light on the . . . sunniest . . . day
> Blinding bright shadow in darkest night!![31]

a six-line recitation by "many people," in Picture II:

> The flowers cover everything, cover everything,
>   cover everything.
> Shut your eyes! Shut your eyes!
> We are looking. We are looking.
> Cover conception with innocence.
> Open your eyes! Open your eyes!
> Gone. Gone.

and the single word "Silence" in Picture IV. Picture III offers a terrified tenor voice "shrieking completely unintelligible words" in which the letter "a" can frequently be heard. As an example of such a word Kandinsky offers "Kalasimuafakola! " a worthy antecedent to Ball's phonic poems and an example of

Kandinsky's own dictum "the sound of the human voice must also be pure, i.e.: without being obscured by words, or by the meaning of words."[32] Picture I presents a chorus "without words," and "singing without words"; Picture V, "whispers," and Picture VI, not a single vocal sound. The literary element has almost completely receded.

The play advances through an interaction of light and music, offset by various backstage sounds often personified in stage directions such as "The music becomes nervous." In his notes to the play, Kandinsky suggests durations for the sound and light effects:

> Picture II:
> (10 minutes of silence) Gradually the blue fog dissolves into white light (20 minutes) . . . . The music (5-10 minutes) is shrill, storm with A and B and A-flat frequently repeated.[33]

These time designations project a work of monumental length and Kandinsky does nothing to dispell this projection when he proposes 30 minutes for the recitation for the 6 line text "The flowers cover everything. . . ." In this vastly extended event, people "dance"—giants with hunched or drooping shoulders turn heads slowly and make simple hand movements, a white figure "makes vague but very rapid movements, sometimes with his arms, sometimes with his legs." At intervals he continues a motion for quite a long time and holds the pose for a few moments. Whole groups join in a "general dance":

> Running, leaping, running to and from each other, falling. While standing, some figures rapidly move only their arms, others only their legs, or their torsos. Some combine all these movements. Sometimes these are group movements. Sometimes whole groups make one and the same movement.[34]

In the final picture, a bright yellow giant with an indistinct white face and large, round, black eyes slowly raises both arms (with palms facing downward) alongside his body and grows taller. When he extends to the full height of the stage, and his figure resembles a cross, it suddenly becomes dark. "The music is as expressive as the action on the stage."

Models for the practical physical possibilities of staging such a drama were not unavailable to Kandinsky. The Munich Artists Theatre was renowned for its effective use of colored light and had in fact increased the conventional spectrum of colored lights to five with the addition of blue. In their 1908 production of *Faust,* the walls of Faust's study "take on a colour as though blood ran from their pores." The curtain changed to deep blue and Faust's silhouette "stood out against it in dark purple."[35] Scriabin's *Prometheus,* described in an essay in *The Blaue Reiter,*[36] provided a further example of the theatrical use of a symphony of colors based on the principle of corresponding sounds and colors. Kandinsky's extraordinary emphasis on dance in the play also had its precedents in Fuch's writing and performance work and Kandinsky was familiar as well with the innovative work in movement of Emile-Jacques Dalcroze[37] and the dances and writings of Isadora Duncan whom he mentions in *Concerning the Spiritual in Art:*

> Isadora Duncan forged a link between Greek dancing and the future. In this she is working parallel to those painters who are looking for inspiration in the primitives. . . . In both mediums we are on the threshold of a future art.[38]

Kandinsky's friend, the dancer Alexander Sacharoff, was spending lots of time at the museums as well, studying forms for Greek dance. It was at his urging that Kandinsky's plans for using a Hans Christian Anderson tale as the basis for a ballet were changed and the Daphnis and Chloe legend substituted.[39] Sacharoff presented his Greek dances at the Munich Odeon theatre in 1910 with von Hartmann composing the music, "un quator à cordes."

Thomas von Hartman was right, however, when he predicted that *The Yellow Sound* would "only be presented in the future." The play has been objected to, misunderstood and dismissed.[40] Only Schoenberg among his contemporaries seems to have provided Kandinsky with an unequivocally positive reaction to the play:

> Your stage composition pleased me infinitely. Your preface as well. I am of your opinion. . . . Did I not attempt the selfsame thing in my "Main Heureuse"? With the only difference being that you have gone farther still than I in renouncing all conscious thought, all action inspired by life. . . . I imagine that the play, when presented will make an extraordinary impression on me.[41]

In 1923 Kandinsky again discussed his concept of a stage-work in an essay entitled "Abstract Stage Synthesis," but only five years later in a stage production which he himself designed for Mussorgsky's *Pictures at an Exhibition,* did the process by which a stage is peopled by color, sound and movement, become clearer. In the production, performed at the Friedrich Theater in Dessau on April 4, 1928,

> The forms appeared simply as surfaces, the stage appeared quite unreal through the use of the black background and lighting, much like the space in Kandinsky's paintings. Next to the movement of forms, the lighting became the time factor and presented a many-sided and rich scale of tonal intensities. The effect of certain procedures was great and magical: the circle floating down before the mysterious darkness, its sudden glow and consequent extinction—or the movement of a white right angle across the stage. The floating down of the arch over the catacombs was unforgettable. The floating, gliding, and standing of the forms, the alternation of colors according to their types and intensities, appeared as a dramatic procedure full of suspense. The image was in constant motion, and every moment was experienced

as an image. At the moment the movement came to a stop, the construction of the composition was completed; this was a dramatic climax. The affinity with the artistic form of the play as such was revealed here in a surprising way.[42]

In only 2 scenes of the 16 tableaux did dancers appear: "The ballet of the chicks in their eggshells," and the "Marketplace of Limoges." The dancers were reduced to marionettes, and in all the other scenes the moving decor became the dramatic spectacle of colored forms which were employed in a purely abstract way for their tonal qualities.

In all of this work, Kandinsky's express purpose was to produce "vibrations" in the audience, equivalent to the "soul-vibrations" of the artist as he creates the work. The value of the work produced was to be measured against its power to evoke just such vibrations in the beholder, although Kandinsky was quick to point out "The observer of today is seldom capable of feeling such vibrations."[43] To increase his ability to heighten his own senses, Kandinsky was, by 1911, doing exercises in "contemplation" following Indian models. Daily he performed exercises in search of those "abilities almost lost by man." He worked to increase the senses of taste and smell and spent time in meditation and concentration. Through continued exercises, he believed, all things would become "spiritually audible," and he did have experiences of "the mastery of the spirit over the frailty of the body."

> Not only the stars, the moon, the forests, and other traditionally poetical subjects, but also a stub in the ashtray, a stray button, a loose calendar leaf, etc. revealed . . . their face, their innermost being, the secret soul.[44]

Kandinsky was led to much of this way of thinking through his attachment to the theosophical movement, an attachment not unqualified yet strong.[45] He was attracted to the works of Annie Besant and C.W. Leadbeater. He had read Mme. Blavatsky in the original Russian and was much influenced by Rudolph Steiner who, in 1913, had broken with the group to found his own Anthroposophical Society. In the works of Steiner and the others, Kandinsky found sources as well as a sympathetic sounding board for many of his ideas. They, as he, believed that the spiritual reality had become accessible to observation and therefore also to representation. The theosophists, who after their move to India in 1879 included a strong Eastern element in their works, also spoke of "forms built by music," and Thomas von Hartmann and the phonic poet Christian Morgenstern were theosophists as well.[46]

In Kandinsky, Ball saw a priest, not a painter. In his occult preoccupations, his contemplation after Indian models, his experiences of healing through faith, his interest in parapsychology and thought transference,[47] Kandinsky as guru presented Ball with many new options in experience. Ball himself experimented with narcotic drugs and meditation. In Kandinsky's notions on

Illustration 4   Man Ray, "Group of Paris Dadaists Playing a Game
of Chance," Paris, 1921

Collection: Timothy Baum, New York

spontaneity and the opposition to any kind of routine in art, his views on "verbal potency" as the key to the future, and his principle of "inner necessity" the artist pointed the way toward a "totalwissenschaft," a synthesis of all knowledge to be achieved in poeticized form. In his theatre work he provided Ball with the most avant-garde models Ball had yet encountered. Only the futurist performance experiments vied in Ball's experience with what Kandinsky had created—and these Ball had not witnessed at first hand. Most crucial, however, was the fact that Kandinsky gave powerful corroboration to Ball's basic belief that a regeneration of society could come about only through art.

The untimely outbreak of the war prevented Kandinsky from producing a book on theater similar in format and equal in significance to *The Blaue Reiter,* and from establishing his projected international society for the arts to patronize a series of theatrical productions. Ball was intimately involved with the writing of the book and the planning of the proposed theatrical venture. In a letter to his sister on May 27, 1914, he wrote:

> . . . I am planning a new book for the first of October, *The New Theater,* together with Kandinsky, Marc, Thomas von Hartmann, Fokine, von Bechtejeff. We jointly want to develop our ideas about the new artistic theater with new scene paintings, music, figurines, etc. . . . Also new architectural plans should be made. A completely new theatre. A new festival house . . . If we succeed in bringing out the brochure before October 1 (Piper, Munich) we will found an "International Society for Modern Art," including not only the theatre, but also modern painting, modern music, modern dance.[48]

and in his diary he noted:

> When I was considering the plan of a new theater in March 1914, this is what I thought: there is a distinct need for a stage for the truly moving passions; a need for an experimental theatre above and beyond the scope of routine daily interests. Europe paints, makes music, and writes in a new way. A fusion of all regenerative ideas, not only of art. Only the theater is capable of creating the new society. The backgrounds, the colors, words, and sounds have only to be taken from the subconscious and animated to engulf the everyday routine along with its misery.
>
> *Diary,* Prologue

The Artists' Theater in the Munich exhibition gardens had been chosen to accommodate this experiment—a theatre which would touch the subconscious, which would use masks and stilts again, which would recall archetypes and use megaphones. "Sun and moon will run across the stage and proclaim their sublime wisdom."

Still under the influence of Max Reinhard's "circus" and "intimate" plays, Ball added an interest in Japanese and Chinese theatre, an interest again reinforced by his talks with Kandinsky.[49] He listened to traditional Japanese theatre music and read Bernhard Kellerman's essay "sasso yo yassa, japanishe tanze," (1911). In the Chinese theatre he discovered a singular example of the evocative power of "noise-song":

> When a general receives orders for a campaign into distant provinces he marches three or four times around the stage, accompanied by a terrible noise of gongs, drums and trumpets and then he stops to let the audience know he has arrived.
> When the dramatist wants to move or shock his audience, he switches over to song . . . The words of the song do not matter; the laws of rhythm are more important.

2.IV.1915

Through Kandinsky as well, Ball met von Hartmann who had recently come from Moscow full of stories about Stanislavsky—especially of how the influence of Indian studies affected the work of the Moscow Art Theater on the plays of Andreyev and Chekov. Ball wrote: "This was different, broader, deeper than we were. And it contributed much to broaden my view and demands for a modern theater."

The strength of Kandinsky's influence is evident in Ball's provisional outline for the new theatre:

An artistic theatre should in theory,
look approximately like this:
Kandinsky . . . . .Total Work of Art
Marc . . . . .Scenes for *The Storm*
Fokine . . . . .On Ballet
Hartmann . . . . .Anarchy of Music
Paul Klee. . . . . .Designs for *The Bacchantes*
Kokoschka. . . . . .Scenes and Plays
Ball . . . . .Expressionism and the Stage
Yevrenov. . . . . .On the psychological element
Mendelsohn . . . . .Stage Architecture
Kubin. . . . . .Sketches for *The Flea in the Fortified House*

Diary, Prologue

The war broke out on July 29, 1914. Plans for the new theatre were momentarily put aside.

Ball and Emmy Hennings: the Move to Zurich
Ball volunteered numbers of times for the German army but was consistently rejected because of a weak heart, though he was never given a permanent discharge. In November 1914, he travelled on his own to the Belgian battlefront to witness the war at first hand. What he saw was fearful, shocking and tragic

beyond anything the theatre could produce. Ball could only recall an exposition of futurists paintings which he had seen at the end of 1913. In the paintings he saw a terrifying vision of a world in agony, a vision which expressed the artist's own "ecstatic sickness." In this ecstatic condition, the depths of the unconscious mobilized to produce a magic, quixotic and highly emotional work of àrt, just the kind of art which Ball was aiming to create in the theatre. Ball's immediate response, however, was escape—into the writing of a novel and the further study of the Oriental theatre. The novel, *Laurentius Tenderenda,* explored certain linguistic, rhythmic and vocal devices which would later appear in his Zurich work. In his study of the Chinese and Japanese theatre, Ball attempted to lose himself once again in a world of music and rhythm. This led him finally back to theatre and the unconscious.

Ball's escapist tendencies, however, had to fight with his activist impulses. In 1915, he and Richard Huelsenbeck organized meetings and poetry readings to commemorate poets killed at the front. These events became more and more aggressive and culminated in an "expressionist evening" in which German "kultur" was condemned, futurist experimentation exalted and the first dadaist techniques were attempted with Huelsenbeck reciting his improvised Negro chants.

In the fall of 1915, Ball was 29 years old and variously torn by his attachments to fervent Catholicism, Bakunian anarchism, mysticism, and the world of the arts. He had linked his life to that of Emmy Hennings, an actress and cabaret singer whom he had met at the Cafe Simplizissimus in Munich in 1913. Tormented, restless and disgusted with Germany which he saw as a "mummy among nations," he fled with her to Zurich, bearing forged papers and under an assumed name.

By the time of her meeting with Ball, Emmy Hennings had lived the wandering actor's life for over 6 years. Unhappily married at 20, she had within a year lost a child and been deserted by her husband. A second child, Anne-Marie, was born while she toured in Silesia and after leaving the child with her mother, she continued to tour Russia, Germany, and Hungary—so often breaking contracts at whim that the German newspapers featured notices by theatre directors, warning of her unscrupulous conduct. She was, however, always in demand, for her stage presence was an electrifying one. In the periodical *Die Aktion* of June 5, 1912, an obscure writer named Ravien Siurlai wrote of Hennings' nightly shows in the Lindenkavett in Berlin, providing a glimpse of the demonic character of her performances:

> She stepped onto the cabaret stage her face waxen, ribboned about the neck, with her cropped yellow hair and the stiffly layered ruffles of her skimpy, dark velvet dress, she was separated from all of humanity . . . many yeared and ravaged, Madame Emmy Hennings. A woman has infinities, Gentlemen, but one does not absolutely have to confuse the erotic with prostitution. . . . Not polite enough to mask herself,

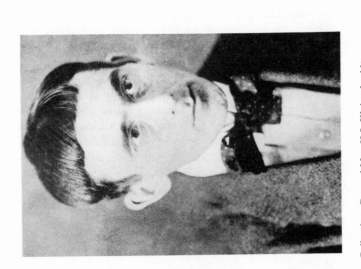

Frau Emmy Hennings revealed to the cavalier that he is the aphrodisiac of the pimp. And again applause indicated that prudence slept. . . . Who can prevent this girl that possesses hysteria, that incendiary quality, the brain-tearing intensity of the litterati, from swelling to an avalanche. . . . Emmy Hennings, very made-up, hypnotizing by Morphine, Absinthe and the bloody flame of the electric "Gloire" torn in extremist distortion of the Gothic, her voice hops across the corpses and will mock them, soulfully trilling like a yellow canary. [50]

From Berlin, Hennings moved to work at the Simplizissimus in Munich where she first met Ball. Ball, then dramaturg at the Kammerspiele, would invite her to sit at his table between numbers and finally offered her the leading woman's role in Andreyev's *The Life of Man*. She accepted his invitation to read the play together and though the production never materialized, the relationship between the two developed and Hennings remained Ball's companion until his death.[51]

At the time of their flight from Germany, both Hennings and Ball were jobless. The Kammerspiele had closed and Hennings, imprisoned for six weeks in Munich on suspicion of forging passports and identification papers for people who wanted to escape to neutral countries, had lost her job at the Simplizissimus.

The move to Switzerland was an escape from an intolerable society, from the war, but an escape out of time as well. Hennings makes it quite clear in her recollections of that period that she feared Ball was in danger of moving into insanity, and that he was possibly a dangerous person not only to himself but to others as well. The impact of the war, his experiments with drugs, his personal failure to that point in achieving any breakthrough in his vision of a program of redemption through the arts—all placed him in a very precarious psychic state. In this state, and almost completely penniless, they arrived in Zurich at the end of May, 1915.

None of the founders of the Cabaret Voltaire came to that venture with the theatre background of Ball and Hennings. In the 10 months that separated their arrival in Zurich from the founding of the Cabaret, Ball, or "Willibald" (his pseudonym), and Hennings, reduced to destitution, found work as performers. Hennings sang at a cabaret and Ball, under still another name, "Gery," was engaged as a pianist with a vaudeville troupe called "Flamingo." The bars and cafes where the Flamingo troupe played were a far cry from the meeting places for intellectuals and artists Ball had frequented in Munich and Berlin. Now, he was eating, sleeping and working among the outcasts of society where neither the artist nor the public had any vital intellectual interests. In addition to eight hours of piano playing every evening, Ball had to spend several hours each day directing and training the players in new parts and new songs because the programs had to be constantly changed. Whatever the depressing aspects of this vaudeville life, there is no doubt that it is in many of its aspects quintessential theatre. There are few better ways to learn to "work" an audience, to construct and reconstruct material for the stage, to be "up," to find sources of energy where there are none, to mold an often banal activity into a theatre piece. Although the player is rarely dealing with the work of actor-as-character, he is always working at the role of actor as performer.

The world Ball lived in surrounded him with "performers." He visited the tattooed lady, Mrs. Koritzky, who, to the music of a zither played by her husband, bared her chest, arms and thighs to guests (30 centimes) and artists (free). Her body was completely covered with portraits and garlanded with flowers. Her behind boasted two enormously butterfly wings. The newspapers advertised that a "demoiselle will perform several rope kissed dances, and curtsies on the tight rope with feet close together and will try her best to ingratiate herself with two curious lovers between heaven and earth" (3.XI.1915). Ball wrote: "morality is irrelevant, art keeps the balance," (4.IX.1915). He met the fat Negress, Miss Ranovalla of Singapore, who hid her bread-loaf arms under a costume of blue smock and red cape, and saw the Sicilian sea lion, blowing the stalactite grottoes of misery on a conch shell. "How confused and hopeless everything is! " he wrote. "What will come of it all? "

Ball had moved from playwriting to theatre scholarship, from acting to stage management, from critical writing to the work of a performer in a mobile variety show. He had lived alongside Kandinsky in the midst of the *Blaue Reiter* circle and had worked with Hennings on Andreyev and on hoofing. Despite the arduous demands of the road-show life, he continued the experiments with words begun in his novel and furthered them through his correspondence with Marinetti, who had sent Ball his own "Parole in libertà." Ball was stunned by the work of the Italian futurist:

> They are just letters of the alphabet on a page; you can roll up such a poem like a map. The syntax has come apart. The letters are scattered and assembled again in a rough-and-ready way. There is no language anymore. . . it has to be invented all over again. Disintegration right in the innermost process of creation.

In November 1915, barely three months before the opening of the cabaret, Ball wrote:

> People who live rashly and precipitately easily lose control over their impressions and are prey to unconscious emotions and motives. The activity of any art (painting, writing, composing) will do them good, provided that they do not pursue any purpose in their subjects, but follow the course of a free unfettered imagination. The independent process of fantasy never fails to bring to light again those things that have crossed the threshold of consciousness without analysis. In an age like ours, when people are assaulted daily by the most monstrous things without being able to keep account of their impressions, in such an age aesthetic production becomes a prescribed course. But all living art will be irrational, primitive and complex; it will

speak a secret language and leave behind documents not of edification but of paradox.

25.XI.1915

By February of 1916 when Ball advertised for artists to join him in establishing an experimental cabaret, he was ripe for the project. Delighted to find himself once again among a group of intellectuals—all uprooted, all revolted by the war, all searching to find release through their art, he directed all the force of his visions and experiments, his visceral recollections of the performing life, the accumulation of theory and talk shared with his friends of the avant-garde, into guiding the work in performance at the Cabaret Voltaire.

Dada Performance: Beginnings

Most of the early programs at the Cabaret Voltaire were catch-as-catch-can, basically literary in intent, and rather conventional cabaret fare. The group's experimental efforts did not spring full-blown with the cabaret's opening. The material was mainly in French and German with its artistic allegiances Franco-German as well: poems by Kandinsky, Werfel and Cendrars, and readings from Max Jacob, Lautréamont and Jarry given alongside the "Sonata for Piano and Cello," op. 32, by Saint-Saens and a Debussy lullaby. A soirée was set aside for the Russians (with humorous pieces by Chekhov, folk songs, and piano music by Rachmaninoff), and a Sunday for the Swiss who, in the cabaret's liberated atmosphere, chose to sing a song about the "Beautiful Virgin Lise." Tzara gave a reading of his poems "which he fished out of his various coat pockets in a rather charming way," and a short, good-natured gentleman from the audience was applauded even before he got onto the stage to perform. "Acts" followed one another in traditional "variety" format—a format which would soon lend itself exceptionally well to the fragmented nature and the compartmentalized structure of the new performing experiments. Quite quickly, however, Ball, Huelsenbeck, Janco, Tzara and Arp developed both a sense of themselves as a "closed" group,[52] as well as a feeling for the structure of the cabaret performances and the nature of the performance experiments.

At one time spontaneous contributions from the audience were accepted:

> Sometimes a young man would get up on the rostrum and read his poetry, sometimes there might be a group asking for permission to give a balalaika concert. We suffered them all in patience and then imperturbably got on with our simultaneous poems.[53]

Soon, however, intrusions of this sort were no longer tolerated, and changes in the cabaret's program came with amazing rapidity. On February 6 and 7, poems were read by Kandinsky, Else Lasker, Wedekind and Cendrars. On February 11,

Huelsenbeck arrived pleading for stronger rhythm (negro rhythm). He preferred to "drum literature into the ground." On February 26 the poems were by Christian Morgenstern, a turn-of-the-century writer of phonetic poetry. On March 2 Ball acknowledged the primacy of poetry as performed:

> Nowhere are the weaknesses of a poem revealed as much as in a public reading. . . . Reciting aloud has become the touchstone of the quality of a poem for me, and I have learned (from the stage) to what extent today's literature is worked out as a problem at the desk and is made for the spectacles of the collector instead of for the ears of living human beings.

> 2.III.1916

and by March 5, he wrote:

> The image of the human form is gradually disappearing from the painting of these times and all objects appear only in fragments. This is one more proof of how ugly and worn the human countenance has become, and of how all the objects of our environment have become repulsive to us. The next step is for poetry to decide to do away with language for similar reasons. These are things that have probably never happened before.

> 5.III.1916

New sights, new sounds filled the small stage—"silence, music—declaration . . . latest rage the big drum . . . cubist tinkle dance . . . great enchanted gyratory movement of 400 persons celebrating . . . music, theories, manifestoes, poems, paintings, costumes, masks. . . ."[54] The more experimental material found expression in:

> Dances and skits, many employing masked performers

> Work with rhythm and music, with "natural sound"—those sounds which the human voice and body is capable of making without the aid of extensions of any kind (e.g., instruments or machines), and noise music ("bruitism")

> Readings of manifestos and of simultaneous and phonic poetry where languages often assumed the values of pure sound and incantation

The unique backgrounds of the "group of 5," and especially Ball's meeting with Kandinsky and his contacts with the *Blaue Reiter* school, had placed an indelible stamp on the fundamental concepts which motivated the performance work.

Masks

The manner in which the group created together is best illustrated by the work with Janco's masks. A number of masks had been made for a new show. They were cardboard cut-outs, painted and glued, and Ball describes them as recalling the Japanese or Ancient Greek theatre, and yet appearing wholly modern. "What fascinates us all about the masks," he writes, "is that they represent not human characters and passions, but characters and passions that are larger than life. The horror of our time, the paralyzing background of events, is made visible." (24.V.1916) Arp recalls them as ". . . terrifying, most of them daubed with bloody red. Out of cardboard, paper, horsehair, wire, and cloth . . . languorous foetuses, . . . Lesbian sardines . . . ecstatic mice."[55] They were designed to make their effect at a distance and in the relatively small space of the cabaret, the result was astonishing:

> We were all there when Janco arrived with his masks, and everyone immediately put one on. Then someting strange happened. Not only did the mask immediately call for a costume; it also demanded a quite definite, passionate gesture, bordering on madness. Although we could not have imagined it five minutes earlier, we were walking around with the most bizarre movements, festooned and draped with impossible objects, each one of us trying to outdo the other in inventiveness. The motive power of these masks was irresistibly conveyed to us. All at once we realized the significance of such a mask for mime and for the theatre. The masks simply demanded that their wearers start to move in a tragic-absurd dance.

> 24.V.1916

An improvisatory situation had been touched off by the stimulus the masks provided and the group proceeded to invent a number of "dances" for which Ball, on the spot, improvised short musical pieces. The dances were largely vehicles for the display of the mask. In themselves they appear hardly more than a single "bar" of dance, showing no development, incapable of being sustained. In this they foreshadow much of the later dada work.

> We called one dance "Flycatching." The only things suitable for this mask were clumsy, fumbling steps and some quick snatches and wide swings of the arms, accompanied by nervous, shrill music. We called the second dance "Nightmare." The dancing figure starts from a crouching position, gets straight up, and moves forward. The mouth of the mask is wide open, the nose is broad and in the wrong place. The performer's arms, menacingly raised, are elongated by special tubes. The third dance we called "Festive Despair." Long, cutout, golden hands on the curved arms. The figure turns a few times to the left and to the right, then slowly turns on its axis, and finally collapses abruptly to return slowly to the first movement.

> 24.V. 1916

Repeatedly we find references to the emphasis on masks. Tzara, in his "Zurich Chronicle," writes, "the most important are the masks and the revolver shots," and a participant at one of the *soirées* in a personal letter wrote:

> All kinds of masks were good for the dadaists. What we don't know is if each chose the mask that suited him best. But the mask was necessary, it took the place of an underground shelter to hide the faces too shocking to be seen.[56]

Ball, in his diary, again and again returns to the image of the mask:

> The dadaist loves the extraordinary and the absurd. . . . He therefore welcomes any kind of mask. Any game of hide-and-seek, with its inherent power to deceive.

> 12.VI.1916

He speaks of dada as "a game in fancy dress," behind which lies a synthesis of the romantic, dandyist and demonic themes of the nineteenth century, and he himself carried around the skull of a dead girl and created a "set" out of his Sant'Abbondio home—"huge rooms painted blue and red, with flowers and hovering birds . . . a chapel . . . decorated and adorned with flowers."

George Burand, in his work *Les Masques,* sees the mask as the key to an understanding of dada performance:

> Man suddenly finds himself placed before an image of himself which he didn't suspect existed and which plunges him into terror. His confidence in himself, in life itself, disappears. He is at the limits of his reason. The horror which the grotesque, degenerate mask communicates is purely negative and destructive. . . . Is it not there rather than in the hedging and polite explanations, that one holds the keystone to dadaist provocation.[57]

The group and their work had not yet become "dada," but slowly there was developing a unity which resulted from no seeming act of will; a pattern of mutual stimulation which, in the coming months, helped the group define itself, both to itself and before its audiences. Much of this self-definition came from the work on simultaneous and phonic poetry, rhythm and natural sound.

Simultaneism

To find the origins of "simultaneism" as developed by the dadaists, we must first look to the painter Robert Delaunay whose work was known to Ball through the *Blaue Reiter Almanac.*[58] In his *Portrait* of 1911, Delaunay painted a monochrome picture with five versions of the figure spreading from a common base along the top of the canvas, and in 1912 he experimented with spectrum-like arrangements of pure color which he called "windows by simultaneous contrast."[59] These color compositions crossed the frontier of non-figurative painting and were celebrated by Apollinaire (who had spent six weeks living with the Delaunays in 1912), in his poem, named as the paintings, "Les Fenêtres":

> The yellow fades from red to green...
> You will lift the curtain
> And now look at the window opening
> Spiders when hands wove the light
> Beauty paleness unfathomable violent tints.

The poem was one of the first in which Apollinaire eliminated punctuation, and it was composed of seemingly disconnected, partially self-sufficient phrases and ideas, which by their placing and interaction, served to evoke both form and atmosphere. For Delaunay's art, Apollinaire revived the ancient term "orphism," a term which points at analogies with the non-imitative qualities of music.[60] In "The Cubist Painters," he lists "Orphism" as the most advanced of the four categories of Cubism and defines it as:

> ... the art of painting new harmonies out of elements borrowed not from visual reality but created entirely by the artist and endowed by him with a powerful presence. The works of Orphist artists should offer simultaneously a sensation of pure aesthetic enjoyment, a structure of which the senses are hardly aware and a profound content, in other words, a subject. This is pure art.[61]

Writing on the "Salon des Indépendents" in March 1913, Apollinaire referred to "L'Orphisme, peinture pure, Simultaneité" and the two terms thus became largely synonymous. It is out of orphism that simultaneism grew. Its birth was not an easy one. Apollinaire and Henri Martin (the author who wrote under the name Barzun) carried on a long and violent polemic over its paternity in the pages of the "Paris-Journal." In his "Manifeste sur le simultanéisme poétique," published in 1913, Barzun claimed to have invented what he called "literary simultaneism." At his side stood a group founded and dominated by the poets Canudo and Valentine Saint-Point who edited *Montjoie*, a review devoted to finding the link between various arts and investigating their common tendencies. This publication and the review *Poème et Drame*, which began publication about 1913-1914, were at the center of the simultaneist movement and published the "poèmes-simultanées" of Barzun and Fernand-Divoire.[62] Apollinaire meanwhile, in defense of his paternity, pointed to the plastic ideas he had championed for so long, as they erupted in the typographical arrangements of his "Calligrams" and his "conversation-poems"—all punctuation is omitted and there is no attempt to clarify the circumstances which produced the disconnected sentences.

While these arguments raged, the artist Sonia Delaunay collaborated with Blaise Cendrars (who frequently called himself "the poet of the Simultanés"), on his *La Prose du Transsibérien et de la petite Jehanne de France*–the first simultaneous book, which they published in October, 1913. Cendrars had written:

> Simultaneity is a technique, and simultaneous contrast is the most recent improvement brought to this technique. The simultaneous contrast is experienced depth-reality-form-construction-representation-life. Depth is the new inspiration.[63]

and the book was a two-meter single sheet of paper, which unfolded accordion style to reveal the lines of the poem, a Michelin map of the Trans-Siberian area, and Delaunay's brightly colored stencil. Twelve different type faces were used in the poem, freely set down upon the page and printed in four different colors.

On her own, Delaunay expanded her experiments in simultaneity to include costume, or as Apollinaire called it, "vestamentary innovation." For their evenings at the popular Bullier dance-hall, Robert Delaunay, Sonia's husband, and himself a painter, would appear in a red coat with a blue collar, red socks, yellow and black shoes, black trousers, a green jacket, sky-blue vest and tiny red tie; Sonia, in a "simultaneous dress" of purple with a purple and green sash, and under the jacket, a blouse "divided into brightly colored zones, delicate or faded, where there is mixed an old rose, yellow-orange color, natter blue, scarlet, etc. . . appearing on different materials, so that wool cloth, taffeta, tulle, flannelette, watered silk and peau de soi are juxtaposed."[64] Writing of Delaunay's use of simultaneous color in 1913, Cendrars called it "that sensuous, irrational, absurd, lyrical element which brings a painting to life surrealistically."[65]

The importance of simultaneism was in its new grasp of structure–a structure which is the "opposite of narration," which represents "an effort to retain a moment of experience without sacrificing its logically unrelated variety."[66] Simultaneism wanted to present a plurality of actions at the same time. Abridged syntax and unpunctuated abruptness tended to merge disparate moments into an "instantané." Passages were set one next to another to encourage feeling the conflict between them rather than the link–the setting of one thing beside another without a connective. From here it is but a short jump to obscurity, illogicality and abruptness, to surprise, shock and "chance."

Finally, however, it was the dadas, as much "poets rooted in painting" as Apollinaire, who took simultaneism to its most complete extension in the area of performance. On March 30, 1916, Huelsenbeck, Tzara and Janco performed "L'Amiral cherche une maison à louer"–the first simultaneous poem:

> a contrapuntal recitative in which three or more voices speak, sing, whistle, etc., simultaneously in such a way that the resulting combinations account for the total effect of the work, elegaic, funny or bizarre.[67]

Here was poetry pushed beyond paper to performance—occupying three-dimensional space and actual time.

Huelsenbeck describes the simultaneous poem as an abstraction referring to the occurrence of different events at the same time:

> It presupposes heightened sensitivity to the passage of things in time . . . and attempts to transform the problem of the ear into a problem of the face. Simultaneity is against what has become, and for what is becoming. While I, for example, become successively aware that I boxed an old woman on the ear yesterday and washed my hands an hour ago, the screeching of a streetcar brake and the crash of a brick falling off the roof next door reach my ear simultaneously and my (outward or inward) eye rouses itself to seize, in the simultaneity of these events, a swift meaning of life. From the everyday events surrounding me (the big city, the Dada circus, crashing, screeching, steam whistles, house fronts, the smell of roast veal), I obtain an impulse which starts me toward direct action, becoming the big X. I become directly aware that I am alive, I feel the form-giving force behind the bustling of the clerks in the Dresdner Bank . . . and so ultimately a simultaneous poem means nothing but "Hurrah for life!"[68]

Experiments in simultaneity led to multiple voices reading poems and manifestos, and the simultaneous reading of unrelated texts (often in different languages). In trying to explain the impact of such poems on the audience, the Bauhaus artist Moholy-Nagy wrote:

> . . . without one's having been able to register its exact meaning, a mutation occurred: clearly, a fabric became comprehensible . . . in a very suggestive unconscious way, through the magic of the words, their affinities and modulations. This was the result of a new lyric expression, like an x-ray revelation, making transparent that which was previously opaque; a new structure and topography of the psychological existence, the rendering of psychological space-time.[69]

This "psychological space-time," evoked by the juxtaposition of unrelated words, verbal free-association, and "inane sonority" comes close to Sergei Eisenstein's concept of "inner speech": a montage concept based on the collision of images:

> If the montage must be compared with something, then a phalanx of montage-pieces, "shots," should be compared to the series of explosions of an internal combustion engine, multiplying themselves into montage dynamics and thereby serving as "impulses" to drive along a tearing motor car or tractor.[70]

The "montage" concept is helpful in looking at much of dada performance. The collision impact in performance is not due to the verbal element alone. There was something visual "going on" on stage as well. At the very least there were the facial expressions of the performers as they moved mouths and focused

Illustration 7   Sonia Delaunay in a simultaneous
dress and veil of her own design which she wore to
the Bal Bullier, 1912-13

Collection: Arthur A. Cohen

eyes in their reading of the texts. Crimped eyes, gaping mouth and focus askew were not the usual diet of a poetry-hungry public. Costume elements and "activity" were added as well. Dada tended to mix the genres and in that rests one of its essential characteristics: tableau-manifestos and poem-drawings, danced songs and simultaneous poems vocally orchestrated. The interpenetration of literary and artistic frontiers was for dada a postulate. Still, the impact of the verbal element remains paramount and the shift was soon made from simultaneous poems based on recognizable words to phonetic freedom.

The Phonetic Poem, Bruitism and Natural Sound

Inducting Officer: Did you write that?
Huelsenbeck: What?
Inducting Officer: Do you write poetry?
Huelsenbeck: Yes, I write poetry.
Officer: Did you write this?
Huelsenbeck: What does it say?
Officer: You write lines like "a horse makes
        himself comfortable in a bird's nest,"
        do you write that?
Huelsenbeck: Yes, I wrote that.
Officer: You'd better go home.

In "L'amiral cherche une maison à louer," the simultaneous poem read by Huelsenbeck, Janco and Tzara, the three came out on stage, "bowed like a yodeling band about to celebrate lakes and forests in song, pulled out their 'scores,' and throwing all restraint to the wind,"[71] each shouted his text at the bewildered spectators. Meaning quickly faded into incantation. Huelsenbeck intoned "Ahoi, ahoi! Des Admirals qwirktes Beinkleid schnell zerfällt," while Janco sang "Where the honny [sic] suckle wine twines itself around," and Tzara shouted "Boumboum boum Il deshabilla sa chair quand les grenouilles humides commencèrent à bruler. . . ." In the rhythmic interludes which followed each stanza, Huelsenbeck pounded on a bass drum and chanted "hihi-Yaboumm," and Tzara endlessly repeated "rougebleu" in rhythm with his castanets while Janco played a counter-rhythm on a whistle. How was one to understand a text that read:

0 0 0 0 0 0

or "prrza chrraz," or "zimzim urallala zimzim urallala zimzim zanzibar zimzallazam." Ball answers, "The subject of the *poème simultané* is the value of the human voice." The phonetic poem in performance had become "an act of respiratory and auditive combinations, firmly tied to a unit of duration."[72]

Illustration 8 *L'amiral cherche une maison à louer*, poème simultan par R. Huelsenbeck, M. Janco, Tr. Tzara; published in *Cabaret Voltaire*, Hugo Ball ed., Zurich, Verlag "Die Arche," June 1916, Little review

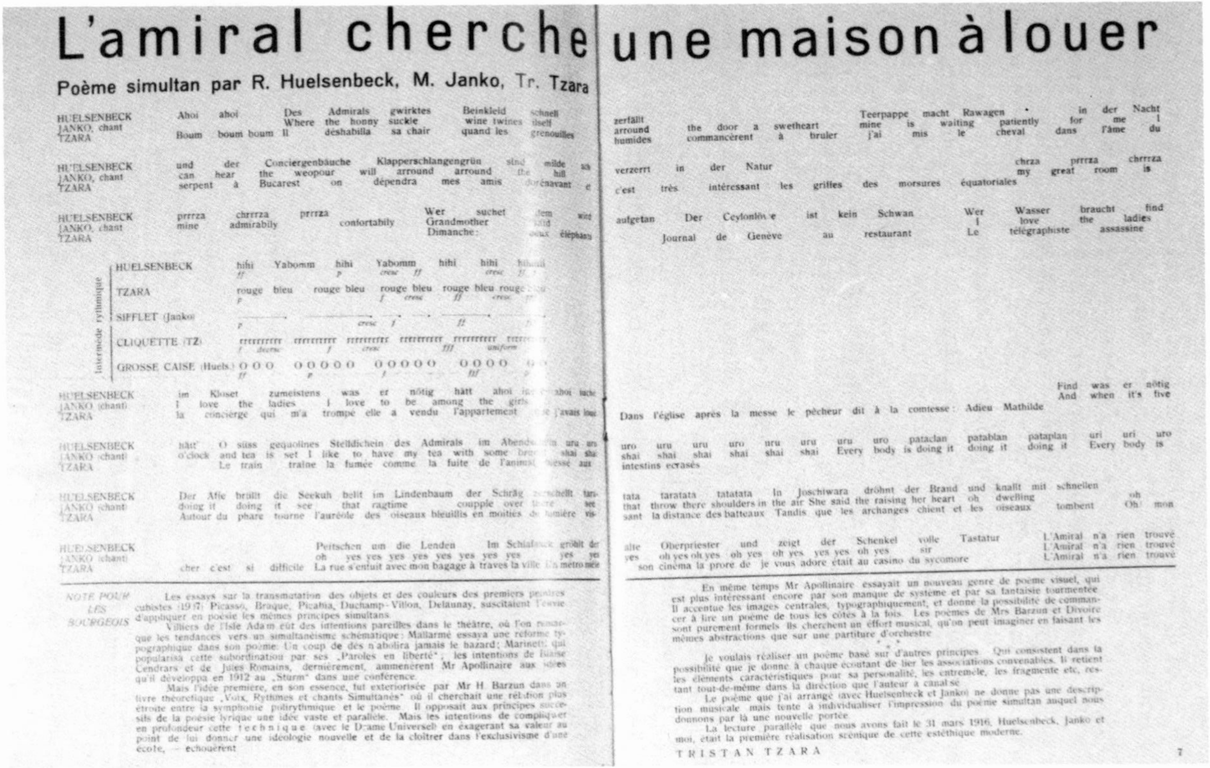
L'amiral cherche une maison à louer

Poème simultan par R. Huelsenbeck, M. Janko, Tr. Tzara

NOTE POUR LES BOURGEOIS

Les essays sur la transmutation des objets et des couleurs des premiers peintres cubistes (1907) Picasso, Braque, Picabia, Duchamp-Villon, Delaunay, suscitaient l'envie d'appliquer en poésie les mêmes principes simultans.

Villiers de l'Isle Adam eût des intentions pareilles dans le théatre, où l'on remarque les tendances vers un simultanéisme schématique; Mallarmé essaya une réforme typographique dans son poème: Un coup de dés n'abolira jamais le hazard; Marinetti qui popularisa cette subordination par ses „Paroles en liberté"; les intentions de Blaise Cendrars et de Jules Romains, dernièrement, ammenèrent Mr Apollinaire aux idées qu'il développa en 1912 au „Sturm" dans une conférence.

Mais l'idée première, en son essence, fut exteriorisée par Mr H. Barzun dans un livre théoretique „Voix, Rythmes et chants Simultanés" où il cherchait une relation plus étroite entre la symphonie polirythmique et le poème. Il opposait aux principes succesifs de la poésie lyrique une idée vaste et paralléle. Mais les intentions de compliquer en profondeur cette t e c h n i q u e (avec le Drame Universel) en exagerant sa valeur au point de lui donner une idéologie nouvelle et de la cloitrer dans l'exclusivisme d'une école, — echouèrent

En même temps Mr Apollinaire essayait un nouveau genre de poème visuel, qui est plus intéressant encore par son manque de systéme et par sa fantaisie tourmentée. Il accentue les images centrales, typographiquement, et donne la possibilité de commancer à lire un poéme de tous les côtés à la fois. Les poémes de Mrs Barzun et Divoire sont purement formels. Ils cherchent un éffort musical, qu'on peut imaginer en faisant les mêmes abstractions que sur une partiture d'orchestre

* * *

Je voulais réaliser un poéme basé sur d'autres principes. Qui consistent dans la possibilité que je donne à chaque écoutant de lier les associations convenables. Il retient les éléments caractéristiques pour sa personalité, les entremêle, les fragmente etc, restant tout-de-même dans la direction que l'auteur a canalisé.

Le poème que j'ai arrangé (avec Huelsenbeck et Janko) ne donne pas une description musicale mais tente à individualiser l'impression du poème simultan auquel nous donnons par là une nouvelle portée.

La lecture paralléle que nous avons fait le 31 mars 1916, Huelsenbeck, Janko et moi, était la première réalisation scénique de cette esthétique moderne.

TRISTAN TZARA

7

Collection: Dr. and Mrs. H.J. Kleinschmidt

The performer wheezed, gasped, wailed and sputtered out the letters and sounds. In Ball's own words, "The poet crows, curses, sighs, stutters, yodels, as he pleases."[73]

Some of these experiments in language may be looked at against a religio-mystical background. The "magic" in religion has often been bound up with power-words like "abracadabra" whose meaning and linguistic provenance is obscure. Here impressiveness derives from unintelligibility. Ball ascribed two-thirds of the "wonderfully plaintive words that no human mind can resist" to "ancient magical texts," (15.VI.1916), and spoke of a mystical interconnection between all things which allowed one to reject normal logic and trust to instinct and the laws of chance. The same militant idealism which prompted Kandinsky to move towards the world of theosophy, drew both Ball and Arp to the works of the seventeenth-century mystic Jacob Boehme in his concern with the "language of Paradise," and Boehme's works were read aloud at the Cabaret Voltaire. Ball was acquainted with the works of the Suabian doctor and poet Justines Kerner who in 1829 published fragments of the "lost language of the soul" spoken by a hypnotic clairvoyant—a coherent but unintelligible language. And Ball himself remarked that modern artists were gnostics who practiced things that priests believed to be long forgotten.

The unintelligible ecstatic stammering which St. Paul called "the gift of tongues" (I Cor.XIV.18) has often been considered the speech of angels. In a more contemporary vein, what is called "speaking with tongues" has been looked at as "an attempt to restore the human word to a new affective basis."[74] An utterance at a Mormon meeting in Manchester, early in the century, sounds very much like the dadas' own sound-poems:

> O me, sontrote krush krammon palassate
> Mount Zion kron cow che and America pa
> palassate pa pau po pe! Sontro von teli
> terattate taw. O me, terrei te-te-te-te!
> O me terrei te! Terrei terrei, te, te-te-te.[75]

Although Ball in his diary (23.VI.1916) claims to have "invented a new genre of poems 'Verse ohne Worte' (poems without words) or 'Lautgedichte' (sound poems)," he was familiar with the work of Barzun and Divoire, as was Tzara.[76] Nor is enough credit given to Kandinsky's influence, through Ball, on the Cabaret Voltaire's experiments with "the word."[77] In *Concerning the Spiritual in Art*, Kandinsky turns to talk about literature:

> frequent repetition of a word (a favorite game of children forgotten in later life) deprives the word of its external reference. Similarly, the symbolic reference of a designated object tends to be forgotten and only the sound is retained. We hear this pure sound, unconsciously perhaps, in relation to the concrete or immaterial object.

But in the latter case pure sound exercises a direct impression on the soul. The soul attains to an objectless vibration, even more complicated, I might say more transcendent, than the reverberations released by the sound of a bell, a stringed instrument, or a fallen board. In this direction lie great possibilities for the literature of the future.[78]

It was in the "verbal potency" of the inner sound of the word and the "vibrations" that it set up in the head, that Kandinsky saw the way of the literature of the future. When, in writing about the form of poetry, Ball stresses solely the "values of the beginning sequence," he speaks of it as being repeated and improvised upon, thus creating hypnotically sounding "vibrations" (23.VI.1916)—using Kandinsky's own word. In Kandinsky's experiments with poems devoid of semantic meaning, *Klänge*[79] (Sounds), the sound of the human voice was applied in pure fashion, "without being darkened by the word, by the meaning of the word." Poems from this collection were recited fot the first time at the Cabaret Voltaire.[80]

For Ball, words were conceived of as being meaningful by being reminiscent of other words, or rather sounds "touching lightly on a hundred ideas without naming them." In August, 1916, setting out a list of directives toward a language project, he wrote:

1. Language is not the only means of expression. It is not capable of communicating the most profound experiences (to be considered when evaluating literature).

2. The destruction of the speech organs can be a means of self-discipline. When communications are broken, when all contact ceases, then estrangement and loneliness occur, and people sink back into themselves.

3. Spit out words: the dreary, lame, empty language of men in society. Simulate gray modesty or madness. But inwardly be in a state of tension. Reach an incomprehensible unconquerable sphere.

16.VIII.1916

The image of the human form was gradually disappearing from the painted canvas. The next step was for poetry to do away with language.

Through Kandinsky, Ball had been introduced to the work of the Russian phoneticists Alexi Kruchenykh and Victor Khlebnikov,[81] who, in their "zaumnyi jazyk," "the creation from existing phonemes of absolutely meaningless combinations in order to obtain freedom from meaning,"[82] had created a transrational language. Ball himself had read the poems of Christian Morgenstern at the Cabaret Voltaire two years after the poet's death. "The big Lalula" from his *Songs of the Gallows* (1905) was especially popular:

Kroklokwafzi? Sememmi:
Seiokrontro—prafriplo:
Bifzi, Bafzi; hulalemi:
quasti basti bo . . .
Lalu, lalu lalu lalula!

Also popular was his "Fish's Nightsong," a poem with no sounds at all.

Work on these sound-poems was particularly suited to a multinational group whose members spoke one another's languages only imperfectly. Arp, an Alsatian, was bilingual. Janco's and Tzara's mother tongue was Rumanian[83] (although Tzara had a fair knowledge of French), while Huelsenbeck and Ball spoke German. An example of a cooperative poem by Arp and Tzara shows each contributing lines in a different language:

Balsam cartouche

Kocht der Adam seine maus zu mus
blattern leicht steinvogler in granit
Kratzt das milde gnu die geigennuss
le gendarme amour qui pisse si vite.
wattehufe tragen dornenmann
esel treibt in sonnenschwamm am tor
coq et glace se couchent sous l'oeil galant
traumern kommt der cactus seltsam vor[84]

The common linguistic denominator of the group was absolute sound,[85] and when he was ready to transcend sound, the dada poet-performer moved on to noise:

Noises (a drawn out rrr sustained for minutes on end, suddenly crashes, sirens wailing) are existentially more powerful than the human voice . . . the noises represent the inarticulate, inexorable and ultimately decisive forces which constitute the background. The poem carries the message that mankind is swallowed up in a mechanistic process. In a generalized and compressed form it represents the battle of the human voice against a world whose rhythms and whose din are inescapable.[86]

Ball composed a noise-concert for shawms and little bells, baby rattles and chants for a human chorus. Perhaps he recalled his visit as a student to Basle on the day of the drumming. At this yearly event, all the citizens turned out in an orgy of rattling for a drummed day of national prayer. On that day Ball had witnessed the craziest convulsions as all that was buried and uncommunicated was suddenly let out, and drummed out.

The drum rhythms that were chosen at the Cabaret were often African, employing real tom-toms to accompany the different "tarred and feathered players" who finally imitated the sound of drums themselves,

damai da dai umbala damo . . .
Sokobauno sokobauno sokobauno.[87]

Huelsenbeck loved the Negro rhythms and even persuaded Jan Ephraim, the proprietor of the cabaret who had spent a good part of his seafaring life in Africa, to help him organize an "African Night." The Dutchman listened to the "umba umba" refrain which Huelsenbeck intoned over and over in his poems. One day he came to the poet with a sheet of paper on which he had scribbled "Trabadya La Modjere/Magamore Mafafere/Trabadja Bono." Huelsenbeck now recited this new "authentic" Negro poem although he refused to omit his own "umba, umba" at the end. He would roar out his lungs more like a side-show barker than a reciter of verse, often waving his cane while drums marked out the rhythm and riding whips cracked the air. Others of the group joined him in black cowls.

The primitive exercised a strong attraction for the dadas. Tzara wrote articles comparing primitive and Western art and published some 40 "African poems."[88] Masks cried out the deepest and most passionate feelings of the actor-performers, and rhythms spoke feelings. Cowbells, drums and blows on the tables joined to excite an audience which had previously sat impassive behind its beer mugs. Huelsenbeck would often recite the poem "Rivers" because it contained extremely daring images and always brought out the audiences' antagonism. Spectators found Huelsenbeck arrogant and belligerent, and even his girlfriend "L" felt that the cabaret was "spawned by insanity." She called the members "immoral" and added "They're good for nothing, they're worthless . . ." When Huelsenbeck presented his mother with a copy of his "Fantastic Prayers," she burst into tears, fearing her son had gone stark raving mad. The press wrote "They are men possessed, outcasts, maniacs, and all for the love of their work. They turn to the public as if asking its help, placing before it the materials to diagnose their sickness."[89]

If these early efforts appeared to be "asking the help" of the audience, it soon became clear that the "group of five" had something else in mind. They, and all those in the later dada-surrealist group who consciously concerned themselves with the use of the theatrical medium, posed as a primary condition for the restoration of a type of primitive theatrical communion, a change in attitude on the part of the public. The passive consenting spectator must give way to a hostile participant, provoked, attacked and beaten by author and actors. As Ribemont-Dessaignes wrote in *déjà jadis* (his recollections of the dada period),

Though the texts were basically childlike, whether imbued with extreme violence or presented by their own author . . . in an inarticulate, particularly odd, provocative way, the audience reacted out of proportion. The essential had been attained. It was necessary to evoke hostility even at the risk of appearing to be sinister imbeciles.[90]

From the small stage of the Cabaret Voltaire, the performers "did not neglect from time to time to tell the fat and utterly uncomprehending Zurich philistines that they regarded them as pigs,"[91] and as Marcel Janco proudly noted, "we made our good fellow citizens roar like lions."[92]

Dada and Futurism

"... resolutely against the future ..."

Tristan Tzara

Illustration 9   Costumes by the futurist Depero for *Machine of 3000,* a mechanical ballet

Collection: Depero Museum, Rovereto, Italy

Both in their theatrical explorations of simultaneity and the art of noise, and in their early attempts to agitate the audience (later to be expanded in the "provocation performances"), the Cabaret Voltaire group was not treading on entirely new ground. Noise had already been christened an art form by the futurists. In 1913 Luigi Russolo had written a manifesto entitled "The Art of Noise," which posited that Western culture to date had accepted only a narrow segment of those infinite possibilities of sound that make music. "It is necessary," he wrote, "to break this restricted circle of pure sounds and conquer the infinite variety of 'noise-sounds.' "[1] All sound should be acceptable material for music:

> Roars, Thunders, Explosions, Bursts, Crashes, Booms, Whistles, Hisses, Puffs, Whispers, Murmurs, Grumbles, Buzzes, Bubblings, Screeches, Creaks, Rustles, Hums, Crackles, Rubs, Percussion noises using: metal, wood, skin, rock, terra-cotta, etc. Voices of animals and humans: Shouts, Shrieks, Moans, Yells, Howls, Laughs, Groans, Sobs.[2]

Russolo, realizing that such a range of sounds could not be produced by traditional instruments, began work on a new group of instruments called "intonarumori" or "noise intoners." These instruments, which were basically rectangular wooden boxes with protruding funnel-shaped megaphones, were run by various motors and mechanisms. They were demonstrated in public for the first time on August 11, 1913, at Marinetti's Casa Rossa in Milan. A year later, at a performance in London, neither critics nor audiences were particularly enchanted:

> the music of the . . . weird, funnel-shaped instruments . . . resembled the sounds heard in the rigging of a channel-steamer during a bad crossing, and it was perhaps unwise of the players—or should we call them the "noisicians?"—to proceed with their second piece . . . after the pathetic cries of "no more" which greeted them from all the excited quarters of the auditorium.[3]

That the intonarumori-players continued despite the pleas of the audience is in no way surprising. Marinetti not only wanted a more active spectator, but was willing to go to great lengths to impel an audience to action. In "The Variety Theatre Manifesto" he suggests:

> Spread a powerful glue on some of the seats, so that the male or female spectator will stay glued down and make everyone laugh . . . sell the same ticket to ten people: traffic jam, bickering, and wrangling. Offer free tickets to gentlemen or ladies who are notoriously unbalanced, irritable or eccentric and likely to provoke uproars with obscene gestures, pinching women, or other freakishness. Sprinkle the seats with dust to make people itch and sneeze.[4]

These devices, plus the inflammatory manifestos loudly declaimed from the stage, achieved their aim and the audiences vented their fury. Reporting on a *serata* (the futurist equivalent of a *"soirée"*), at the Margherita Hall in Rome, the London Times says:

> Few of the scenes could be understood because showers of beans, potatoes, toma-toes, and apples often drove the actors off the stage . . . When the futurist artists came on the stage carrying paintings they had achieved they used their masterpieces quite frankly as shields.[5]

In Naples, Marinetti stood on the stage "ducking potatoes and apples with great aplomb and shaking his fist at the mob while he shouted to them that it would take a microscope to see their souls."[6]

Hans Richter's admission of the ties between dada and futurism,

> Like all newborn movements, we were convinced that the world began anew in us; but in fact we had swallowed futurism—bones, feathers, and all. It is true that in the process of digestion all sorts of bones and feathers had been regurgitated.[7]

stands in contrast to the dadas' usually explicit and vociferous rejections of any relation with the futurists (as with schools of art and "isms" in general). This need to refute any possible association with established movements, avant-garde or otherwise, often assumed childish proportions. When Marinetti declared in his "Foundation and Manifesto of Futurism"

> We declare that a racing car is more beautiful than the Victory of Samothrace.[8]

Tzara found it necessary to retort:

> We declare that the automobile is a feeling that has sufficiently coddled us in the slowness of its abstraction like steamships, noises and ideas.[9]

Moreover Breton in the first of his two dada manifestos quite categorically states ". . . futurism was a political movement. DADA is a state of mind. To oppose one to the other reveals ignorance or bad faith."[10] It seems clear, how-ever, that at least the basic tenets of futurism and probably some of its operative methods as well were familiar to the Zurich dadas when they began their experi-mental work in 1916. We know that by 1916 both Tzara and Ball were in corre-spondence with Marinetti, and that Ball in his diary speaks of extending even further the experiments in syntax and grammar called for by the futurist leader in his manifesto of 1913 "L'imagination sans fils et les mots en liberté." In 1916 as well, Tzara had met futurist set designer Enrico Prampolini in Rome, and that same year Prampolini participated in the "International Dada Exhibition" in

Zurich. Tracing the connections backwards, however, it appears that the initial meetings between dada and futurism were not direct but rather achieved via the Paris grapevine which linked Marinetti to Apollinaire and Pierre Albert-Birot, and through them, Marinetti to Tzara. By 1913 Marinetti was a familiar figure to the French literary avant-garde. His first futurist manifesto had been published on the front page of *Le Figaro* in February 1909, and in April of that year his play *Le Roi bombace* caused a scandal at the *Théâtre de l'Oeuvre*. His book *Le Futurisme*, a history of the movement, appeared in Paris in 1911, and in 1912 *Le Figaro* published his "manifeste technique de la littérature futuriste" which extolled the virtues of the machine, speed, and a liberated vocabulary and syntax. In addition, through the early years of the century, Marinetti had been on the board of directors of three French "arts" journals: *La Vogue, La Critique internationale,* and *Akademos.*

Apollinaire was probably the vital link in channeling futurist materials to the dadas, for he was friendly with Marinetti, and wrote a number of articles on futurism starting in 1913. We know that Apollinaire was in correspondence with Tzara by 1916, for the first issue of *Le Cabaret Voltaire* features his work as well as that of Tzara, Picasso, and Marinetti. Tzara, in 1917, contributed to Pierre Albert-Birot's journal *SIC,* and Albert-Birot contributed to Tzara's *Dada.* Albert-Birot's studio was in the same building as that of Gino Severini, a friend of Marinetti and an artist (whose wedding in 1913 had been attended by Apollinaire). *SIC,* in 1917, featured a description of the futurist movement written by Luciano Folgore, a futurist himself:

> Futurism is not a school. It's a trend. It's a leap forward. It's the inexhaustible love of the new. . . . Futurism has no laws, doesn't want to impose fixed rules. . . . Futurism proclaims in some cases the superiority of certain modes of expression, not in order to establish artistic dogmas, but merely to extol its conquests. . . . Futurism has thrown its grand creations into the ring of understanding: synthetic lyricism, freed words, plastic dynamism, the art of noises and the sounds and smells of painting.[11]

By 1917 then, a network for the transferring of information between the futurists and the Zurich dadas clearly existed.

> Through Tzara we were also in relation with the futurist movement and carried on a correspondence with Marinetti . . . we were glad to take over the concept of simultaneity, of which we made so much use. Tzara for the first time had poems recited simultaneously on the stage . . . although the "poème simultanée" had already been introduced in France by Deremé and others. From Marinetti we also borrowed "bruitism" . . . [12]

Many common elements are to be found in dada and futurist performances. Short theatrical pieces, simultaneous and phonic poetry, declaimed manifestos and bruitist music were part of the programs of both movements. In music though, the dadas never devoted themselves to experiments as technological and mechaniatic as Rusollo's "intonarumori." Their instruments were home-made, their noise-craft more naive. Natural sound took priority over the machine. Hugo Ball's phonic poems, such as *O Gadji Beri Bimba*,

> gadji beri bimba glandridi laula lonni
> cadori
> gadjama gramma berida bimbala glandri
> galassassa laulitalomini
> gadju beri bin glassa glassala alula lonni
> cadorsu sassala bim
> Gadjama tuffm i zimzalla binban gligia
> wowolimai bin beri ban[13]

resemble the invented language of a poem such as the futurist Balla's "Discussion of Futurism by Two Sudanese Critics":

> Farcionisgnaco gurninfuturo bordubalota-
> pompimagnusa
> sfacataca mimitirichita plucu sbumu
> farufutusmaca
> sgnacgnacgnac chr chr chr stechestecheteretere
> maumauziaititititititi.[14]

The revolution in typography proposed by the futurists can also be studied in the dada journals, and the works of the futurist poets Buzzi, Cangiullo, and Marinetti himself were presented at the Cabaret Voltaire. In both movements the poems and manifestos were more often than not meant to be read aloud and were performed by multiple voices. The futurists were even more extreme than the dadas in their use of the techniques of simultaneity. In Marinetti's play *I Vasi Communicanti* (the title was later adopted by Breton), the action on stage goes on in three different unrelated locations at the same time. Linear and homogeneous time was out; in its place stood a new dynamism to be achieved by the simultaneous reduction and overlapping of time and space.

Some of the futurist *sintesi* (very brief theatre pieces) are similar, especially in tone and impact, to the "staged moments" of the dada performers. In *Atto Negativa* by Bruno Corra and Emilio Settimelli,

> A man enters, busy, preoccupied. He takes off his overcoat, his hat, and walks furiously.
> Man: What a fantastic thing! Incredible!
> (He turns toward the public, is irritated to see them, then coming to the apron, says categorically:)
> I have absolutely nothing to tell you . . .
> Bring down the curtain!
> CURTAIN[15]

In recalling a "play" by Paul Eluard, Tzara recounts,

Two characters meet on the stage. The first says: "The post office is across the street." The second replies: "What's that to me?"

CURTAIN[16]

Both plays, in their brevity, seem to be little more than a staged gag. In the first, the sense of anticipation aroused by the character's excitement is short-circuited by the actor acknowledging the audience and quickly insulting and dismissing it. In the second, anticipation is generated by the meeting of the two characters. The reply of the second leaves the piece nowhere to go and the curtain falls.

Sections of Mario Carli's *States of Mind* in their unintelligibility and their exploration of phonic language resemble the dialogues of Tzara's *Première aventure céleste de M. Antipyrine.* Carli uses generic "characters":

The Deputy (with great oratorical gestures and a thundering voice): Mirafago prorfon caralazz brugun fala deidor prokolifrogotipo campogofu tlombo!

The Lovers (to each other): Pci ni hai vit cir pui pui pui pui tu cchiu glu glu glu ingin vl n slin fuffi doddo dai dai dai dai

The Poet (with ecstatic eyes toward the sky): Shudder mystery wings sunset icily. Showers lover moon suffered breathtaking murmur supine foliage strutting zooms rose-colored sighs blue.[17]

Tzara, though inventing names for his characters, provides essentially the same material:

Pipi: amertume sans église allons allons charbon chameau synthétise amertume sur l'église isisise les rideaux dodododo

Mr. Antipyrine: Coco Bgai Affahou
Zoumbai zoumbai zoumbai zoum

Mr. Cricri: il n'y a pas d'humanité il y a les reverbères et les chiens
dzin aha dzin aha bobobo Tyao oahiii hio hii
bebooum ihea ieho.[18]

All the plays are brief. All, in their rejection of logic, have no need for the traditional theatrical forms which stress exposition and development and demand adequate characterization. In Marinetti's "Teatro futurista sintetica" (1915), and in Tzara's "Manifèste de M. Antipyrine" (1916) and "Manifèste de M. aa l'Antiphilosophe" (1919), both authors reject all classical forms of dramatic literature. All theatre that progressively develops an intrigue, delves into psychological analysis, or hints at verisimilitude must be abolished as "stupid" and "passéiste." In its place will come "all the discoveries (no matter how unlikely, weird, and anti-theatrical) that our talent is discovering in the subconscious, in ill-defined forces, in pure abstraction, in the purely cerebral, the purely fantastic, in record-setting and body madness."[19] Tzara cries out: "We are circus directors and whistle amid the winds of fairs. . ."[20]

What undoubtedly links the two movements is an "esprit provocant." If Marinetti was delighted to "épater le bourgeois," so was Tzara. Inasmuch as the futurists could be counted on to shock, goad and provoke an audience, Tzara was for them; and one can see in dada the aggressively direct approach to the public and the acts of provocation which were part of the futurist *serate*.

Paris had had its first taste of Marinetti in 1909 when his play *Le Roi bombace—tragédie satirique* (written in French in 1905), was performed at Lugné Poe's *Théâtre de l'Oeuvre*. The play, described by Francesco Flora as

> . . . the caricature of the Past . . . of world bolshevism, of stupid putrescence . . . the abdominal imbecility of the boredom of a constant reality. . .[21]

employed masks, music, and several elaborate "trucs" and relied heavily on oral-anal metaphors to create the scandal it did. The strong audience response was aided by the several farts emitted by a priest in the second act. In another of Marinetti's plays performed in Paris in 1909, *Poupées électriques,* an American engineer plies his hobby constructing life-size automatons of his in-laws in order to have them clear their throats in the room where he is making love to his wife.

In a Paris where the gods were changing faster than anyone could keep track, scandal was in its heyday. Romantics were followed by parnassiens, and then symbolists, naturalists, impressionists, fauves and cubists. Soon orphists, vorticists, imagists, intimists, cloissonists, paroxyists, dynamists, and vitalists crowded the market. In the struggle to attract a public, he who provoked best reigned, and the dadas were not unimpressed by the futurists' abilities to carry a crowd. At a lecture he gave in 1914 at the Galerie Bernheim in Paris, Marinetti contrived to utilize all the methods at his disposal to create a scandal:

> Standing on a table, his moustache flying in the wind, his eyes flashing, he directed curses at the past with its false poetry, at the manifestations of art hallowed by tradition and under the effect of a senile love . . . he praised to the sky, with hyperbole and rash metaphors, the new artistic, plastic and poetic motifs such as the automobile, electricity . . .[22]

Today, this may appear so much puerility, but at that time the attachment of "l'homme moyen sensuel" to the rites of his art was religious in character and every attempt at change threatened the security of his daily life. Both futurism and dada learned to use this factor to the utmost.

For all the similarities between the two movements, the divergent elements are quite apparent. The futurists were one of the few groups of contemporary artists anywhere to preach a war-oriented politics. Extremely nationalistic, they staged, in addition to their *serate,* anti-pacificist demonstrations, while within the theatre-evenings themselves much of the material was polemical or quasi-political. Their linking of war propaganda and the theatre was generally unequivocal—"The only way to inspire Italy with the warlike spirit today is through the theatre."[23] In the 1930s many of the futurists were themselves fascists and Marinetti was a personal friend of Mussolini. The Zurich dadas, by contrast, were essentially refugees fleeing the war: an international melange of Germans, Rumanians, and French, who, though almost entirely apolitical (only in Berlin-dada did politics play a significant role), were surely against the war. Futurism was directed against all the confining isms of the past and toward a more liberated future. Dada, though it too espoused an anti-passéism, was "resolutely against the future."[24] Whereas futurism urged a "daily spit on the altar of Art,"[25] dada went a step further and rejected the concept of Art entirely. Most important perhaps, the works of futurism were part of a "program" and designed to fulfill that program:

> War—futurism intensified—obliges us to march and not to rot in libraries and reading rooms . . . ninety percent of Italians go to the theatre, whereas only ten percent read books and reviews . . . [26]

If theatre could attract nine times as many people as written works, the futurists would make theatre. Dada had no program and was against all programs. If dada turned to theatre, it was because only by playing could the dada discover who he was.

Whatever they had taken from futurism, the dadas were erratic in their loves and hates, and by the time Marinetti brought his bruitist concerts to Paris, dada was screaming, "We have enough cubist and futurist academies."[27] At the *Théâtre des Champs Elysées,* dadas spurred the audience to whistle and jeer at Russolo's music until Marinetti requested that if they could not respect the music, they at least respect the musicians who had conducted themselves as befits heroes during the war. To this the outcry was even more vociferous:

> heros, all the more reason to boo them, poor things . . . who asked them to make war![28]

In the relationship dada-futurism, the wheel seemed to have come full circle.

The Dada Actor and Performance Theory

"Are you one of those people who call them-
selves dadaists . . .?"
"Yessir," I said, stiffly clicking my heels on
Zurich's neutral soil.
"Well," he said in a paternal and almost
melancholy tone of voice, "you'll be
hearing from us."
"Yessir," I replied in an even stiffer tone (if
that was possible.)
The army doctor looked back at me as he was
about to step through the doorway:
"Be careful and avoid excitement."

Richard Huelsenbeck, *Memoirs of a Dada
Drummer*

It's too idiotic to be schizophrenic.

Carl Jung, on the dada productions

Illustration 10   Hugo Ball reciting "Karawane" at the Cabaret Voltaire, 1916

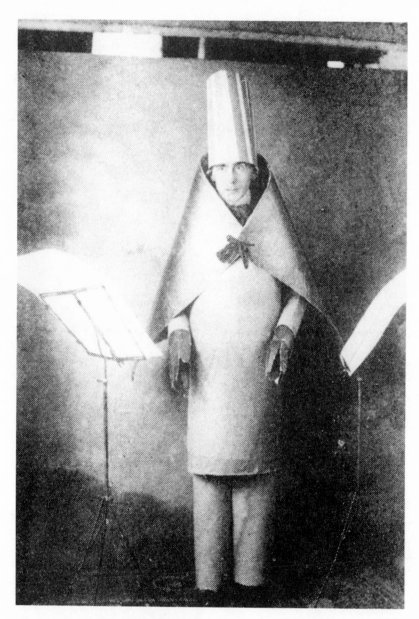

Collection: Dr. and Mrs. H.J. Kleinschmidt

Dada Becomes a Movement

Dada is a tomato.
Dada is a spook.
Dada is a chameleon of rapid, interested
  change.
Dada is never right.
Dada is soft boiled happiness.
Dada is idiotic.
Dada is life. Dada is that which changes.
Dada means nothing.
Everything is Dada.

Dada manifestos, *passim*.

After the first few months of experimentation, the group at the Cabaret Voltaire chose the word "dada" to describe their work. Despite the great controversy over the origin of the name and its meaning, Hans Arp wrote:

> I am convinced that this word is of no importance and that only imbeciles and Spanish professors can take an interest in dates. What interests us is the Dada spirit, and we were all Dada before Dada came into existence.[1]

Dada's raging manifestos do not help clarify the movement; rather, they reinforce its many ambiguities. Dada comes out against Art ("Art is useless and impossible to justify"—Francis Picabia), and yet makes art. Its spokesmen cry: Dada wants nothing Dada means nothing All real Dadas are against Dada—and yet its adherents continue to create. Destruction becomes synonymous with creation: "order-disorder; ego-nonego; affirmation-negation."[2] How is one to define a movement which cannot be identified with any one personality or place, viewpoint or subject, which affected all of the arts, which had a continually shifting focus and which was moreover intentionally negative, ephemeral and illogical. What does emerge from the manifestos, journals and recorded diatribes of the "movement" is the opposition to anything that smacks of traditionalism in literature and the arts:

> Dada was born of a need for independence, of a distrust toward unity. Those who are with us preserve their freedom. We recognize no theory. We have enough cubist and futurist academies: laboratories of formal ideas . . . I am against systems, the most acceptable system is a principle to have none.[3]

Dada would not succumb to the procrustean bed of bourgeois values, and in fact, the only consistent aim of the movement was a subverting of the values of bourgeois society and of bourgeois complacency itself. Logic, and with it the traditional use of language was to be abolished: "We need works that are strong, straight, precise and forever beyond understanding." No systems were to be served, no ties would bind. Dada was against the past and "decidedly against the future." It was, in fact, opposed to the concept of Art as a whole. Tzara assigned art "a subordinate place in the supreme movement measured only in terms of life" and he wrote: "art is not as important as we mercenaries of the spirit have been proclaiming for centuries . . ."[4] Art is going to sleep for a new world to be born. 'ART'—parrot word—replaced by DADA."[5]

Dada was at its inception a movement more involved with a style of life than with a system of aesthetics, more involved with existence than with art. "The pure Dadaist," the art critic William Rubin writes, "was not a painter at all, or even a poet, but someone whose essence was expressed equally in all his acts." Huelsenbeck set few limits on who could be a dadaist:

> The bartender in the Manhattan Bar, who pours our Curaçao with one hand and gathers up his gonorrhea with the other, is a Dadaist. The gentleman in the raincoat, who is about to start his seventh trip around the world, is a Dadaist. The Dadaist should be a man who has fully understood that one is entitled to have ideas only if one can transform them into life—the completely active type, who lives only through action, because it holds the possibility of his achieving knowledge.[6]

The dadas were nonetheless poets, painters, and performers and as such their anti-art stand posed them a serious problem: how to express themselves without art when all means of expression are potentially artistic. As attempted solutions, a Duchamp "ready made," such as his "Bottle Rack" (1914) was a mass-produced commercial object on which he conferred the status "sculpture": at once an artistic yet anti-art gesture. At the "Premier Vendredi" *matinée* in Paris (1920), Breton erased Picabia's blackboard drawing, reinforcing the dada stand against art, history and permanence. Dada would exist only in the present—it would provide no models for the future. Spontaneity would be recognized as the basis for the creative act:

> Dada, absolute and incontestable belief in every god that is the immediate product of spontaneity. . . . What we want now is spontaneity. Not because it is better or more beautiful than anything else. But because everything that issues freely from ourselves, without the intervention of speculative ideas, represents us. We must intensify this quality of life . . .[7]

Every spontaneous impulse, every message from within, was therefore greeted as an expression of pure reality, and every possible artistic technique was acceptable to provoke these impulses. Absolute spontaneity, chance regarded as the intervention of mysterious and wonderful forces, pure automatism as a revelation over which consciousness has no control—these became the techniques that opened the way to a more comprehensive view of the relationship between Self and the world. In some respects the call for a new order that would accommodate the expression and acting-out of irrational and unconscious impulses harks back to Rousseau and Romanticism. The notion that the human being was stunted or deformed by social conventions that failed to allow for his irrational side never seemed so plausible as it did to the generation that came of age with World War I. But dada's "unreasoned order" was more radical than the dualism proposed by the Romantic-Symbolist tradition. Rejecting the gradual attuning of irrational drives to rational controls, it opted in favor of anarchic spontaneity.

This combined stand of anti-art, anti-history, anti-permanence and pro-spontaneity makes it quite a simple step to an understanding of the dadas' valuing of "process" (the manner by which the work is accomplished) above "product" (the work itself):

> The efficacy of art to the extent that Dada admitted it at all, lay in the purposeful act of making it. The object created was not an end in itself and consequently nothing to be prized.[8]

The Dada Actor

Who wants to act now, or even see acting.

Hugo Ball, 2.IV.1915

For an actor, process and product merge. Though there are many moments in performance which are the products of rehearsal "decisions," still the creative art in its totality must occur at every performance anew, and to truly work his art, the actor must constantly remain open and "in the process of . . . ." Once the actor has finished his performance, nothing of his "art" remains visible. This is in perfect accord with the dadas' expressed desire to leave behind as few completed works as possible, and it is perhaps for this reason that the dada-artist became an actor. Placing himself and the moment of his creation at the center of the artistic event, the dada performer explored the boundary between primitive exaltation and manic excess. This performer, who did not find it inappropriate to combat insanity with what appeared as well to be insanity, is at the center of dada theatre.

The dada actor is an anti-actor. All craft is ignored. He uses his unskilled body and a spirit capable of spontaneous emanations, allows himself manifestos and poems, some pots and bells, cardboard and paint, a chair or two and perhaps a bed-sheet. Rehearsal and the work of the director are basically ignored. Improvisation takes over:

all our sketches were of an improvised nature, full of fantasy, freshness and the unexpected. There were few costumes, little direction, and few sets.[9]

If we divide "actors" into three main categories: the "skilled" actor, the "masked" actor, and the "personal" actor, the dada performer falls into the last group. The "skilled" actor is one most clearly recognized by the "skill" he presents before the audience: the acrobat and his bodily contortions, the tightrope walker and his daring abilities. Rather than seeing the actor (him), we see the skill (it). We look at the actor's virtuosity; we are thrilled and aghast by what he can do that we cannot do. The dada performer had no such skill. With the exception of Laban's dancers (who, though they were not dadas, did participate in dada performance), no dada who ventured on stage did so with a performing skill greater than that of the average "artist" in the street. That he had more daring, and quite specific and driving motivation for his performances, is for the moment beside the point.

The "masked" actor works behind a mask or role. He is most simply the actor within the traditional play. Watching him perform, we know him as "Faustus" or "Oedipus" and with our "willing suspension of disbelief" we allow him to take us into the life of his character. He will excite us only inasmuch as we are moved by the character he "lives" on the stage. Afterwards, the more sophisticated may comment, "look at who he (the actor) can become." The average spectator will remain entranced by the mask. No one ever went home from the Cabaret Voltaire speaking of the characters "X" or "Y," and though the dadas used real masks, they never so lost themselves to the mask that one was not always aware, "Oh, there's Tzara, kicking up his feet."

The dada actor was the "personal" actor, still tied on stage to the name, the identity which marked his offstage life. He is, in this, most readily recognized as the nightclub star: Frank Sinatra, who sings to us as Frank Sinatra; Buddy Hackett, the stand-up comedian who, while moving through the characters of his routine, remains Buddy Hackett. Film and television have blurred these distinctions by deifying the actor and in so doing have washed out the line between the personal and masked performer. We can hardly look at Dustin Hoffman in a role without seeing Dustin Hoffman. The stage still manages to retain some of this categorical difference. On stage at the Cabaret Voltaire, the public saw Tristan Tzara, Hugo Ball, Marcel Janco, never losing sight of the performer as an identifiable person. As for the actor: Tzara presented Tzara, Ball presented Ball. The personal dada actor then, outfitted either in his clothes of everyday or in the hastily put-together trappings of some outlandish masquerade, performed his phonetic intonings, masked dances and rhythmic instrumentals.

The setting for these performances was what Michael Kirby calls a "non-matrixed environment."[10] Kirby speaks of the performer in traditional theatre as performing within a matrix, a created world of time, place and character. The dada performer, inasmuch as he is a personal actor, performs outside the matrix of character and time. The time is now, the performer is himself. There are no "given" circumstances. The actors works within no physical setting. The stage, whether it was the small slightly raised platform at the Cabaret Voltaire, or the larger stages of the "provocation performances" was usually bare, or furnished with an occasional backdrop of abstract shapes painted by the members of the group. Such a backdrop was the one painted by Arp and Hans Richter for one of the *grandes soirées:*

> We began from opposite ends of immensely long strips of paper about two yards wide, painting huge black abstracts. Arp's shapes looked like gigantic cucumbers. I followed his example and we painted miles of cucumber plantation . . . before we finally met in the middle. Then the whole thing was nailed onto pieces of wood and rolled up until the performance.[11]

Performing "before" such a backdrop, never "within" it, the dada actor was working in completely "unlocalized" space. The stage represented no-place, it was the stage. For the dadas it was important that it remain a stage—a clear dividing line between the actor and the audience. For all their innovative work in performance, the dadas still guarded the line that separates actor from audience. It was not the proscenium that they protected (for they had no need of a picture frame of any sort to confine a theatre of illusion), but the slightly thrust stage of the presentational performer; a stage which allows the performer at times to address his audience directly and then again to withdraw to a position where the audience must regard him as separate from itself.

The role played by the audience remains ambivalent. On the one hand Tzara claims "Art is a private affair, the artist does it for himself," and the dadas give us many examples of purely gratuitous acts performed for the doer's own gratification. The pervading feeling, however, is that the audience was indispensable to the dada performer. It served to stimulate, delight and enrage him. Before it, he became a circus act, a breathing collage, a chanting, incanting medicine man, a provocateur.

The dadas in their manifestos never concern themselves with the theory of performance *per se* and in this, they do the theatre critic a service. All too often theoretical doctrines restrict the observing eye inasmuch as they present a mold into which one then attempts to fit the examples. No anti-artist could even be expected to consistently follow his principles and what Albert Einstein said, speaking of theoretical physicists, well applies to the dadas:

> If you want to find out anything about the methods they use . . . I advise you to stick closely to one principle: don't listen to their words, fix your attention on their deeds.[12]

Programs and Performances

The name "dada" may have lent a new notoriety to the young movement, but the nature of the performing experiments remained basically the same. The work with sounds and language, with simultaneous poetry, with costumes and masks, as well as the attacks on the audience, all grew in scope and intensity. Marcel Janco perpetuated a *soirée* at the Cabaret Voltaire in a painting which is annotated by Arp:

> On a platform in an overcrowded room, splotched with color, are seated several fantastic characters who are supposed to represent Tzara, Janco, Ball, Huelsenbeck, and your humble servant. We are putting on one of our big Sabbaths. The people around us are shouting, laughing, gesticulating. We reply with sighs of love, salvos of hiccups, poems, and the bow-wows and meows of medieval bruitists. Tzara makes his bottom jump like the belly of an oriental dancer. Janco plays an invisible violin and bows down to the ground. Madame Hennings with a face like a madonna attempts a split. Huelsenbeck keeps pounding on a big drum, while Ball, pale as a plaster dummy, accompanies him on the piano.[13]

Ball's emotional stamina, however, was being drained by this "playground for crazy emotions":

> The cabaret needs a rest. With all the tension, the daily performances are just exhausting, they are crippling. In the middle of the crowds I start to tremble all over. Then I simply cannot take anything in, drop everything and flee.

> 15.III.1916

By April of that year, Ball could say "I am anxious to support the cabaret and then to leave it." (21.IV.1916), and on June 23, 1916, Ball offered the cabaret audience a final performance of his sound poems. His recollections of the reading of his poems on that June evening are one of the clearest descriptions we have of a dada performance event. Before his recitation, Ball read a few introductory words:

> With these sound poems we should renounce the language devastated and made impossible by journalism. . . . We should stop making poems second-hand; we should no longer take over words (not even to speak of sentences) which we did not invent absolutely anew, for our own use.

Of the performance itself Ball writes:

> I had made myself a special costume. . . . My legs were in a cylinder of shiny blue cardboard, which came up to my hips so that I looked like an obelisk. Over it I wore a huge coat collar cut out of carboard, scarlet inside and gold outside. It was

fastened at the neck in such a way that I could give the impression of winglike movement by raising and lowering my elbows. I also wore a high, blue-and-white-striped witchdoctor's hat.

On all three sides of the stage I had set up music stands facing the audience, and I put my red-penciled manuscript on them; I officiated at one stand after another. Tzara knew about my preparations, so there was a real little premiere. Everyone was curious. I could not walk inside the cylinder so I was carried onto the stage in the dark and began slowly and solemnly:

> gadji beri bimba
> glandridi lauli lonni cadori
> gadjama bim beri glassala
> glandridi glassala tuffm i zimbrabim
> blassa galassasa tuffm izimbrabim . . .

23.VI.1916

After an initial period of confusion, the audience exploded, laughing, screaming, applauding. Ball, immobilized in his costume, faced them and continued:

The stresses became heavier, the emphasis was increased as the sound of the consonants became sharper. Soon, I realized that, if I wanted to remain serious (and I wanted to at all costs), my method of expression would not be equal to the pomp of my staging. I saw Brupbacher, Jelmoli, Laban, Mrs. Wigman in the audience. I feared a disgrace and pulled myself together. I had now completed "Labada's Song to the Clouds" at the music stand on the right and the "Elephant Caravan" on the left and turned back to the middle one, flapping my wings energetically. The heavy vowel sequences and the plodding rhythm of the elephants had given me one last crescendo. But how was I to get to the end? Then I noticed that my voice had no choice but to take on the ancient cadence of priestly lamentation, that style of liturgical singing that wails in all the Catholic churches of East and West.

I do not know what gave me the idea of this music, but I began to chant my vowel sequences in a church style like a recitative, and tried not only to look serious but to force myself to be serious. For a moment it seemed as if there were a pale, bewildered face in my cubist mask, that half-frightened, half-curious face of a ten-year-old boy, trembling and hanging avidly on the priest's words in the requiems and high masses in his home parish. Then the lights went out, as I had ordered, and bathed in sweat, I was carried down off the stage like a magical bishop.

23.VI.1916

Ball was perfectly aware of the primitive and "magical" import of his metrical and phonetic experiments:

We have charged the word with forces and energies which made it possible for us to rediscover the evangelical concept of the "word" (logos) as a magical complex of images.[14]

In his writing he withdrew to this "innermost alchemy of the word," surrendering the word as a promoter of logic, in favor of Tzara's dictum "thought is made in the mouth."[15] It was in performance, however, that the impact of the spontaneously formed, alogical, rhythm-linked word reached its full power. With drum beats in the background and a dead-serious expression on his face, Ball presented himself, a multi-colored obelisk, before his audience. The three music stands on which his texts of phonetic poetry rested demarcated the boundaries of his small stage. The tubular cardboard shapes which encased him prevented almost any movement but the mock-heroic flapping of his wings and were of the same ready-made materials as the other dada costumes: cardboard tacked and pasted, and patches of colored paint.

Ball's priestly garb as well as his tubular costume on another dada occasion, both products of the rectilinear vocabulary of Cubism, are striking in their resemblance to the "abstract-puppets" of Hans Arp and his wife Sophie Taeuber, as well as to the conical forms of Depero's Futurist figures. The puppets, which consisted mostly of thread spools joined together, were used in performances at the Cabaret Voltaire.[16] Their mechanical and robot-like appearance was occasionally relieved by a bit of feather or a drape of rag, but by and large they were formed like the futurist figures and Ball's cardboard encasement—of geometric shapes and harsh joints, of chimney heads and pointers for hands. No longer locked into a tradition linked to "reality,"

> They reveled in a new world of spatial rhythms, of objects reduced to their most elementary forms. Taeuber, uninterested in external bodily attributes, moved toward an idea as unreal as a dream, and yet tied to a more important reality which everyone feels in himself when the familiar external world suddenly appears singularly impassable.[17]

The actor, as the dada puppet, had been abstracted and the dada costume itself stood as a reaction against the "arts" of sewing and design, against permanence and against any sort of subtlety in characterization. Ball's costume and others consistently evoke the feeling of a school play, a masquerade or a birthday party: something infantile, amateurish and hastily put together. This attraction to that which is childlike is linked to the dada-work at many levels. The phonetic gibberish and cacophony of natural sound which the dada performer reveled in is as suggestive of a move toward childhood as the name "dada" itself. Ball wrote that the aim of the dadaist was to "surpass oneself in naiveté and childishness,"[18] and he described in no uncertain terms his unswerving attraction to childhood:

> childhood as a new world, and everything childlike and fantastic, everything childlike and direct, everything childlike and symbolical in opposition to the senilities of the world of grown ups.[19]

He promoted as well a certain "hermaphrodite" quality for the artist, a sexual changeability that would enable him to change from the male to the female viewpoint at will, thereby permitting "that multiplicity of reflection that produces ideas."

On that evening of June 23, the costumed Ball had been carried on stage in a darkness heavy with anticipation and was suddenly revealed to begin his incantatory chants. Though all this was meant to arouse and shock the audience, a feeling remains (a feeling corroborated by the performer's own recounting of the event), that the ensemble of performer, costume, mask, phonetic text and drum, plus the permission to ululate and crow, was intended at least as much to affect the performer as to work its effect on the public. In the dada struggle for primacy between process and product, process emerged victor, and here, as with much of the contemporary psychophysically oriented work in performance, one often has the uneasy feeling (uneasy because it places the spectator at a disadvantage), that the actor is having a fuller, more satisfying experience than the audience. While Ball is carried offstage in a state of such fevered exaltation that it results in his nervous collapse, the audience is, at best, roused to "shouting and fighting in the hall" and one can even find "several elderly Englishwomen taking careful notes."[20] As opposed to the performer's intense involvement with what was going on onstage, the audience, despite its often vocal participation, remained at a basic remove. The quality of experience that the performer sought for himself was different from that which he offered his audience. While for the audience, the performance remained largely an experience of agitation and arousal, for the dada performer, the performing experience was an artistic one.

There was, however, another more intimate audience whose presence cannot be ignored and whose experiences of the performance more closely resembled the dada performer's own. That audience was the dada group itself, and there can be little doubt that the dadas created and performed for one another with at least as much relish as they manipulated their audiences. The importance of "the group" was paramount. In the "Café de la Terasse," their first meeting place in Zurich, Tzara, Serner and Arp together wrote a cycle of poems entitled "The Hyperbole of the Crocodile's Hairdresser and the Walking Stick." The meeting place was soon transferred to the "Odéon" (in sympathy with a waiters' strike at the "Terrace") where two or three tables were not sufficient to hold the dadas' burgeoning circle of friends. They would end up reserving half of the Rami-Strasse corner of the "Odéon" for themselves. Here, the group sat for hours, introducing one another to those various people who chanced into their midst: Dr. Oscar Goldberg, the numerologist; Erich Unger who had studied classical philosophy and the Kabbalah; the heavy-bearded Giacometti and the fiery Spaniard del Vajo who vied with Ball for the affections of Emmy Hennings. It was open house every day, but the center held. When not at the "Odéon," the group might be drinking in the Bazerba, a Spanish wine-cellar, browsing at Hack's bookshop, or ogling the young dancers at Laban's dance studio: Sophie Taeuber (who later became Mrs. Jan Arp), Mary Wigman, Suzanne Perrottet, Maya Kruseck (Tzara's "petite amie"), Maria Vanselow (who went around with Georges Janco) and her friend who eventually became Marcel Janco's wife. When all else paled, members of the group might walk along the Limmatquai, opening one restaurant door after another to shout "Vive, dada!" And then there was always the work of putting out the journal *Cabaret Voltaire* and its successor *Dada,* or working on the editions of the "Dada Library," which succeeded in bringing out two publications: Tzara's short play *La première aventure céleste de M. Antipyrine,* with illustrations by Janco, and Huelsenbeck's *Fantastic Prayers,* illustrated by Arp. Huelsenbeck had used Ball's typewriter to copy out some of his poems, often stopping at a phrase to ask Ball "Is this perhaps yours?" Evenings found the group reunited at the Cabaret where they often stayed till the early hours of the morning:

> I go home in the morning light
> The clock strikes five, the sky grows pale,
> A light still burns in the hotel;
> The cabaret shuts for the night.

> Emmy Hennings "After the Cabaret"

When Zurich lay asleep under the pale sickle of the moon, Hennings went home with Ball, Richter and Tzara to adjoining rooms in the Hotel Louisatquai. Only Janco and Arp went to their respective lodgings: Janco with his French wife, their son and his two younger brothers in the familial enclave of a bourgeois apartment, and Arp to his seclusion with Sophie Taeuber on the outskirts of Zurich. Even for the night they group barely separated.

Under these conditions it is not surprising to point out the importance of the group for its individual members:

> There was the emphatic energy of our group. One member was always trying to surpass the other by intensifying demands and stress.

> 18.VI.1916

Quite clearly the circle of people who best understood and delighted in the series of nightly devotions and exorcisms at the Cabaret was that very circle of people who planned and executed them.

First and foremost, however, the dada actor performed for himself, performed in the search for himself. As Apollinaire wrote in his poem "Cortège":

One day
One day
I said to myself Guillaume it's time you turned up
So I could know just who I am . . .
All those who turned up and were not myself
Brought one by one the pieces of myself.[21]

the dadas tracked the "pieces of themselves": Ball in his incantatory "trips," Huelsenbeck, banging on the big drum, and Tzara codifying the principle by writing, "Art is a private affair, the artist produces it for himself."[22] Richter as well points to the importance of individual creation for each member of the group:

> The Cabaret Voltaire was a six-piece band. Each played his instrument, i.e., himself, passionately and with all his soul. Each of them, different as he was from all the others, was his own music, his own words, his own rhythm. Each sang his own song with all his might. . . .[23]

Spontaneity and Chance

Most significant, in this performing for oneself, which the dada practiced, is the liberating creative method which it fostered and out of which it grew.

> The artist cedes a measure of his control (and hence of his ego) to the materials and what transpires between them, placing himself partially in the role of discoverer or spectator as well as that of originator.[24]

The elements of "chance" and the "spontaneous act" took on a new significance for the performing artist. Chance was the basis of Tzara's paper-bag poetry (shake the words and select at random), and much of Arp's poetry as well:

> I tore apart sentences, words, syllables. I tried to break down the language into atoms, in order to approach the creative . . . Chance opened up perceptions to me, immediate spiritual insights.[25]

Hans Richter recounts in an anecdote the workings of chance in Arp's painting:

> Dissatisfied with a drawing he had been working on for some time, Arp finally tore it up, and let the pieces flutter to the floor of his studio on the Zeltweg. Some time later he happened to notice these same scraps of paper as they lay on the floor, and was struck by the pattern they formed. It had all the expressive power that he had tried in vain to achieve. How meaningful! How telling! Chance movements of his hand and of the fluttering scraps of paper had achieved what all his efforts had failed to achieve, namely expression. He accepted this challenge from chance as a decision of fate and carefully pasted the scraps down in the pattern which chance had predetermined.[26]

Arp himself wrote:

> In 1915 Sophie Taeuber and I made in painting, embroidery and collage, the first works derived from the simplest forms. . . . We rejected everything that was copy or description, and allowed the Elementary and Spontaneous to react in full freedom. . . . I declared that these works . . . were ordered "according to the laws of chance."[27]

Later, Arp attempted to record the process of his improvisational methodology in the work on "automatic drawings." The starting point in the creation of these works was the notion of vitality in the movement of the creative hand. First the artist would paint an entirely black surface.

> The black grows deeper and deeper, darker and darker before me. It menaces like a black gullet. I can bear it no longer. It is monstrous. It is unfathomable. As the thought comes to me to exorcize and transform this black with a white drawing, it has already become a surface. Now I have lost all fear and begin to draw on the black surface. I draw and dance at once, twisting and winding, twining soft, white flowery round. A snail-like wreath . . . turns in, grows. White shoots dart this way and that. Three of them begin to form snakes' heads. Cautiously the two lower ones approach one another.[28]

One may hesitate to take such descriptions of the use of "chance" and "automatism" at face value, preferring to see chance as only one way for the artist to stimulate his imagination; a starting point for images later consciously rearranged. While this possibility of rearrangement may be granted the painter and the poet, it is hardly viable for the unrehearsed dada performer. Ball came on stage, costumed and text-laden, but with only the most general idea of what he was going to do. In his work with Janco's masks, Ball improvised, on the spot, a piece of music for the dances, which themselves emerged out of movements which five minutes before had been unanticipated and unpredictable. "What we want now," Tzara explained, "is spontaneity. Not because it is better or more beautiful than anything else. But because everything that issues freely from ourselves without the intervention of speculative ideas, represents us."[29]

The elements of chance and spontaneity in the immediacy of the creative act were championed by the dada painters, poets and performers alike.[30] The Laban dancers danced in front of Arp's biomorphic cucumbers—plastic representations of an internal event. Ernst's "collages" are the visual counterpart of the simultaneous poem, instantly presenting contradictory data in the tradition of Lautréamont's "chance meeting of a sewing machine and an umbrella on a dissection table," while Apollinaire's radical defense of collage and "papiers collés" in *The Cubist Painters* (1913), opened the way not only for an incredible liberation of the plastic arts, but of the performing arts as well:

You may paint with whatever material you please, with pipes, postage stamps, post-cards or playing cards, candalabras, pieces of oil cloth, collars, painted paper, news-paper.[31]

The art repertory had been expanded to all existing sights and objects. Art, no longer in the service of religion, ethics, history or government, saluted an end to descriptive content. If painting increasingly came to be about "the possibilities of painting," then theatre, re-searching for the possibilities of theatre, returned to its origins in the actor as performer.

Wagg Hall: July 14, 1916

One major performance climaxed this first period of Zurich dada while pointing the way for a second phase in which Tzara's more negative, more nihilistic drives would eventually force Ball's complete retirement from the group. This was the "Dada Night," of July 14, 1916:

In the presence of a compact crowd Tzara demonstrates, we demand the right to piss in different colors, Huelsenbeck demonstrates, Ball demonstrates . . . the dogs bay and the dissection of Panama on the piano . . . shouted poem–shouting and fighting in the hall, first row approves second row declares itself incompetent the rest shout, who is the strongest, the big drum is brought in Huelsenbeck against 2000, *Ho esenlatz?* accentuated by the very big drum and little bells on his left foot and the people protest shout smash windowpanes kill each other demolish fight here come the police interruption.[32]

The program, perhaps because of the holiday evening "quatorze juillet," per-haps because of Tzara's growing desire to reach a larger public, had been moved out of the confines of the Cabaret Voltaire and into the larger "Zunfthaus zur Wagg." The nature of the events remained basically the same in an evening advertised to include "music, the dance, theory, manifestos, poems, pictures, costumes, and masks." The costumes, as usual, were "paper, cardboard, materi-als of all colors stuck together with pins."[33] They were perishable, temporary, ugly, absurd: all intended to reinforce a sense of spontaneity and to fight any impression of formal, aesthetic coordination. Original musical compositions by the composer Heusser were played, and a Cubist dance was performed: "each man his own big drum on his head, noise, Negro music." Five literary experi-ments were performed by Tzara "in tails before the curtain": a gymnastic poem, concert of vowels, bruitist poem, static poem and vowel poem. The vowel poem was simply a sequence of vowels: aao, ieo, aii, etc. The static poem involved chairs on which placards, each containing a word, were placed. A curtain was lowered and raised, each time revealing a new ordering of the words. "To make a dadaist poem," Tzara wrote:

Take a newspaper
Take a pair of scissors
Choose an article as long as you are planning to make your poem
Cut out the article
Then cut out each of the words that make up this article and put them in a bag.
Shake it gently
Then take out the scraps one after the other in the order in which they left the bag
Copy consecutively.

That same July evening saw the first production of Tzara's *La Première aventure céleste de M'Antipyrine,* a play in one act capped by a lengthy manifesto-monologue.[34] The manifesto is recited by a character called "Tristan Tzara," who joins the nine other characters: Messrs. Bleubleu, Cricri, BoumBoum, Antipyrine (the hero of the title), Pipi, Npala Garoo, La Parapole, and the Manager. There is also a pregnant woman. We don't know who played each role, though we do have the cast list for the play's second performance in Paris in 1920. Since in Paris Tzara played the role designated him in the text, it is likely that he did the same in Zurich. The text, with woodcuts by Janco, was published on July 28, 1916, in an edition limited to 10 copies. Janco's woodcuts are abstract and offer no iconographic evidence as to the Zurich production. The text itself has no stage directions. What we are left with, then, is a text of some 238 lines divided among 10 characters: the first dada play.

The text, at first reading, is a maze of impenetrable phrases, interspersed with pseudo-Africanisms (Soco Bgai Affahous), phonetic gibberish (dzin aha dzin aha bobobo), and freestanding vowels and syllables (Oi oi oi oi . . . u u u un pht). The title itself is a source of confusion since "Antypyrine" has been translated as "Fire-Extinguisher," but the word was also the name of a common Swiss headache remedy. The emphasis is clearly on sound rather than on meaning—in the repetition of syllables (immense, pause, pense et pense pense . . . la cathedrale, drale . . . . drale . . . rendre, prendre, entre), in internal and half rhymes (amertume sans église allons allons charbon chameau synthétise amertume sur l'église isisise les rideaux/dododo), in the names of the characters with their childish sing-song (CriCri, PiPi), and in the clearly alogical syntax and nonsense sequiturs resembling the verbal collages of the simultaneous poem.

In his use of the exotic rhythmic words of a pseudo-African tongue, Tzara was merely following the same muse that had led him to write of the art of Africa and Oceania, to seek out African drum rhythms and use them to shock the sensibilities of the Zurich bourgeoisie. The handiest reference a Continental burgher of 1916 had to the men of the dark continent was the image of the towering Senegalese mercenary brought to fight in the front lines of the war. From this he might well conclude that they were savages. This impression is reinforced in the play by the coupling of these exotic-Africanisms with the fantasy images of sex and excrement:

> The sexual organ is square, is covered with lead
> is thicker than the volcano which erupts below Mgabati.
>
> the big one named Bleubleu clambers up in his
> despair and then shits his manifestos

Add to this a series of lists without purpose:

> Four hundred horses, sixty camels, three hundred
> sable pelts, five hundred ermine skins
> her husband is sick
> twenty yellow fox skins . . .
> one hundred white and yellow fox skins . . .

and two simultaneously recited poems of phonetic chants, and the dada aim of incensing its public was sure to be achieved.

Tzara termed the text a "double quadralogue," and it begins with the introduction of four characters: Bleubleu, CriCri, the pregnant woman and Mr. Antipyrine, each reciting his own introductory monologue. The four, plus Pipi, exchange ripostes which, on paper, are set up as dialogues, yet are incomprehensible—in themselves as well as in their relationship to one another. The play's opening lines seem to indicate activity such as might be given in a stage direction:

> penetrates the desert
> howls while digging the road in the sticky sand
> listens to the vibration

In looking at the text which follows, however, it is difficult to propose (or forbid for that matter) any activities whatever that might have been associated with the text, or to justify in any way the dividing of the play into analyzable segments. Any resemblance to theatre conventions is denied. Only a few "numbers" or "acts" are identifiable within the piece. There are the two simultaneous poems bringing together first one, and then another combination of the five characters met so far, and then introducing the sixth, "the Manager," who says two of the play's more coherent lines: "he is dead," and "and then they sang." The latter is indeed followed by a "song" in the form of the second simultaneous poem. Outstanding as well is Tzara's long monologue. Suddenly, in the midst of all the confusion, here is a manifesto, clearly didactic and quite comprehensible. The show stops for a moment and its chief barker permits himself a few choice words which, if there were any doubts, make clear the dadas' purposeful violation of the audience:

> A harsh necessity without discipline or morality and we spit on humanity. Dada remains within the European frame of weakness it's shit after all but from now on we mean to shit in assorted colors and bedeck the artistic zoo with the flags of every consulate.

Tzara was taking no chances. If, for some reason, the audience "took to" the phonetic gibberish of the play, or merely laughed, Tzara had provided himself with an infallible instrument of attack in the form of the manifesto. Not many Frenchmen could avoid being offended by the lines:

> psychologie psychologie hi hi
> Science Science Science
> vive la France

and to top it all off, Tzara ended with kisses to the audience, "dear listeners, I love you so, I love you so, I assure you, and I adore you."

Two long monologues bring the play to its concluding line "and then they left," which is truly an exit line.

All told, the reader has little to hang on to. What seems to move the play more than the energy of a comprehensible activity is the acoustical energy, the thrust of the music of the lines which, in performance, was augmented by the visual aspects of the performance and the shape of the audience's response.

We know nothing of the Zurich performance. We can, however, put together some details of the Paris première three and a half years later. Since Tzara participated in both productions, it is possible that some elements of the first carried over into the second. More likely, though, with the passage of time, within the new Paris-dada framework, and with new collaborating artists (it was Picabia who designed the Paris costumes and sets, Janco the Zurich ones), the performance had changed. The scenic details of the Paris production, however, present a staging not far different from what we have seen of Zurich-dada performance.

For the occasion, Tzara had invented "a diabolical machine composed of a Klaxon and three successive invisible echoes, for the purpose of impressing on the minds of the audience certain phases describing the aims of Dada."[35] The sets and costumes (the characters enclosed in huge, variously colored paper sacs, each with his name written on a large placard and hung around his neck), were described by the critic of *Commoedia* as "astonishing, unexpected, ridiculous." He continued:

> They clearly evoke drawings conceived by the mad, and correspond perfectly to the inconceivable text of Mr. Tristan Tzara. . . . The transparent set, placed in front of the performers and not behind them—composed of a bicycle wheel, several ropes strung across the stage and some cartons containing hermetic inscriptions ("Paralysis is the onset of wisdom," "Stretch out your hands, your friends will cut them off"), perfectly completed the whole.[36]

Tzara's own recollections of the performance are quite clear:

> This play is a boxing match with words. The characters, confined in sacks and trunks, recite their parts without moving, and one can easily imagine the effect this produced—performed in a greenish light—on the already excited public. It was impossible to hear a single word of the play.[37]

For Tzara, this successful inciting of the public was what he most desired. For Ball, the frenzy had exhausted him. At the Waag Hall evening, Ball still participated with the reading of some of his sound-poems. In addition, however, he read out a manifesto which he later admitted was "a thinly disguised break with friends." (6.VIII.1916) The jabs at Tzara were quite clear: "To make of Dada an artistic tendency must mean that one is anticipating complications . . . and yourselves, honored poets, who are always writing with words but never writing the word itself, who are always writing around the actual point."[38] The thrust of the manifesto was clear as well: "The word, gentlemen, is a public concern of the first importance." Ball's fight to dispense with conventional language had peaked. No longer did he want words which other people had invented. He wanted his own words, his own rhythms and vowels and consonants too. Of Tzara and his followers he wrote: "When things are finished, I cannot spend any more time with them. That is how I am; if I tried to be different, it would be no use." (6.VIII.1916)

In July, 1916, Hugo Ball and Emmy Hennings left for the small Italian village of Vira-Magadinot. Ball's departure was very difficult for Huelsenbeck, and the young man responded with insomnia, a nervous stomach, vomiting and depression. By October, Huelsenbeck decided to leave the cabaret as well and wrote to Ball: "I too have always been greatly opposed to this art." By the fall of 1916, then, both internal and external pressures determined the closing of the Cabaret Voltaire less than a year after it had opened. Herr Ephraim, the proprietor, was fed up with the public complaints at the nightly excesses committed on his premises and announced that the dadas would have to seek a new home. Tzara, however, was indomitable. Taking over complete leadership, he carried on. The cabaret phase of the movement had ended. Tzara would now seek bigger and bigger forums for his manifestations. Eventually he would burn himself out.

Theatre at the Dada Gallery

We have surmounted the barbarisms of the
  cabaret.

Hugo Ball, 22.III.1917

the DADAIST Theatre. Above all, masks,
and revolver effects, the effigy of the director.
Bravo! and Boom boom!

Tristan Tzara, 14.IV.1917

Galerie Dada

Zürich,   Bahnhofstrasse 19,   Eingang Tiefenhöfe 12.

Neue Kunst und Literatur,   Antiquitäten.

Sturm-Ausstellung

II. Serie

9. bis 30. April 1917

Albert Bloch,   Fritz Baumann,   Max Ernst,
Lyonel Feininger, Johannes Itten, Kandinsky,
Paul Klee, Oscar Kokoschka, Ottakar Kubin,
Georg Muche, Maria Uhden.

Täglich 2 - 6 Uhr,   Eintritt Fr. 1.-.

Jeden Mittwoch, 4 Uhr nachmittags
Führung durch die Galerie

Samstag, 14. April, abends 8½ Uhr

Sturm-Soirée

Literatur und Musik von:

G. Apollinaire, A. Berg, B. Cendrars, A. Ehrenstein, J. van Hoddis,
Kandinsky, F. T. Marinetti, A. Schönberg, P. Scheerbart, Herwart Walden.

Negertanz

getanzt von 5 Personen

Premiere

Sphinx und Strohmann

Kuriosum von O. Kokoschka.
Inszenierung und Masken von Marcel Janco.

Auskunft an der Kasse der Galerie.

Collection: Dr. and Mrs. H.J. Kleinschmidt

The Dada Gallery

Hugo Ball returned to Zurich in November, 1916. Tzara had urged his return ("Tzara, Arp and Janco have written me a letter from Zurich saying I must definitely go there: my presence is urgently desired" 3.X.1916), and Ball allowed himself to be influenced, though his interest in Tzara and dada was very ambivalent. In October he wrote in his *Diary* "I finished Flametti today . . . a gloss to dadaism, it will disappear along with dadaism for all I care," and upon his arrival in Zurich he promptly lost a whole package of new poems given him by Tzara. "It's your subconscious," his friend Leonhard Frannk told him, "They are not important to you any more." Still, by March of 1917, Ball was partying with the dadas at Mary Wigman's and on March 18, he and Tzara once again joined forces to open the Dada Gallery, Bahnhofstrasse 19:

> We have surmounted the barbarisms of the cabaret. There is a span of time between Voltaire and the Galerie Dada in which everyone has worked very hard and has gathered new impressions and experiences.

> 22.III.1917

Perhaps this new venture was spurred by Ball's desire to have one last try at putting into practice Kandinsky's idea of the union of all the arts, for in April, Ball lectured at the Gallery on Kandinsky, noting in his diary:

> Yesterday I gave my lecture on Kandinsky. I have realized a favorite old plan of mine: Total art: pictures, music, dances, poems. . . .

> 8.IV.1917

The gallery was to be a combination art gallery and cabaret. The former practice of daily performances at the Cabaret Voltaire was abandoned and alongside the exhibitions (the Sturm group, the dadaists themselves, Negro art, Prampolini), lectures and guided tours stressed the new educative aim of the enterprise. A café called the Kandinsky Room was open in the evenings, and afternoon teas were instituted in an attempt to draw a more genteel clientele. It is this aspect that Huelsenbeck mocked, referring to the gallery as a "little art business . . . a manicure salon of the fine arts characterized by tea-drinking old ladies trying to revive their vanishing sexual powers with the help of 'something mad'."[1] The concept of the Gallery seems to have Ball's more temperate hand in it. But the conflict between Ball and Tzara was by no means resolved.

In the 11 weeks of its existence, the Dada Gallery sponsored six soirées in which Tzara's continuing efforts to provoke the audience are very much in evidence.

The grand opening ceremonies on March 29, 1917, are recorded by Tzara in his "Zurich Chronicle" as:

> Red lamps mattresses social sensation Piano: Heusser, Perrottet, Recitations: Hennings, A. Ehrenstein, Tzara, Ball, Dances: Mlle. Taeuber/costumes by Arp/c. Walter, etc. etc. great enchanted gyratory movement of 400 persons celebrating.[2]

All of this sounds quite *comme il faut* for the dadas, as do the recollections of Gabrielle Buffet-Picabia:

> Huelsenbeck recited a poem with the endlessly recurring refrain "And the pastor buttons his fly." Tzara paraded around the stage in a top hat crowned with a lighted candle. The protests of the public mingled with the uproar created by the actors: respectable members of the audience shouted with rage.[3]

Ball records the opening program more soberly:

> Abstract dances (by Sophie Taeuber; poems by Ball; masks by Arp. Frederic Clauser: poems. Hans Heusser: compositions. Emmy Hennings: poems Olly Jacques: Prose by Mynona. H.L. Neitzel: poems by Hans Arp. Mme Perrottet: new music. Tristan Tzara: Negro poems. Claire Walter: expressionist dances.
>
> 29.III.17

He lists some of the more prominent members of the audience of ninety—Mary Wigman, von Laban, members of the Psychoanalytic Club [4]—and notes that what impressed him most among the program's events were the fantastic movements of Sophie Taeuber's abstract dance, "Song of the Flying Fish and the Sea Horses."

> All around Taeuber is the radiance of the sun and the miracle that replaces tradition. She is full of invention, caprice, fantasy . . . an onomatopoetic plaint. It was a dance full of flashes and fishbones, of dazzling lights, a dance of penetrating intensity. The lines of her body break, every gesture decomposes into a hundred precise, angular, incisive movements. The buffoonery of perspective, lighting and atmosphere is for her hypersensitive nervous system the pretext for drollery full of irony and wit. The figures of her dance are at once mysterious, grotesque and ecstatic.[5]

The difference between Ball's recall of this first Dada Gallery evening and Tzara's again displays the unbridgeable gulf between the two men in their approach to art and a performance aesthetic. Ball's need to move toward a studied, sensitive exploration was set against Tzara's desire to shock.

Gallery Performances

The second Dada Gallery performance, the "Sturm Soirée," on April 14, 1917, did not neglect the "shock" element. It was linked to an exhibit of "Sturm" paintings,[6] and the works of Jarry, Marinetti, Apollinaire, van Hoddis, Cendrars and Kandinsky were read by the usual cast of performers.[7] Music by Heusser was featured alongside Ball's laban-danced "Negro-dances." But the highlight of the evening was the performance of Oskar Kokoschka's play *Sphinx and Strawman,* featuring Ball as Herr Firdusi ("an enormous swiveling straw-head with arms and legs, carrying a pig's-bladder-balloon on a string"),[8] Wolfgang Hartmann as Mr. Rubberman ("an educated snake-like Rubberman"), Emmy Hennings as Anima (the womanly soul), and Frederic Clauser as Death. Tzara writes of the event:

> This performance decided the role of our theatre, which will entrust the stage direction to the subtle invention of the explosive wind, scenario in the audience, visible direction, grotesque props: the DADAIST theatre. Above all, masks and revolver effects, the effigy of the director. Bravo! & Boom boom![9]

The plot of the play, one of Kokoschka's early expressionist works, is simply told. Mr. Firdusi, having loved and lost, sues to love again. The object of his affections is Anima, the female soul, who so succeeds in turning Firdusi's head that she literally turns it on its axis so that his nose overlooks his posterior and he is forever incapable of seeing her. Mr. Rubberman, the "doctor" who arrives to cure Firdusi of his love, instead seduces Anima in the adjoining room while Papagei, a parrot, reports on the proceedings, echoing the sighs of the womanly spirit, "O my sweet Mr. Rubberman! O my sweet Mr. Rubberman!" Firdusi shoots himself but expires only after having sung a number of short death-arias. He is chanted to his final end by a chorus of men whose bodies are painted on a drop which descends, and whose top hats rest on the empty holes in the curtain. The dadas did not concern themselves with spirits, nor were they interested in the causes of love or its cures. What attracted them was the heavy language, filled with aphorisms and nonsense, and often bordering on incomprehensibility, and the possibilities inherent in the staging. The play, written by Kokoschka on a bet in 1907, was first produced at the Vienna School of Arts and Crafts before his colleagues. It was composed mainly during rehearsals with some young actors who were Kokoschka's friends. The dadas were perhaps attracted by the scandal that had followed the Vienna production of another of the artist's plays, *Mörder: Hoffnung der Frauen,* where spectators and soldiers with drawn swords clashed at the sight of a half-naked woman throwing herself about the stage.

In *Sphinx and Strawman,* the playwright provided a vehicle for the deployment of many of the dadas' scenic games:

The play was performed in two adjoining rooms; the actors wore body masks. Mine was so big that I could read my script inside it quite comfortably. The head of the mask was electrically lighted; it must have looked strange in the darkened room, with the light coming out of the eyes. Emmy was the only one not wearing a mask. She appeared as half sylph, half angel, lilac and light blue. The seats went right up to the actors. Tzara was in the back room, and his job was to take care of the "thunder and lightning" as well as to say "Anima, sweet Anima!" parrot fashion. But he was taking care of the entrances and exits at the same time, thundered and lightninged in the wrong place, and gave the absolute impression that this was a special effect of the production, an intentional confusion of backgrounds.

Finally, when Mr. Firdusi had to fall, everything got tangled up in the tightly stretched wires and lights. For a few minutes there was total darkness and confusion: then the gallery looked just the same as before.

14.IV.1917

Ball's brief recollection of the production provides several important insights into the way the dadas worked. In writing that Tzara looked after "entrances and exits" Ball recalls the methods of the *commedia dell'arte* where there were such confusions of entrances and exits that plot-sheets were hung in the wings to remind the performers of the order of their various comings and goings. Here Tzara served this function. This, the fact that Ball read his text from within his huge mask, and Tzara's working of sound effects at the wrong moments, all seem to verify the limited rehearsal process, and a generally carefree attitude as regards the resultant "product." Again, masks served to delight both performer and audience, while the figures with holes for heads painted on the finale-backdrop, reversed the figure-ground relationship of mask and face—the painted drop becoming a mask for the body, the real body set as a mask atop the drawn figure and inserted in the blank "mask" of the hole. Kokoschka's own explanation for this painted chorus would have been quite to the dadas' taste:

> . . . in order to economise on actors, which were few, and on material, of which there was none, I used for the first time the trick of painting minor parts and props not essential for action on the background . . .[10]

Tristan Tzara and Zurich Dada Performance

The performances at the Dada Gallery continued with the conflict for artistic leadership between Tzara and Ball played out in the background. The third soirée, on April 28, 1917, was named by Tzara "New Art Night" and he recounts it, placing himself in a position of importance, and mentioning Ball only in passing:

Tzara: Cold Light, simultaneous poem by several persons. Clauser: poems, Negro music and dances. Janco: paintings, Mme. Perrottet: Music by Laban, Schönberg, etc. Ball, Hennings, etc. F. Hardekopf reads from his works.[11]

Ball, in his diary, relegates Tzara to a less than starring role and provides a full description of his own:

I: S. Perrottet: Compositions by Schönberg, Laban and Perrottet (piano and violin)

Clauser: "Father," "Objects" (Poems)

Leon Bloy: "Excerpts from the Exegesis of Commonplaces" (Translated by Frederic Clauser)

Ball: "Grand Hotel Metaphysics" (prose in costume)

II: Janco: "On Cubism and My Own Pictures"

S. Perrottet: Compositions by Schönberg, Laban, and Perrottet (piano)

Emmy Hennings: "Criticism of the Corpse," "Notes"

Tzara: "Cold Light" (simultaneous poem, read by seven people)[12]

The last three Dada Gallery performances on May 12 ("Old and New Dada Night"), May 19 and May 25 were patterned on the same principles, events and experiments as the three that preceded them, and both Ball and Tzara absented themselves from the stage for a while. The program for May 12 was listed by performers:

Alberto Spaini:

Jacopone da Todi, and the Anonymous Popular Poets of the Thirteenth Century

Corrado Alvaro, "Cantata"

Francesco Meriano, "Jewel"

Hans Heusser:

Prelude and Fugue

Exotic Procession (piano)

Emmy Hennings:

"O You Saints" (poems)

From the book of the *Flowing Light of the Divinity* (1212-94):
Sister Machtild

From the book *Der Johanser zum Grünen Werde zu Strassburg:*
Be Unfathomably One

The Monk of Halsbrune: "Truth is a Hoax" (1320)

Hans Arp

Chronicle of Duke Ernst (1480): "How he fought on an island with huge birds and defeated them"

From Dürer's diary: The Dutch Journey

Jakob Böhme: The Rising Dawn: On the Bitter Quality, On the Description of Cold (1612)

Marcel Janco:

"Principles of Ancient Architecture (Brunelleschi, L.B. Alberti., F. Blondel, 15th-18th century), Concerning Painting and Abstract Art"

12.V.1917

This program was successful enough to be repeated on May 19, with the addition of "psychoanalytical debates," after the soirée. The officiating Dr. Hoch-. dorb, in a tuxedo, was "very appropriate."

A gallery tour for workmen was scheduled for Sunday April 20: "One single workman turns up." The final soirée on May 25 was devoted to the music of Hans Heusser, who throughout had provided background accompaniment to the other performances.

On May 11, 1917, Ball wrote:

> The gallery has three faces. By day it is a teaching body for schoolgirls and upper-class ladies. In the evening the candlelit Kandinsky room is a club for the most esoteric philosophies. At the soirées, however, the parties have a brilliance and a frenzy such as Zurich has never seen before.

Still, the Gallery had accumulated a debt of 313 francs and its closing was imminent. A great tension existed within the group. Tzara, demanding that the performance work advance in ever more aggressive channels, had drawn Janco to his camp. Opposing them were Ball and Huelsenbeck—Ball, withdrawing at the merest sign of a conflict, and Huelsenbeck, furious with Tzara's audacity, but eventually withdrawing as well. Of Tzara at the time, Huelsenbeck wrote:

> Tristan Tzara was devoured by ambition to move in international artistic circles as an equal or even a "leader." He was all ambition and restlessness. For his restlessness he sought a pole and for his ambition a ribbon. . . . He worked indefatigably. He wrapped, pasted, addressed, he bombarded the French and Italians with letters; slowly he made himself the "focal point."[13]

On the first of June, 1917, the Dada Gallery went on "unlimited vacation." Ball was spent and tormented. He did not want to leave the project ("It's a pity we have to close. I would very much like to continue." 15.V.1917), but his views and Tzara's on the development of dada were showing themselves to be more and more at odds. Tzara was rapidly moving away from all modern art and towards a path of pure provocation, a "new transmutation that signifies nothing, and was the most formidable blasphemy mass combat speed prayer tranquillity private guerrilla negation and chocolate of the desperate."[14] For Ball, who as early as 1915 had declared, "I have examined myself carefully and I could never bid chaos welcome," the split with Tzara was final.[15] Ball left Zurich for good at the end of June, 1917, while Tzara, in a euphoric mood at his new emergent leadership, wrote:

> Mysterious creation! magic revolver
> The DADA MOVEMENT is launched.[16]

Tzara was now on his own. He continued to edit the journal *Dada*, but his letters of the period attest to his state of nervous alarm, and in fact no major dada manifestation was organized for a year following Ball's departure (July, 1917-July, 1918).[17] What seems to have broken the stalemate was the arrival in Zurich of Francis Picabia in the Fall of 1919. Tzara had been in correspondence with Picabia since August, 1918. The two shared a revolutionary attitude to art and a nihilistic approach to life. Encouraged by Picabia, Tzara served up one more dada performance before leaving for Paris.

The climax of Zurich dada theatre was the "Grand Soirée" in the Saal zur Kaufleuten of April 9, 1919. That the evening is remembered in great detail by numbers of the dadas emphasizes the impact of the "Greatest-Ever-DADA-Show" on both audience and participants. It is at once the finale and prototype of Zurich dada theatre, featuring the usual cast (all but Ball) in their usual roles, by now as familiar as those of a circus family. Chief barker and "tamer of acrobats": Tristan Tzara (who had organized the evening "with the magnificent precision of a ring-master marshalling his menagerie of lions, elephants, snakes and crocodiles"). Sets by Hans Arp and Hans Richter (it was at this performance that Arp's biomorphic cucumbers were used as a backdrop for the Laban dances). Masks by Janco and music by Hans Heusser. Choreography by Suzanne Perrottet and Sophie Taeuber.

The program itself was divided into three parts, each succeeding in bringing the audience to a higher peak of excitement and rage:

Eggling appeared first[18] . . . and delivered a very serious speech about elementary "Gestaltung" and abstract art. This only disturbed the audience insofar as they wanted to be disturbed but weren't. Then followed Susanne Perrottet's dances to compositions by Schönberg, Satie and others. She wore a Negroid mask by Janco, but they let that pass. Some poems by Huelsenbeck and Kandinsky, recited by Kathe Wulff, were greated with laughter and catcalls by a few members of the audience. Then all hell broke loose. A "Poème simultané" by Tristan Tzara, performed by twenty people who did not always keep in time with each other. This was what the audience and especially its younger members, had been waiting for. Shouts, whistles, chanting in unison, laughter . . . all of which mingled more or less anti-harmoniously with the bellowing of the twenty on the platform.[19]

Tzara had skillfully arranged things so that this simultaneous poem closed the first half of the program. If not, the passionate response of the audience would have overwhelmed the performers on stage. Instead the members of the audience used the intermission to regroup their forces for the second act.

The second part of the program began with Richter's address, "Against, Without, For Dada" which Tzara had called, "Malicious, elegant, Dada, Dada, Dada," and in which Richter consigned the audience to the underworld and cursed them "with moderation." This was followed by the "anti-tunes" of Hans Heusser, dances by Perrottet and a piece by Arp entitled "Wolkenpumpe"

("Cloud Pump") which the audience greeted with laughter and cries of "Rubbish." Walter Serner, the Austrian poet and revolutionary who had joined the group toward the end of 1916, appeared next. Dressed as if for a wedding in a black frock coat, striped pants and a grey cravat, the tall, elegant Serner came on stage carrying a headless tailor's dummy. He then went back to get a bouquet of artificial flowers, offering a smell at the place where the headless dummy's nose would have been, and then laying the bouquet at its feet. Finally he brought a chair on stage and settling himself on it with his back to the audience, proceeded to read from his anarchistic credo, "Final Dissolution." This was what the audience had been waiting for:

> The tension in the hall became unbearable. At first it was so quiet that you could have heard a pin drop. Then the catcalls began, scornful at first, then furious. "Rat, bastard, you've got a nerve!" until the noise almost entirely drowned Serner's voice, which could be heard, during a momentary lull, saying the words "Napoleon was a big, strong oaf, after all."
> That really did it. What Napoleon had to do with it, I don't know. He wasn't Swiss. But the young men, most of whom were in the gallery, leaped onto the stage, brandishing pieces of balustrade (which had survived intact for several hundred years), chased Serner into the wings and out of the building, smashed the tailor's dummy and the chair, and stamped on the bouquet. The whole place was in an uproar.[20]

A reporter Richter knew grabbed him by the tie and shouted over and over "You're a sensible man normally." Madness had transformed the audience into a mob. The "cretinization of the public" had been achieved. The performance was stopped and the lights went on. During the 20-minute intermission which followed, the audience "gained in self-awareness." The rage subsided and in its place emerged the realization not only that Serner's provocatory acts had partaken of the inhuman, but that the audience's rage had been inhuman as well. Performers and public had found some kind of meeting ground and in the calm that ensued the third part of the program reached its end without incident. The Laban dancers performed the ballet "Noir Kakadu" with Janco's savage Negro masks and abstract costumes, and even Serner returned to the stage to recite his poems. Tzara declaimed his "Proclamation 1919" and the evening concluded with more of Heusser's atonal music. "The public was tamed," and for Tzara, the 1500 spectators in the audience had finally vindicated his belief in the potential impact of dada. He wrote in his diary:

> Dada had succeeded in establishing the circuit of absolute unconsciousness in the audience which forgot the frontiers of education, of prejudices, experienced the commotion of the NEW. Final victory of Dada.[21]

Yet the "victory" was a slightly tarnished one. One interesting proof of dada's fundamentally theatrical base was its need for constantly virginal audiences. Three years in Zurich had virtually used up such a public. With the end of the war, many of the activists cloistered in Zurich were returning to their native countries. Dada theatre's voracious appetite for material had not lessened and Tzara was beginning to feel both the audience and the dada group strain. The intimate dada group had fed on itself for too long. It was time for dada to move on, and Tzara packed his bags for Paris.

Laban, Wigman and Dada:
the New German Dance and Dada Performance

Just as in music or in painting there is no such
thing as an "ugly" sound or outward "disso-
nance," so too in the dance the inner value
of every movement will soon be felt, and the
inner beauty will replace outward beauty.
From unbeautiful movements issues an un-
recognized force and living power. From this
moment on, the dance of the future begins.

Hugo Ball, 1917

Illustration 12   Mary Wigman, ca. 1919

Photo: Charlotte Rudolph, Dresden

It was to Zurich as well, in 1916, just as the Cabaret Voltaire settled into the Spiegelgasse, that Rudolph von Laban moved his experimental dance studio. With him came his star pupil and collaborator Mary Wigman, and there, the small circle of dancers who had already worked with Laban in Munich and Ascona, regrouped: Suzanne Perrottet who, like Wigman, had originally been a student of Jacques-Dalcroze, Gertrud Leistikow, Clothide van Derp and her husband Alexander Sakharoff (who had left Kandinsky's Munich circle to dance with Laban), the artist Sophie Taeuber, Clair ter Val, the Falke sisters (daughters of the well-known German poet Gustav Falke), Laura Oesterreich and Katja Wulff. Almost all of these dancers later performed at the Zurich dada events, for if the dada group's terrestrial base was the Café Odéon, its "celestial head-quarters" was Laban's Zurich studio. Richard Huelsenbeck makes light of the group's relationship with the "laban-girls":

> There was a "laban" group in Zurich. Maestro Laban had revolutionary ideas, dance ideas. He would gather the most beautiful girls from near and far for his group. I really can't say whether I was drawn more to the beauty of the girls or the newness of the dancing. But since I've never particularly cared for, or understood much about the dance, I tend to think that I was drawn more to the beauty of the girls. I must say that we behaved quite aggressively toward them. We ran after them, asking for dates (although we didn't have the money to take them anywhere), and making every effort to draw them into our erotic fantasies.[1]

Yet the meeting between the Laban-Wigman dancers and the dada performers is one of the most interesting artistic liaisons in the history of avant-garde performance.

Rudolph von Laban

Rudolph von Laban[2] was born on December 15, 1879 in Poszony, Hungary. His uncle was a theatre director in Bucharest and his father, a high-ranking officer in the Austro-Hungarian army, was military governor of Bosnia and Herzegovina—at that time a primitive area populated almost entirely by Moslems. While visiting his father, Laban first saw the exercises of dervishes, an experience which had a lasting influence on his vision of dance:

> . . . the dervish-dances . . . are, at first sight, completely incomprehensible, even almost repulsive in the wild whirling which goes on till the dancers froth at the mouth. It all seems quite mad to us, but it is probably in the madness that the sense lies.[3]

From 1900-1907 Laban lived off and on in Paris, drawing caricatures for journals, arranging and performing in small revue-type shows, and painting. To better understand anatomy and human movement, he enrolled in the dancing classes at the Opera and suddenly found himself dancing. Once, asked by the *maître de ballet* for an opinion of a new dance, Laban suggested that the dancers discard their toe shoes in order to more effectively assume some of the intricate poses of the ballet. Horrified, the *maître de ballet* responded "What sir? Do you take the Paris Opera for a cheese shop!"

The Opera was no cheese shop but neither was it the proper school for an artist of Laban's radical bent. In 1908 he moved to Munich where he lived until the outbreak of the war, painting and experimenting with movement in his "Dance-Sound-Word" *("Tanz-Ton-Wort")*[4] —a visionary work of art which would combine dance, music and poetry. To earn his living, he directed performances for holiday festivals. Rehearsing large numbers of exuberant amateurs, Laban recalls:

> When at last the time came, we could not stand on ceremony very much, but simply called out: "Shoes off!" "Ladies, corsets off!" "Bend your knees!" "Walk!" "Run!"[5]

In these simple directions quietly lurks a revolution in dance. Bare feet would make contact with the stage and there discover a new grounding. Corsets off meant a body freed of restraints, free to accept itself and discover its wide-ranging potential for expressiveness in movement. Bent-knees, the exploration of walking and running all led away from movement as a means of expressing character and place and gave way to a consideration of movement for its own sake. For here it was but a step to the eliminating of the story element which had played so central a part in classical dance. Ever since toe shoes had been introduced during the reign of Napoleon I, nothing much had changed in the classical dance. Based on the famous five positions set during the reign of Louis XIV, it strove to attain brilliance in technique and especially in elevation, and had conditioned its audience to beauty of form, fluidity of movement and a harmonious and programmatic meeting with music. The ballet dancer of that time was not fit for dance as Laban envisioned it, and modern dance had not yet come into being. Laban had to create the dance and the dancer as well. He needed a new style of dance for a new type of dancer; a dance based on the natural organic movement of the human body and the principles of tension and relaxation. Describing this new dance at the earliest stages of its development, André Levinson, the noted French dance critic, wrote:

> The new dance demands a painful tension of the whole being. The dancer's eyes exclaim, her fingers flare; her body writhes with terror; she squirms on the ground, stamps furiously, collapses exhausted. To all the flexions and tractions of her

members she lends a spasmodic violence. The classic dancer, by her balloon-like rebounding, by the elasticity of her supple ankle and practised kick, gives us the illusion of an imponderable soaring. She defies gravity and twits the world of weight. The modern German moves, implacable, with her whole bulk, accenting heavily each tread or tap of her unshod heel. The classic ballerina aims at grace; Mrs. Wigman's pupils seek their effects in a rupture of the harmony of the body, in an elegant deformation.[6]

From 1912-1914, Laban and his pupils summered on a dance-farm in Ascona (Ticino, Switzerland) at the Monte Verità colony—a spot frequented by prominent members of the European intelligentsia, artists and writers, theosophists and anthroposophists.[7] Surrounded by trees and meadows in the lovely lake country, the group made a serious attempt at communal living:

> Every morning . . . I sounded a gong and everyone turned up for work. Tools were distributed and before breakfast groups went to various gardens to weed, dig, plant and do other necessary jobs.
> Groups of women went into the sewing room where they made dance-costumes and sandals. We had a bakery and later even two weavers' looms which produced the fabric we needed. Fruit was preserved and meals prepared and cooked in various shifts.[8]

In this colony of vegetarians, alongside the courses of dried fruits and to the sound of cracking nuts, the dance experiments continued. In the open air, Laban worked to discover movements bigger and freer than those he could find in cramped indoor facilities. In the workshop, Laban, drum in hand, made his dancers move—to words, phrases, little poems they invented by themselves. Wigman gives us an example of such a "poetical improvisation":

> The eight or ten of us had formed a circle facing each other, concentrating, waiting. Then a face was lifted, the gesture of an arm followed, and a voice, deepened by emotion, could be heard:
>
> "The night is dark . . ."
> A second movement and a second voice:
> "Dark is the night . . ."
> A third:
> ". . . and blue . . ."
> Then the chorus shifting to the right, *mezzoforte:*
> ". . . blue night . . ."
> Then to the left, *piano:*
> ". . . dark night . . ."
> Coming to a standstill, all faces and arms lifted up, *pianissimo:*
> ". . . beautiful . . ."

Anybody watching this improvised performance must have thought us a bunch of crazy idiots. To us, however, it meant one more exciting adventure and dance experience.[9]

In the obligatory sketching classes, Laban, the painter and designer, taught his dancers how to draw. Through invoking their imagination on paper, his instruction turned into a lesson in improvisation, and in the final result, into dance. With them he searched for a "system" in dance, but as yet there were no limits, no strict laws to be followed, no theoretical lines drawn.

Mary Wigman and the Laban School

Mary Wigman came to Ascona in 1913. She had been sent to Laban by the painter Emil Nolde who, after seeing her improvise, had told her "he moves as you do and he dances as you do—without music."[10] In 1913, to dance without music was heretical and audiences and critics who later viewed the "soundless" performances offered no applause for what they considered "weird," "crude," and "morbid." Even Jacques-Dalcroze, himself so much an innovator in the field of movement-performance could not accept the elimination of music for the dance and when, in 1910, he was presented by Marie Rambert, one of his star pupils, with an essay defending dance without music and proposing that dance was an independent art and that direct expression could be made through it alone, he was horrified. His own work might be performed in shocking black bathing suits, but never in silence. To the resounding silence, critics ranted: "The dance without music—unbearable, fatiguing."

Perhaps the most reasoned critical response to the silence was that of the German critic Alfred Schlee, who later wrote:

> Ears refuse to go on strike. They hear the sighing of the stage boards, the rumbling of projectors, the creaking of chairs, the coughs of the spectators, the breathing of the dancers. And since the absence of music provides for no distraction, these endless small noises are heard as even stronger. They brusquely create an accompaniment and their autonomous disorder forms a counterpoint which too often leads the dancers into the realm of the ridiculous. Therefore dance without music becomes impossible.[11]

For Laban, there was a non-musical rhythm which had to be explored by the dancer. If the extent of Alexander Sakharoff's revolt was to state "We ... do not dance to music, or with musical accompaniment, we dance *the music*," Laban's went much farther. A Laban dancer explored rhythm in soundless space:

> ... rhythm is experienced by the dancer as plastic (three dimensional). Rhythm is for him not time-duration divided by force accents as one tries to interpret this concept in music. Rhythm is the law of gesture according to which it proceeds at one time more *fluently* and at another time less *fluently* in its sequence in *space* within a sequence of time (duration). As a result tensing and detensing (relaxation) originating within the body whole are *force* nuances.[12]

Yet even Laban, though he championed performing without music admitted:

> Most people find it almost impossible to dance without an audible stimulus. Only through intense self-awareness can inner and outer inertia be overcome.[13]

Four years after the music-less performances of the pre-1919 period, a critic at a Wigman performance, demonstrating so effectively that process by which avant-garde techniques move into the mainstream of performance and gain unqualified acceptance, wrote:

> The tragic will of her body movements becomes more poignant when music is silent. . . . Her body of steel . . . relaxed in silent loveliness.[14]

Wigman's choice of a career in dance was a break from a traditional upbringing in Hanover, where she was born on November 13, 1886. While at school abroad she saw a number of performances of "avant-garde" dance: a Dalcroze children's performance in Amsterdam and a concert by Grete Weisenthal in Berlin. Weisenthal, at that time one of the most innovative of German dancers,[15] rejected Wigman's petition to study, saying she was too old and too big, and so in 1910, at the age of 24, Wigman enrolled at the Dalcroze school in Hellerau near Dresden. But the Dalcroze method of movement was too binding for her and she found herself experimenting with her strong and bony body in ways which neither the classical dance nor Dalcroze found suitable. Yet despite her eclectic bent she was impressive enough as a dancer so that when Nolde directed her to Laban, she had just been offered a contract to head a branch of the Dalcroze school in Berlin. But in her meeting with Laban at Ascona, she found the liberation in movement she had been seeking: "I danced, danced, danced." The Berlin job was rejected. Laban became Wigman's first real teacher and she, his first real disciple and collaborator.

With the outbreak of the war, Laban's students scattered. Only Wigman remained with him in Ascona where for months they threw themselves with incredible intensity into work on Laban's search for a dance notation system and the working out of his "Theory of Harmony and Movement." This theory, later developed as "Eukinetics," (or Effort-Shape analysis), was to evolve as a description and understanding of movement dynamics (the movement equivalents of the musical descriptions *forte, pianissimo,* etc.), alongside a complementary study of spatial harmonies, designs and scales (later called "Choreutics"). This great dream of an analysis of movement and the translating of it into a recordable script of signs—a cross, bar and point system—was codified by Laban in 1928 to become Labanotation.[16]

In 1914, working with Wigman in her small room, Laban instructed her in deep breathing exercises followed by combinations of organic movements which were to lead to the perfect harmony of his movement scale. With Wigman, Laban explored and analyzed supports and gestures in various rhythms, bent limb positions were used, shifting centers of weight and torso rotations were investigated. The movements coupled a spatial geometry with some secret mystical science, much in line with Kandinsky's experiments of the same time. With Wigman demonstrating, Laban would repeatedly design and reject movements, occasionally exploding at Wigman's intense self-expression with "You clown, you grotesque monster, with your terrific intensity you ruin my whole theory of harmony."[17] Laban's outburst, what Susanne Langer might call a "self-revealing utterance of the artist," foreshadows the eventual break between Laban's work and Wigman's own—a rupture which had so reached a peak by the late 1920s that at the Congress of German Dancers which attracted over 1,000 delegates to Essen in June, 1928, the debate on the New German Dance which had been inspired by Duncan and founded on the research into rhythm and expressiveness by Dalcroze, centered on the conflict between the school of Laban and the school of Wigman.[18]

In 1914, however, Wigman was still Laban's protégée and although she did not present a full evening of her own dances until 1918, her work was featured in Laban's performances from 1914 and her influence in the studio work was dominant. Nearly all of her most original dances were unaccompanied by music and when music was used, it was written by the composer working in collaboration with the dancers. Neither Wigman nor Laban ever composed a dance to a piece of existing music. Wigman especially was almost categorically anti-music and in the new relationship which emerged between music (or non-music) and the dance rests one of her most radical changes and innovative contributions. The subordination of dance to music was to be ended. Even an intimate link between the two was suspect. Not only was the dancer to be liberated from literature, but from music as well. The new emphasis was on rhythm, and dances, often called "forms," used gongs, clappers and rattles as accompaniment. Dances often had no titles at all and no program descriptions were available to relieve the uneasy audience. On stage, a crouched figure in a two-piece black gym suit[19] might work herself into a frenzy with an offstage rattle keeping pace. On the verge of rising to normal height for the first time, she would suddenly fall prone, the lights would go out, the number ended. The frame of the conception of nineteenth-century dance had been broken.

In 1914, Laban mounted one of his earliest works, "The Earth," performed with musical interludes composed by him and based on a scale of his own fashioning in which each tone is of equal importance. The music was noted without bars and was to be interpreted vocally by Suzanne Perrottet and Maja Lederer (Laban's second wife). It had been very difficult for Laban to find "suitable artists" to present the work and in the end Lederer alone sang the songs intended for a large chorus while Perrottet joined the dancers, often moving to

Illustration 13   Mary Wigman, ca. 1916

Collection: Performing Arts Research Center, The New York Public Library at
Lincoln Center

the challenge of complete silence. The unprepared audience, fearing it was being mocked, responded by "sending eggs, overripe plums and pieces of wood flying onto the stage." Laban was generous to his detractors:

> It is not at all easy to follow the movements of a dancer with one's eyes, and what one cannot see one obviously cannot really judge.[20]

Continuing his experiments in sound and movement, Laban worked on a piece called *The Dancing Drumstick*. Using as a stimulus a book on the meaning of old Mexican drum messages—primitive movement made audible—Laban tried to move over from sound as an audible gesture to dance—a visible language:

> To primitive man the language of the drum seems nothing other than the rhythm of his body made audible. Therefore, as long as the European tries to investigate it with his intellect, it will always remain a mystery to him.[21]

A further area of experimentation was in the dancer's relation to space. The forms of nineteenth-century ballet, though executed in space, basically remained subtle plays of the body with itself, largely irrespective of space. The dancer moved in space but not into it. Group dancing was mass movement: patterns of dividing and joining in space but no shaping of the space itself. Group dances were not the bearers of "space functions."[22] Fascinated by the dancer's use of space, Laban used a "machine" called a "space crystal"— "a cage made of wire in the form of a polyhedron, in which the pupil is enclosed, to enter into affinity with space and so to be galvanized into contact with the fourth dimension,"[23] and one of Wigman's principle themes was "space feeling"—the dancing filling the space of the stage, leaving no room for vague or unncessary movements, making each gesture expressive and decisive. For Wigman, space was to be used as an emotional element, an active partner in the dance. The dancer would grapple with space as with an opponent, would embrace it as a living thing, would carve it to suit her subjective purpose:

> Standing in the center of the space, eyes closed, the danseuse feels the weight of the atmosphere resting upon her limbs. Hesitatingly she lifts her arm, cleaving the invisible body of space, pressing forward, the feet following—thus creating the direction. Space appears to be reaching for her, pulling back from the newly created road; counter direction—a game, up and down, forward and back, a meeting of one's self, a struggle in space for space—the Dance . . . she lowers her arms, again remains standing still, observes the bare space—the dancer's realm![24]

Dada and the New German Dance

Much of the experimental work in performance at the Cabaret Voltaire was based on dance. Ball, in planning his ideal theatre, had included "modern

Illustration 15   Rudolph von Laban in dance-mask

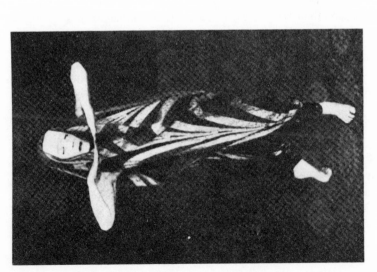

Illustration 14   Mary Wigman: masked dance

painting, modern music, modern dance,"[25] and his closeness to Kandinsky had put him in touch with the painter's experiments in art and the dance (the dancer "dancing the painting") as well as the artist's experiments in movement in *The Yellow Sound*. Ball wrote short musical pieces for "dances" which the dadas improvised and Janco's masks inspired "a tragic-absurd dance."

The importance of the mask for the dadas as a stimulus for the dance is echoed by Wigman. Recalling the composition of an early work she said:

> I realized that the figures had to wear masks—to give each of the three dancers a proportion outside the distinctively personal. A young sculptor came and worked on the masks—and since my experience taught me that such a dance could be formed only after seeing the masks, I waited for them before beginning to compose. They came—wonderful . . . the mask of the old woman, which I wanted to wear myself . . . it frightened me. . . . It expressed something so remote and beyond life that I could visualize for it only motionless silence. . . . And then it happened. . . . Suddenly my entire body was tense, unbearably tense, my hand grasping my tightly closed coat; I was straightening, growing in a struggle within and without me, prancing, three steps wide into the dark empty room—a rhythm forced my arm upward—the theme was born.[26]

By the time a visit to the Dada Gallery by "Laban and his ladies," is formally recorded by Ball in his diary (2.IV.1916), it is quite clear that a strong interaction was already in progress between the dada painter-poet-performers and the makers of the new German dance. Ball partied with the other dadas at Wigman's house, wrote at length of Sophie Taeuber's abstract dance "Song of the Flying Fish and the Sea Horses," and saw Wigman dance to Oriental poems at Zurich's Pfauens Theater. He also saw her "dance Nietzsche" at the Café des Banques. In the center of a self-made circle and "conceived deeper than day," she waved Zarathoustra around "left, right, left, right."[27]

The influence of the one group of artists on the other is undeniable though it is sometimes not clear in which direction the influence is flowing. Describing one of Wigman's performances, a critic in 1918 wrote:

> The curtain divided on the first dance and we saw a motionless figure, dressed in a yellow bell shaped costume hooped over at the lower edge. Over her hair she wore some metallic lace work, and over her face a strange, immobile, slit-eyed mask. A gong off-stage sounded and the figure moved. Nothing can describe the uncanny effect of this dehumanized mechanism. All the movements were mannered and rhythmically tuned to synchronize with the beating of the gong.[28]

Though this critique is fairly late as a signpost for a stage of creative reciprocity between Wigman and the dadas, it is quite clear from earlier photographs that Wigman's use of the gong antedates this performance, and by 1917, Ball in his diary had written of dancers and the gong—relating both to his own experiments in sound and movement:

> Abstract dances: a gong beat is enough to stimulate the dancer's body to make the most fantastic movements. The dance has become an end in itself. The nervous system exhausts all the vibrations of the sound and perhaps all the hidden emotions of the gong beater, too, and turns them into an image—a poetic sequence of words is enough to make each of the individual word particles produce the strangest visible effect on the hundred-jointed body of the dancer.[29]

The dry violence of non-melodic drums and gongs was very much in tune with the grotesque movements of the dancer. Some of this emphasis on percussive accompaniment may be related to Ball's intense involvement with Oriental theatre.

Laban and Wigman, both students of the arts of the East, favored the rhythmic designs of harsh instruments and Wigman's use of Eastern movements can be seen in her pre-1923 photograph which, when set alongside similar portraits of Ruth St. Denis and Sent M'Ahesa, shows the more generalized use of the Eastern dance as a basis for the work of the contemporary "modern" dancer. St. Denis had just completed a three year European tour with her *Radha*, a sacred Hindu dance, while Sent M'Ahesa (a Swedish dancer whose program belied her ancestry) had just done a series of performances in Zurich and Berlin. M'Ahesa used Egyptian and Indian models, tambourines, drums, cymbals, and the triangle for accompaniment, and stressed the effects of make-up and costume.

Ball, writing of the dance, speaks of "vibrations," a term he had learned from Kandinsky to apply to the work of the artist, and Hanya Holm, an early student of Wigman's wrote of her work in the dancer's studio:

> One day the problem of vibration was brought up. . . . We found the answer to it by sitting on a sofa a whole night, with the springs helping us to bounce back. Then on our feet, without any outward help, the demands of the momentum carried us gradually further until the repetition of the movement finally broke down any mental opposition and vibration became a true experience for us.[30]

The primacy of group work for Ball was echoed by Wigman:

> It is not the soloists achievement which is pregnant with future. This will always remain a single and purely maximum achievement. . . . But the young dance generation should put all emphasis on the group dance. There are all possibilities, there is a future.[31]

and when Wigman describes the work in the new Dresden studio to which she moved late in 1919, she might well have been describing the Cabaret Voltaire-Dada Gallery experience:

> We . . . were a small experimental club in which everything was tried out which the imagination would yield and which the bodily abilities would permit. But we all without exception were fanatics, obsessed with what we were doing.[32]

Wigman, as Ball, was conscious of the devotion necessary for the task of experimentation:

> Fatigue and exhaustion were states of transition . . . the most difficult was to experiment.[33]

By April of 1917, Ball was writing repeatedly of the dance. In dance he saw an art of the closest and most direct material, "very close to the art of tatooing and to all primitive representative efforts that aim at personification."[34] His own search was for "absolute dance,"—a minimum of impressions enough to evoke visual images; while critics who saw the Wigman performances spoke of a "pure" dance—aiming to express nothing but itself.

At the second Dada Gallery performance of April 14, 1917, five Laban ladies performed a piece choreographed by Ball himself. Dressed as Negresses in long black caftans and face masks, the five moved symmetrically to a strongly emphasized rhythm with mimicry of a studied, deformed ugliness. The concept of "ugliness" was a liberating one for dada as well as for the "modern" dancer— a concept which Kandinsky had pointed to in 1912 in his *Concerning the Spiritual in Art:*

> In dance . . . we are on the threshold of a future art . . . Conventional beauty must go and the literary element, "story-telling" or "anecdote," must be abandoned. . . . Painting and dance must learn from music that every harmony and every discord that springs from internal necessity is beautiful (i.e., Functional): but it is essential that they spring from internal necessity alone. The "ugly" movements suddenly become beautiful and emanate an undreamt-of strength and living force. At this point the dance of the future begins.[35]

Seeming to paraphrase Kandinsky in his lecture on the painter delivered at the Dada Gallery, Ball said:

> Just as in music or in painting there is no such thing as an "ugly" sound or outward "dissonance," so too in the dance the inner value of every movement will soon be felt, and the inner beauty will replace outward beauty. From unbeautiful movements issues an unrecognized force and living power. From this moment on, the dance of the future begins.[36]

Discarding as models the "beautiful" movements of ballet's mimed storytelling, the dancer could begin by accepting first her own body and then in turn its limitless potential for expression. No more was a small, dainty body necessary

Illustration 16   Laban dancers in the nude

for the dance. The demand for such a body would have eliminated the strong-boned, muscular, full-breasted Wigman (as well as Isadora Duncan and Loie Fuller before her). Moving in this liberating direction, a new and compelling equilibrium developed for the dancer of the new dance. New permission allowed her to be neither young nor old, neither beautiful nor ugly, neither masculine nor feminine:

> The sex of a German rhythmician is practically abolished. Mannish, positive, wide of womb, robustly underpinned, she functions forcefully and frankly. These neutral nymphs often affect the masculine uniform—a blouse and trousers to the ankle, or the trunks of the gymnast which leave the muscular flanks free. Their ejaculatory movements forbid grace or fragility.[37]

Ball as well promoted a certain "hermaphrodite" quality for the artist; a sexual changeability that would enable him to change from the male to the female viewpoint at will, thereby permitting "that multiplicity of reflection that produces ideas."

Ball would not be trapped in a masculine posture and Wigman, the frizzled brunette, had nothing of the "Gretchen" about her. She would dance what she thought, felt and lived. Her body could now express both static and dynamic patterns, could explore new temporal and spatial rhythms, could cling to the floor, could aspire upwards and outwards. To intensify this new meeting with her body, and in an attempt to make of her body a perfect instrument of her will to dance, Wigman went into a retreat in a religious monastic community near Zurich.[38] There she worked outdoors "like the great Isadora Duncan," freeing herself from as much clothing as possible, to the dismay of the decorous novitiates. Modern dance performances in the nude were not uncommon at that time and German books on the dance between 1913 and 1920 feature nude photos and sketches of Grete Weisenthal and Gertrud Leistikow as well as the dancers of the Laban school.

Working on her first dance cycle *The Seven Dances of Life* (not presented until 1921), Wigman used those "aimless improvisations" which had so intoxicated her in the early work with Laban, and which implied a permission to allow "ugly" movements to appear. Her dance could weep, scream and complain. A dance with a skeleton's skull was an actual event and Hugo Ball always carried with him the skull of a young girl.

The New German Dance in Performance

The new German dance of Wigman and Laban was as unacceptable to critics and audience as were the dada performances. A child of expressionism, it had evolved from a totally new way of looking at art in the world—expression as a direct reaction to experience. The canons of formal beauty which characterized classical dance were out. Possibilities for body movement would now be probed in detail while emotion determined form and the inner life emerged. The crude slams with the whole of the bare foot against the floor, the walking, running, and lying on the stage, the spiral placement of the torso and asymmetrical positioning of the legs were met with responses of "ridiculous," "idiotic," "imbecilic dislocation of the joints." What accompaniment there was was labeled "a mad frenzy," "the drum and gong—earsplitting, tortuous," "an excruciating din." Even Michel Fokine, so innovative a choreographer within the classical forms, found Wigman "soulless, stiff and strained," and wrote of her performance:

> In order to glorify her a novel method is used: Wigman is not beautiful in movements, therefore beauty is considered as something old fashioned. She is not feminine, therefore femininity, it is said, no longer should belong to women. She has poor musical sense, therefore there is no music.[39]

In their more controlled moments, critics of the new German dance saw its deficiencies in its highly developed perception of geometric design which continually overreached what they considered its rudimentary sense of motion. With the torso quiescent and the extremities in violent activity, the patterns were seen as constantly degenerating into pantomime and emotionalism.

While the critical concern was solely with the result, what was foremost for the Laban-Wigman school, as in the dada work, was the primacy of "process." Laban, predating the surrealists' experiments with automatic creation, would stimulate a faltering improvisatory situation with "Look here, if nothing else occurs to you at least jump!"[40] and Wigman wrote:

> . . . the idea for a dance comes to the creative dancer, so to speak, in his sleep, in other words, suddenly it is here. As a musician hits upon a melody without knowing where it comes from, thus the dancer's movements come spontaneously to his mind.[41]

By 1917, a stable working relationship is evident between the Laban-Wigman dancers and the Dada Gallery performers. All dance events at the Gallery were performed by dancers of the Laban-Wigman school and whether choreographed by one or another of the dancers or by Ball or another of the dadas, a semblance of stylistic unity, an agreement on medium and method seems apparent. Barefoot bodies, in draped cloth or athletic costumes, often masked, moved in group or solo dances to the beat of a gong, a drum or to the sound of silence. The costumes were neither meant to reveal nor conceal, only to add to the effect of the dance idea by whatever texture, color or line seemed best, and to allow the dancer the greatest liberty of movement. Costume, scenery, "music," were all subordinated to the "idea" of the dance. Simple, essential gestures spoke a new vocabulary of movement while experimental creations in time furthered the development of a new temporal rhythm in the dance. Designs in time and space would now arouse an audience by sheer power of aesthetic form.

As with the dada work in performance, the ecstasy of the first recitals of German dance could never be repeated. The emotional stimulus became dull and although the dance had not been created with intent to shock, still some of its force diminished as its shock value dissipated.

Avant-Garde Performance in Paris

It's all a joke isn't it?

Jules Lemaitre, at the opening of Jarry's
Ubu Roi, 1896

Jean, astonish me!

Diaghilev to Cocteau about the scenario
for his new ballet, *Parade,* 1915

. . . the most tremendous hoax and practical
joke . . .

de Champclos, *Le Petit Bleu,* at the opening
of Apollinaire's *The Breasts of Tirésias,* 1917

Illustration 17　Guillaume Apollinaire and members of the cast of *Les Mamelles de Tirésias*, June 24, 1917 (*La Rampe*, July 12, 1917)

When dada performance zoomed into Paris with Tristan Tzara in 1920, the dada theatre imported from Zurich seemed so strikingly new, daring and defiant, that it tended to eclipse all signs of an already resident theatre avant-garde. Yet Paris had spawned its own share of *Hernanis,* and although Alfred Jarry had been dead for over 13 years, the spirit of his conical père Ubu, chubby king who scandalized the French public in 1896, continued to hover, patron to a flourishing of the most contemporary and controversial of the arts.

As early as 1909, Lugné-Poe had produced Marinetti's *Le roi bombace* with its scatalogical assaults on the spectator, and in 1911, Ferdinand Divoire, poet at the center of the simultaneist movement had published five plays by the futurist leader in *l'Intransigeant.* He called them "explosive capsules." In that same year, Apollinaire, who was in correspondence with Marinetti, wrote an article on futurist painting almost before the theory and the painting had fully developed. Between 1914 and 1919, a rash of futurist plays were produced in Paris, and in the delighted rebellion against conventional modes of representation, "marinettismo" was hard to avoid.

By 1912 the tests of the Swiss Dr. Rorschach were in use in Paris: "chance pictures," whose interpretation served to show the relationship between perception and personality, between a certain psychic predisposition and the creative act. Freud had been translated into French and the painter Odilon Redon had acknowledged the primacy of the unconscious in the creative process. "Nothing is achieved in art by the will alone . . . everything is achieved by docile submission to the advent of the unconscious."

The traditional limits of art had fallen by the wayside. Collage had brought nails and newsprint to the canvas, and "extraplastic phenomena," such as noise, were now considered a part of painting as well. Painting was even changing the movement of performers on the stage. In 1913, a conservative critic stated that in Debussy's *Jeux,* Nijinsky had forced himself and his two female partners into cubist distortions; that he had "twisted Karsavina's precious limbs in the name of Matisse, Metzinger and Picasso." Although the static architecture of cubism was fundamentally opposed to the representation of movement in the action of a play, this school of art had succeeded in proposing a new relationship to space. Volumes now unfolded themselves on a flat surface and several views of the same object became common. Guillaume Apollinaire, art critic and promoter of the French avant-garde had sympathies with both the analytic and synthetic tendencies of cubism—the first reconstructing the world of nature according to the rigid rules of geometry and best represented by the French Braque, Gleizes and Metzinger—the second, stressing creation, surprise, and spontaneity as in the works of the Spanish Picasso, Gris, Picabia. But it was finally

Picasso, with his concept for the Managers in *Parade*—carrying the sets and costumes as one on their backs, blurring the line between actor and object—who found the way to advance beyond collage and step over into movement and performance. The audience stood by shaking its head and muttering like the Father at the end of Hebbel's 1843 drama *Maria Magdalena*, "I don't understand the world any more."

The avant-garde performances which scandalized Paris before the advent of dada were Jarry's *Ubu Roi* (1896), the Cocteau-Picasso-Satie ballet *Parade* executed by Diaghilev's Ballets Russe (1917), and Apollinaire's *Les Mamelles de Tirésias* (1917). All three explored the use of a performing arena filled with the objects, games, "plastique" quality and elements of shock which would later mark Paris dada theatre. The Apollinaire and Cocteau pieces were both striking in their physical conception, in their treatment of the actor as object, in their inaugural coupling of the "real," and the "sur-real." To all three performances, the audience reacted with a virulence and vitality born of threat and of the new; with varieties of anger and joy depending on which side of the cultural fence you sat. All three performances comprise the beginnings of a theatrical continuum in Paris that leads through the arrival of dada performance and the growth of surrealist theatre, to the experiments of the Autant-Lara's *Théâtre Art et Action* and of Artaud's *Théâtre Alfred Jarry,* into the most contemporary of avant-garde performances.

Alfred Jarry's Ubu Roi

The origins of *Ubu* are well known. Professor Hébert, a well-meaning but hopelessly incompetent teacher of physics at the local lycée at Rennes, was parodied by his young students Alfred Jarry, then 15, and Henri and Charles Morin. They immortalized Hébert in a series of epic poems and plays featuring the obese, misshapen unfortunate (whose name had undergone transformations from Héb through Hébé to Ubu) in an endless series of adventures and mishaps. The ur-*Ubu* was first performed in the Morin and Jarry attics in 1888 using marionettes of a small theatre which Jarry père had presented to his children. Five years later the character of Ubu was still alive and Jarry, in Paris, published a few fragmentary dialogues entitled "guignol," in which père Ubu was first introduced to the public at large.[1] Jarry was barely 20 and lived in a small apartment on the Boulevard St. Germain. There he had installed a marionette theatre to entertain his friends, those members of the symbolist cenacle who clustered around Alfred Valette (editor of *Mercure de France*), and his wife Madame Rachilde. Valette and Rachilde were to remain active participants in the theatrical avant-garde through the years of dada and surrealism.

By 1896, Jarry had published six different fragments of the *Ubu* text and in the spring of that year, Paul Fort, former director of the Théâtre d'Art,

Illustration 18   Firmin Gémier as Ubu with the "Cheval à Phynance" (Act III), March 28, 1908 (*Commoedia,* November 4, 1921)

Collection: Département des Arts du Spectacle, Bibliothèque de l'Arsenal

published a full-length play called *Ubu Roi* in his review *Le livre d'Art*. There was a large reading public for such small literary reviews and by the summer of 1896 when the play appeared in book form, *Ubu* already had a following.

Upon his arrival in Paris in October 1891, Jarry moved into the world of young writers, editors and theatre-makers of the avant-garde. In 1894 he became co-director of a small review entitled *l'Ymagier,* and it was through the offices of *l'Ymagier* that Jarry made his first overtures to the director Lugné-Poe, sending him the first issue of the magazine with "tout sa sympathie d'Art," and expressing enthusiasm at the forthcoming second season of his theatre. Aurelian Lugné-Poe, at 25, had just become director of the *Théâtre de l'Oeuvre* (a theatre, descendent of Paul Fort's short-lived experiment in symbolism, the *Théâtre d'Art*), and the young Jarry at 21 was attracted by Lugné-Poe's youth, his poverty, his boldness. With A. Ferdinand-Hérold (a member of the *Mercure* group), as intermediary, the two men met in the Fall of 1894 and the empathy was mutual. Lugné-Poe writes of Jarry at that time:

> I had faith in him and he aroused my curiosity. His owlish looks, his voice hammering out phrases on two notes . . .[2]

Lugné-Poe's attraction was coupled with the fact that he knew that Jarry was preparing a play for the *l'Oeuvre* although he confesses "I was far from conceiving the type of play he was preparing for me."[3]

Jarry first offered Lugné-Poe *Les Polyhedres* (which later became *Ubu Cocu*), for production, but while this was under consideration, he promoted *Ubu Roi* as well (perhaps hoping that the young director would mount them both). In a letter to Lugné-Poe dated January 8, 1896, Jarry formally suggests *Ubu,* and lists his now famous six points to consider in the play's production:

1) Mask for the principal character, Ubu; I could get this for you, if necessary. And, in any case, I believe that you yourself have been studying the whole question of masks in the theatre.

2) A cardboard horse's head which he would hang around his neck, as they did on the medieval English stage, for the only two equestrian scenes; all these details fit in with the mood of the play, since my intention was, in any case, to write a puppet play.

3) One single stage-set or, better still, a plain backdrop, thus avoiding the raising and dropping of the curtain during the single act. A formally dressed individual would walk on stage, just as he does in puppet shows, and hang up a placard indicating where the next scene takes place. (By the way, I am absolutely convinced that a descriptive placard has far more "suggestive" power than any stage scenery. No scenery, no array of walkers-on could really evoke "the Polish Army marching across the Ukraine.")

4) The abolition of crowds which usually put on a terrible collective performance and are an insult to the intelligence. So, just a single soldier in the army parade scene, and just one in the scuffle when Ubu says "What a slaughter, what a mob, etc. . ."

hoice of a special "accent," or, better still, a special "voice" for the principal character.

6) Costumes as divorced as far as possible from local color or chronology (which will thus help to give the impression of something eternal): modern costumes, preferably, since the satire is modern, and shoddy ones, too, to make the play even more wretched and horrible.[4]

When he first received *Ubu,* Lugné-Poe confesses "I didn't know which end to take hold of in order to stage it."[5] He did, however, propose that Jarry replace Adolphe van Beven, the *l'Oeuvre* stage-manager, who, in the summer of 1896, was forced to retire for reasons of health. By the time Jarry moved into this position at the theatre, the form of address in his letters to Lugné-Poe had shifted from "Monsieur," to "cher Monsieur," to "cher Lugné," and when Lugné-Poe himself left for a vacation in Brittany, the letters of Jarry—"sécre-taire, régisseur, acteur"—followed him with the plans for an imminent *Ubu* production always kept alive.[6] Meanwhile, Jarry opened the mail at the theatre, ran the office and organized publicity for the coming season. In his letters to the vacationing Lugné-Poe, amidst the talk of ads submitted and gas bills paid, again and again the Ubu project crops up:

Don't you think it will perhaps be fun, so that everything will be unusual when we stage Ubu, to have Bougrelas played by an intelligent youngster of the appropriate age and thereby react against a tradition of "travesti" which no one has dared over-throw since that one phrase in *The Marriage of Figaro?* . . . I met one in Montmartre who is very handsome. . . He is thirteen years old and quite intelligent . . . this would excite the old ladies and certainly give rise to a scandal.[7]

Playing up to Lugné-Poe's mania for long neglected "foreign" plays he offered to unearth information about some German works (mainly Grabbe), never before translated and bearing resemblance to the comic vein of *Ubu*—always *Ubu* in the background.

The fourth season at the *l'Oeuvre* approached and Lugné-Poe sent out a manifesto with a plea for new plays:

Should someone from afar bring us a rough, unpolished work written with disregard for the rules of the theatre, with complete ignorance of what one calls dramatic art . . . we would receive it with joy.[8]

Ubu Roi had indeed been promised for production that season and Jarry, in anticipation of the mounting of his own play, had worked with devotion on the *l'Oeuvre's Peer Gynt:* researching the music, reshaping the troll's scene (whose humour was very difficult to follow in the French) and acting the role of the King of the trolls. The play was a success, and Lugné-Poe felt that he must now keep his promise to Jarry and mount *Ubu.* But he could not dispell his

112

anxiety about the project and sought encouragement from Mme. Rachilde, his friend and a patron of Jarry's. He received a letter full of gentle chiding and support.

> Look . . . if you didn't sense success when you accepted the play, then why did you, the director of the theatre who knows what makes for a success (that it is sometimes simply a lot of noise), accept it? . . . I keep hearing and re-hearing in my circle, that all the younger generation and a few of the "oldies" who like a good joke, are all eagerly awaiting this production. So what's the problem? Perhaps it won't be a smashing success but rather an oddity which will marvellously substantiate your eclecticism. Strive as much as you can for guignol, avoid the lecture! One needn't explain to us how to laugh . . . Yes, the l'Oeuvre must mount it. . . .[9]

And so *Ubu* was mounted. And the play which was first performed on December 9, 1896,[10] was a fitting antecedent to the theatre of dada which would be born 20 years later.

Once decided on the project, Lugné-Poe assembled a cast of stars. The director's artist friends Serusier and Bonnard, assisted by Vuillard, Toulouse-Lautrec and Ranson designed the sets and made sketches for the production. Claude Terrasse, married to Bonnard's sister, and a newcomer to Paris, prepared the score. Lugné-Poe had originally considered himself for the part of Ubu but finally, deciding that he had too many other responsibilities to undertake the role, he approached Firmin Gémier, an established actor of the *Comédie Française* who was known to be friendly to the avant-garde. Gémier was at the time playing in Villier de l'Isle Adam's *La Révolte* at the *Odéon,* but he succeeded in receiving permission to absent himself from the production for two evenings. Mère Ubu was to be played by Louise France, a seasoned member of the *l'Oeuvre* troupe, and Bordure by the actor Flandre who had been suggested by Jarry because of his physical appearance, tall and thin in contrast to Gémier's bulk. Jarry was full of other suggestions as to how the play should be mounted. For young Bougrelas he chose a handsome 14-year-old boy whom he had met in Montmartre (an unheard-of choice at the time). Jarry's six suggestions in his letter to Lugné-Poe show the influence of the symbolist movement of the time: the plain backdrop or "no scenery," the abolition of crowds, and costuming divorced from local color or chronology. His suggestions for the use of masks and his inclination to relate the production to the puppet theatre he knew so well are ideas he developed further in two brief articles published in 1896 and 1897. The first, "On the Futility of the 'Theatrical' in the Theatre,"[11] appeared in the *Mercure de France* in September of 1896, three months before the premiere of *Ubu.* In it, Jarry stresses the importance of the mask as embodying the eternal nature of the character:

> The actor should use a mask to envelop his head, thus replacing it by the effigy of the CHARACTER. His mask should not follow the masks in the Greek theater to

Illustration 19   Two views of the original *Ubu Roi* marionette (*Les Soirées de Paris*, No. 24, May 15, 1914)

Collection: Département des Arts du Spectacle, Bibliothèque de l'Arsenal

indicate simply tears or laughter, but should indicate the nature of the character: the Miser, the Waverer, the Covetous Man accumulating crimes. . . .[12]

These masks, to be further effective, must be illuminated by a gyroscope or kaleidoscope to achieve the maximum interplay of light and shadow, and the actor himself must learn to gain, from the slow nodding and lateral movements of his head, the greatest expressiveness. Jarry cites no examples of how this is to be done, for he says the examples "vary according to the nature of the mask and because everyone who knows how to watch a puppet show will have been able to observe this for himself."[13] The actor will, in addition, have to discover the particular voice and body quality appropriate to the role. Jarry's second article, "Theatre Questions," published in *La Revue Blanche* just a month after *Ubu*'s premiere, is in large part an attack on the audience: that group of "idiots" who did not know whether to cheer or boo at the December premiere.

The evening itself opened with a brief lecture, as was the custom at the *Théâtre de l'Oeuvre*.[14] Usually some qualified person said a few words about the new dramatist being presented (often Ibsen or Maeterlinck). On this occasion it was the author himself who spoke. Jarry, dressed in a baggy suit, white shirt and flowing chiffon scarf, his hair down to his shoulders, approached a small wooden table which had been draped with a piece of sacking, and on it placed his notes. A carafe of water and a glass awaited him but it is doubtful that he drank any for fear of smudging the white pancake make-up with which he had covered his entire face, lending himself the appearance of some dandied-up Pierrot. Those in the audience who knew Jarry were probably not surprised, for the young writer was renowned for appearing at various social functions in the most unlikely costumes. His usual dress was that of a bicycle racer: tight sweater, short coat and pants tucked into his socks, and he thought nothing of appearing at Mallarmé's funeral in this get-up, having added for effect a pair of Mme. Rachilde's bright yellow shoes. To the opera he wore a dirty canvas suit and a paper shirt with a tie painted on in India ink, and when he sensed his impending death, he laid out for himself a mauve shirt so that he would "disappear in the color scheme of *Le Mercure*."[15]

Such was the author who now stood before the two to three thousand people who filled to capacity the Nouveau Théâtre on the evening of December 9, 1896. The man, whose army discharge papers carried the classification "precocious imbecility," addressed the crowd in a low voice intended to hide his emotion:

Ladies and Gentlemen,
It should be quite unnecessary (apart from being slightly absurd for an author to talk about his own play) for me to come up here with a few words before the production of *Ubu Roi* after so many more distinguished people have spoken kindly of it: among whom I would especially like to thank Messieurs Silvestre, Mendes, Scholl,

Lorrain and Bauer—in fact, my only excuse for speaking to you now is that I am afraid that their generosity found Ubu's belly far more swollen with satirical symbols than we have really been able to stuff it with for this evening's entertainment.

The Swedenborgian Doctor Mises has quite rightly compared rudimentary works with the most perfect achievements, and embryonic forms with the most evolved creatures, pointing out that the former categories lack any special characteristics, leaving them a practically spherical form like the ovule or Mister Ubu; and, equally, that the latter possess so many personal attributes that they too take on a spherical form, by virtue of the axiom that the smoothest body is the one presenting the greatest number of different facets. Which is why you are free to see in Mister Ubu as many allusions as you like, or, if you prefer, just a plain puppet, a schoolboy's caricature of one of his teachers who represented for him everything in the world that is grotesque.

This is the point of view that the *Théâtre de l'Oeuvre* is going to give you this evening. A few actors have agreed to lose their own personalities during two consecutive evenings by performing with masks over their faces so that they can mirror the mind and soul of the man-sized marionettes that you are about to see. As the play has been put on in some haste and in a spirit of friendly improvisation, Ubu has not had time to obtain his own real mask, which would have been very awkward to wear in any case, and his confederates, too, will be decked out in only approximate disguise. It was very important that, if the actors were to be as much like marionettes as possible, we should have fairground music scored for brass and gongs and megaphones—which we simply did not have time to get together. But let us not be too hard on the *Théâtre de l'Oeuvre:* our main intention is to bring Ubu to life through the versatile genius of Monsieur Gémier, and tonight and tomorrow are the only evenings when Monsieur Ginisty—and the current production of Villiers de l'Isle-Adam—is free to let us borrow him. We are going to make do with three complete acts, followed by two acts incorporating some cuts. I have made all the cuts the actors wanted (even sacrificing several passages essential to the understanding of the play), and for their benefit I have kept in scenes which I would have been only too happy to eliminate. For, however much we may have wanted to be marionettes, we have not quite hung each character from a string, which may not necessarily have been an absurd idea but would certainly have been rather awkward for us, and in any case we were not quite sure exactly how many people were going to be available for our crowd scenes, whereas with real marionettes a handful of pulleys and strings serves to control a whole army. So in order to fill our stage you will see leading characters such as Ubu and the Czar talking to each other while prancing around on their cardboard horses (which, incidentally, we have been up all night painting). At least the first three acts and the closing scenes will be played in full, just as they were written.

And we also have the ideal setting, for just as a play can be set in Eternity by, say, letting people fire revolvers in the year one thousand or thereabouts, so you will see doors opening onto snow-covered plains under blue skies, mantelpieces with clocks on them swinging open to turn into doorways, and palm trees flourishing at the foot of beds so that little elephants perching on bookshelves can graze on them.

As for our nonexistent orchestra, we shall have to conjure up in our imagination all its sound and fury, contenting ourselves meanwhile with a few drums and pianos executing Ubu's themes from the wings.

And the action, which is about to start, takes place in Poland, that is to say Nowhere.[16]

The public applauded politely though there was, perhaps in light of the general tumult, later disagreement as to the clarity and comprehensibility of the opening remarks. A. Ferdinand Hérold of the *Mercure de France* found the talk witty and in fact the most appropriate commentary on the play while Fouquier of *Le Figaro* claimed that he could not catch a single word, which mattered little for the talk had been distributed in print with the program and even as such, Fouquier claimed, it was incoherent. Jarry was helped off with the table and Claude Terrasse the huge and frizzy-haired composer, and his wife, playing four-hand on the piano, began the overture with an off-stage orchestra as the curtain opened to reveal the set of what Arthur Symons, the English critic present at the evening, referred to as a "symbolist farce."

> . . . the scenery was painted to represent, by a child's conventions, indoors and out of doors, and even the torrid, temperate, and arctic zones at once. Opposite you, at the back of the stage, you saw apple trees in bloom, under a blue sky, and against the sky a small closed window and a fireplace . . . through the very midst of which . . . trooped in and out the clamorous and sanguinary persons of the drama. On the left was painted a bed, and at the foot of the bed a bare tree and snow falling. On the right there were palm trees . . . a door opened against the sky, and beside the door a skeleton dangled. A venerable gentleman in evening dress . . . trotted across the stage on the points of his toes between every scene and hung the new placard on its nail.[17]

Symon's description paints the set as a Surrealists' delight with the juxtaposition of incongruous objects, suited to a dream life. Gémier's own recollection of the set is by contrast far more pallid:

> The sole set was an inside-out baroque living room, and everything in it was left to the imagination of the audience.[18]

while the critic Paul Chauveau, similarly describes a more standard "interior,"

> . . . with, at the back, a fireplace flanked by two trees, and which, as we had been informed, opened in two to permit the characters to pass through.[19]

Max Maurey, on the other hand, brings us back to a sense of the fantastic by recalling at the left a wide bed beneath which was the inevitable chamber pot, and on the right, painted on the wall, a gallows and views of the sea, woods and open country. The fireplace door at the rear opened despite a clock and candelabra on the mantelpiece.[20]

When the curtain opened, Gémier and Marie France were already on stage, Gémier sporting a huge belly and wearing a heavy mask which had been designed by Jarry. The actor had vacillated until the last moment about appearing in the role, fearing that it might endanger his reputation and complaining to Lugné-Poe that he could find no way to work on the character. The director finally suggested to him to imitate Jarry's own peculiar manner of speaking which moved basically between two tones and with this in mind and after very little rehearsal, Gémier opened with the play's infamous "Merdre."

The resulting pandemonium has been chronicled by many critics. Laughter, hisses, cries of anger and applause vied with each other for prominence. The Decadent writer, Jean Lorraine left, immediately followed by a baffled Sarcey shrugging his shoulders. Jules Lemaitre anxiously asked, "It's all a joke isn't it?," while Georges Courteline shouted abusively "Don't you see that the author is dumping on us?" Tristan Bernard and Jules Renard screamed and whistled, enjoying themselves enormously in the confusion, while monocled and restrained Edmond Rostand smiled indulgently. In an effort to calm the crowd, Ferdinand Hérold, in the wings (where he was responsible for the lighting), switched on the houselights. This brought only a momentary lull as members of the audience suddenly saw each other with hands raised and mouths agape. On stage Gémier fumed behind his huge mask,

> . . . imprisoned in this carcass, I was hot . . . I was terribly furious. Up to this point I'd always gotten the better of the audience; feeling my impotence under this mask made me boil.[21]

Professional that he was, Gémier turned his fury to good use. Recognizing the impossibility of using his face to regain the audience, he set about dancing a florid jig which climaxed in a fall into the prompter's box, legs akimbo. There was a momentary truce as the audience applauded him and the play continued, but only to be interrupted again and again. Gémier chose to sit on the edge of the stage with his feet in the audience only to be greeted by the cry "This way's the exit!" At the moment when Ubu comes to visit Captain Bordure in prison, an actor, representing the prison door, stood on stage with his left hand extended. Gémier approached him and inserted a key between his fingers as into a lock, making the sound, "cric-crac" and at the same time moving the hand as if to open the door. The audience, primed to respond at the slightest stimulation went off on another wave of whistling and shouting. Nor were they silent when 40 life-sized straw mannequins which had been rented by Jarry were tumbled into the pit in Ubu's famous "crochet à phynnances."

In the days that followed the critics continued to stoke the smouldering fire of outrage. The general conclusion was unanimous "A scandal . . . no other word will do." The defense, small but staunch, was led by Henry Bauer of the *Echo de Paris,* who wrote one of five favorable reviews.[22] He maintained that the audience should have understood Jarry's satirical intent, he loved the charming buffoonery of Terrasse's score and praised the excellent interpretation of the characters. He concluded "The mad, the extraordinary evening!" For his trouble he was ousted from his position at *l'Echo,* and though he subsequently took over the drama column at *La Petite République,* his column was thereafter censored.

The opposition position, led by Henry Fouquier of *Le Figaro,* reigned. Fouquier, speaking for a loyal bourgeois following, saw no justification for incoherent satire. He termed the characters musical comedy puppets and as for the language he dismissed it as a mere "superficial pastiche of the language of Rabelais, of which particularly the muck is retained and repeated with love."

It was the Irish poet W.B. Yeats, however, sitting in the audience that night (and later recording the event in his autobiography), who more than anyone else pointed the direction which would ultimately mark Jarry as the idol of dadas and surrealists alike. For Jarry had started a move toward an art which, as it delighted, would both frighten and scandalize; an art which worshipped a "Savage God."

> I go to the first performance of Jarry's *Ubu Roi,* at the *Théâtre de l'Oeuvre,* with Rhymer who had been so attractive to the girl in the bicycling costume. The audience shake their fists at one another, and Rhymer whispers to me, 'There are often duels after these performances,' and explains to me what is happening on stage. The players are supposed to be dolls, toys, marionettes, and now they are all hopping like wooden frogs, and I can see for myself that the chief personage, who is some kind of king, carries for a sceptre a brush of the kind that we use to clean a closet. Feeling bound to support the most spirited party, we have shouted for the play, but that night at the Hotel Corneille I am very sad, for comedy, objectively, has displayed its growing power once more. I say, after S. Mallarme, after Verlaine, after G. Moreau, after Puvis de Chavannes, after our own verse, after the faint mixed tints of Conder, what more is possible? After us the Savage God.

Jarry was 23. In the 12 years which remained to him, he lived his life to its dada best. Taking life as art, refusing as the dadas did to acknowledge any separation between the two, he moved within the Paris literary world of the early 1900s, carrying his pistol, riding his bicycle and more and more sliding into the role of the living-Ubu. His flat at 7 rue Cassette was one which the landlord had divided horizontally for the use of tenants "of small stature." There he lived with two cats and an owl, sporting a head of hair all white at the ends from brushing the whitewash off the ceiling. In speech he assumed the royal "we," and spoke with great pomposity of the wind as "that which blows," and of a bird as "that which chirps." In dress he continued to imitate the circus clown and in his activities he was remembered for those aggressive anti-establishment incidents which would later identify the dadas. One day he fired a pistol into a hedge and a lady shot up from behind it in a fury. "Sir, my child is playing about here, and you might have killed him!" "Madame," Jarry answered gallantly, "I would have given you another." Seated in the upper balcony of a theatre because of his bizarre dress, he took his revenge on the management by complaining in a loud voice just as the curtain went up, "I don't see why they allow the audience in the first three rows to come in carrying musical instruments."[23] At a banquet given for his artist and writer friends, he thought nothing of announcing at the dessert "This (pointing to the chocolate mousse) represents the left breast of the giant Negress of the carnival in the *Place du Torn.* Madame Rachilde copied it from life in chocolate and vanilla, using the milk of Madame Fontaine (pointing to the wife of a local resident) who, as the whole countryside knows, sleeps with her goat . . ."[24] The newspapers began to refer to him as "Father Ubu, himself," and the young writers who would help pass on his spirit flocked to be at his side: Guillaume Apollinaire, André Salmon and Max Jacob. André Breton would later write of him,

> We maintain that beginning with Jarry . . . the differentiation long considered necessary between art and life has been challenged, to wind up annihilated as a principle.

and Gide in no uncertain terms maintained,

> . . . the Surrealists invented nothing better . . . they had good reason to recognize him as a forerunner.[25]

Five months after Jarry's death, on March 28, 1908, *Ubu* was revived at the *Théâtre Antoine* with Gémier again playing the lead role. This time the directorial concept was Gémier's own, but for all of his being a fine actor, Gémier had none of Jarry's eccentric daring. The performance was pallid, the audience calm and fairly indifferent. The decor had been tempered into a geometric vista of harlequin-squared meadows in whose midst rose a Slavo-Arab palace, its dome echoing the pear shaped head of Ubu. Mère and père Ubu entered from opposite sides of the stage at a trot, collided and remained stunned for an instant, arms akimbo. Gémier with his stomach padded as in the original production had, however, forsaken his mask for two puffed cheeks and a conical skull. In the third act Ubu trades this costume for the resplendent garb of a hussar. Mère Ubu was fat in a flowered Indian dress, her face and hands painted red, alongside a wind-up-toy Captain Bordure. Wenceslas sported sign which read "Roy" and the Czar was a jack-in-the-box, emerging on cue from his packing crate marked "FRAGILE". Bougrelas' royal family wore grotesque masks but strangest of all was the conclusion:

> All the characters, living and dead, revived, and spread out in a single line; and down to the young Bougrelas, they draped themselves over the neck of the 'Cheval à Phynance,' and slept, heads bent and quite clearly snoring.[26]

The excitement of the guignol in the original production had faded into the more common tricks of slapstick and the more polite humor of political satire.

The text had been abridged to make it more digestible for the audience. Gémier had forced *Ubu* to grow up and in so doing, had robbed the play of its most vital parts. The magic and vulnerability of childhood and the elements of shock and "merveille" so admired by the dadas and surrealists, which had worked their effect in the 1896 production, were obviously not inherent in the text of the play alone but in a whole series of circumstances which had combined to produce the *Théâtre de l'Oeuvre*'s most famous scandal. In the wide gap which separates the audience's responses to the two *Ubu* productions, we have a foreshadowing of the problems dada would face in its move to Paris, and which would cause its eventual demise. Eliciting a shocked response in an audience is either the product of a very fine understanding of a particular society at a particular moment, or a haphazard stroke of well-placed defiance. In either case the response is a very difficult one to sustain. The "merdre" of 1896 was no longer startling when uttered by the chubby king in 1908. Times had changed and Gémier, to shock anew with *Ubu*, would have had to work through some new performance concept to startle and agitate his public. But Gémier's intention was surely different from Jarry's; Gémier was apparently satisfied to mount a well-honed museum piece to be regarded through a glass and admired.

In 1903 Guillaume Apollinaire sought out Jarry in his *Grande Chasublerie* and there spent many hours with the eccentric writer who was barely seven years his senior. In 1904, he wrote the first major article to be published on Jarry. In the decade which followed, Apollinaire, himself the most influential French art critic of the early years of the century, found the way to meet, support and bring together that group of young poets and artists who in 1920 would make "le scandale" an aesthetic principle. At the time of his meeting with Jarry, Apollinaire was also introduced to André Salmon, Max Jacob and Picasso, and the four soon formed an inseparable group much inspired by Jarry's bravado. The clique of the three Parisians and the Spanish painter soon drew to itself all those younger avant-gardists who were to become first the followers of Tzara and dada, and then the founders of the surrealist movement.

Parade

With the onset of World War I, theatrical activity in Paris was vastly diminished. It was through the ballet that new concepts of performance began to evidence themselves. Jean Cocteau, young poet of the avant-garde, had maintained contact with Diaghilev ever since his first Paris season in 1909, and had designed posters for the Russian ballet company's 1910 and 1911 seasons. By 1915 Diaghilev was eager to receive from Cocteau the scenario for a unique ultramodern ballet. "Jean, astonish me," he had written, but Cocteau was already three steps ahead of him. In October of 1915 he had left a pile of notes with Erik Satie, then 48 and a composer recognized in the fashionable Paris salons.

Satie, he had decided, would write the music for the new ballet. In the fall of 1915, the composer of "noise-music" (bruitism), Edgar Varèse, introduced Cocteau (then 26) to Picasso and by September of 1916 the *Parade* group had been formed.

The scenario which Cocteau suggested for *Parade*[27] was not in itself innovative. In front of a fair booth set on a Parisian boulevard one Sunday afternoon, a Chinese magician, an acrobat and a young girl perform their music-hall routines in an effort to draw a crowd inside. Three "managers" direct the goings-on. The crowd, so entranced by the performers, takes them to be the show itself and departs without entering the booth. What did occur to cause the varied boos, whistles and applause in the audience on the evening of May 17, 1917 was a product of the elements of production. Cocteau had originally envisaged as a complement for the dances a series of raucous sound effects in the bruitist tradition of the futurists:

> After each music-hall routine, an anonymous voice issuing from an amplifying orifice (a theatrical imitation of a circus megaphone, the mask of antiquity in modern guise), was to sing a type-phrase outlining the performer's activity so as to open up the world of make-believe.[28]

This suggestion was vetoed by Satie and Picasso, but Cocteau later incorporated it into his conception for *Les Mariés de la Tour Eiffel*. What remained of the desire for a kind of noise-music was incorporated by Satie into the score with parts written for typewriters, sirens, airplane propellers, Morse tappers and lottery wheels. No critic failed to mention the typewriters. As to the other "instruments," it seems that they proved greater production problems than had been anticipated and few were actually used in the performance. Another of Cocteau's ideas, of delivering lines through holes in the scenery, was brushed aside as Picasso took the lead in formulating the conception of the performance. Picasso, taking off from the sheet-metal constructions with which he was then experimenting, proceeded to do what was most startling to the public. Moving towards a totally plastique conception of the stage, he gave the set a new active role by building it onto the characters. Two "managers," their costumes rising 10 feet high, moved like enormous skyscrapers across the stage, making actor and costume identical. The third manager, a horse formed by two dancers, did his capers amidst the noise-effects and concert jazz. The dancers detested the costumes, which were a torture to move about in, but Picasso had explained, "how effective it would be to exploit the contrast between three characters as pasted 'chromos' in a canvas, and the more solemnly tranposed inhuman, or superhuman characters who would become in fact the false reality on stage, to the point of reducing the real dancers to the stature of puppets."[29]

Whatever his explanation, this contrasting of two realities was enough to fire up the audience to cries of "It's scandalous—Bring down the curtain!." One woman could not restrain herself from shouting "You are all idiots!," while another loudly claimed, "I know Picasso: what he adores is noise, publicity. I know that he himself paid the hiss-ers and the boo-ers."[30]

This was the performance which Apollinaire had blessed (in his "Introduction" to the program) with being "the point of departure for a whole series of manifestations of the New Spirit . . . the thing that has most profoundly stirred the arts in the course of the last ten years."[31] It was *Parade* to which Apollinaire had affixed the word "sur-réaliste," a word that had never been used before. The public was confused. Here was the cubist Picasso, working with Cocteau to produce what the poet considered a new "realism" and which Apollinaire called "sur-réaliste." After all the whistling and shouting had subsided, one woman in the audience, naive enough to comment on the Emperor's new clothes, asked bewilderedly "In short, sir, what should one think: is it a success?"

Cocteau himself was confused. On the one hand, Apollinaire, dressed in his soldier's uniform, had had to rescue him, Picasso and Satie from a group of attacking women armed with hatpins. Here certainly was an assurance that he had succeeded in creating a new kind of theatre that would provoke and surprise. On the other hand, the collaboration with Picasso and Satie had left him restless and dissatisfied. Both were far more scandal-mongering than he. Both had forced major revisions in his original performance concept. Just what part of *Parade* was his? Gide in his *Journals* recalls:

> . . . went to see *Parade*—one doesn't know whether to admire most its pretension or its poverty. Cocteau is walking in the wings where I go to see him: aging, contracted, miserable. He knows very well that the sets, the costumes, are by Picasso, that the music is by Satie, but he wonders if Picasso and Satie are not by Cocteau.[32]

The critics were most vociferous in their response. There were no raves. Mostly there was a sense of anger as if one had somehow been duped. Was this "del'art (?) nouveau"—a bunch of typewriters in the orchestra and a two-person horse? But the critics hardly knew what was awaiting them.

Guillaume Apollinaire's *The Breasts of Tirésias*

By 1917, the year of the premiere of his first full-length play, *Les Mamelles de Tirésias*,[33] Guillaume Apollinaire was, without a doubt, the main French impresario of the avant-garde. It was thanks to him that Picasso and Braque met in 1907. As early as 1909, he had written the first major article to be published on Alfred Jarry, and it was he who helped organize the cubist Room 41 at the "Salon des Indépendants" of 1911. In 1912 he vacationed with the Spanish painter Picabia who, for his work at the "Salone d'Automne," had received the dubious plaudit, "The prize for idiocy this year is retained by

M. Picabia" (*Paris Journal* 30 September 1912). In the same year he met with the Italian painter de Chirico who had written, "To become truly immortal, a work of art must escape all human limits, logic and common sense will only interfere."

Apollinaire had baptized orphism, moved in the center of the simultaneist movement and was a staunch supporter of Futurism—his own Futurist manifesto, "L'anti-tradition futuriste," proclaiming "suppression of poetic grief in syntax, punctuation, lines and verses, houses, boredom." He had launched and directed the journal *Soirées de Paris,* one of the principal organs of the avant-garde before the war, had promoted the dada poems of Tristan Tzara in the review *Nord-Sud,* and in 1917, barely a month before the opening of *Les Mamelles,* was attending rehearsals of the Diaghilev-Picasso-Satie-Cocteau ballet, *Parade* (for which he would write the program's "Introduction"). He was, in *plein pouvoir,* a dean of the "esprit nouveau."

Naturally, Apollinaire had a coterie of followers, and when on Sunday, June 24, 1917, the small theatre of the Conservatorie Renée Maubel on the rue de l'Orient in Montmartre opened its doors for the premiere of his first play—"drame surrealiste en deux actes et un prologue, choeurs, musiques et costumes selon l'esprit nouveau,"—an audience of nearly 500 artists, poets, critics, and bizarre types seized on the opportunity to revel amidst the grim soberness of wartime Paris.

Among the crowd that late afternoon[34] were Paul Fort, Gallimard and Mme. Rachilde (who had promoted Jarry's *Ubu*), André Breton and Louis Aragon (21 and 22 years old, who had just been introduced to Tzara's dada poems *chez Apollinaire*), the actors Pierre Bertin and Louise Lara (who arrived by bicycle), and the critics of all the major newspapers—all the "opinion parisienne." While a number of the guests finished their aperitifs at the nearby cafes, Apollinaire moved among the crowd. Eye-catching dress was de rigeur. Mme. Maubel, mistress of the conservatory, wore a dress of "violent emerald," and two young ladies, "conspicuously cubist," painted their faces a raw yellow while smearing their eyelids with blue. The critic of *La Rampe* afterwards lamented:

> How I regretted not having sported a suit the color of unripe lemon and a red paper gendarme's hat. One can't think of everything.

(G. Davin de Campclos, *La Rampe,* 12.7.17)

Jean Cocteau was there as well, but rather somber—barely have recovered from the excitement generated by his ballet *Parade,* produced a month earlier. It is not surprising that Apollinaire's "drame surréaliste" was compared to the Cocteau-Picasso-Satie work. Here again was that new word "surréaliste"[35] which Apollinaire had first employed in his "Introduction" to the program of *Parade,* and though many people saw the text of *Les Mamelles* as a rather conventional *pièce à thèse:*

> Essentially Guillaume Apollinaire is a traditionalist, and beneath the apparent disorder of ideas, beneath his raucous clowning, fantasy and guignol, he demands a return to order.

(Guillot de Szis, *Le théâtre*, 29.6.17)

there was no doubt that the production was directly in line with such scandal-evoking "cubist" events as were produced by the Diaghilev ballet.

> The novelty of this play, so violently drafted, is less in the subject matter, which wants to be merely an interesting fantasy, than in the synthetic decor which envelops it.

(Jean Gourmont, "Une esthetique nouvelle," *Mercure de France*, 25.6.17)

The masks, the patchwork houses of the backdrop, the gendarme's horse, were all reminiscent of Picasso's designs for *Parade*, which Apollinaire, in his "Introduction," had signalled as having for the first time achieved an alliance with theatre that heralded a more comprehensive art to come.

> This new alliance—I say new, because until now scenery and costumes were linked only by factitious bonds—has given rise, in *Parade*, to a kind of sur-realism which I consider to be the point of departure for a whole series of manifestations of the New Spirit that is making itself felt today, and that will certainly appeal to our best minds.

(Program for *Parade*, 18.5.17)[36]

The expectations of the spectators at the *Les Mamelles* premiere ran high, and inside the hall, the audience, primed with anticipation, was restless. Stamping feet demanded that the play begin, while outside the theatre, an angry crowd who could not get in banged on the locked doors. Pierre Albert-Birot, editor of the avant-garde journal *SIC*,[37] which had sponsored the performance, later published an apology:

> We sincerely apologize to the people who could not get in, for it was only with the greatest regret that we shut the doors—but the additional number of spectators in the hall was such, that we were compelled to make this radical decision so as to avoid riots or accidents.

(*SIC*, No. 18, June, 1917)

Aragon, speaking for those who did get in, later wrote:

> One expected anything—it was something else.
>
> ("Le 24 juin 1917," *SIC*, No. 27, May 1918)

Admission was free, but the public was required to pay one franc for a program which bore a suggestive drawing by Picasso and a Matisse woodcut. A classic blue curtain hid the stage and amidst the tumult, Mme. Rachilde called out "The curtain is too blue . . . remove the blue." Finally a somberly dressed Edmond Valée, in the role of the "director," emerged from the promptor's box to vaunt in the medieval tradition—"So here I am once more among you,"— and to deliver the prologue. Apollinaire's invitation in this prologue to his French comrades to recall the tragedies of the war was later unanimously commended:

> remarkable—an ardent poem in which is inscribed the tragic mirage of a night of war . . .
>
> (*L'heure*, 26.6.17)

But no one seems to have noticed the author's use of the prologue to propose a new kind of theatre as well: "a theatre in the round with two stages, one at the center, the other surrounding the spectators." No one, that is, but the management of *SIC*, whose invitations for that afternoon proposed that the public attend as well a lecture entitled "The spirit of the avant-garde (à propos cubism, futurism, and nunism.)"

"Nunism," derived from the Greek word "nun" (now), was the name Pierre Albert-Birot had given to his own study of a new type of theatre, "le théâtre nunique." In a number of brief articles which he published in *SIC* (Nos. 8, 9, 10—August, September, October, 1916), Albert-Birot described this theatre: having left the three unities behind, it would now focus on acrobatics, sounds, projections, pantomimes, and cinematographic elements. It would be a "grand simultaneity" encompassing all the methods and all the emotions capable of communicating life in its vitality and intensity to the spectator. In order to convey this intensity, multiple actions would take place simultaneously onstage as well as in the auditorium. Being bound to no unity of time or place, these scenes could take place "in Paris, in New York, in Tokyo, in a house, beneath the sea, underground, in the air, in prehistoric times, in the middle-ages, in 1916, in the year 2,000." The scenes would therefore be set by light alone, using a wide palette of colors to create the appropriate atmosphere. The theatre area itself would be a vast circus-like expanse with the audience placed at the center, while on a rotating platform on the periphery the actors would play their various scenes. It is quite likely that Apollinaire was influenced by Albert-Birot's concept of the Nunique stage when he described his new theatre as:

> A circular theatre with two stages
> One in the middle and the other like a ring
> Around the spectators permitting
> The free unfolding of our modern art
> Often connecting in unseen ways as in life
> Sounds gestures colors cries tumults
> Music dancing acrobatics poetry painting
> Choruses actions and multiple sets
>
> ("Prologue," *The Breasts of Tirésias*)[38]

A year earlier, in an interview in SIC,[39] he had already advocated a type of circus theatre which would have a more widespread appeal because of its new simplicity and broad effects.

Albert-Birot relates that it was he, in 1916, who asked Apollinaire to write, for production and publication by *SIC,* a play that would illustrate some of Apollinaire's own theatrical ideas, including the wish he had one day expressed that the theatre of the future be free of "odious realism."[40] Albert-Birot claims as well to have been influential in Apollinaire's choosing the phrase "surrealist" for his first play:

> When Apollinaire and I, in 1917, searched for a term to describe *Les Mamelles de Tirésias,* Apollinaire suggested "surnaturaliste," and I cried out, No! No!, "surnaturalisme" is something entirely different. In principle, the "surnaturel" is a miracle. Immediately Apollinaire replied, "That's right—let's put in then "drame surréaliste."[41]

It was only at the last minute that the word was rushed to the printer.

Whatever the source of the inspiration, Apollinaire, in his own defense of the term, wrote: " 'Surréalisme' is not yet in the dictionary and it will be more convenient than 'Surnaturalisme,' which is already used by the philosophers." As for the meaning of the word, he wrote:

> In order to attempt, if not a renovation of the theatre, at least an original effort, I thought it necessary to come back to nature itself, but without copying it photographically. When man wanted to imitate walking he created the wheel, which does not resemble a leg. In the same way he has created surrealism.[42]

Albert-Birot's strong involvement in the project, however, is undeniable. His wife, Germaine, wrote the music for the piece. As for the directing of the play, it seems to have been a joint effort, with Albert-Birot largely responsible but

Illustration 20   Design for Théâtres Nuniques by Pierre Albert-Birot (*SIC,* Nos. 21-22, September-October, 1917)

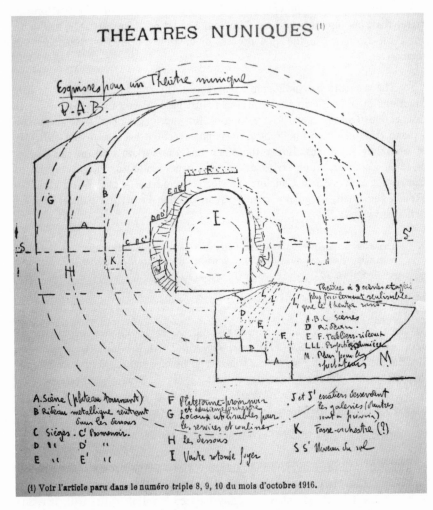

with Apollinaire himself taking an active part. In an article written on the production of the poet's following play, *Couleur de Temps,* Albert-Birot expresses regret that, because of his illness, Apollinaire could not take part as he had in his work on *Tirésias,* "in the vital process of creation inspired by the rehearsals themselves."[43]

The overture to Apollinaire's play about Thérèse, who rejects her female functions in order to do as she pleases ("Just because you made love to me in Connecticut/Doesn't mean I have to cook for you in Zanzibar"), was begun on a piano (the full score for orchestra was not executed because of the difficulty of obtaining musicians during the war), and the curtain rose on the market place in Zanzibar. Long strips of colored paper, patched with rectangles of contrasting colors "à la Gauguin cubiste," covered the wings. When asked to explain the small, irregularly pasted squares, Serge Férat, the painter and designer, answered:

> Those, why they're windows, and look, that piece of blue paper there on the white rectangle—it's a curtain behind the window. It's all to indicate the intimacy of a family setting.

(*La Rampe,* 12.7.17)

At stage left stood an actor-cum-newsstand, covered with newspapers of the day: *Le Journal, L'action Française, Paris-Midi.* At the back were scrawled illegible inscriptions in red, green, yellow and blue. When asked how he had put the set together, Férat ingenuously replied:

> Lord—I bought seven francs worth of paper which I cut up—that's all.

(*La Rampe,* 12.7.17)

The costumed characters and their activities were no less startling. Thérèse-Tirésias (Louise-Marion) entered in blackface with a long dress on which the painter Irène Lagut had splashed highly colored tropical fruits. With her, she carried all those "instruments" relating to her role as housewife, and as a climax to her opening tirade against the making of children, she removed the two huge celluloid balloons—her breasts—and threw them to a startled audience as a beard suddenly shot up about her face. The crowd went wild. A baby started to cry and someone shouted, "Pass him your breasts, Tirésias . . . the baby wants some milk." "If it's ugliness he wants," a nearby scoffer replied, "why that's already been served up!"[44] ("Les on dit," n.p.1.7.17)

Meanwhile, upstage, the actor Howard, in redface, playing the role of "the people of Zanzibar," occupied himself with all manner of musical sound

Illustration 21   Characters in costume from *Les Mamelles de Tirésias*, June 24, 1917 (*La Rampe*, July 12, 1917)

effects, using a toy flute, cymbals, an accordion, wood blocks and broken dishes to punctuate the speeches of the actors. Niny Guyard backed him up with eccentric and dissonant music on a piano which stood onstage throughout the entire performance.

Having thrown all her household utensils at the audience, Thérèse achieved the final transformation into Tirésias by forcibly dressing her husband (Marcel Herrand)[45] in her own clothes. Simultaneously, in the auditorium, Messrs. Presto and Lacouf (played by Edmond Vallée and Yeta Daesslé), two "bourgeois," started a quarrel as to whether they were in Paris or in Zanzibar. The audience soon joined in shouting invectives. The two mounted the stage to fight a duel which finished them both off, while Tirésias, frightened by the noise, ran off. A gendarme (Juliette Norville), astride a cardboard horse, entered to restore order and wound up seducing the husband in drag, while the latter, still raging at his wife's refusal to bear more children, cried out: "If woman won't make more, why then man will do it." The husband promised to produce a huge progeny within nine days. On this battle cry, the first act ended.

Even for Apollinaire, who in his "Calligrams" had already tested the physical restraints of the printed page, the release from the restrictions of flat black on white was an exhilarating experience. The first act was marked by the sensuous assault of shapes and sounds. Cries from the audience mingled with the text—itself accompanied by music and sound effects. Visually, splashes of color, clusters of flying props, and a great deal of traffic between the stage and the hall made for a fast-paced spectacle, vaudevillian in tempo. Just as in all his poetry beginning with *Alcoöls* (1913), Apollinaire admitted no punctuation, in *Les Mamelles,* the action rants on, admitting no stops, delighting in the new grammar of a liberated imagination. The use of a single actor to represent the entire "people of Zanzibar," recalled Jarry's instruction for *Ubu,* that a single soldier represent the entire Polish army, and the Press itself continually recalled *Ubu:*

It's Jarry Montmartre-ized, modernized, and martyrized.

(*La Griffe,* 6.7.17)

It's an art which makes one think of Jarry, Jarry to the twentieth power.

(*L'heure,* 25.6.17)

One thought himself at *Ubu Roi.*

(n.p.n.d.)

Most interesting, however, was the use of simultaneous action—such as Tirésias "raped" into his wife's clothes onstage as Presto and Lacouf begin their quarrel in the auditorium. The Presto-Lacouf episode is unrelated to the main action of the text, but, in performance, received equal focus with the Thérèse-Tirésias combat. The inclusion of such an experiment in simultaneity is not a chance occurrence for Apollinaire, for simultaneity was well in the forefront of his interests, and, as he wrote in his "Preface" to the play, "it is legitimate, in my opinion to bring to the theatre new and striking aesthetic principles which accentuate the roles of the actors and increase the effect of the production."

In the production of Les Mamelles, instances of simultaneism abound. From the opening scene, sensual assaults on the audience overlapped from several areas on stage simultaneously. "The people of Zanzibar," feather sticking out of his head and occupied with the making of noise-music,[46] shared the focus with Thérèse who herself "attempted to dominate the sound of the orchestra." The human kiosk (who, with its proprietress, was "one" and simultaneously "two"), could be expected to enter the activity at any moment; the at-one-with-his-horse-gendarme (again the many-faceted actor/object), pranced off and on; and, if all the onstage happenings proved insufficient, there were also voices of women "(in the wings)." The characters of Thérèse-Tirésias themselves played out their own rondelay of a multiplicity of masks—they changed roles before they changed clothes, but even in drag, each of them was never quite identical with himself.[47]

The performance was full of "doing." The extent of commotion and activity which reigned on stage recalls the well-made play (then still enjoying a huge success at the boulevard theatres)—but with the intrigue-machinery gone awry. In Les Mamelles it was distressing to try to recapitulate the plot, for the impact was in the overlay and crowding of events. The narrative dimension had been critically attenuated, and the "events" or "activities" which remained were difficult to keep in focus serially, for they had almost no causal relationship. Time as well was no longer a matter of chronology, but merely of will. No sooner did Thérèse will to become a man than the change took place. Later, she rose in rank as fast as the titles could be pronounced: "long live Tirésias, long live General Tirésias, long live deputy Tirésias." Finally, at the end of the play, she is "head of the army in Room A at City Hall" as well as being a fortune teller and the lover of three influential ladies. The husband is equally prodigious in his accomplishments, for he wills, and in one day creates, 40,050 children who, while still crying in their cradles, have already taken their places in the world: the novelist, the poet, the divorcée, the journalist.[48]

Apollinaire was far from unaware of the Futurists' uses of simultaneity, or the dada experiments which had been carried out at the Cabaret Voltaire in the year which preceded the Les Mamelles premiere. In line with dadaist performance, the intermission of Les Mamelles provided its own excitement. Jacques Vaché, a follower of the tradition of Jarry-Ubu who lived in his own world of "umour," had entered the theatre with a revolver. Master of the provocative gesture and the openly destructive act, and excited by the scandal of the performance, he had brandished the gun at the intermission audience, threatening to fire into the crowd. André Breton was filled with admiration for this contemporary of dada and later recalled Vaché's act in his "Second Surrealist Manifesto" where he wrote that "the simple surrealist act consists of going out into the street revolver in hand, and firing at random into the crowd as often as possible."[49]

Simultaneous activity was continued as the second act opened with a chorus in the form of a simultaneous song, not printed in the text:

> You who cry watching the play
> Wishing the children to be the winners
> See the imponderable ardour
> Born of sex-change.[50]

Max Jacob and Paul Morisse sang the verses plus a number of encores while the post-natal husband rocked his many children in their cradles (designed by M. Sternberg). Throughout this act as well, the audience continued to interrupt the performance.

> The public was at a feverish pitch. Seeing that the play was a farce, they participated fully, including themselves in the proceedings. The performance played itself out in the hall as well as on stage.
>
> (Paul Sonday, "une pièce cubiste," *Paris-Midi*, 26.6.17)
>
> 'One must create life,' I heard one enthusiast cry. But what was created was tumult.
>
> (Bernard Lecastre, "La Vache enragée," n.p.n.d.)

Animal noises were among the sounds voiced, and Mme. Rachilde cried out, "Go call the police, there are some crackpots in the house."

Only for a moment did an attentive hush fall on the audience, as the husband began to enumerate the qualities of a good journalist and loudspeakers on stage proceeded to answer questions about specific "colleagues" in the profession. But riot was soon restored as a fortune-teller in a luminous headdress quarreled with the gendarme and strangled him. It was a repentant Thérèse in disguise, and she revealed herself, as the gendarme (who had merely fainted), joined the now happy couple for an upbeat end to the play.

In the days which followed, the critics were hard put to it as to what to call the performance. They tried "futurist," "simultaneist," and "cubist," and Gaston Picard, editor of *Le Pays*, asked Apollinaire himself, "Which -ism seems most appropriate to you?" Apollinaire answered:

How little the epithet matters. Time will decide. We carry through history labels which usage has consecrated. As for myself, I do have my preferences—Orphisme or surnaturalism—that is, an art which is not merely photographic naturalism but which nonetheless reflects nature—that interior nature of unsuspected marvels: imponderable, pitiless and joyous.

For his part, Picard concluded:

> . . . let people say cubist or futurist according to their preference, or surnaturalist with Monsieur Apollinaire. We will say "apollinairien!"

> ("Interviews: M. Guillaume Apollinaire et *la Nouvelle Ecole Littéraire,*" *Le Pays,* 24.6.17)

The interview drew a host of angry responses—most violent among them, from a group of cubist painters who were outraged at the word "cubist" being so bandied around. In a letter to Picard, they wrote:

> As cubist painters and sculptors, we protest against the unfortunate link which people are straining to establish between our work and certain theatrical or literary fantasies which are none of our business to judge.
> Those among us who were present at the *SIC* and *Art et Liberté*[51] manifestations, formally declare that they have nothing in common with our plastic experiments.

> ("Lettres," *Le Pays,* 29.6.17)

The letter was signed: Metzinger, Juan Gris, Diego Rivera, Lipschitz, Henri Hayden, André Lhote, Kissling, Gino Severini. The painters, however, had merely leaped into the fray. The press had declared "Allah is cubist and M. Birot is his prophet," and nothing was about to stop the battle of the nomenclature. The critic Victor Basch decided that what Apollinaire really meant by the word "surrealist" was "symbolic," while other critics connected the new term with what was eccentric and dissonant. The only thing that seemed clear was that no one had been left indifferent. André Breton later said:

> Never again, as at that evening, did I plumb the depths of the gap which would separate the new generation from that preceding it.[52]

and Aragon wrote:

> I will always cherish, from that afternoon of the 24th of June, 1917, the souvenir of a unique freedom which permits one to foresee a theatre liberated from the philosopher's cares.

> (*SIC,* No. 27, May, 1918)

Not everyone was so impressed. The critic of *L'heure* angrily wrote:

> This prank might be amusing, recounted by a bantering and unctuous Apollinaire one Tuesday, or acted by Max Jacob in a left-bank studio, but to baptise it "drame surréaliste," and to present it seriously to an audience, is to say the least, indecent . . . The play was acted by people whose profession was obviously not acting. The sets . . . stolen!

(26.6.17)

Léo Poldes could not contain himself and burst out:

> Let the artists pardon me, let the reader excuse me, three words spill from my pen in summation—"Ah, the swine."

(La Grimace)

In *Le Petit Bleu,* Davin de Champclos ranted:

> The "new spirit"? . . . I must be awfully regressed, backward, conventional, traditionalist, sodden and reactionary, because this new spirit seemed to me to the most tremendous hoax and practical joke.

and for the critic of *Le Cri France,* a single sentence sufficed:

> *Les Mamelles de Tirésias* has alienated from Guillaume Apollinaire many of his admirers.

As for Apollinaire, he did not take the criticism lightly. Four days after the premiere, he wrote to his friend Pierre Reverdy:

> I have just experienced the greatest joy, and with it the greatest pain in my life. I've given the most personal, the most lyric, the most joyous thing in *Les Mamelles de Tirésias,* which has had the greatest success except for Metzinger, Gris, and other asses of that kind.[53]

The following November, in a lecture entitled "L'Esprit Nouveau et les poètes," and given at the Théâtre du Vieux Colombier, Apollinaire himself turned to answer his detractors,[54] and specifically championed the element of surprise as the most exacting defining characteristic of the new movement.

> Surprise is the greatest source of what is new. It is by surprise, by the important position that has been given to surprise that the new spirit distinguishes itself from all the literary and artistic movements which have preceded it.

("L'esprit nouveau et les poètes," *Mercure de France,* ler décembre, 1918)

Apollinaire was given little chance to continue his experiments. Less than a year after the premiere of *Les Mamelles,* on November 9, 1918, he succumbed to an attack of influenza. He had begged the doctor to cure him, saying, "I want to live, I still have so many things to say."[55]

Apollinaire's mark on avant-garde performance had, however, been indelibly made. For people such as Breton and Aragon, young "littérateurs," who would later participate in the experiments of Paris-dada performance, the 1917 productions of *Les Mamelles de Tirésias* and *Parade* and what they had heard and read of Jarry's *Ubu* served to embody the basic elements of a tradition of radical theatre. Surprise and shock were paramount, preferably raised to the level of scandal. The text emerged as peripheral and the performance elements, as conceived and executed by director, actors and designer, became the crucial elements of the production. Sets and costumes often merged, with the actor carrying both as one on his back. Wearing a huge mask, or painting his face, walking within a box, or padding himself beyond recognition, the actor often moved in the gray zone between actor and object. Shock and surprise had forged a bridge in the gap that traditionally separated the audience from the stage, and a new oneness was felt between the public and the performer even as they taunted one another.

Both in his play and in his last essay, Apollinaire had made a forceful impression upon that generation of young writers who were looking for new loyalties after the war. As the dadaists and surrealists of the next decade, they would initiate a wave of experiments in performance whose like would not be seen again until the Happenings of the 1950s.

Paris Dada

What are you doing, parked there like serious
oysters? . . . you're all idiots.

Picabia, *Manifeste Cannibale,* read by Breton
at the *Théâtre de l'Oeuvre,* 27.III.1920

You don't understand what we are doing, do
you? Well dear friends, we understand it
still less.

Dada Manifesto, 1920

Illustration 22   *Manifestation Dada,* Francis Picabia, Paris, Maison de l'Oeuvre, Salle Berlioz; Saturday, March 27. Program

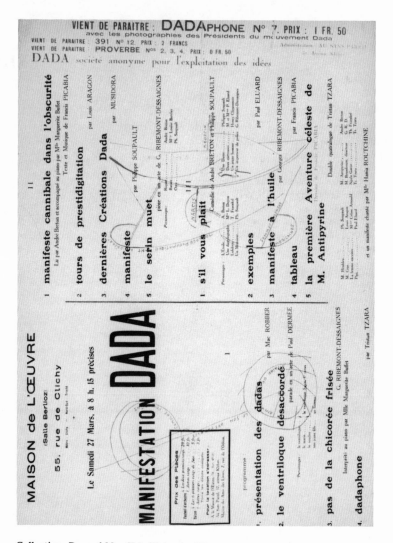

Collection: Dr. and Mrs. H.J. Kleinschmidt

Paris Dada: the Major Manifestations

Paris dada was a child born to the *Littérature* group out of Tzara through Ball. This group, which awaited Tzara "like the messiah," was a floating commune of young writers who met at *Certa's* in the *Passage de l'Opéra,* at its annex *Le Petit Grillon,* and occasionally at the restaurants of Mme. Saulinier a few steps away on the *rue du Mont-Thabor.* Its members were 20 years old in 1920, and gathered around the periodical *Littérature.*[1] This small yellow-covered magazine, which published the works of Gide, Max Jacob, Reverdy, Cendrars and Isadore Ducasse, Comte de Lautréamont, had set out to make a sweeping indictment of traditional literature. The magazine had three editors: André Breton, at 24, the guru; Philippe Soupault, 23, with yellow-brown tiger eyes and curly brown hair, the strongest devotee of dada who loved all things African and who once appeared costumed as the President of the Liberian Republic; and Louis Aragon, 23, tall and delicate with a thin moustache, already a leading figure in the French cultural avant-garde, and a precocious literary success. About these three there gathered Paul Eluard who worked in his father's real-estate business during the day and wrote poetry at night, Roger Vitrac, a nonchalant young giant of 21 who was to become the group's most serious dramatist, and Jacques Baron, at 17 the youngest. This was the "surrealist"-group in 1920 before there was a surrealism and at the moment of Tzara's arrival in Paris.

When Tzara came to Paris there was no dada group there. Pierre Albert-Birot's journal, *SIC,* was considered futurist in tendency; *Nord-Sud,* edited by Pierre Reverdy, identified itself with cubism; and *Littérature,* while from the first it was referred to as "dadaisante," had steered clear of dada in its first 12 issues. Moreover, although Breton and Soupault had published their poems in *Dada III* (December, 1918), (that same issue of the journal which had brought to Paris Tzara's *Manifeste Dada I 1918* with its strident declaration of war against all the bastions of culture), they were still more involved with the state of mind produced by *l'esprit nouveau,* a new sense of freedom in the choice of subject matter and poetic devices, than with Tzara's all-out rebellion.

The shift seemed to come at the beginning of 1919. That year is generally characterized by historians as a year of internal political reaction, and a time of widespread disappointment over the terms of peace. For the Europeans there had been over 20 million casualties. The greater part of Breton's, Soupault's and Aragon's generation had been killed or maimed. Those who survived were not left merely with a sense of being "lost" but were in Gertrude Stein's words, "a lost generation." The demobilization was gradual. Breton himself was not discharged from the army until September, 1919. The days of a strange new freedom were spent musing at the desk in his hotel-room, walking aimlessly through Paris, or sitting alone on a bench at the *Place du Châtelet*. Of his mood at the time, Breton recalled:

> . . . as for me, released from the military yoke, I tried my best to evade any new constraints. Come what might . . .[2]

During the war, Paris could not house and encourage the types of organized artistic activity which had flourished in Zurich, and although Breton had seen a copy of *DADA I* in 1917 *(chez Apollinaire)*, it was only in 1919 that he, Aragon and Soupault caught up with what dada had been doing in Zurich. In the fall of that year Marcel Janco arrived in Paris for a few weeks, bringing with him the first live reports of Tzara's work in Zurich. Janco was no longer on the best of terms with Tzara, and the portrait he painted of the pale dark-haired little man with the monocle was intended to offend rather than please. Breton and Soupault seemed to thrive on the offensive details. By March of 1919 Breton and Tzara were corresponding, and the period of waiting for the new prophet had begun.

When Tzara arrived in Paris, his voiced purpose was to continue his "métier de poète." Not long before, however, he had written in an open letter to Jacques Rivière:

> If one writes, that is nothing but an escape: in any case I don't write as a profession and have no literary ambitions.

Littérature 7

Tzara was redefining the role of the "poète." In him the poet became an impresario, director and actor. He wrote a language aggressive and destructive in its incoherence; he staged it and performed it himself, making it come alive with sound effects and palpable rhythms. He gathered around him a community of like-minded artists and with them went on stage to create in the "now" before a live audience. In Paris of 1920 the basic features of the dada-experience as lived in Zurich began to appear once again: "shameless publicity, provocation, lies, insults."

In the planning of the *premier vendredi* sponsored by *Littérature,* Tzara acted with restraint by not imposing on Breton, Soupault, and Aragon, one week after his arrival, the full measure of his Zurich-dada-experience. This restraint however was short-lived. A few weeks after his arrival, he exploded in a frenzy of activity:

His hotel, to the great terror of the manager, became a sort of headquarters. Tzara had become an impresario, magazine director, ticket seller, publicity chief, typographer, editor, organist . . .[3]

The second program had been set for February 5, 1920, barely two weeks after the *premier vendredi*. This *Manifestation Dada* at the Grand Palais was to be presented within the framework of the *Salon des Artistes Indépendants,* a series of 12 performances of music, literature, and the dance. The programs were planned to run from the February 5 to 28, with the participation of such groups as *Art et Action,*[4] *Idéal et Realité,* and *La Maison des artistes.* Tzara, however, rushed to obtain his own type of publicity. Utilizing the gullibility of both press and public, he spread the news that Charlie Chaplin would participate in the second dada event:

Charlie Chaplin, the illustrious Charlot has just arrived in Paris. He will be presented to us so that we may applaud him; his friends, "the poets of the dada movement," invite us to the *Matinée* which they are organizing. . . . The famous American actor will there take the floor. . . .

Journal du peuple, February 2, 1920

Charlot, of course, never appeared and instead the audience was treated to the *Bulletin Dada,* distributed at the door, and a program which promised seven manifestos read by "10, 9, 8, 7, 6, 5, 4, (and a journalist)," persons. The manifestos were recited, chanted and acted out in the midst of great confusion. Aragon's began with the phrase "Me—everything which is not me is incomprehensible"; Soupault read a list of responses to the question "Why have you written a manifesto?" and Breton did a playlet-parody of Baudelaire's *l'Etranger* in a dada-idiom:

— What is your name? (he shrugs his shoulders).
— Where are you? At the *Grand Palais* on the *Champs Elysées.*
— What day is it? Thursday, February, 1920[5]

The audience threw coins, and Tzara recalls "An old man in the audience gave himself up to behavior of a character more or less intimate . . . somebody set off some flashing powder and a pregnant woman had to be taken out."[6] Picabia, who was to have taken part in the demonstration, disappeared as soon as it began, continuing the practice of absenting himself, begun at the *premier vendredi.* It was a practice he would observe for all the remaining manifestations, for he was unable to submit himself to the indignities of clowning before an angry mob. André Gide, who was present that afternoon, recalls the event with some disappointment. The young participants, unused to their performing roles, were still quite a bit more inhibited than the audience response would seem to indicate:

I had hoped to enjoy myself more and that the dadas would have drawn out a stronger reaction from the unsophisticated stupor of the public. The young men, stiff, stilted, bound, mounted the stage. . . . From the back of the audience someone called out "Make some movements!"; and everyone laughed for it seemed that precisely for fear of jeopardizing themselves, no one dared budge.[7]

Tzara, aware that his co-performers were still novices, scheduled his own manifesto for the end, relying finally on his own ability to bring the performance to its rousing conclusion. His manifesto took the form of an harangue by "the king of Fakirs," a man who predicts the future every day. The audience went wild and the lights had to be turned out in order to bring the meeting to an end. Despite the seeming success of the conclusion, Tzara knew that Paris-dada had not yet arrived. He therefore accepted two interim "performances" while planning the next major dada soirée for March 27.

After the matinée at the *Salon des Indépendants,* Léo Poldes invited the dadas to participate in an evening at the Club Faubourg of which he was director. The Club specialized in public discussions of hot issues of the day and the dadas hoped to find an audience of workers before whom to present their "show." They decided to repeat the *Indépendants* program of manifestos, for the two days' notice (February 7) had given them little time to prepare anything new. Still, they reserved the right to change the manifestos at will, and perhaps to improvise some new ones on the spot. At the Club, however, they barely had time to mount the stage when the audience, composed of young intellectuals and members of the avant-garde, began whistling and shouting. The dadas' "name" had preceded them and the public was set to enjoy a riot. Aragon, "un peu snob," was quite put out by the disturbance and attempted to reprimand the audience and get on with the manifestos. They shouted him down and even the efforts of the toga-clad Raymond Duncan (brother of Isadora who was on intimate terms with Picabia) to subdue them were of no avail. At the *Université Populaire du Faubourg Saint-Antoine* on February 19, the group met its first audience composed entirely of the working class. The dadas had publicized the evening in the press:

The 291 male and female presidents of the dada movement have appointed Messers. Breton, Aragon, Dermée, Eluard, Fraenkel, Picabia, Ribemont-Dessaignes, Soupault and Tzara to deal with the following questions: locomotion, life, dada skating; pastry, architecture, dada morals; chemistry, tatooing, dada finances and typewriters: this Thursday at 8:30 at the *Université Populaire du Faubourg Saint-Antoine.*[8]

Despite this provocative announcement, the audience was ready to try in good faith to understand what it was being forced to undergo. The workers had not anticipated a scandal, nor did they particularly want one, but Tzara was dedicated to activating the passive crowd and when the violent attacks on cubism and modern poetry merely elicited polite requests for explanations, he struck out against Lenin and Marx. This the workers refused to accept and though they did not break out in a riot, they held the dadas for hours, forcing them to explain their position again and again.

Tzara was still working to find his way within the Paris-dada group, which had by now expanded to include Picabia's long-time friend, the eclectic artist-writer Georges Ribemont-Dessaignes, Breton's childhood friend Théodore Fraenkel, and the "cubists" Paul Dermée and his wife Celine Arnaud. Enthusiasm for dada was high and yet there is a sense even in these first manifestations that Tzara's provocative tactics were not tailored to the needs of the group of young Parisian poets and artists. Picabia found it necessary to absent himself on every occasion and neither Breton, Aragon, nor Soupault seemed to be finding the way to match their personalities with Tzara's. Two more *Grandes Manifestations* were to prove to Tzara that he could in fact achieve in Paris what he had in Zurich. What would be proved to the *Littérature* group was that Tzara's path was not its own.

The first of the two major evenings was March 27, 1920, at the *Théâtre de l'Oeuvre*, the same theatre where 25 years earlier Jarry's *Ubu* had been played. The second evening was two months later, on May 26 at the *Salle Gaveau*. The programs for the two evenings are striking in their similarity, both to each other and to Tzara's Zurich soirées. Both were compartmental in structure, featuring short numbers: musical selections, the reading of manifestos, the showing of paintings, simultaneous selections and "plays."

What is immediately striking about the Paris evenings, as compared to the Zurich events, is the great increase in the number of skits and plays. Four plays were presented at the *Oeuvre*, and two at the *Salle Gaveau*, whereas the entire Zurich period provided only two plays: Tzara's *Première Aventure céleste* and Kokoschka's *Sphinx and Stawman*. Tzara's *Première Aventure* at the *Oeuvre* was paralleled by his *Deuxième Aventure* at the *Salle Gaveau*. Breton and Soupault presented their sketch *S'il vous plaît* at the *Oeuvre* and *Vous m'oublierez* at the *Gaveau*. Georges Ribemont-Dessaignes contributed a one-act play, *Le Sérin Muet*, a manifesto and a dance for the first evening and a musical number, manifesto and dance for the second.

About a dozen performers participated in each evening,[9] all of them dadas and their friends. At the *Oeuvre*, the audience, (so numerous that Tzara claims that even after 1200 were turned away, there were 3 spectators left for every seat), arrived carrying musical instruments with which to harass the dada performers. They got what they were waiting for. Paul Dermée's sketch featured a ventriloquist playing three roles and a man playing the role of a woman. Ribemont-Dessaignes' piano selection "no endive," which had been composed according to the laws of chance, created such an outcry that the author, who had seated himself next to his pianist Marguerite Buffet[10] in order to turn the pages of the score, found himself engulfed in

> an extraordinary uproar, caused by the disconsonant music, the constant murmuring in the audience—its shouts and whistle blasts which joined to create the strangest effect of the sound of breaking glass.[11]

In complete darkness Breton read Picabia's *Manifeste Cannibale,* using direct address to intimidate the audience:

> You are all defendents, rise . . . stand up before DADA, which represents life and which accuses you of liking everything from snobbism, just as long as it's expensive . . . What are you doing, parked there like serious oysters—for you *are* serious, aren't you? . . . Hoot, laugh, beat me up, and then? and then? I'll still tell you that you're all idiots . . . [12]

The audience in response threw down from the balconies copies of the antidada journal *Non* in which the dadas were described as lunatics. With the short plays of Ribemont-Dessaignes, Breton and Soupault, and Tzara's own *Première Aventure,* the audience was admitted into a world filled with visual and verbal oddities. In Ribemont-Dessaignes' *Le Sérin Muet* (a piece written in 1919, not prepared specifically for the dada evening), Breton set himself atop a ladder, playing the character of Riquet "hunter of panthers," husband to Barate, "hunter of men." In *S'il vous plaît,* only the second act was played with the authors appearing in starring roles and Breton sporting a wreath of revolvers around his head. In Tzara's *Première Aventure,* the characters, immobilized in large colored sacks, chanted their incomprehensible lines behind a free-floating bicycle wheel and a web of ropes. Tzara wore his name across his belly and the stage was hung with signs reading "Paralysis is the beginning of wisdom," and "Extend your arms, your friends will cut them off." Picabia presented his *Portrait of Cézanne* (having searched in vain for a live monkey to place in his still-life, he finally settled for a stuffed one), and the program closed in a finale worthy of its name. Mlle. Hania Routchine, a known soprano, had been scheduled to sing the *Clair de lune* of Duparc. This serious end to the scandalous evening was planned as a joke in itself, but the unfortunate soprano had not been let in on the prank and she innocently implored the audience "I hope you will do me the honor of listening." Following upon the incomprehensible *Première Aventure,* however, the audience was in no mood for her tender lyrics and the stupefied singer dissolved in a flood of tears as the public vented its anger.

Everyone seemed pleased with the results of the performance. The spectator, for a ticket of from 3 to 20 francs, had received a printed program and a

Illustration 23   *Festival Dada;* Tristan Tzara, Paris, Salle Gaveau, Wed.
May 26, 1920. Poster

Collection: Morton G. Neumann, Chicago

copy of the journal *391* with Picabia's moustached Mona Lisa on the cover. He had both witnessed and helped to create the scandal he had expected. The dadas finally felt themselves coming into their own, and Lugné-Poe, director of the *Théâtre de l'Oeuvre* and sponsor of the evening, enchanted with the furor, declared himself willing to consider future dada scripts for production.[13] On the eve of the performance, the critic Jacques-Emile Blanche had predicted the theatre-events to come:

> I know, especially about this manifestation what the program has in store for me. There will be a lot of talk about the novelty of the staging. The costumes and the set will be one and the same. The music will be composed by a man who has never before written any. One will hear the plays of Paul Dermée which remind me a bit of fancy-dress, "modern" shows . . . they sacrifice less to the play of light and color than they do to ideas.

Commoedia, March 26, 1920

Blanche was not disappointed, and after the event, he and his fellow journalists took to their pens with a vengeance.

The public awareness of the scandal that was dada was sealed. The press cried: "they should all be burned in the public square,"

> The public has lashed out against, boo-ed and jeered at the dadas who received their injuries with grinning faces. One would have thought oneself at a madhouse, and the spirit of madness shrieked from the stage as well as in the hall. The dadas have exasperated their spectators and I think that this is exactly what they wanted to do.

Georges Charensol, *Commoedia,* March 29, 1920

The chansonniers rushed to include the topical dadas in their repertoire. The intellectual decadence evidenced in the "dirty paper" which was dada was blamed on the war which, while strengthening the strong had also further perverted the perverts and encouraged fools in their folly.

As for the dadas, their delight in themselves was at a new height. Soupault, in the April, 1920 edition of Picabia's journal *Cannibale,* wrote a litany in dada praise of the coterie:

> Breton sees better without spectacles
> Francis Picabia doesn't have syphilis
> Fraenkel doesn't wear glasses
> Soupault doesn't wear glasses
> Aragon (Louis) doesn't wear glasses
> Fraenkel doesn't wear glasses
> Fraenkel doesn't wear glasses

Fraenkel doesn't wear glasses
Tristan (Tzara) needs a doctor
Breton forgets his purse
and then
and then
  Shit!

Tzara gave his public but short respite. On May 3, an exhibit of the collages of Max Ernst opened in a darkened cellar, where the dadas gave themselves
free rein in a new series of pranks. Without ties but wearing white gloves, they
paced back and forth, Breton chewing matches, Ribemont-Dessaignes screaming
"It's raining on a skull," Aragon improvising with natural sounds, while Soupault
and Tzara played hide and seek. Groans arose from a trap door, someone hidden
in a closet heaped insults on the guests, Benjamin Peret shook hands with Char-
choune every other minute, and Jacques Rigaut, at the door, counted aloud
the cars and pearls of the lady visitors. This was merely a warm-up for the
second major dada manifestation three weeks later on May 26, 1920 at the *Salle
Gaveau*. The impact of the *Salle Gaveau* performance is clear in A. d'Esparbes'
review:

> It is very difficult for me to describe what I have seen this afternoon at the "dada
> festival," my poor head refuses to help me. . . . That which we could see and hear
> surpasses all that reason can imagine.

Commoedia, May 27, 1920

Provocative publicity had announced that all the dadas would cut off their
hair on stage, "sodomistic" music would be played, a static dance and two plays
performed, and finally one would be able to identify the sex of dada. The "sex
of dada," a phallic cylinder of white cardboard resting on two balloons opened
the program. As the heat in the auditorium began to affect the balloons, they
slowly shrank, carrying the paper phallus with them and sending Tzara into the
wings shouting "the sex is collapsing." Philippe Soupault in his role as "the
famous magician" appeared in blackface, wrapped in a huge white bathrobe with
a knife in his hand. Opening a trunk he released five colored balloons bearing the
names of Benoît XV, Mme. Rachilde, Clemenceau, Pétain and Jean Cocteau.
This last balloon he savagely cut, signalling a formal rupture between Cocteau
and the dadas,[14] a rupture brought on by Cocteau's publishing in *Le Coq*
(the official organ of literary cubism) insults and accusations against the dadas.
Georges Ribemont-Dessaignes and Mlle. Marguerite Buffet contributed a musical
number similar to their "no endive" at the *Oeuvre* and Ribemont-Dessaignes
alone prepared a "motionless frontier-dance," the upper part of his body
encased in an immense cardboard funnel which served to catch the tomatoes,
carrots, turnips, cabbages, oranges and "for the first time anywhere in the

world," beefsteaks, hurled by the audience. Picabia's permanent setting featured two walls of false greenery, cut in the formal French manner, lining a set of steps on either side of the stage. In front of the huge pipes of the *Salle Gaveau* organ,[15] he placed a tall yellow and white striped stove-pipe with an open umbrella inscribed, "Francis Loustic," at its top. Scattered about the stage were large wrapped cartons labeled "Tzara," "Aragon," and "Soupault," and near the grand piano stood a barrel. In this setting six dadas appeared with white cylinders planted on their heads to perform Tzara's *Deuxième Aventure céleste.* The tallest cylinder was labeled "Tristan Tzara," and had a huge mask on top. Later, Paul Eluard, in a yellow sack and a wool wig, played the part of "Sewing Machine" in Breton and Soupault's sketch *Vous m'oublierez* and Breton, wearing large glasses and a sandwich board designed by Picabia, read out the artist's *Farsighted Festival Manifesto:*

> I am Picabia, that is my disability. I am like a blonde sacrificed to St. Antoine. Negresses has a spherical c . . . and a sex of white iron. . . .

The concluding number, Tzara's *Vaseline Symphonique,* was a cacophony of sounds with 10 people making natural sounds on the syllables "cra . . . cra . . . cra" and "cri . . . cri . . . cri'" on a rising scale. Breton, after 5 minutes of the intolerable racket, could take no more, and left for an adjoining room.

Two hours of interminable harangues from the stage had brought audience and critics to the breaking point. The Gaveau family, attending the festival, turned pale at having their great organ used to play a popular fox-trot and Mme. Gaveau herself was hit by several flying tomatoes. Gide, Romains, Allard, Barzun, Dorgeles, Reboux, Brancusi, Gleizes, Leger, Metzinger, and Lugné-Poe, all present in the audience, were rocked and buffeted by the whistles, squeaks and animals cries hurled between the crowd and the stage. Benjamin Peret, making his first contact with the dadas at this event, cried out "Long life France and chips," and Mme. Rachilde, who had championed *Ubu,* outraged now by the independent young dadas, urged her followers against them. Among the throwers of fruit and shouters of invective were not only members of the artistic avant-garde, but also those "five o'clock littéraires," those of *belles-dames* who gathered to hear the sparkling verse of the Comte Robert de Montesquieu. André Germaine writes of sitting between a charming "Lausannoise" and a vigorous and opulent quinquagenarian bourgeoise who, in order to somehow regain her composure, would repeat at intervals "Cocteau is nonetheless nice."[16]

There was little critical sympathy from the press. The dadas were condemned for the intense boredom they inspired, for the resounding inanity of the manifestos, and for their acting:

Illustration 24 *Excursion et Visites Dada*, Tristan Tzara, Paris, Eglise Saint
Julien le Pauvre, Thurs. April 14, 1921. Prospectus

Collection: Dr. and Mrs. H.J. Kleinschmidt

Illustration 25   "Trial of Maurice Barrès," Hall of Learned Societies, Paris,
May 13, 1921

Collection: Timothy Baum, New York

One hardly heard them, so inarticulate . . . writers transformed into actors who threw themselves on stage with awkwardness and fearlessness like novice swimmers into the sea.

Nouvelle Revue Française, May 27, 1920

There was nothing worth mentioning on stage unless one was interested in

a few paper costumes of doubtful imaginativeness, and some scatalogical vulgarities recited like at school, by pale youngsters . . .

L'Echo de Paris, May 27, 1920

Critics seemed to agree that the most fitting eulogy one could give the dada performances would be not to speak of them at all. Yet Jean Paulhan was prophetic in saying:

If you must speak of Dada you must speak of Dada. If you must not speak of Dada you must still speak of Dada.[17]

Tongues wagged and words tipped over themselves rushing into print. Amidst all the fracas and name-calling, André Germaine, writing in the *Nouvelle Revue Française,* was one of the few critics to pose an interesting question. Describing the members of the group, in all the diversity of their literary-artistic talents, he asked:

Since these people can do other things, why the exhibitionism and martyrdom of the day before yesterday? Why so deliberately seek out insults and scorn when one is capable of gathering sweeter crowns?

Nouvelle Revue Française, May 29, 1920

Germaine attempted an answer: following the call of their guru, Tzara ("thus spoke Tzara . . . Thoustra"), the *Littérature* group had mounted the pillory of the *Salle Gaveau.* The "method," the intense and naked light in which they bared themselves before a howling audience—Tzara's and their participation in such grotesqueries—could only be explained as one somehow accepts the sullied muse who apologizes for her unkempt appearance by saying, "Please understand, I met the coal-merchant going up the stairs; he was so handsome I just had to hug him."

There was surely something entrancing about Tzara and his methods, and yet the *Littérature* group couldn't suffer its own self-abnegation. Following every dada demonstration, there was collective nervous depression. Though on the surface all was going as planned with the defiant postures leading to reams of scandalous publicity, within the group the sentiments were quite different. As the time approached to plan each new soirée Picabia would call everyone together at his home where they would all be pumped for ideas. A sort of hysteria seemed to accompany this search, "Ideas, ideas, finding ideas . . . it all rests in that."[18] But the ideas came fewer and farther between. Tzara would insist on the inevitable first, second, umpteenth *Aventure céleste de M. Antipyrine,* and once again there would be tall cylinders of cardboard and raucous music. The *littérateurs* were disillusioned and dissatisfied, but Tzara, oblivious to what was going on around him, continued to move in a state of perpetual exaltation.

> He sacrified to "Dada" anyone who escaped its rule, hoping that the God would return to him a hundred-fold, these human sacrifices. Similarly, he ruled over his own company—with monastic strictness, admitting neither discussion nor controversy, nor the slightest personal initiatives which might have, as their end, the singling out of the individual at the expense of Dada.[19]

Breton, Soupault and Aragon were young, and as Breton later wrote:

> The greatest disillusionment of that time—disillusionment for many of us—came from the fact that Tzara was not that which we had supposed . . . [20]

But the hullabaloo which surrounded the Rumanian poet was like a drug and the young *littérateurs* were still doped on Tristan Tzara.

The Period of Rupture: Tzara vs. Breton

The break between Tzara and the *Littérature* group began in 1921, but rumblings had already been felt in the major manifestations. Picabia, though he participated actively in the planning of the manifestations, did not find it possible to perform with the group. Perhaps it was true, as Ribemont-Dessaignes said, that the artist lacked courage. Nevertheless, by his actions Picabia expressed a negative attitude towards Tzara's performing tactics. In the spring of 1921, Picabia issued a "communiqué" to the newspapers entitled "M. Picabia quits the dadaists," in which he accused dada of repeating itself:

> The Dada spirit really existed only from 1913 to 1918, during which time it never ceased evolving and transforming itself and after which time it became as uninteresting as the productions of the Beaux-Arts or the static lucubrations offered by the *NRF* and certain members of the Institute. In wishing to prolong itself, Dada became enclosed within itself.[21]

A half year later, he officially broke with Tzara, attacking him (as well as Cocteau, the cubists, and a number of other dadas) in a pamphlet called "La

Pomme des Pins." Picabia's rupture with dada was violent and unforgiving. Even years later, when questioned as to the motives for his leaving the movement of which he had been one of the chief ornaments, he replied, "I was sick of living in the midst of a gang of people who, having no ideas of their own, spent their time asking me for ideas."[22]

Breton, who had written to Tzara as early as 1919, "I have, to the same degree that you do, the passion to destroy, but mustn't one conceal it? Sooner or later you risk discrediting yourself. . . ."[23] finally walked out on Tzara's piece "Vaseline Symphonique" at the *Salle Gaveau.* He was later to describe the spring of 1921 as the period of "the obsequies of Dada." "Dadaism," he wrote, "cannot be said to have served any other purpose than to keep us in the perfect state of availability in which we are at present, and from which we shall now, in all lucidity, depart towards that which calls us."[24]

As in Zurich, dada in Paris had lost its spontaneity, had rechewed its material to the point of tastelessness, had alienated not only its public but its own members as well. If the planning of the manifestations was becoming laborious work, their execution was becoming even more painful. Except for Tzara, Picabia (who never appeared) and Ribemont-Dessaignes (classified by Breton as one of the few true dadas), the others suffered miserably at the hands of both the audience and their own consciences. Even worse perhaps, dada was securing itself a place in the Establishment. At the end of 1920, Jacques Rivière, editor of the *NRF,* printed in his journal an article entitled "Gratitude to Dada," welcoming dada to the hallowed halls of the French intelligentsia. For Breton and Aragon this could mean nothing but a further calcification of Tzara's already stale methodology. The ends of dada remained valid; the means, though, had to be called into question. "We were," Breton said, "for a radical renovation of the means, for the pursuit of the same ends, but by determinedly different ways."[25]

The idea of the manifestation was not yet to be abandoned. The theatrical nature of the movement remained intact. There were, however, to be new activities. First among them was a series of "visits" to various sites around Paris. In the "found-environments" of the Morgue, the St. Lazare train station and the Church of St. Julien le Pauvre, the dadas would gather to read their manifestos and poems. Only the St. Julien "visit" took place and that, in a teeming rain and with a sense that the proper medium had not yet been found.

The second experiment was both more ambitious and more successful. Expressly against the wishes of Tzara, Breton moved to organize the Barrès trial, in effect a trial of dada itself. On Friday, May 13, 1920, Maurice Barrès, once liberal author of *Un Homme Libre,* a testimony to the supremacy of sensation in the development of the inner self ("le culte de Moi"), was indicted and tried by dada. The philosophy behind the trial of this respectable writer who, in the eyes of Breton, had compromised his spiritual integrity by becoming increasingly chauvinist (he had in fact become President of the League of

Patriots) and bourgeois, was overshadowed by its theatrical aspects. The crowd that had assembled was prepared for another dada carnival of chaos. What it got instead was a highly organized evening of theatre. The emergence of Breton and the theatre of surrealism was at hand.

On the stage at the *Salle des Savants,* costumed dadas, resplendent in their white robes and clerical caps, faced a haberdasher's mannequin who represented the accused Barrès. Aragon and Soupault, counsels for the defense in red caps, asked for the death of their client. Ribemont-Dessaignes, the public prosecutor, called a list of witnesses which included Tzara, Marguerite Buffet, Drieu la Rochelle, Mme. Rachilde, and Benjamin Peret (who appeared dressed as the German Unknown Soldier and testified in German). Breton sat as judge with Théodore Fraenkel and Pierre Deval as his associates. Tzara, determined to "dada" the proceedings, was impudent when addressed, but received in response only the stern wrath of Breton:

> The Witness, Tristan Tzara,: You will agree with me, Sir, that we are all nothing but a pack of fools, and that consequently the little differences—bigger fools or smaller fools, make no difference.

> The president, André Breton: Does the witness insist on acting like an utter imbecile, or is he trying to get himself put away?[26]

When Breton, exasperated, asked Tzara if there was anyone whom he respected, Tzara replied, "Well, I myself am really a charming fellow." The relationship between the two men was fast deteriorating, and the entire dada group was beginning to splinter. Ten days after the Barrès trial, three matinee performances were given of the short plays of Max Jacob *(La Femme fatale),* Erik Satie *(La Piège de Meduse),* Raymond Radiguet *(Les Pélican),* and Cocteau, Radiguet and Poulenc *(Le Gendarme Incompris).* The authors and director, Pierre Bertin, were all one time dadas or dada-associates. No mention was made of Tzara and although the critics partook of another "quite improbable dose of incoherence," there was no scandal, no riot, no shouting. The possibility of performing some new kind of theatre without resorting to Tzara's tactics was becoming evident.

Tzara, determined not to forego his position of leadership in the movement, set about planning a new series of manifestations, a dada Salon to be held at the Galerie Montaigne beginning June 6, 1921. In the course of this exhibition a soirée and two matinees were to be given. The soirée, on June 10, was again in the tradition of the *Grandes Manifestations.* On the small stage placed within the gallery stood a mirror and a piano. Above, a balcony protruded. It could be reached by a ladder at whose side stood a mannequin in evening dress. The opening number, a musical rendering of the exposition's catalogue, was enlivened by one M. Jolibois, a craftsman of the sixth

arrondissement, who repaired porcelain. The unwitting fellow was pushed onstage by Tzara to join in the singing and by doing his best, received the howling acclaim of the audience. Philippe Soupault, masked and fitted out as the President of the Liberian Republic, passed among the audience and alongside the canvases which hung on the walls of the gallery. He was followed by an entourage of dadas who initiated a ritual of matches and candles suited to the title of the event, "The Match-box." Shaking hands all about and never stopping the incoherent babble which poured from his lips, Soupault lit a candle before each dada he met, then extinguished it and returned the candle stub to his pocket. When wearying of this he distributed candles and matches to his followers who amused themselves and the audience with the fire and wax drippings. Suddenly all attention was focused on the balcony, Aragon appeared, and in evangelical style delivered a mock sermon. These and the acts which followed were still in the tradition of Tzara. The Russian dancer Valentin Parnak did a dance of the miraculous-fowl, descending the ladder from the chicken-coop-balcony, dressed in tennis shoes with wings attached to his back. Strapped to his right hand was one of those enormous metal models of a foot which adorned the display windows of podiatrists. Ribemont-Dessaignes read a long, scatological poem entitled "The Book of Kings," and Benjamin Peret recited a poem of Eluard's—motionless, and with intonations exactly contrary to the sense of the piece. Philippe Soupault's number "Diableret" involved the entire dada group, arguing about the comprehensibility of incomprehensible phrases. The audience dissolved into chaos, forcing an intermission.

Tzara's play *The Gas Heart,* featuring Soupault in the part of "Ear," Ribemont-Dessaignes as "Mouth," Théodore Fraenkel as "Nose," Louis Aragon, "Eye," Peret, "Neck," and the author as "Eyebrow," climaxed the evening. The play, which Tzara liked to refer to as "the biggest swindle of the century in three acts," and which he claimed would make happy only the industrialized imbeciles who believe in the existence of men of genius, was to be played by the actors with the seriousness due a *Macbeth*. But, wrote Tzara,

> Treat the author, who is not a genius, with little respect and . . . note the lack of seriousness of the text which contributes nothing new to the technique of the theatre.[27]

The play was howled down by the audience who left the theatre as it was being performed. Its revival two years later, however, led to one of the most memorable battles of the declining years of dada and signalled the end to all relations between Tzara and Breton.

What is notable about the Dada Salon Manifestation is Breton's absence. Eluard, Aragon and Soupault, though ambivalent, all participated. Even Picabia, who had already made public his break with dada, helped in the planning.

Illustration 27   Poet René Crevel and novelist Madame X (Jacqueline Chaumont) in costumes by Sonia Delaunay for Tzara's *Le Coeur à Gaz* at the
Théâtre Michel, July 6, 1923

Collection: Arthur A. Cohen

Breton absented himself completely, and in the two years which followed made his rift with Tzara more and more evident.

Wanting to explore his conception of a "new-art," an art which would move in a constructive direction, Breton convened an "International congress for the determination of the direction and defense of the modern spirit." Inviting Tzara to participate, Breton was turned down politely, through a letter which stated, "Modernism doesn't interest me at all."[28]

Though Tzara stoutly maintained that there was nothing personal in his refusal, Breton reacted very strongly and a battle of words was carried on in the press. The congress collapsed and the dadas divided into two opposing camps. Breton was fast emerging as the leader of a group which he would list and welcome in the manifesto "Leave everything!"

> Picabia, Duchamp, Picasso are still with us. I grasp your hands, Louis Aragon, Paul Eluard, Philippe Soupault, my dear friends forever . . . Jacques Baron, Robert Desnos, Max Morise, Roger Vitrac, Pierre de Massot are waiting for us.[29]

The new call was to leave everything: wife and mistress, children, hopes and fears, but mostly "leave dada." This last separation was not so easy to achieve. Dada had gripped Breton and his friends at an impressionable period in their lives. Now, the attempts to leave seemed to resemble nothing so much as dada itself.

In the winter of 1922, after the collapse of the congress, Breton began to tie the group to him by setting up new idols and planning new activities. The first new "God" was Raymond Roussel and the activity, a dada-like scandal in support of the little known playwright at the revival of his play *Locus Solus*.

Roussel (1877-1933), called in his time "a difficult author," or "madman," was hailed as a "mesmerizer" by Breton. The choice of this work left Breton free to leave vague the reasons for his adulation of Roussel, but it seems probable that the ordered nightmares and mysteries which filled Roussel's works were reason enough to deify him. Roussel's world was more than merely theatrical. It was a world of dream images and of an imagination run riot. Roussel himself underwent a psychic collapse in his youth and was treated by the noted psychiatrist Pierre Janet, who greatly influenced the surrealists. Roussel, who had remained unproduced since 1912,[30] was eager to mount *Locus Solus*, which had been originally written as a book. Rich enough to support the entire production, he hired Pierre Frondaie, a popular playwright and novelist, to adapt the work for the stage. The tale of a group of visitors making the rounds of the incredible marvels which are part of Locus Solus, the estate of Martial Cantarel, rich scientist, magician and illusionist, presented the audience with bizarre scenes and characters. A huge wooden hammer suspended from a dirigible balloon was operated automatically to create a mosaic of variously discolored teeth; a gigantic glass tank containing highly oxygenated water housed human beings, sea horses trained in aquatic sports, an entirely depilated Siamese cat and the brain, nerves and musculature of Danton's head. These the cat, through a special mechanism, was able to galvanize into speech. Behind the glass tank were various "mansions" in the tradition of *"décor simultané":* a ruined chapel in Italy, the actual stage of a theatre, a sculptor's workshop. At each mansion a corpse with paid attendants recreated the most significant moments of his life. Tiny insects lived within a pack of cards and a gallinacious bird, beautifully adorned, formed letters in its congested throat and coughed them out in blood on a tablet of ivory.

The production was greeted with anger by the public and scorn by the press. Roussel, furious, closed the show for two days, claiming a breakdown of machinery. When he opened again on December 11, 1922, Breton and his entourage were on hand to lend their newest favorite author support. Throughout the production, Breton, Aragon, Picabia, Desnos, and Vitrac applauded, shouted and whistled their approval for Roussel. In the third act, Roussel, still steaming under the impact of public and critical disapproval, had removed a particularly poetic section and introduced in its place a series of dada invectives hurled at the audience. At the play's closing, to show his further disdain, he substituted, for his own finale, a one-act boulevard play, screamingly sentimental and full of love for the "patrie." At this, the Breton-dadas erupted with renewed vigor, crying "idiots," "Hélas" and "It's false," at performers and audience alike. To answer one actor whose line "Well? " was met by a brief silence, Aragon shouted from the balcony, "Well, shit." In the grand dada tradition, the play was irrevocably interrupted and the audience fled the theatre in chaos. Breton's tactics on this occasion seem undeniably dada but a crucial difference existed. The Breton group that had broken with dada raised its first collective voice in support of someone, rather than in vacuous riot.

Tzara's dada played its last scene at the "Evening of the bearded heart," on July 6, 1923 at the *Théâtre Michel.* Tzara, deprived of his former friends and rejected by theatre managers as being too dangerous a producer to allow into their auditoriums, had been forced to make new alliances. He joined with Ilia Zdanevitch, a Russian expatriate who directed a theatre group of Russian amateurs entitled "Tcherez." Zdanevitch, who had participated in previous dada events, was sympathetic to Tzara and had theatre connections as well. These enabled him to rent the *Théâtre Michel* and to bring to the program a full staff of technicians and designers. The program, therefore, necessarily became a collaborative effort and though resembling the dada manifestations with their alternating offerings of music, poetry and sketches, it was barely dada in tone and surely not in intention. Tzara's comedown was therefore complete even before the curtain rose. Unable to work without his group, Tzara could do little more than contribute his play *The Gas Heart,* and this time he neither acted in it nor directed.

No matter the program, the clique of former dadas headed by Breton had come to perform their own rites at the obsequies of dada, and if they were not to be provided with sufficient stimuli to react against, they would somehow manufacture the stimuli themselves. So it was that the mention of Picasso's name in an innocuous poem of Pierre de Massot, set off the first wave of fighting in which Breton broke the arm of the young Massot and was taken into custody by the police.[31] A wave of shouting was set off by the reading of a poem of Soupault's, and Tzara's own play brought down the curtain with a further volley of recriminations from Breton's claque. Eluard, battling on stage, fell through the scenery, for which he was later fined 8,000 francs.

The play itself hardly merited all the tumult. Designed and costumed by Sonia Delaunay, the actors[32] found themselves encased in thick cardboard trapezoids which divided the body into angular parts and recalled the object-actor of Picasso's *Parade* designs. In contrast, however, with Picasso's dancer-figures who were fully plastique forms (forms built for movement), Delaunay's creations were meant to be seen face forward. They were flat surfaces, podiums on which rested the head of an immobilized, reciting actor. The striped trousers and tie, the festooned bars across the skirt and the two discs which marked the breasts of the actress created an "op" effect, while the set curtain reflected the motionless, posturing quality of the performance. Germaine Everling-Picabia was prophetic in remarking that "a scandal which lasts is no longer a scandal."[33] Even the critics were quite sure that they were witnessing only the final tremors of something that had in fact, already died:

> Dada, in fact, is quite dead. One has known it for a few years. . . . The performance began a half an hour late. That's certainly a minimum. Dada is behind much more than that.
>
> Charles Gilbert, "Mort de Dada," *Le Figaro,* July 8, 1923

Tzara retreated. He corresponded with dadas outside of France, worked on his poetry and wrote a fourth play, *Handkerchief of Clouds.* The stage was set for a new movement and a new leader.

Dada Performance and the Surrealist Sketch

Miro: Should one go to see Picabia or Breton?
Masson: Picabia is already the past, Breton is
the future.

Conversation between Miro and Masson, 1923

Illustration 28   The Surrealists, 1924. Standing from left to right: Charles Baron, Raymond Queneau, Pierre Naville, André Breton, J.A. Boiffard, Giorgio di Chirico, Roger Vitrac, Paul Eluard, Philippe Soupault, Robert Desnos, Louis Aragon. Seated from left to right: Simone Breton, Max Morise, Mick Soupault

The "Family" of the Surrealist Sketch

Here are elephants with women's heads and
flying lions.

André Breton, *First Manifesto of Surrealism*

After Apollinaire's use of the word "sur-réalisme," in the program for *Parade* in 1917, and later as a subtitle for his own "drame surréaliste," *The Breasts of Tirésias,* the word floated in avant-garde circles vaguely present but hardly defined. In the August 1920 issue of *La Nouvelle Revue Française,* Breton, in his article, "For Dada," used the adjective "surréaliste" and referred to two of the areas which would soon concern the surrealist movement: the riches of the unconscious, and the essential nature of inspiration. In April 1922, Breton was shouting "Leave everything, leave dada," and by November of that year he had written:

> Up to a certain point one knows what my friends and I mean by *Surréalisme*. This word, which is not our invention and which we could have abandoned to the most vague critical vocabulary, is used by us in a precise sense. By it, we mean to designate a certain psychic automatism that corresponds rather closely to the state of dreaming, a state that is today extremely difficult to delimit.[1]

By 1924, the word had surfaced in a magazine called *Surréalisme,* edited by Yvan Goll and an "office of surrealist research," opened at 15 rue de Grenelle. The office was manned by the group that surrounded Breton and was administered by Antonin Artaud. This group, which now included Pierre Naville, Benjamin Peret, Soupault, Aragon, Eluard and Roger Vitrac, published a journal entitled *La Révolution Surréaliste,* which chose a scientific format (modeled on the well-known scientific journal *La Nature*), to emphasize its desire to pursue research and experiment. In 1924, Breton published his *First Manifesto of Surrealism* with a definition of the term:

> SURREALISM, n. Psychic automatism in its pure state, by which one proposes to express—verbally, by means of the written word, or in any other manner—the actual functioning of thought. Dictated by thought, in the absence of any control exercised by reason, exempt from any aesthetic or moral concern.

> ENCYCLOPEDIA. Philosophy. Surrealism is based on the belief in the superior reality of certain forms of previously neglected associations, in the omnipotence of dream, in the disinterested play of thought. It tends to ruin once and for all all other psychic mechanisms and to substitute itself for them in solving all the principal problems of life.[2]

By 1924, then, Breton and the group that surrounded him had evolved into a new movement.

The movement, however, proved a highly unstable one. By 1925, the "friendly group" had dissolved. Surrealism had entered the period of numerous arguments regarding philosophy and political action. By 1925, most of the plays that the members of the surrealist group were to write, had been written, and the group had ceased to function as an acting-producing unit. After 1925, those surrealist plays produced were done by avant-garde theatres outside the periphery of the group, by professional actors and often with the group's outspoken disapproval. Aragon's *Au pied du mur,* scheduled for production at the Vieux-Colombier in June of 1925, was successfully sabotaged by the surrealists,[3] and the author's *The Mirror Wardrobe, One Fine Evening,* was performed at the *Théâtre Art et Action* in March, 1926, after Aragon had specifically denied permission for its presentation. Vitrac's *The Mysteries of Love* opened the *Théâtre Alfred Jarry* in 1927 to the hoots and catcalls of the surrealists, while Vitrac along with Artaud had already been banished from the surrealist circle for yielding to what Breton considered commercial instincts in wanting to produce plays in the framework of a professional theatre.

The attempts of both the *Théâtre Art et Action* and the *Théâtre Alfred Jarry* to produce surrealist texts merits a full study of its own. After 1924, however, the surrealist group was no longer performance-oriented and the clique of young poets that had served its apprenticeship under Tzara fragmented and split. The "Office of surrealist research," which had been manned by Artaud, closed its doors. Soupault was expelled from the movement for engaging in "the stupid literary adventure," Breton became the sole editor of *La Révolution Surréaliste,* and the movement began to take a decidedly political turn. By 1925, then, the type of performance which had its beginnings with Tzara in Zurich had stopped to catch its breath. During the next 30 years, it would rear its head in the works of individual theatre-people of the avant-garde: Artaud, for instance. Not until the late 1950s, however, would it again find the soil in which it could grow most fertily—that of performing groups such as the communal Living Theatre, the Open Theatre with playwrights in residence, or the theatre of happening created by an intimate group of artists and their friends.

Ludwig Wittgenstein, in the famous counsel set forth in his Philosophical Investigation, writes:

> Consider for example the proceedings that we call "games." I mean board-games, card-games, ball-games, Olympic games, and so on. What is common to them all?—Don't say: "There must be something common, or they would not be called 'games'—but *look* and *see* whether there is anything common to all. For if you look at them, you will not see something that is common to all, but similarities, relationships, and a whole series of them at that . . . we see a complicated network of similarities

overlapping and criss-crossing; sometimes overall similarities, sometimes similarities of detail. . . .

I can think of no better expression to characterize these similarities than "family resemblances"; for the various resemblances between members of a family: build, colour of eyes, features, gait, temperament, etc. etc. overlap and criss-cross in the same way.—And I shall say: "Games" form a family.[4]

It would be critically unproductive to make too narrow a definition of which poet/playwrights may be included in the family of the surrealist sketch. If, to name a poet/playwright "surrealist," we simply accept exploration into the labyrinth of the unconscious, the reconciliation of dream and reality, the generous list of precursors and contemporaries who at one time or another received acclaim from Breton and his followers, we obtain an understandable, though specious, vision of poetic creation. And what is to be done with the fearful stumbling block posed by Breton in his *First Manifesto of Surrealism,* to the effect that the true surrealist will operate "in the absence of any control exercised by reason"? The domains offered the poet/playwright by the surrealist outlook were vast indeed: in method—automatic writing, simulated madness, games and violent provocation; in outlook—the realm of the unconscious, the power of dreams, the freeing of the psyche's menagerie, the revolt against the logical, the liberation from tradition. All these were some of its points of departure, its loci of inspiration. For some, reason was the great prostitute. For others, the greatest temptation was to try operating magically on things, first of all on one's own self.

The focus should remain, then, on the original nucleus of the surrealist group—that group of young writers who had lived the Paris-dada experience and were present at the founding of surrealism. This group immediately included André Breton, Philippe Soupault, Louis Aragon, Georges Ribemont-Dessaignes, Roger Vitrac, Jean Cocteau, Robert Desnos, Pierre Albert-Birot and Antonin Artaud. Tristan Tzara, though the acknowledged papa of dada, must also be included here. That Soupault remained more true to Tzara than to Breton, that Aragon left Breton's cenacle and that Cocteau staunchly denied ever having been part of it; that Ribemont-Dessaignes was considered one of the few true "dadas," and that Artaud has hardly been talked about in relation to surrealism—these are truths which do not infringe on the category I am proposing. For it is the nature of the theatre pieces written by these people, the models of performance chosen for their execution, the experience with performance in the early 1920s which shaped the authors and pieces alike, the cultural and theatrical milieu of the Parisian avant-garde which they shared, that allows the grouping of these people and labelling of them as the makers of the surrealist sketch.[5]

In writing his "Project on contemporary literary history" in 1922, Louis Aragon included the names of almost all the people, works and events crucial to a performance history of the surrealist sketch:

Futurism . . . The *Ballets Russes* . . . Nick Carter . . . The Duncans . . . Guillaume Apollinaire . . . The Movies, Charlie Chaplin and the Vampires . . . *SIC . . . Parade . . . The Breasts of Tirésias* . . . the influence of Jarry . . . Pierre Bertin[6] . . . Madame Lara[7] . . . *Art et Vie* becomes *Art et Action* . . . Dada . . . Cocteau takes shape . . . Raymound Radiguet . . . Fraenkel . . . Ivan Goll . . . *The Magnetic Fields* Picabia . . . Tzara . . . Ribemont-Dessaignes . . . Le premier vendredi de *Littérature* . . . period of Manifestations: *Grand Palais, Faubourg,* popular University, *Oeuvre* . . . the *Salle Gaveau* . . . *Le Boeuf sur le toît* and Cocteau's productions . . . the Barrès affair . . . André Breton separates from Dada . . . *Les Mariées de la Tour Eiffel* . . . Roger Vitrac . . . The Bearded Heart . . . Robert Desnos . . .[8]

During the five years between Breton and Soupault's experiments in writing in *The Magnetic Fields (Les Champs Magnétiques,* 1919), and 1924, by which time surrealism became preoccupied with other things, the surrealist playwrights penned and mounted some 15 pieces for the theatre, among them: Breton and Soupault's *S'il vous plaît* (1919) and *Vous m'oublierez* (1920), Pierre Albert-Birot's *Le Bondieu* (1920), *L'homme coupé en morceaux* and *Les femmes pliantes* (1921), Raymond Radiguet's *Les Pélican* (1921), Jean Cocteau's *Les Mariés de la Tour Eiffel* (1921), George Ribemont-Dessaignes' *Le Sérin Muet, Zizi de Dada* and *Les partage des os* (1921), Tristan Tzara's *Le Coeur à Gaz* (1922), Roger Vitrac's *Entrée Libre* (1922), and *Les Mystères de l'Amour* (1923), Louis Aragon's *L'Armoire à glace un beau soir,* and *Au pied du mur* (1923), and Antonin Artaud's *le jet du sang* (1924).

The most striking of the family resemblances among these plays, and their most salient feature, is the dislocation of language from its usual function of rational communication. The surrealists gave precedence to the liberation of language, for, as Breton had written in his *Second Surrealist Manifesto:*

> The problem of social action is . . . but one of the forms of a more general problem . . . which is that of human expression in all its forms. Whoever says expression, says, to begin with, language. You must not be surprised then, to see surrealism situated first of all almost exclusively on the plane of language.[9]

The liberties the surrealists took in their relationship to a text were not, however, as with the dadas, expressions of hostility, or a stand against the academies, but were based on a new set of priorities. No longer would dialogue work essentially to support and develop plot. On the contrary, to the extent that plot would count at all in surrealist theatre, it would tend to function mainly as a support for dialogue—while the dialogue itself would be allowed to push forward on a level of exchange where common sense and normal sequence surrender their claim to attention.

J.H. Matthews, in his book *The Theatre in Dada and Surrealism* states:

The major discovery made in the name of surrealism, is that theatre is compatible with poetry, as surrealists understood this, but that on stage it is frequently necessary to liberate poetry through language at the expense of drama. Hence surrealism's impact upon playwrighting rests mainly upon diversion of theatre from dramatic to poetic ends. This is the significance of plot discontinuity and inconsistency in character and behavior, called upon to play its part in setting the theatre free from its restricted role as mirror to reality.[10]

But let there be no illusions. Surrealism had not sought to develop an aesthetic for the theatre, but rather had abducted a literary genre for its own purposes.[11] Just as the surrealist text itself is often difficult to grapple with, on the theoretical level the reader will have to struggle with the absence of a consistent and consecutive approach to drama as well as the absence of a unified program for the stage. It is often then, now new conventions which strike the reader/viewer, but the distant echoes of old ones, as established theatrical schemata are subverted to mark the direction of a new pathfinder.

Surrealism vs. Dada

One's resemblance to one's parents is always
strong enough without putting on their
clothes.

Juan Gris, 1921

In order to trace the path of the surrealist sketch, it is necessary to look a bit more closely at the relationship between dada and surrealism for too many critics have blithely assumed that surrealism is merely an extension of dada, or, no less tendentious, that dada is surrealism in search of its true identity.

Surrealism has again and again been compared to dada: dadas were basically the destroyers, surrealists, the creators; dada had only the vaguest concern for the future (or none at all), while surrealism saw the reconstruction of the future as an objective problem. There is something misleading in such neat accounts of the two movements, and recent critical comment evidences a new approach to their comparison. What the two movements shared—intense revolt, provocation, mystification—is greater than what separated them. As Sanouillet puts it, "there is a surrealist aspect to Dada and a dada aspect to Surrealisme,"[12] and Breton himself says in the *Entretiens:*

It is therefore inexact and chronologically improper to present surrealism as a movement born of dada or to see in it the re-erecting of dada on a constructive plane.[13]

Roger Shattuck goes so far as to say, "I have been taking sightings and soundings on Dada and Surrealism for many years, and cannot find a more satisfactory distinction between the two than straight chronology."[14] This statement, however, should give us pause, for surely, if the original question was how to find some careful discrimination between dada and surrealism, then Shattuck's modest proposal is not a solution but rather a restatement of the problem. What Shattuck is actually saying is that there is a date upon which he had fixed, for him 1921, which marks the end of the appearance of certain "dada" characteristics in the arts, and the beginning of the appearance of those qualities he will associate with surrealism. The problem is, of course, that other critical historians have suggested other dates: 1922—the year of the Barrès trial; 1924—the year in which Breton published his *First Manifesto of Surrealism*. Straight chronology, then, is not so much a matter of fact as a matter of critical choice. For our purposes, in the search for the beginnings of a theatre of surrealism, a year which bears serious consideration is 1919.

Automatic Writing

The alleged instinct for causality is nothing
more than the fear of the unusual.

Nietzsche

In the summer of 1919, six months before Tristan Tzara arrived in Paris, André Breton and Philippe Soupault sat down to write what Breton was later to call the first surrealist text: *The Magnetic Fields (Les Champs Magnétiques)*. This was to be done according to the principles of automatic writing—the direct transcription of thought, "in the absence of all critical intervention":[15]

> After you have settled yourself in a place as favorable as possible to the concentration of your mind upon itself, have writing materials brought to you. Put yourself in as passive, or receptive, a state of mind as you can. Forget about your genius, your talents, and the talents of everyone else. Keep reminding yourself that literature is one of the saddest roads that leads to everything. Write quickly, without any preconceived subject, fast enough so that you will not remember what you're writing and be tempted to reread what you have written. The first sentence will come spontaneously, so compelling is the truth that with every passing second there is a sentence unknown to our consciousness which is only crying out to be heard. . . . Go on as long as you like. Put your trust in the inexhaustible nature of the murmur. If silence threatens to settle in if you should ever happen to make a mistake . . . break off without hesitation with an overly clear line. Following a word the origin of which seems suspicious to you, place any letter whatsoever, the letter "l" for example, always the letter "l", and bring the arbitrary back by making this letter the first of the following word.[16]

I quote this statement, which is in effect the "how to . . ." of automatic writing, for both *The Magnetic Fields* and its correspondent methodology are important to this study—the date of its writing (1919), and the date of Breton's recording of the method (1924) forming the chronological perimeters of an investigation of the surrealist sketch. Among the pieces in the volume which comprised *The Magnetic Fields* is *If You Please*, the play presented at the major dada manifestation at the *Théâtre de l'Oeuvre* (March 27, 1920), but written before Tzara's arrival in Paris.[17]

Michel Sanouillet makes a strong claim for dada's paternity in the case of automatic writing—and points in particular to an untitled page, written jointly by Picabia and Tzara to signal their joining of forces in Zurich in 1919:

> This page is composed of two texts, drafted by automatic writing, simultaneously and on the same sheet of paper.[18]

Consciously or not, he claims, Breton and Soupault were influenced by this experiment in writing which they had seen in the journal *391*. In addition, he notes, similar techniques had been employed in such texts as Apollinaires' *Onirocritique* (much admired by Breton and Aragon), in the futurists' "parole in libertà," and in the works of Raymond Roussel.

Anna Balakian, in her critical biography of Breton,[19] challenges these claims through her investigation of Breton's debt to Dr. Pierre Janet, professor of psychiatric medicine and chronologically an intermediary between Charcot and Freud. His thick volume *L'Automatisme psychologique* (first edition 1889, 9th edition 1921) was required reading of all medical students of Breton's vintage (Breton was a medical student before the war and had spent some of his wartime service in a hospital for shell-shocked and crazed soldiers where he observed new psychoanalytic methods and work with dreams at first hand). Breton's meeting with Janet's experiments in automatic writing was crucially important, for Janet was constantly alert to the uses of this technique not only as a channel for therapy, but as a tool for the exploration of the normal mind as well. In man, Janet claims, there is a most primordial area in which volition plays no part, and of which man is not aware unless it interferes with his conscious thought. This intrusion occurs in the mentally ill where, however, it is of no use to the subject because he has lost, at the same time, his sense of awareness of the intervention. If the normal person cannot lift the self-censuring mechanism of reason that bars access to automatic thought, he can, in a moment of inattentive writing, squeeze out the data stored in the deep recesses of the mind. "Let the pen wander," he says, "automatically, on the page, even as the medium interrogates his mind."[20] This, Balakian claims, is the premise on which the surrealist notion of automatic writing is founded. Although what emerges in this automatic writing appears in a form that is grammatically rational, the effect produced on the hearer (or reader) is irrational for the spewing forth is that of a mind unburdened by the overwhelming armor of patterns that are called "rational" because of collective social agreement.[21] This process, though accidental in the insane, could, according to Janet, be induced without the aid of exterior stimuli, and much of Breton's displeasure with his colleagues during the "époque de sommeil" was caused by their use of alcohol or drugs as stimuli in these experiments. "It was a time," wrote Aragon, "when we would meet each evening like hunters, giving account of the day's catch: the number of beasts invented, the fantastic plants, the images excavated."[22]

Functioning uniquely within this epidemic of trances was Robert Desnos, master of the art of falling asleep at will:

> In a cafe, amidst the noise of voices, the full light . . . Robert Desnos has only to close his eyes and he speaks, and in the middle of the beer steins and flying saucers, an entire ocean gives way with its prophetic din and its vapours, adorned with long banners. Those who interrogate this incredible sleeper need barely greet him and suddenly the preaching, the tone of magic, of revelation, of revolution, the tone of the fanatic and the apostle appear.[23]

In *Les Pas Perdus,* Breton describes his own initiation into this kind of experimentation:

> In 1919, my attention was fixed on those more or less incomplete phrases which, in complete solitude, at the approach of sleep, became perceptible to the mind without it being possible to discover for them, a previous determination. These phrases, remarkably vivid and in perfectly correct syntax, seemed to me poetic elements of the first order. I restricted myself, first of all, to remembering them. It was only later that Soupault and I dreamed of voluntarily reproducing in ourselves the state in which they had been formed.[24]

It is difficult to understand how one can write a play by a method of gratuitous pen-pushing. How does one acknowledge the end of one section of dialogue and the beginning of another, the division into acts or scenes? Do the character's names spontaneously enter the consciousness of the playwright, and what makes them speak, first A, then B, then A again? When the writing is a collaborative effort, when does one author write, when the other?[25] In an interview with Philippe Soupault in 1971,[26] I questioned the poet about the writing and production of the two plays on which he had collaborated with Breton. Noting that there were certain differences between the texts as originally published in *Cannibale* and *Littérature*[27] and then in the definitive edition issued by Gallimard in 1967, I asked Soupault how he explained this in the light of the precepts of automatic writing. The question was perhaps unfair[28] for Aragon had already written the definitive apology in his *Traité du Style:*

> Surrealism is inspiration recognized, accepted and practiced. No longer as an inexplicable visitation, but as a skill which one can practice. Normally limited by fatigue.

Of variable breadth depending on individual strengths. And the results of which are of unequal interest . . . legend has it that it is sufficient to get the knack of it and immediately, texts of great interest, flow from the pen or no matter whom, like an inexhaustible diarrhea . . . But if you write, according to a surrealist system, sad idiocies, they will be sad idiocies, without excuse.[29]

What Soupault answered about the "corrections" was, perhaps Breton corrected the proofs, or Picabia, but not "me." Breton himself, in *Point du jour,* points out the difficulties of remaining for long in the desirable state of receptivity for such writing, and that one must always be wary of "involuntary retouching." Occasionally, he writes, even the vanity of the author can falsify the experience.

Here perhaps the subject should rest. It is hardly likely that *If you please* (or the later *You will forget me—Vous m'oublierez,* or the small sketch that comprises section 31 of *Soluble Fish*—all written by the method of automatic writing), was written entirely without editing. This does not mean to disclaim the pretentions of the method, to diminish the importance of using it, nor to deny the unique qualities of the resulting work, but to recognize that automatism was never chemically pure—it constituted an outer limit toward which the author could strive but which he could attain only sporadically. Still, merely the decision to test this method of writing against dramatic form is an artistic contribution which deserves focus.

In his emphasis on automatic writing, Breton was moving, as did dada, to stress the importance of process over product—to allow the artist to shift into an entirely different gearing of the mechanics of creation. In the collaborative efforts of Breton and Soupault there are immediately two "speakers" who, in joining their "unedited" efforts, produce a kind of dialogue. Anna Balakian, in writing her critical biography of Breton, had access to the original marked-up manuscript of *The Magnetic Fields* which indicated which parts were written by which poet. With this help, what Balakian calls the "dialogue quality" of the work becomes clear, making the automatic writing appear "like a game of ping-pong."[30] In entering into a discussion of this dialogue-quality aspect of Breton and Soupault's collaborative writing, Balakian cannot avoid mentioning that the two poets did produce two pieces for the theatre. She is, however, too ready to dismiss the results of these efforts as "dramatic fragments which today are of no more than documentary interest."[31] If Balakian were not so convinced that the theatre experiments of the surrealists were quite worthless, an opinion she has only recently begun to revise,[32] she might have found "the dialogue quality of a play," a more apt phrase than "a game of ping-pong," by which to describe the quotations from *The Magnetic Fields:*

— Have you forgotten that the police have arrived and that they have never been able to stop the sun?

— No thank-you, I know the time. Have you been locked in this cage long? What I need is the address of your tailor.

A careful exploration of Breton's writing reveals that there is an intimate link in his mind between surrealism and dramatic form.

André Breton and Surrealist Theatre

Breton's attitude to the theatre was ambivalent. In 1924, in his "Introduction au discours sur le peu de réalité," he wrote:

> O eternal theatre, you demand that not only to act the role of another, but even to dictate this role, we mask ourselves to resemble it, that the mirror before which we pass reflect a foreign image of ourselves. Imagination has every power except that of identifying us in spite of our appearance as a person other than ourselves.[33]

Here, Breton seems to indicate a fear of so being taken in by the role as to be unable to separate the mask from the self. In *Nadja* (1928), he confided, "I have never been able to tolerate the theatre."[34] Perhaps by this he means the theatre of convention, which takes itself seriously, for he is quite ready to say that the plays at the boulevard theatres such as the *Théâtre Moderne* (with the rudimentary acting of the performers who paid only the faintest attention to their parts and scarcely listened to one another—so busy were they making dates with the audience) "correspond perfectly" to his ideal.[35] He goes out of his way to comment on *Les Détraquées* by Palau which, to him, was an extraordinary play because of the latent element of "strangeness" lurking within a totally naturalistic setting, and because of the intense impact of the play on his dream life. In his poem "Rideau, rideau," the poet's life is played out on the stage of a theatre, in a baroque spectacle which includes not only the actor playing Breton, but another man in a Breton mask and on a level below the stage, a silhouette of Breton, with a bullet in his heart, outlined in fire on a white wall. In *Les Vases Communicants,* he compares the dream's formal unity and integrity to that of a classical tragedy, while in *L'Amour fou,* he presents the reader with his own highly theatrical dream—costumes, stage directions and all. He speaks of having been possessed by a mental theatre in which he tried to construct the ideal play. He envisages a scene in which seven or nine symbolic men, dressed in black habits, participate in a mysterious rite. They are first perceived sitting on a bench engaged in an imperceptible dialogue, but always staring straight ahead. At dusk, they ritually wander to the shore in single file, skirting the waves. A further scene introduces seven or nine women clad in the most beautiful light clothing. Through the dream a juxtaposition of simultaneous monologues presents itself, completely disregarding the linguistic function of communication. It is here, in the potential for new uses of language, that theatre looms most attractive for Breton.

In his *First Manifesto of Surrealism* (1924), Breton states "The forms of surrealist language adapt themselves best to dialogue," and speaks of "dialogue" and "soliloquy" in a passage which is revealing to an understanding of the disordered conversations which tend to mark the surrealist plays:

> Poetic surrealism, which is the subject of this study, has focused in its efforts up to this point on re-establishing dialogue in its absolute truth by freeing both interlocutors from any obligations of politeness. Each of them simply pursues his soliloquy without trying to derive any special dialectical pleasure from it and without trying to impose anything whatsoever upon his neighbor. The remarks exchanged are not, as is generally the case, meant to develop some theses, however unimportant it may be; they are as disaffected as possible. As for the reply that they elicit, it is, in principle, totally indifferent to the personal pride of the person speaking.[36]

To illustrate this surrealist dialogue, Breton quotes a conversation with a mental patient whose reponses (which seem illogical and capricious) are actually triggered by sound mechanisms, poetic associations or dream musings and imagery:

> Q. "How old are you?"
> A. "You." (Echolalia)
> Q. "What is your name?"
> A. "Forty-five houses." (Ganser syndrome, or beside the point replies)[37]

When he comes to writing *If You Please*, Breton, in collaboration with Soupault, records the following sequence:

> Gilda: Are your eyes really that color?
> Maxime: Elbow on the tale like naughty children. The fruit of a Christian primary education, if books didn't lie, everything that is golden.
> Gilda: In the huts of fishermen one finds those artificial bouquets made up of periwinkles and even a bunch of grapes.
> Maxime: The globe must be lifted up if it is not transparent enough. . . .[38]

Here are the multiple "short-circuits" which Breton discusses in his *Second Manifesto of Surrealism,* here is the sabotaging of the usual "insanities" which form the realistic current of life.

Breton calls himself and Soupault "interlocutors," and although the most common definition of the word is someone who takes part in a conversation or dialogue, questions or cross-examines, the first dictionary definition of the word is, "the man in the middle of the line of performers of a minstrel troupe who carries on a conversation with the end men."

It is not surprising to find Breton writing with words from a theatre vocabulary, for theatricality had been a compelling part of the dada experience. His experiences at the major dada manifestations left him no longer afraid of boos and shouted expletives. He was used to painters and musicians, poets and ballet-masters, participating in a revue-type pastiche of movement, noise and assaulting activity. All theatrical stops were out. The body—clowning, naked, grotesquely sexual or reshaped by costumes and masks, took center stage. Activities, absurd in their pointlessness or unrelatedness, defiant in their flaunting of stage as well as social custom, filled the playing time. Most striking perhaps was the "white" quality ("white" as in Satie's "white music," or the recent technological sedative, "white noise") of many of the pieces: that is, their absolute refusal to develop. This was perhaps dada's greatest legacy. Not merely were the unities dispensed with, but so was any consistent regard for characterization and any concept of sequence which might send one vaulting to a climax. Gide, who was writing his "cubist" novel, *Lafcadio's Adventures,* at the time, complained in his *Journal* of the difficulty of having to start anew with each chapter because of the coreless sequence of events. This, despite the fact that he had himself chosen for a motto, "Never take advantage of momentum,"[39] Dada theatrical schemas most nearly resembled the *cadavre exquis,* that collective collage so delighted in by the surrealists, in which they wrote down a word or drew a line, folded the paper, and passed it on for the next contribution.

Theatricality reigned above all. Beginning a lecture at the Ateneo in Barcelona on November 17, 1922, Breton said:

> In general I consider that a critical study is quite out of place in the present circumstances and that the smallest theatrical effect would serve my purposes better.[40]

Dada had introduced the young surrealists to a new kind of relationship with the audience: the passive spectator must be converted to a hostile participant, beaten by the provocations of author and actors. And though occasionally they vacillated, the surrealists as performers or "claque" did not depart from this proscription. It was not until 1929 that Breton, in his *Second Manifesto of Surrealism,* recorded the departure of surrealism from this attitude towards the spectator: "We absolutely must stop the public entering if we want to avoid confusion."

The Surrealist Plays of Breton and Soupault

André Breton and Philippe Soupault sat down to write *S'il vous plaît* in 1919, before Tzara's arrival in Paris.[41] What was foremost then in their minds was the attempt to explore the potential of language by the methodology of automatic writing. Whatever the product, it would be acceptable. The models turned out to be the schemas of a traditional theatre, bending to the whims of the unconscious. By the time the two set out to write *Vous m'oublierez,* however, barely a year later in April of 1920,[42] they had already been through the rodage of four dada months which had included performances at the *Palais des Fêtes,* the *Salon des Indépendents,* the *Club de Faubourg* and the *Université populaire.* Visions of Tzara-ian stage pictures danced in their heads and fragments of schemata of dada theatre had been imprinted on their consciousness. All that remained now was to join the mad rondel of dada performance and Philippe Soupault had made the willingness quite clear:

> *Vous m'oublierez* was written especially for a dada manifestation. We wanted to do something completely different from the regular theatre . . . to do something scandalous . . . against the academies.[43]

Vous m'oublierez strikingly exhibits surrealism's attempt to assimilate dada performance. The qualities which link this sketch to the earlier *S'il vous plaît,* however, stand out just as clearly. They indicate the independent direction taken by the surrealist sketch, which even dada could not divert.

S'il vous plaît was written during the winter of 1919, and messages about it were quickly sent by Breton to Tzara, who was still in Zurich. On Friday, December 26, 1919, Breton wrote: "I have just completed, with Soupault, a play in four acts."[44] On Wednesday, January 14, 1920, only three days before Tzara's arrival in Paris, Breton sent off: "I have just completed a play in collaboration with Soupault: *S'il vous plaît,* a drama in four acts. We plan to perform it next spring."[45]

The play itself is composed of four acts, divided into 25 scenes in the French manner, at the entrance or exit of any character. There are 30 characters none of whom appears in more than a single act of the play. Each act, then, is a self-contained unit with its own setting, characters, activities. There is a whore called Gilda, a husband and wife—Valentine and Françoise—Paul the lover, an office boy and an Algerian peddler. The characters kiss, they look in mirrors, knock on doors, shake hands and smoke cigarettes. They type, make phone calls and play cards. The characters are "like real people." The authors are writing relationships. What then is strange?

Each of the first three acts has a recognizable context, and is, in fact, modeled on one or another of the standard schemata of boulevard drama:[46] Act I—the wife and lover interrupted by the husband; Act II—the heavy intrigue of an office linked with public affairs, the law, the police, the signing of papers; Act III—a whore and a gentleman meet in a cafe. From act to act, however, there is no continuity. No act bears any relation to the other acts in the play. The build-up of intrigue associated with the well-made play, and anticipated by the audience because of the nature of the character-types and activites in the act, is effectively thwarted.

At the end of Act I, Valentine, the wife, is killed. The audience may think it has discovered the lover, Paul, as murderer in Act II, scene 10:

Létoile: (to the policeman) Arrest that man.
The young Man: What's going on? You're out of your mind.
Létoile: Resistance is useless (to the policeman) I make a formal accusation against this man for murdering his mistress, Madame Valentine Saint-Cervan.

but there is no mention of Paul in that scene, or afterwards in the act, or in the rest of the play—and the man accused is visibly younger than Paul and sports a blonde moustache. At the end of Act II, Létoile, in whose business office the act takes place, is himself arrested and in true anti-climactic fashion says "What does that matter to me." The curtain falls. His response is almost identical with that of Maxime, the gentleman, who, at the end of Act III, after being told by Gilda the whore that she has "the syph," responds "Who cares." Another curtain. What do Maxime and Gilda have to do with Létoile? What does Act II have to do with Act I? The answer seems to be—nothing.

Within the acts themselves, although the nature of the activity is recognizable, there is something new and confusing occurring with the energies of the characters. Roger Shattuck has pointed to three of Breton's favorite metaphors, all drawn from the language of physics: interference, the short circuit, and communicating vessels.[47] All three are helpful in trying to pinpoint just what it is that gives these almost recognizable scenes their quality of being off-balance, and therefore unsettling. In the first segment of Act I, Paul and Valentine converse. The audience is set down on the frontier of a known language: I think I understand it, I must understand it for I understand all the words, but in fact I don't understand.

Paul: I love you. (long kiss)
Valentine: A cloud of milk in a cup of tea

The level of frustration at almost-understanding is far greater than that of not understanding at all, and is one of the significant tensions which work through the surrealist sketch.

Here we are close to the world of the painting of Matisse and Masson whose works, no matter how abstract they become, always allude, however elliptically, to a subject. Masson and Matisse, spending a few weeks together in the country in 1932, explained to one another their manner of working. Masson described,

I begin without any image or plan in mind, but just draw or paint rapidly according to my impulses. Gradually, in the marks I make, I see suggestions of figures or objects. I encourage these to emerge, trying to bring out their implications even as I now consciously try to give order to the composition.[48]

Matisse replied,

> That's curious, with me it's just the reverse. I always starts with something—a chair, a table—but as the work proceeds, I become less conscious of it. By the end, I am hardly aware of the subject with which I started.[49]

For both painters, the subject is always present and Breton himself, in discussing surrealist painting, makes it quite clear that no matter how abstract the painting may appear, "it moves in favor of the subject."

What the painters did with their brush strokes to bring the subject into focus or allow it to fade to the edge of awareness, Breton and Soupault achieved with their verbal flights and the shaping of the scenes. Valentine and Paul never stop relating to one another, so that when the listener is buffeted by the juxtaposition of a sequence of dialogue such as:

> Paul: Did you hear him come in?
> Valentine: Current morality: it makes me think of a current of water.
> Paul: The charm lies in that lovely liquid song, the spelling out of the catechism by children.

he can still hang onto the "subject" of the scene. There is no doubt that the scene is a love-scene.

It is this balance between abstraction and an ever-present subject which is a striking quality of the surrealist sketch. It is this quality that gives the sense of the world-in-the-scene as being slightly unfocussed, a blurriness which provides an enticing tension. This lack-of-focus-tension, however, is extremely hard to maintain in the theatre, for everything that is put on stage cries for focus. What the playwrights resort to, therefore, to maintain this off-focus tension, are techniques of interference and short-circuiting. Valentine suddenly pushes the energies in the scene to a climax with "I dreamt that we were drowning"—a sexual image of identification. Paul's response is a short-circuit: "It's a long time since the charming statue on top of the Tour Saint-Jacques let fall . . . etc." Here are Breton's interlocutors, "freed from the obligations of politeness."

The short-circuiting in the second act (the only act performed at the *Théâtre de l'Oeuvre*)[50] takes place between scenes, for within each scene, many lines proceed as in a boulevard play:

> Létoile (speaks heatedly; during the whole scene his eyes do not leave the other man): Sir, I'm sorry to say I can't give you more than a few moments. I was about to go out when you card was sent in. Be so good as to take a seat. (He remains standing).
>
> The Man: Yesterday evening my wife and I came home after having been to the theatre. I should tell you that the dressing room is quite some distance

> from our bedroom. Before undressing, my wife put her necklace and rings on the mantelpiece. I remained in the study.
>
> Létoile: Excuse me, were you smoking?
>
> The Man: (after taking time to reflect): Yes. Several minutes later . . .
>
> Létoile: Several minutes, you say.
>
> The Man (troubled): Well, about ten minutes. The jewels had disappeared.

It is from scene to scene that the major interference occurs. No pattern of energies is allowed to develop. Characters disappear never to be seen again. The concluding of activities begun is indefinitely postponed.

In Act III, it is possible to abstract from the running dialogue a 12-line text, more like an acting exercise, which gives the actors rather neutral lines on which to build characters:

> Maxime: Aren't you bored?
> Gilda: Why?
> Maxime: Aren't you waiting for someone?
> Gilda: No (she smiles)
> Maxime: (sitting down opposite her): With your permission. (A pause.)
> Gilda: You haven't finished your letter . . . Someone has dared to sadden you.
> Maxime: I don't think so; I've only just come in.
> Gilda: Are your eyes really that color? . . . Why do you laugh? (A pause.)
> Gilda: Call me Gilda.
> Maxime: Where do you live?
> Gilda: (giving him her hand): Let me leave alone . . . you'll regret it. I've got the syph.
> Maxime: Who cares?
>   (They leave.)

Any two actors could fill this skeleton scene with a hundred different people. But in between these lines, Breton and Soupault have filled in cloudy recollections of children ("I was dreaming I was still in boarding school"), a truth which two people know but seldom utter aloud ("I won't love you always"), with sentences whose syntax we understand but in whose noun-subject positions sit sensuous dream words ("Corridors and clouds are my whole life"). In the text the combination reads as follows:

> Maxime (sitting down opposite her): With your permission.
>   (A pause.)
> Gilda: I was dreaming that I was still in boarding school, I was wearing that lace collar one last time. They kept a sharp eye on my correspondence: an unknown man will climb over the garden wall this evening. He said to me: "You've been crying because of my mother of pearl cheeks." Night will fall. Soon there will be nothing but the windmills.

Maxime: You can take it or leave it. Interior elegance and the maddest acts of despair. To leave the church throwing candy around.

Gilda: You're not like the others.

Maxime: How can one not say to oneself several times every day: that won't come back again!

(A pause.)

Gilda: You haven't finished your letter.

Maxime: What's the good forgiving a sign of life for too long a time.

The dialogue rests on the edge of the subliminal. The syntax is deceptive. What looks like a reassuringly logical succession of phrases collapses as sentences reach their conclusion or as one sentence follows another. The first three acts do, however, subscribe to the basically conventional theatrical acceptance of character, setting, subject and activity, and to the convention of a fourth wall as well.

Act IV is a fascinating study of a different kind. The first three Acts of *S'il vous plaît* were published in *Littérature* with the exhortation at their end "The authors of *S'il vous plaît* wish the text of the 4th Act not to be published." Benedikt, writing before the fourth act had been recovered, concluded that "This is one of the many outward signs of the then contemporary movement, Dada"[51] But the act, discovered a number of years ago among Breton's papers, has since appeared in the Gallimard edition of *The Magnetic Fields*. Since it has not yet been translated into English, I quote it here in its entirety.

ACT IV

Scene 1:

The auditorium is plunged into a half-darkness. The curtain rises on a front door. Two insignificant characters, one with a cane in his hand, stop in front of the door.

X: (consulting his watch) Look at the time, I'm leaving.
    They shake hands.
Y: (paces back and forth in front of the door without saying a word. He looks upwards, rubs his arms with his hands, blows his nose).

Scene II:

A spectator in the orchestra: "That's all?"
The pacer on stage stops, looks at the interruptor with surprise, then lifts his eyes skyward and continues pacing.
    The spectator: Will you be finished soon?
One hears: Shhh!
    A second spectator: I don't understand anything. It's idiotic.
    Someone shouts from the balcony: Will you please shut up!
    The second spectator (standing): I do have the right to say what I think.
    From the balcony: You have the right to leave.
The actor is stopped.

The second spectator: I paid for my seat just like you.

The wife of the second spectator: Please, Edward, be quiet.

A voice from the audience: If at least it were amusing.

The second spectator: I repeat that I understand nothing (Applause).

It is probable that I'm not the only one (Standing on his seat). For some time now, under pretext of originality and independence, our fine art has been sabotaged by a bunch of individuals, whose number increases every day and who are for the most part, strange types, lazy fellows or practical jokers.

The curtain falls. Applause.

It is easier to get yourself talked about in this fashion than to attain true glory at the cost of hard work. Are we going to put up with the most contradictory ideas and aesthetic theories, the beautiful and the ugly, talent and force without style being placed on the same footing? I appeal to our traditional good sense. It shall not be said that the sons of Montaigne, Voltaire, Renan . . .

The spectator from the balcony: Throw him out. Continue.

The three knocks are sounded.

Scene III:

Same as the first scene. When Y pulls out his handkerchief, the second spectator stands:

The second spectator: Enough!

Cries: Yes, enough, etc.

The second spectator (to his wife): Let's go.

They exit noisily but before leaving the auditorium, the second spectator shakes his fist at the stage.

The second spectator: It's shameful.

Tumult. The curtain falls. One hears cries of "Vive la France," "Continue," etc. One calls for the authors. Two actors bow in their stead.

Curtain.

The fourth wall has crumbled and actors and audience join in a pre-dada jamboree. "Plants" have been placed in the audience, and the spectators argue among themselves as well as with the performers. The subject has disappeared, the performers have become "personal actors" and have extended to the audience, an invitation to chaos. Clearly, Breton and Soupault had sketched out for themselves a distinctive departure from conventional theatre before Tzara's arrival in Paris.

The critics who do approach the play are hard put to it to come to grips with the text. Sanouillet succumbs to calling it "play . . . composed of a series of sketches, constructed according to the best rules of dramatic art, but perfectly incoherent."[52] Esslin dismisses it as "bizarre and largely improvised,"[53] while Béhar records its plot but generally avoids any further discussion. Even Michael Benedikt dismisses the author's attempts, by describing them merely as the desire to "flaunt the usual literary goal of homogeneity of style."[54] It is only

Matthews who agrees to see the structuring of the play as "willfully discontinuous." He writes:

> Intention, not incompetence . . . underlies the incoherent plot structure . . . In aggressive fashion, Breton and Soupault demonstrate how proven ingredients can be arranged in a manner that shakes the stability of dramatic convention.[55]

Tzara had come to Paris in 1920, carrying with him the text of *La Première aventure céleste de M. Antipyrine,* and the surrealists suddenly found themselves on stage in the roles of Pipi and CriCri, standing up to their necks in paper bags and singing "zdranga, zdranga, di, di, di." Tzara's play had no identifiable context at all. It was basically 239 lines divided among 9 characters and capped by a lengthy manifesto-monologue. It was filled with pseudo-Africanese, phonetic gibberish and simultaneous-poem-chants. In performance it brought down the house.

As their contribution to the *Salle Gaveau* manifestation (May 26, 1920) Breton and Soupault brought Tzara *Vous m'oublierez,* a sketch they had written especially for the occasion. Coming to the play with this knowledge, it is hard not to see the young poets' attempts to bring an offering which would please their "master," which would be acceptable to him and which he would include in his great manifestation rites.[56] They had called their characters Umbrella, Sewing Machine, and Bathrobe, (the first two coming from that phrase of Lautréamont's which seemed to haunt the surrealists, about the fortuitous meeting of an umbrella and a sewing machine on a dissection table), in an attempt to bring them closer to M. Bleubleu than to Valentine and Paul. They had again and again repeated the meaningless question: "What then is that tree, that young leopard whom I caressed the other day upon coming home?" (four times within the first nine speeches), just to be provocative.[57] They plotted non sequitur activities (Umbrella recalls a visit to a Chateau on the Loire; Bathrobe kneels down to pray) in an attempt to destroy context. But though Tzara's obfuscated dialogue in the *Antipyrine* plays and his energy-stunted schematic configurations had had their effect on Breton and Soupault, although *Vous m'oublierez* strikingly exhibits surrealism's attempt to work within criteria set up by dada performance, the qualities which link this sketch to the earlier *S'il vous plaît,* stand out just as clearly. They indicate the independent direction taken by the surrealist sketch, which even dada could not divert.[58]

In moving so thoroughly to incorporate Lautréamont's psychosexual image into the sketch:

> The force of the image depends upon the fact that the umbrella cannot here but represent man, the sewing machine, woman (this is true in most cases of machines, except that here we deal with a machine frequently used by women, as we know for onanistic purposes), and the dissection table, the bed. . . .[59]

Breton and Soupault are bowing in a direction other than Tzara's—a fervent tribute to Lautréamont[60] and a step into a private esoteric enclave where the audience could not reach them.

> Sewing Machine: Explain it to me, and I'll leave.
> Bathrobe: No explanations.

Again, what is unique in this attempt at a dada text is that the characters relate to one another. Sewing Machine is decidedly female in the text. She says, "That means nothing to you, the honor of a woman," and one can trace her attempts to seduce Umbrella while brushing aside Bathrobe with an affectionate, "Shut up rabbit," "Shh! you red hooligan." Bathrobe is the odd man out in the love-triangle, an affectionate old geezer ("he is deaf and blue, with thunder on his hands, but in fact he's not a demanding old guy"), constantly rising from his search for some unknown object to ask "What?" as the conversation continues around him. The Lautréamont phrase and the repeated "What?" take on the rhythm of those repeated game-routines we recognize in the plays of Beckett and Ionesco,[61] even to the mocking of theatre with "This play, will it ever be over?" and "my ears are buzzing, I beg of you, be quiet . . . This has gone on long enough."

Even in a play which they wrote under Tzara's tutelage, Breton and Soupault could not abandon the experiments they had begun in *S'il vous plaît*, and in *The Magnetic Fields*. The language of surrealism was to aim at reducing reason, at persuading the imagination to surrender before the enticing images of the marvellous. It allowed a new freedom "for" rather than the dada freedom "from". The customary bearings were gone, but here was a challenge to reason rather than mere provocation. Within the surrealist sketch, poetry abounds at the expense of dialogue continuity. Bizarre images reminiscent of Breton's "There is a man cut in two by the window" which first prompted him to investigate automatic writing, recur. Such dialogue steers the mind towards a much more ephemeral seeing of the "light of the image," to which it is infinitely sensitive. Automatism had left its indelible mark. Breton and Soupault were moving forward, faithful to their program of "giving language back its full purpose" and "making cognition take a big step forward."[62]

The attitude of Breton and Soupault to these two plays and the nature of the plays in production emerges from two interviews I held with Philippe Soupault in Paris in the summer of 1971. Although some of the "facts" in the interview are contradictory or unclear, the value of this personal recollection rests in the vivid sense it provides of the young poets and their attempt at making theatre.

MELZER: M. Soupault, you and André Breton together wrote two plays which were presented at the dada manifestations in 1920. Can you tell me something about *S'il vous plaît?*

SOUPAULT: Fifty years ago, we wrote it without any hope that it would be played. We didn't know how to stage it. It was written "on a table"—not so much with the idea of staging it—so many problems: we were no actors, no director wanted to direct it, we had to do everything ourselves.

MELZER: Why did you decide to write plays at all?

SOUPAULT: Breton and I wrote *The Magnetic Fields* and we decided it would be interesting to try writing a play using these same techniques. That was *S'il vous plaît.*

MELZER: Can you tell me something about the production?

SOUPAULT: It was an extremely simple staging—"giving the importance to the text"—there was no stage setting.

MELZER: Who decided who played the roles?

SOUPAULT: André Breton and I, Breton played l'Étoile and I played "a woman" and "a man." Mlle. Doyon played the secretary. She was a friend of ours. Fraenkel agreed to play out of friendship too. There were the parts of the "two women alms-collectors." No women wanted to agree to take the parts because the characters were robbers. Paul Eluard played one and his wife, the other (Mme. Eluard is not afraid of anything). The other characters were played by "extras," young people who were part of the *Théâtre de l'Oeuvre* and who agreed to play these small roles. We rehearsed a number of times "to learn the parts," and we presented only the second act.

MELZER: Why only the second act?

SOUPAULT: The whole thing would have been too long . . . perhaps three hours. The second act was the most "spectacular." It had the greatest amount of movement, lots of entrances and exits. The other acts were more static. It was also simple to stage—it took place in an office. Also Breton wanted to play the part of Létoile and his part was biggest there.

MELZER: What ideas did you have about the staging?

SOUPAULT: There were no strange things in this act. Breton wanted it to be almost "realistic," as opposed to the first and third acts . . . the office of a businessman. I borrowed my mother's clothes to play the role of the woman. My mother was very big like me. Eluard borrowed from his mother too. Other than that the costumes were "normal." We wore no grotesque clothes, only normal make-up, and we wore hats as the women. The important thing about *S'il vous plaît* is that, it is a different kind of theatre, "a loosening of the theatre." One act had nothing to do with the other.

MELZER: Can you tell me about this mysterious fourth act which was not printed until the Gallimard edition of 1967?

SOUPAULT: The fourth act was lost. After Breton's death we looked over his papers and found it. It's very important because it's no longer just the authors who present, but the actors too. There is in this, anti-theatre—a part is given to the public. This was not usual at the time . . . an invitation for the audience to participate in the performance.

MELZER: How was the play received?

SOUPAULT: The public listened to the second act with a certain amount of attention . . . but no one understood the fourth act because there was such excitement in the audience.

(ed. at this point there was a bit of confusion for M. Soupault said that the fourth act was presented at another manifestation, then that it was presented at the *Oeuvre* after the second act, with Breton playing x, and himself, y. The question was not resolved.)

MELZER: What of *Vous m'oublierez?*

SOUPAULT: That was written especially for a dada manifestation, we wanted to do something completely different from the regular theatre . . . the theatre at that period was commercial. We were not interested in that.

MELZER: Was the production really "completely different?"

SOUPAULT: The only thing really bizarre was that Breton wore a crown of revolvers. I appeared as "Bathrobe," in a regular shirt . . . anything so as not to wear a bathrobe. Breton played "Umbrella" all in black, and Eluard played a woman, "Sewing Machine," all in white.

MELZER: What was the set like?

SOUPAULT: There was just an armchair. Breton sat in the armchair and Eluard and I moved in a circle around him saying terrible things . . . a kind of parody of classic theatre . . . a kind of tragedy.

MELZER: What is the significance of the continuing refrain, "What then is that tree, that young leopard whom I caressed the other day upon coming home?"

SOUPAULT: It had no particular meaning . . . only to create a sense of anticipation. We were a group of friends who wanted to do something scandalous . . . against the academies.

Illustration 29   The cast of Cocteau's *Le Boeuf sur le toit*, February 1920 (*Commoedia*, February 23, 1920)

Collection: Département des Arts du Spectacle, Bibliothèque de l'Arsenal

Other Theatre Influences on the Surrealists

There's no need to call ourselves artists; let
us leave that name to artists and chiropodists.

Erik Satie

While surrealist theatrics leaned heavily on the dada heritage, other performances of the period as well helped to shape a surrealist sense of the stage.

In 1920, Cocteau, continuing what had been a productive alliance with a spectacle theatre of movement and music, mounted *Le Boeuf sur le toît*, a pantomime-farce for clowns with music by Darius Milhaud. Cocteau, reacting to the mis-labeling of *Parade* as a "farce" (among other misnomers), decided to mount a real farce, modeled on Charlie Chaplin and the new art of the cinema. The production starred the Fratellini brothers (Paul, François, and Albert), famous European clowns, in the parts of the barman, the redhead, and the "woman with the décolletée." The scene was a bar in which two women, a boxer, and a Negro dwarf play billiards, throw dice and flirt. The place is raided by a policeman, but the bartender saves the day by lowering a rotating electric fan which decapitates the officer. One of the women dances triumphantly on her hands, but in the finale the bartender revives the policeman, restores his head and for this service, presents him with a bill three yards long. The cast, wearing huge papier-mâché masks,[63] appeared to be more puppets than people, which was quite in keeping with Cocteau's intention of getting away from "a false reality of real objects, real furniture, real faces."[64] There were to be no particular activities performed by the actors, and whatever was done on stage was to have no relation to the music played. The music in fact was played twice: once before the curtain rose, and again as the actors went through their paces.

The dada-surrealists turned out to see this Cocteau farce as well as his second "ballet," done a year later with the *Ballets Suédois*. *Les Mariés de la Tour Eiffel* was part of that theatrical genre which was not properly speaking ballet, nor Opera, nor Opera-Comique, surely not a "play," but a new experiment which employed dance, acrobatics, mime, drama, satire, music and the spoken word. In a twilight zone between the established theatrical genres, the rules of the game were being revised.

In *Les Mariés*, Cocteau felt that he had crystallized the theatrical schema he had been experimenting with in *Parade* and *Le Boeuf sur le toît*. Here again actor merged with object: two phonographs with actors' bodies and megaphone mouths. The two, who spoke the text of the ballet, were stationed at either side of the stage like masters of ceremonies at the music hall. The masked dancers performed a sequence of activities narrated by the two megaphone-bodies. A party of wedding guests interrupts the hunt for an ostrich on the first platform of the Eiffel Tower. The guests in turn are interrupted by a cyclist, a bathing

Illustration 30   Scenes from *Les Mariés de la Tour Eiffel* (Léon Moussinac, *"Tendances nouvelles du théâtre,"* Editions Albert Lévy) Note the two megaphones at the sides of the stage in the upper photo

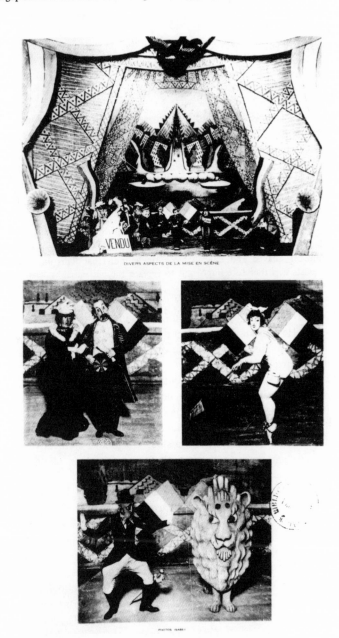

DIVERS ASPECTS DE LA MISE EN SCÈNE

beauty and a fat little boy who is hailed in a style which we associate with the Ionesco of *The Bald Soprano:*

> – He's the image of his mother.
> – He's the image of his father.
> – He's the image of his grandmother.
> – He's the image of his grandfather.

The wedding party is massacred and then reassembled; there is a dance of the telegrams, a dirge for a General, and a series of disappearing acts into the photographer's camera. All this takes place to boos and hisses from the audience at the "infantile marionettes," while the actors are having a fine time. It sounds familiar.

A year later, in 1922, in his preface to the scenario of the ballet, Cocteau wrote:

> A theatrical piece ought to be written, presented, costumed, furnished with musical accompaniment, played and danced by a single individual. This universal athlete does not exist. It is therefore important to replace the individual by what resembles an individual most: a friendly group.[65]

Cocteau's "friendly group" included *les Six,* Picasso and the ballet-masters of the new-ballet. He had moved in and out of the friendly group that was dada, and already forming in the 1921 audience of *Les Mariés* was the friendly group that would mould surrealism.

The ballet continued to furnish a vital experimental stage for the avant-garde, and what the legitimate theatre could not dare and the avant-garde could not afford, the ballet could and did. In the late spring of 1924, Picasso once again joined with Satie to mount what was to be the artist's last major work for the theatre. Working with Massine, Diaghilev's innovative choreographer, he conceived *Mercure,* a ballet with more mime than real dancing, revolving around a series of incidents in which Mercury figured. The episodes were described as "plastique poses" and in his attempt to evolve an even newer concept of the moving, set-linked actor, Picasso went further than he had gone in *Parade.* Unlike the giant mobile columns of the *Parade* managers, Picasso now created marionette-like figures, each of which was manipulated by a concealed dancer: schematic "doubles" outlined in twisted rattan on cardboard cutouts. In the scene of "The bath of the three graces," the dancers first fused with the stylized, non-perspective scenery. Collage-like, the upper bodies of the three graces emerged from a large rectangular construction whose inner surface, painted blue and tilted slightly upwards, represented water. The graces, appearing through holes cut in the surface, were men wearing long black wigs and sprouting outsize breasts painted red (recall the exaggerated breasts in *The*

Breasts of Tirésias). Emerging from the bath, the graces then appeared, each behind his own "practicable," whose rattan lattice-work allowed the head to move up and down. Accompanying them was the figure of Cerberus, another "practicable" consisting of a large circle and two legs, decorated with a group of animal heads.

This ballet was received with almost as much hostility as *Parade*. The audience found it derisive and offensively erotic with intent to shock. Even Cyril Beaumont of the Diaghilev ballet called the whole thing "incredibly stupid, vulgar and pointless."[66] The surrealists in the audience were distressed for their own particular reasons. The ballet had been presented under the auspices of the Comte Étienne de Beaumont, as part of a season of ultra modern works for the benefit of the Aid to War Widows and the Committee for Aid to Russian Refugees. This group had won the patronage of M. le Président de la République and Mme. Millerand, M. le Président du Conseil and Mme. Poincaré, M. le Maréchal Foch and his wife, as well as a group of diplomats and ambassadors. The surrealists, incensed that Picasso, one of their idols, should agree to work "for the benefit of the international aristocracy," could not restrain themselves from demonstrating violently on the evening of the performance.[67] They could not, however, deny Picasso's impressive, imaginative daring, and so, after the screaming and yelling was over, a letter of apology appeared in the *Paris Journal* of June 20, 1924. It was entitled "Hommage à Picasso."

> There have been so many anodyne manifestations in the realms of art and thought during recent years that we have lost sight of their real purpose and even of the way things are developing, which is all that matters. The public and the critics are in agreement to encourage only mediocrity and every sort of concession. It is therefore our duty to put on record our deep and whole-hearted admiration for Picasso, who defies consecration and goes on creating a troubling modernity at the highest levels of expression.
>
> > signed: Louis Aragon, Georges Auric, André Breton, Robert Desnos, Max Ernst, Benjamin Peret, Francis Poulenc, Philippe Soupault, Roger Vitrac.[68]

In that same year, 1924, Picabia, long wearied of the dadas and already engaged in a private feud with Breton, mounted his own ballet, *Relâche (Performance Cancelled)*, in collaboration with Erik Satie and the Ballets Suédois. Though Picasso was at that moment in favor with the surrealists, Satie was not, and Picabia's collaboration with Satie was the beginning of a theatrical spit-in-the-eye at Breton. Picabia, the anti-dada dada, would out-dada them all with his performance concept.

The name of the ballet was the first provocative act: *Performance Cancelled*. The scenario was composed of two acts, a cinematic intermission, and "the dog's tail" at the end. There was no decor.[69] The set consisted of three doorways; one behind the other, covered with circular metal disks, each of which had an electric bulb shining in the center. Short scenes followed one another in the manner of the music hall. A chain-smoking fireman spent the whole evening pouring water from one bucket to another. Man Ray sat out the performance on a chair near the edge of the stage. Occasionally he would stand and walk back and forth. Spot-lights were beamed directly into the eyes of the audience, making it difficult to see what was going on, and a naked man and woman (the man was Marcel Duchamp) in the poses of Cranach's *Adam and Eve* were intermittently illuminated. The intermission featured Picabia's film "Entr'acte," directed with the assistance of René Clair, a then unknown cameraman. This was not the first time that an intermission had been filled with performance elements;[70] it was, however, the first time that music had been especially written for a film. The film itself was full of astonishing visual conceits. Jean Borlin, dressed in a gauze ballet "tutu," performed his leaps, the camera catching him from below through a glass plate. Marcel Duchamp and Man Ray were seen playing a game of chess on the roof of the *Théâtre des Champs-Elysées* (in which theatre the performance was actually taking place). Erik Satie, who had composed the music for the film, stood by, overseeing the game. In the dada tradition, the group was unable to get away from using itself as subject and object, as creator, performer, and audience at the same time. Finally there came a funeral procession in slow motion, the hearse plastered with posters, the sobbing members of the family bearing wreaths of bread, only to be astonished by the emergence of a grinning corpse from the coffin, a corpse who proceeded to make all the mourners disappear as if by magic.

In the second act of *Relâche*, the provocation increased. Costumes were changed in full view of the audience. Posters hung across the stage saying "Satie is the greatest musician in the world," and "If you're not satisfied, buy a whistle for two sous from the attendant." As a fitting finale, the authors drove onto the stage in a 5 h.p. Citroën to the jeers and catcalls of the audience.

For Rolf de Maré, the performance was traumatic, for it forced the dissolution of his *Ballets Suédois:*

> Relâche was too much for all of us. This conception was contrary to our Nordic spirit. If the ballet was going to move in this direction, then we Scandinavians could no longer 'humbly' serve art as in the past . . . it was impossible for us to go forward, to remain on the path that opened in front of us, and equally impossible to turn back. Up to now we had felt the breath of modern life and translated it into dances; but now we had reached the decisive point at which its downward slope was anathema to us.[71]

Not everyone felt that way. Fernand Léger championed the performance, writing,

. . . to hell with the scenario and all literature! *Relâche* is a lot of kicks in a lot of backsides, whether hallowed or not. . . . The author, the dancer, the acrobat, the screen, the stage, all these means of "presenting a performance" are integrated and organized to achieve a total effect. One single aim: to bring the stage to life. All prejudices come crashing down.[72]

Avant-garde performances, however, were not the only ones to attract the young surrealists. Another kind of theatre continued to play the Parisian boards week after week, creating no scandals but always filling the house. This was the theatre of the boulevards where Sacha Guitry moved the hearts of husbands, wives and lovers around the stage ("Two men are not too many to give a woman all the love she needs"), where Maurice Donnay spoke of money to the *nouveau riche* of the *après-guerre,* and where Feydeau (who died in 1921) raced his characters in and out of doors in frenetic meetings and flights.

The war had effected certain changes in the boulevard theatres. The artist's flat had replaced the living room, telephone calls served instead of unexpected visits, and the lover had discarded his moustache. But the emphasis on craftsmanship which stemmed from the formula of the well-made play, with its neatly turned plots, comic objects, and series of coincidences, still reigned. And the emphasis on temperament and the passion of love continued to satisfy the public. On one level, a play such as Aragon's *L'Armoire à glace un beau soir,*[73] exists as a parody of that genre of boulevard drama which had the husband coming home after a hard day's business, only to discover his wife's lover hidden in the wardrobe.[74] Writing for an audience familiar with this schema, Aragon was assured of causing laughter by the manipulation of several well-recognized formulae. The husband, in contrast to the boulevard pattern of action, persists in delaying the opening of the closet while the wife, confessing that indeed she has taken a lover, urges her mate to open the wardrobe door. The author indulges in high-flown romantic language which always lacks just enough thrust to remain high-flown: "I'm going to clutch you in my arms as the young handsome Roman does the Sabine woman in the painting a copy of which is at the lady attorney's office."[75] He mocks the passions of this drama, and its clichés ("Madame, you're deceiving me"):

Lenore: Oh, Oh, here is his anger now. He'll begin to beat you, to crush you beneath his blows . . . Don't pull my hair, don't bruise my wrists.
Jules: Come on now, Leni, aren't you going to cook supper?

He chooses specific activities easily associated with well known farces: Jules, playing with the matches he has collected from the floor, proceeds to count them and set them in rows while talking with Lenore:

Jules: One, two; one, two; one, two ...
Lenore: The hammer, if I have a lover.
Jules: Not savage enough, one two ...
Lenore: You've loved me like the morning air.
Jules: One, two, the fragrance of strawberries, one two ...

In a similar scene in *Pots of Money* by Labiche and Delacour, the characters Boursey and Felix continue to count the coins in a pot while engaging in serious conversation:

Felix: Two, three ... to experience a feeling that can only be called ...
Boursey: One, two ...
Felix: Six, seven ... that can only be called love.

In addition, Aragon uses the phrase "the drama" to create that self-conscious awareness of the mocking of a theatre, the awareness of a game being played:

Jules: The drama: but I'm going to clutch you in my arms ...
Lenore: Blunderer: drama gone wrong ...
Jules: I can't stand these dramas we keep playing.

Fascinated by popular culture, the surrealists

crowded to the Cinéma Parisiana to see *L'Étreinte de la Pieuvre* (the Grip of the Octopus), to the *Théâtre Moderne* to enjoy the stupid plays performed there, or at the *Porte Saint-Martin*. The most ridiculous shows were the most prized, for they put on the stage the popular sentiments and emotions that had not yet been spoiled by culture.[76]

The new American cinema was especially attractive to the Breton group. They flocked to the films of Charlie Chaplin (which arrived in Paris in March, 1915), to the Mack Sennet Keystones, and the Pearl White serials. As Matthew Josephson recalls:

I also furnished them with a goodly store of recent "Americana" in the form of "Krazy Kat" cartoon serials by George Herriman. . . . These were exhibited to my French friends Soupault, Aragon, Breton as "pure American Dada humor."[77]

In the cinema, a new tempo jostled the audience—broken rhythms and a speed of change in place and time that allowed for no time to sit back. The American girl in Cocteau's *Parade* imitated Chaplin's peculiar walk and Soupault, for a time, gave himself over wholly to film as an inspiration for his "poèmes cinématographiques." *Fantômas* and Detective Juve influenced the second Act of *S'il vous plaît* and Max Jacob wrote a four-part poem about the dedicated detective and the arch-criminal. Here were a series of influences generally considered antithetical to accepted literary tradition, but as Soupault wrote, "Littérature alone does not suffice the new generation."

Tzara's Fourth Play

By 1924, Tzara himself had written a play which seemed to signal the end of dada performance. If the dada master could write *Mouchoir de Nuages (Handkerchief of Clouds)*, then the movement, in performance terms, had truly worked itself out.

> *Mouchoir de Nuages* is an ironic tragedy or a tragic farce in fifteen short acts, separated by fifteen commentaries. The action, which partakes of the realm of the serialized novel and the cinema, takes place on a platform set in the middle of the stage.[78]

In taking off from the cinema of Mack Sennet and the Perils of Pauline, or the endless *Fantômas* series, Tzara was remaining true to a first love of the dada/surrealists. The play itself, however, embodies a serious commitment to the art of the stage, a commitment no one would have dared expected of Tzara in 1920. A page and a half of stage directions opens the text, giving careful details as to the manner in which the work is to be mounted:

> The action takes place in a closed space, like a box, from which the actors cannot leave. All five sets are the same color. In the back, at a certain height, there is a screen that indicates where the action occurs, by means of reproductions blown up from illustrated post cards. These are rolled up on two rollers by a stagehand, who is visible at all times to the audience.
>
> In the middle of the playing area there is a platform. To the right and the left are chairs, makeup tables, properties and the actors' costumes. The actors are on the set for the duration of the play. When they are not performing, they turn their backs to the audience, change costumes, or talk among themselves.
>
> The primary action in each act takes place on the platform, while the Commentators operate in the playing area in front and to the side. At the end of each act, the lighting changes abruptly so that only the Commentators are lit; the actors then leave the stage. The lighting also changes abruptly at the end of each Commentary, when the light projectors light only the platform. The electricians and the reflectors are also visible.
>
> Two stagehands bring on or take off the props from the stage. All the actors in the play keep their own names. In the present edition, the characters have the names of the actors who created their roles. The Poet, the Wife of the Banker and the Banker are the principal characters. A, B, C, D, and E are the Commentators, who also play all the secondary roles.[79]

That Tzara would take such care to spell out directives on the art of the theatre, is a new departure for the former dada. The style he chooses takes as much from

Pirandello as from the cinema: the actor remains "on stage" throughout the performance, changes costumes and make-up before the audience, and is addressed by his real name instead of bearing the name of a character. Here Tzara recalls as well his own work as the "personal actor" in Zurich and at the Paris manifestations. The audience had come to see Tzara on stage—in *La Première aventure céleste,* he read his manifesto as "Tristan Tzara." In *Mouchoir de Nuages,* however, Tzara has left M. Antipyrine far behind.

Tzara's fourth play has a clear plot which works itself out through some 70 pages of text. The characters speak and relate directly to one another and there's not a simultaneous poem to be found. As in Aragon's *L'Armoire à glace,* many moments have the ring of boulevard theatre:

> The Poet: (Seated. A valet hands him a letter. He reads it aloud:)
> "Dear Sir,
>> Though the times are hard and not very propitious for adventure, and in spite of the omens that the Heavens send me every day in different forms, just like the rates of exchange and the values of the stock market of the heart, I still let myself write to you.

or,

> Andrea: But why so quickly, so quickly . . . I would like you to have a memento . . . What can I give you? . . . Take this black velvet half-mask, souvenir of the masked ball—in the middle of which you taught me to live a life contrary to that which I had in me.

yet with just enough humour to let the audience know where the playwright stands:

> Andrea: . . . Excuse me sir, could you tell me the name of this place?

> Stationmaster: You are in the "Peak of the Sentimental Consolidation," some miles from the border, 2,300 meters in altitude, on the 37th Meridian, pleasant climate, especially recommended by leading doctors to people who have nothing wrong them. Strong alpine sensations. Winter sports. The "Peak of the Sentimental Consolidation" is nicknamed the "Himalaya of the Poor."

Tzara was cautious as well to dissociate himself from any connection with the surrealists by making it quite clear that any discontinuity, use of gauze curtain, or flashback technique had nothing to do with the world of the dream:

> The vagueness of forms has nothing to do with the dream. It merely indicates that the scenes, in their logical progression within the acts, do not take place within the normal flow of time.[80]

Conclusion

By 1924, the attraction of the dada manifestations and the dada variety of scandal had paled. With the departure of Tzara from the dada-surrealist cenacle, no one remained who was capable of revitalizing the realigned surrealists into a new performing unit, and the performing of plays was taken over by professional or semi-professional theatres. What had happened to the movement's strong theatrical bent? Perhaps Breton associated the general depression that afflicted him between 1921 and 1924 with the ranging series of performances he had compelled himself to participate in, all the while denying the many negative feelings the performances had raised in him.

By 1924 however, it no longer seemed that surrealism's inability or unwillingness to continue dada performance, or any performance at all, was simply a product of Breton's temperament. Nor was it even a decision made on artistic grounds, e.g. that something in the nature of dada-surrealist performance itself was self-defeating. With his shift into the political arena, Breton became more conscious of what he considered the compromising role *all* theatre assumed in relation to its audience. Theatre was the celebrant at society's feast and Breton, who was just beginning to crystallize his revolt against society, was unwilling to play lackey to any commercial venture. Artaud and Vitrac were bounced from the movement for dealing in tickets and auditoriums. Picasso was castigated for contributing (with his *Mercure*), to the evening-out of Maréchal Foch. And when Tzara himself had his most recent play performed before Paris high-society (*Mouchoir de Nuages,* 1924), Breton's rage knew no bounds. The revolt was not against dada performance, or against the medium of theatre itself, but rather against the theatre's parasitic need for society once that theatre had been taken out of the context of the "groupe amical"—Cocteau's "friendly group" which was capable of creating and maintaining a theatre without impresarios or box offices, without professional performers or a dependence upon an audience. Tzara had retreated from the Paris-dadas in 1923. Within a year of his departure the former dada group had splintered about Breton. Breton himself was incapable of fashioning a performance group, nor did he want to. As he watched his former performing colleagues taking their plays to professional theatres, he showered on them all the wrath of a young politician fiercely feeling the need to make his revolutionary politics visible.

By the end of 1924, then, the playing arena of surrealist performance had shifted. So had the attitudes of the surrealists towards performance itself. Whatever family resemblances there had been among the surrealist sketches blurred as the members of the family separated and moved on.

This has been the story of André Breton, "the glass of water in a storm," Philippe Soupault, "the musical urinal," Louis Aragon, "the glass syringe,"

Georges Ribemont-Dessaignes, "the steam man," Hans Arp, "clear wrinkles," Théodore Fraenkel, "the great Earth serpent,"[81] and their meeting with the pale, dark-haired, grey-eyed little man who wore a monocle. "If I had come to Paris to improve myself," Tzara had stated in 1920, "I would read *Littré*, the big *Littré* dictionary. There is an admirable work of the highest art. I keep it at my bedside; begin reading at 'Z' and go backwards."[82]

Tzara's arrival in Paris, however, had nothing to do with improving himself. The dada Emperor from Zurich ravaged the French capital in an attempt to satisfy the rapacious appetites of his monster-manifestations. Before the hungry jaws he set audience after audience and the morning papers implored, "For God's sake, don't write about it, and maybe it will go away."

Yet dada was a force which would not just go away. Dada had cried "We want nothing, above all nothing new," and yet dada had "made cubism dance on the stage." Dada had cried "there is a great negative work of destruction to be accomplished," but dada was surely more than a destructive movement. As William Seitz points out,

> despite themselves, in pointing to negative values they encountered beauty . . . in stressing unsureness, accident, confusion, disunity and discontinuity, Dada released a constellation of physical and intellectual energies through which the artist could (and still can) operate in a way that at least in the West, was previously impossible.[83]

The currents of the post-war Parisian avant-garde and Tzara's dada met and ignited the *Littérature* poets in 1920, and for two years Paris burned. Not only was the blue of the flame felt in the theatre, but through performance, the long fortified barriers between the arts came tumbling down. Painting became partner to poetry, poetry turned to sound and music. Arp and Janco became actors and Satie wrote a play. Duchamp appeared nude on stage and even the stage-shy Picabia finally crossed the proscenium in his own ballet. Max Ernst's "frottage" technique yielded the images of animal, vegetable, and cosmological fantasies. Breton, Desnos and Peret wrote a play for insects and monkeys. De Chirico's brother, the poet Savinio, had been in close contact with the Zurich dadas and had invented a "manichino," an anthropomorphic thing-figure. De Chirico himself drew hallucinatory visions of the object and in Desnos' *La Place de l'Etoile*, hundreds of starfish proliferate over the world of the scene. Breton in "Le Surréalisme et la Peinture" wrote: "The eye exists in a savage state," and Buñuel, in his early film *Un Chien Andalou*, shows a razorblade slicing into an eyeball, as a crescent moon cuts into a cloud. All of the techniques of one art seemed to stand ready to serve all the others. There were simultaneous poems and costumes painted in simultaneous color, bruitist concerts were given with intruments and as part of the readings of poems, with voices. "Spontaneity" and "chance" invaded the atelier and the auditorium.

In Paris, as in Zurich, a sense of "group" had been of paramount importance. Breton chose to live among the artists of Montparnasse; Miro and Masson shared adjoining studios on the rue Blomet; Eluard, Dali and Gala lived a *ménage à trois*. The entire group of *Littérature* poets turned out to see Picasso's work on *Parade* and *Mercure*, Cocteau's *Les Mariés and Le Boeuf*, and performed their various gallery-stints among the paintings of their colleagues. In writing as in performing, "collaboration" was the word.

Conditioned as we are to anti-theatre, to expressions of the futility of attempts at communication, to attacks on the audience, we may tend to underestimate the impact and unsettling nature of dada and surrealist performance in its time. Dada and surrealism were the *delirium tremens* of the crisis of sensibility which began with romanticism. The hallucinations and the dances of the convulsive state were played out before an audience for as long as the audience held and until the group disintegrated.

When Artaud wrote *Le jet de sang* in 1924, his nurse with the big breasts which disappear echoed Apollinaire's Tirésias, his hands, feet, colonnades and temples falling slowly as if in a vacuum repeated the world of de Chirico's 1914 paintings. By then the period of the dada-surrealist group and the great dada-surrealist theatre events had drawn to a close. At the end of 1924, Yvan Goll planned the opening of his "Théâtre surréaliste." It was to mount the plays of Apollinaire, Albert-Birot, Georg Kaiser and Mayakowski, directed by Meyerhold, the futurist Prampolini, and Gaston Baty. The project had been planned and announced months in advance. Internationally noted directors had been invited to mount the plays of authors who were part of the avant-garde establishment. A respectable theatre had been rented and the entire project was under the artistic direction of one man, Goll. The project never materialized, but even if it had, this "surrealist theatre" would have been a far cry from the dada performances. On the other hand, though much had been written about Artaud's 1927 venture, the *Théâtre Alfred Jarry*, this avant-garde theatre venture has not yet been placed in its correct context—a theatre surely influenced by all the dada-surrealist performance work which Artaud had witnessed.

Tristan Tzara, recalled by Gide as a charming man with a young wife who was "even more charming,"[84] fought with the French Resistance during World War II and later joined the Communist party. André Breton, when he died in 1966, was accompanied to his grave by "waves of young men and young girls often in couples, with arms entwined." They had come from all over France to pay him tribute. Philippe Soupault became a respected editor, critic and radio commentator and Louis Aragon moved to the forefront of the French Communist party—a highly successful historical novelist who disliked talking about his days as a surrealist. There are moments when the whole dada-surrealist performance world looks like some great dada swindle perpetrated on the only too fallible researcher and critic. It is all true, however. Tzara paraded around the stage in a top hat crowned with a lighted candle, Hugo Ball was carried off in a sweat after having recited "gadgi beri bimba." Mme. Gaveau was splashed with rotten tomatoes. Eluard fell into the scenery of *Le Coeur à Gaz*. It remains only to believe it.

A Note on Kurt Schwitters
and Berlin Dada Performance

All that an artist spits out is art.

Kurt Schwitters

In the transition from dada to surrealist performance, the work of the Zurich group proves most important, for Tzara, through his personal relationship with Picabia, his correspondence with Breton, and his editorship of *Dada* I, II, and III, forged the ties that were to move dada performance into the Parisian theatrical avant-garde. Still, outside of the Zurich circle there was the theatre of Berlin dada, and the one-man performance art of Kurt Schwitters.

Schwitters met the dadas in Berlin in 1918. At that time he was living in Hanover, writing poetry, and working on collages made of cheese wrappers, old shoe-soles, wires, feathers—the flotsam and jetsam of everyday life. These works he called MERZ, a label taken from the word COMMERZ (which had once found its way into one of his collages), and applied throughout his career to all the varied art-works he produced. There were Merz pictures and Merz plastics; his home, each room worked into a different private environment, he called "Merzbau" and finally he identified himself as "Merz." In this autobiographical bias, Schwitters resembled the dadas in their desire to fuse art and life. His aesthetic discipline became a way of life: the objects he lived with he worked into his art, his "Merzbau"[1] became a backdrop and set for his real life. By 1919, the walls and the floors had become so crowded with collages and free-standing objects that there was no distinction between the room and the interior architecture. The rooms in their different settings were given names: Cathedral of Erotic Misery, Great Grotto of Love, Lavatory Attendant of Life, Sex-Murder Cave. From here it was but a small step to a concept of theatre which Schwitters began to develop in *Sturm-Bühne* (1919), a volume devoted to theatre projects. In 1920 he wrote:

> . . . the composite Merz work of art, par excellence . . . is the Merz stage . . . all parts of the Merz stage-work are inseparably bound up together; it cannot be written, read or listened to, it can only be produced in the theatre. Up until now, a distinction was made between stage-set, text and score in theatrical performances. Each factor was separately prepared and could also be separately enjoyed. The Merz stage knows only the fusing of all factors into a composite work. Materials for the stage-set are

all solid, liquid and gaseous bodies, such as white wall, man, barbed wire entangle-
ment, blue distance, light cone. Use is made of compressible surfaces, or surfaces
capable of dissolving into mushes; surfaces that fold like curtains, expand or shrink.
Objects will be allowed to move and revolve, and lines will be allowed to broaden
into surfaces. Parts will be inserted into the set and parts will be taken out.[2]

While this sense of the function of the stage echoes Wagner's concept of "Gesamtkunstwerk," its real link is rather with dada, in its blurring of the distinctions between the arts (rather than integrating them into an organic whole), and
its using the various media and their parts not to create an orderly synthesis but
rather an anarchic confusion. The materials were not to be used logically, and in
fact the more intensively the work of art destroyed rational objective logic, the
greater its artistic potential. Materials for the text were "all experiences," but
most important was "forget the written word."[3] The movement of the set may
take place silently, or accompanied by noises or music. The score, (as in the
music of the futurists and in the later dada experiments) is composed of "all
tones and noises capable of being produced by violin, drum, trombone, sewing
machine, grandfather clock, stream of water, etc."[4] All of experience in its
primal disorder may be brought into play:

> Take gigantic surfaces, conceived as infinite, cloak them in color and shift them
> menacingly. . . . Paste smoothing surfaces over one another. . . . Make lines fight
> together and caress one another in generous tenderness. . . . Bend the lines, crack
> and smash angles . . . let a line rush by, tangible in wire. . . . Then take wheels and
> axles, hurl them up and make them sing (mighty erections of aquatic giants). Axles
> dance mid wheel roll globes barrels. Cogs flair teeth, find a sewing machine that
> yawns. . . . Take a dentist's drill, a meat grinder, a car-track scraper, take buses and
> pleasure cars, bicycles, tandems, and their tires, also ersatz wartime tires and deform
> them. . . . Take petticoats and other kindred articles, shoes and false hair, also ice
> skates and throw them into place where they belong, and always at the right
> time. . . . Inner tubes are highly recommended. Take in short everything from the
> hairnet of the high-class lady to the propeller of the S/S Leviathan, always bearing in
> mind the dimensions required by the work.
> Even people can be used. . . .
> Now begin to wed your materials to one another. For example you marry the
> oilcloth table cover to the Home Owners' Loan Association, you bring the lamp
> cleaner into a relationship with the marriage between Anna Blume and A-natural,
> concert pitch. . . . You make a human walk on his (her) hands and wear a hat on his
> (her) feet. . . . A splashing of foam.
> And now begins the fire of musical saturation. Organs backstage sing and say:
> "Futt, futt." The sewing machine rattles along in the lead. A man in the wings says:
> "Bah." Another suddenly enters and says "I am stupid." (All rights reserved.) Be-
> tween them a clergy man kneels upside down, and cries out and prays in a loud
> voice: "Oh mercy seethe and swarm disintegration of amazement Hallelujah boy,
> boy marry drop of water." A water pipe drips uninhibited monotony. Eight.[5]

The Merz stage was never actualized. Although it interested the actor and director Franz Rolan who had related ideas, Schwitters himself felt it unrealizable. He nonetheless continued work on the stage through 1923, developing the plans for a less radical theatre which he called "Normalbühne Merz." For this he conceived of a space stage in which the machinery constituted a visible part of the aesthetic of the event. Here, however, there was none of the visionary intoxication of the Merzbühne: the stage was functional, written work was restored, the actor returned in a role of primary importance while once again the stage returned to an accompanying position:

> The stage is an accompaniment to the action of the play. It should be as simple and inconspicuous as possible, so that the action comes to the fore. The normal stage employs the simplest forms and colors—straight lines, the circle, the flat surface, cubes, parts of cubes—black, gray, white, red. The parts are constructed and painted so simply that it is easy to relate them to one another. . . . Everything should be built as lightly as possible to make changing the scene and transporting the production on tour as easy as possible. The normal stage should provide a background and accompaniment for any play that, as good drama ought to be, is essentially action. . . . The normal stage is objective, is practical is inexpensive.[6]

Except for a warm and continuing relationship with Arp, Schwitters' meeting with the Berlin and Zurich dada groups was not a fruitful one. In 1918, Huelsenbeck rejected his attempt to join the dadas because of his "bourgeois face"[7] and the Berlin dadas resented his close attachments to *Der Sturm* which they attacked as a stronghold of Expressionism. They also resented Schwitters' refusal to take part in their program of political agitation. Schwitters was rebuffed by George Grosz in a scene worthy of dada. Schwitters, arriving at the home of Grosz, rang the bell and Grosz opened the door:

> "Good morning, Herr Grosz. My name is Schwitters."
> "I am not Grosz," answered the other and slammed the door. There was nothing to be done.
> Halfway down the stairs, Schwitters stopped suddenly and said, "Just a moment."
> Up the stairs he went, and once more rang Grosz's bell. Grosz, enraged by this continual jangling, opened the door, but before he could say a word, Schwitters said, "I am not Schwitters, either." And went downstairs again.[8]

The two men never met again, and Schwitters remained basically a loner.

In 1919, in the Polish periodical *Blok*, Schwitters wrote:

> Blok has asked me to write about Dadaism, actually I am not a Dadaist. . . . In his encounter with Dadaism the individual senses a mortal enemy, and starts to fight back. . . . In those days, Dada had to pick fights with everyone and everything.[9]

Schwitters' work, however, remained close to that of the dadas. The process whereby the work was created, remained for Schwitters as for the dadas, more important than the product. In his 1920 essay on "Merz" he declared, "The medium is as unimportant as I myself. Essential is only the forming."[10] In his experiments with process Schwitters became a performer: he roamed Prague, Holland, Switzerland and France performing with Theo van Doesburg (the dean of Dutch dada and leader of the de Stijl movement), toured Czechoslovakia with Raoul Hausmann and performed in his native Hanover as well. In 1922, Schwitters wrote to Van Doesburg:

> I very much like your proposal for a Dada tour of Holland. I shall be glad to take part and I write to tell you so immediately. You ask what I'd like to do on the tour. We must discuss this. I have a number of turns, material enough for several evenings. But if all the other gentlemen you name take part, there'll only be a quarter hour for each. If we could rehearse, we might do something all together, maybe a sketch in 5 languages, nobody understanding the others. The grouping is very good. . . . We could rehearse at Hausmann's or at my place. We already were planning to do something together, making a racket. If Hausmann can find the time, we'll work it up. What we have in mind is a lecture alternating abstract poetry and dance with a noisy accompaniment of our own. Should I have to recite something myself, the question is whether I can speak German in Holland. In any case, people will want to hear me recite my Anna Blume poem, and I can do it in German, English, and French, one right after the other. Also I could recite the poem "Wand" (made up of one word), 3 number-poems (if you'll tell me the numbers in Dutch), and some phonetic poems, which, without sense and without language, can be understood by any Dutch-man—Ddssnnr-Je-M-Mp-Mpf-Mpft-Mpftl-etc. I'm sure with a little thought we can come up with the right thing. As for the honorarium, I hope and assume it will be share and share alike. . . .[11]

The evolution of this type of poetry-performance allowed Schwitters to do dramatic recitations of the alphabet or merely simple recitations of letters in sequence. The most famous of Schwitters experiments in phonetic poetry were his "Anna Blume" published in *Der Sturm* in 1919, and his "Ursonate," created in 1923. The "Ursonate," which begins with the line "Fümms bö wö tää zää Uu." was inspired by a phonetic poem of Raoul Hausmann's which begins, "fmsbwtäzäu." Schwitters had met Hausmann in Berlin in 1918, and in the fall of 1921 they went to Prague where they gave a soirée at the Produce exchange. Of his experience with Schwitters, Hausmann wrote:

> The day after the soirée we began our return trip. Schwitters . . . did not mention my phonetic poem until the day we visited a famous waterfall in the Saxon Alps. The first thing that morning, Kurt began: "fmsbwtazau, fmsbwtazau, pgiff, pgiff, mu—"; he did not stop all day until we saw that hydraulic miracle. . . . On our way back, Schwitters again started on his "fms, fms," and "fmsbw," it became a bit much. This was the starting point of his "Ursonate." First Schwitters recited my poem at the Sturm, calling it "Portrat Raoul Hausmann," and later, around 1923,

Illustration 31   *Merz 24* "Ursonate," Kurt Schwitters, Merzverlag, Hanover, 1932

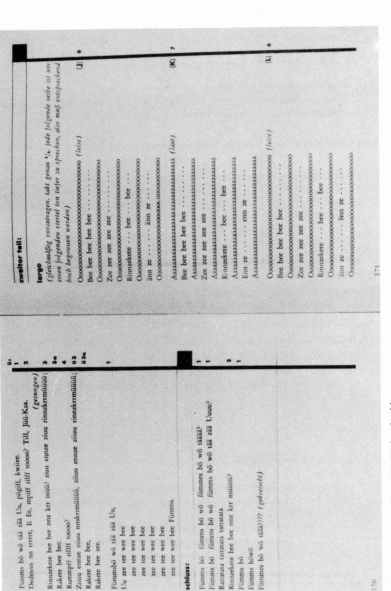

Collection: Dr. and Mrs. H.J. Kleinschmidt

he enlarged it considerably by repeating lines as many as fifty times, and lastly, in 1932, he composed the Scherzo "lanke trr gll" and other parts and published the whole under the heading "Ursonate" in his "Merz no. 24."[12]

For Schwitters the value of abstract poetry was to nail down word against word, as in a collage, object against object:

You wear your hat upon your feet and walk around on your hands, upon your hands you walk. Halloo, your red dress, sawn [sic] up in white pleats. Red I love Anna Blume, red I love your!–you ye you your, I your, you my.–We?[13]

Schwitters' poetry was theatre, valid and coming alive only when recited:

Sound poetry is only consistent with logic when it is created in actual performance and not written down. . . . To the reciter, written poetry is merely raw material. It makes no difference to him whether his raw material is poetry or not. It is possible to speak the alphabet, which is purely functional in its origins in such a way that the result is a word [sic] of art.[14]

At one soirée, Schwitters performed a poem consisting only of the letter "W". He started to recite it "with slowly rising voice. The consonant varied from a whisper to the sound of a wailing siren till at the end he barked with a shockingly loud tone."[15] Letters had no absolute sounds, they only contained the empirical possibilities of sounds which could be interpreted by the performer. Arp, recalling Schwitters at practice on the 'Ursonate,' wrote:

He hissed, whistled, chirped, fluted, spelled letters. The sounds he made were superhuman, seductive, siren-like; they might have sparked a new theory, like the twelve-tone system.[16]

And Hans Richter wrote:

But what Schwitters made of the poem, and the way he spoke it, were totally unlike Hausmann. Hausmann always gave the impression that he harboured a dark menacing hostility to the world. His extremely interesting phonetic poems, resembled as he spoke them, imprecations distorted by rage, cries of anguish, bathed in cold sweat of tormented demons.

Schwitters was a totally free spirit; he was ruled by Nature. No stored-up grudges, no repressed impulses. Everything came straight from the depths, without hesitation, like Athena from the head of Zeus, ready-made, fully-armed and never seen before.[17]

On paper the text looked like the grammar of some little known language but in a letter to Hausmann, Schwitters sent his friend a "key" to the pronunciation of his phonetic poems–definitely having decided to adopt German spelling and pronunciation.

The poetry-performances were satisfying for Schwitters and he was continually offering himself for readings. In *Merz 20* (1927), he wrote:

> My poems led me to public readings, and I have already appeared in many places, among others, Amsterdam, Berlin, Braunschweig, Bremen, Delft, Dragten, Dresden, Einbeck, The Hague, Haarlem, Hamburg, Hanover, s'Hertogenbosch, Hildesheim, Holzminden, Jena, Leer, Leiden, Leipzig, Luneburg, Magdeburg, Prague, Rotterdam, Sellin, Utrecht, Weimar, Zwickau. Now it is one place, now another. Wiesbaden, Frankfurt, Paris, and Cologne are in prospect. I recite willingly and with great enthusiasm, and I should be grateful for opportunities elsewhere. Please write to me.[18]

Schwitters first performed his "Ursonate" in 1924 at the home of a Frau Kiepenhauer in Potsdam. The poem lasted 35 minutes in performance, contained four movements, a prelude, and a cadenza in the fourth movement. The "words" used do not exist in any language though they might exist in any language. They have no logical, only an emotional context, and affect the listener with their phonetic vibration, like music.

Those invited to the Potsdam performance were the elite of the city: a corps of retired generals and the remnants of Prussian nobility. Such an audience, with absolutely no experience whatever of anything modern, was caught unaware by Schwitters' hisses, roars and crowings.

> At first they were completely baffled, but after a few minutes the shock began to wear off. For another five minutes, protest was held in check by the respect due to Frau Kiepenhauer's house. But this restraint served only to increase the inner tension . . . two generals pursed their lips as hard as they could to stop themselves laughing. Their faces, above their upright collars, turned first red, then slightly bluish. And then they lost control. They burst out laughing, and the whole audience, freed from the pressure that had been building up inside them, exploded in an orgy of laughter. The dignified old ladies, the stiff generals, shrieked with laughter, gasped for breath, slapped their thighs, choked themselves.[19]

Schwitters, all six feet of him, not in the least put out by the response, only increased the volume of his recitation and improvised a melodic line above the continuo of the laughter, riding out the storm until somehow the mood shifted. A sudden calm descended upon the audience who now heard the poem out to its end. Their response was unexpected:

> The same generals, the same rich ladies, who had previously laughed until they cried, now came to Schwitters, again with tears in their eyes, almost stuttering with admiration and gratitude. Something had been opened up within them. Something they had never expected to feel: a great joy.[20]

In his travels as a performing artist, Schwitters further experimented in natural sound and with the performer-audience relationship as well. With Raoul

Hausmann, Schwitters performed in Prague in September of 1921, at a recital entitled "Anti-Dada and Merz." The audience, which had come expecting a scandal, was disarmed by the "novelty and perfection" of the program. With Hausmann again, Schwitters gave a Merz-matinée in Hanover on December 30, 1923. One of the acts consisted of the two men standing on a darkened stage: Hausmann held the switch to an electric light while Schwitters recited one of his poems. After every other line Hausmann turned on the light revealing himself in a grotesque pose. What resulted was an alternation between noisy darkness and the visual impact of Hausmann's silent grotesqueries.

With Theo van Doesburg, Schwitters appeared at the inaugural lecture of what was to be a dada Congress in The Hague in 1923. The Congress itself never materialized, for the dadas, a bit anxious about the reaction they would get in "respectable" Holland, never appeared. Van Doesburg and Schwitters, however, were a smash success. It had been decided that van Doesburg would explain dada and Schwitters would provide an example of a dada act. Van Doesburg appeared on the platform in a tuxedo and tails, monocled, and with his face painted white. Sometime during the lecture, van Doesburg was to stop for a drink of water. That would serve as a cue for Schwitters (who spoke no Dutch). Everything went as planned. Just as van Doesburg started to drink, Schwitters—a perfect stranger sitting in the audience—began barking wildly. As Schwitters reports it:

> The barking netted us a second evening in Haarlem; as a matter of fact it was sold out, because everyone was curious to see van Doesburg take a drink of water and then hear me suddenly and unexpectedly bark.[21]

At the second performance, Schwitters did not bark.

By the time the two reached Amsterdam, the audience could not wait out the suspense. They raged and laughed hysterically and one woman was carried out in a faint. None of this experience was wasted on Schwitters. In the small dramatic fragment which he calls an "Anxiety Play," Schwitters shows himself well aware of what it means to manipulate an audience:

a. Sir.
b. Yes?
a. You are under arrest.
b. No.
a. You are under arrest, Sir.
b. No.
a. I shall shoot, Sir.
b. No.
a. I shall shoot, Sir.
b. No.
a. I shall shoot, Sir.

b. No.
a. I hate you.
b. No.
a. I shall crucify you.
b. Not so.
a. I shall poison you.
b. Not so.
a. I shall murder you.
b. Not so.
a. Think of the winter.
b. Never.
a. I am going to kill you.
b. As I said, never.
a. I shall shoot.
b. You have already said that once.
a. Now come along.
b. You can't arrest me.
a. Why not?
b. You can take me into custody, but no more.
a. Then I shall take you into custody.
b. By all means.
    b. allows himself to be taken into custody and led away. The stage grows dark. The audience feels duped and there are catcalls and whistles. The chorus cries: "Where's the author? Throw him out! Rubbish![22]

In practice, Schwitters is unquestionably linked with dada performance though in his theoretical statements he stands diametrically opposed to dada's anti-art aesthetic:

Art is a primordial concept, exalted as the godhead. . . . Merz stands for freedom from all fetters, for the sake of an artistic creation . . . As a matter of principle, Merz aims only at art. . . .[23]

Dada performance, though centered in Zurich was not limited to that city alone. The Dada Club, Berlin's dada center, which included among its members Raoul Hausmann, Richard Huelsenbeck, George Grosz, Walter Mehring, and Johannes Baader, engaged in many of the same activities as the Cabaret Voltaire. The Berlin dadas were not gentle with their public and amidst the already recognizable dada diet of bruitism, simultaneous poetry and masked dances, they would heap invectives upon the audience.

We would say "You heap of dung, down there, yes, you, with the umbrella, you simple fool." Or, "Hey, you on the right, don't laugh, you ox." If they answered us, as they naturally did, we would say as they do in the army: "Shut your trap or you'll get kicked in the butt."[24]

Occasionally one of the dadas would be reciting something "very ridiculous" on stage while Grosz would go down into the audience to intimidate, cajole or even threaten the spectators into giving him money for the Club. If anyone objected, Grosz would hurl at him "Shut up! . . . You kept your mouths shut for four years during the war. Now keep them shut a little while longer."[25] Sometimes the insults would emerge from a staged situation. Walter Mehring would pound away at his typewriter, reading aloud the poem he was composing on the spot and Heartfeld or Hausmann or Grosz would come from backstage and shout "Stop, you aren't going to hand out real art to those dumbells, are you?"[26]

When they weren't swearing at the audience the Berlin-dadas staged "artistic" acts. Sometimes these skits were prepared but usually they were improvised and generally they were belligerent. Since there was often some drinking backstage before the performances, the battles that began in the wings were merely carried onto the stage and continued before the audience. The police came, sometimes taken for dadas in disguise, and were assaulted with the assortment of fruits and vegetables prepared for the occasion. Hausmann recalled that it took considerable courage to appear before such audiences which often numbered more than 2,000, and he kept in reserve a little dance called "sixty-one-steps" which seemed to have a calming effect on the crowd and which he would perform at difficult moments.

The atmosphere in Berlin, however, was different from that in Zurich, and Berlin dada assumed a much more political tone. Richard Huelsenbeck, returning from Zurich to Berlin in January 1917, was struck by the difference, and returned disillusioned with what he described as Tzara's willingness to turn dada into just another form of abstract art. For him the dada artist must be a political animal, he must be willing to "Make literature with a gun in his hand."[27] Still, Huelsenbeck could not free himself from the impact of Zurich dada theatrics and when he envisioned his art-cum-politics movement, it involved the use of dada simultaneous poems as state prayers and the setting up of one hundred and fifty dada circuses for the enlightenment of the proletariat. Although these projects were never realized, in Berlin, dada took to the streets. Anti-militarist songs were sung and theatre returned to one of its possible origins in the form of ceremonial processions. On one occasion, the procession was to publicize and sell a dada periodical called *Every Man His Own Football:*

> We hired a *char-a-banc* of the sort used for Whitsuntide outings, and also a little band, complete with frock coats and top hats, who used to play at ex-servicemen's funerals. We, the editorial staff, paced behind, six strong, bearing bundles of *Every Man His Own Football* instead of wreaths. In the sophisticated west end of the city, we earned more taunts than pennies, but our sales mounted sharply as we entered the lower-middle class and working-class districts of north and east Berlin. Along the streets of dingy grey tenements . . . the band was greeted with cheers and

applause as it played its two star pieces, which were the sentimental military airs "Ich hatt' einen Kamaraden," and "Die Rosenbank am Elterngrab."[28]

The Berlin dadas found it as difficult as their Zurich colleagues to separate theatre from life. On a beautiful summer evening in 1918, Raoul Hausmann and Johannes Baader suddenly recalled that it was Gottfried Keller's hundredth birthday:

> We were in the middle of the Rheinstrasse in Friedenau. The sky was orange. A gentle twilight hovered in the wide streets flanked with tall buildings . . .
> "Have you got anything by Keller on you?"
> "Yes, I've got *Green Henry*."
> "Good, let's celebrate."
> Without wasting a word, we made for the middle of the street and stood under a powerful electric street light . . . We took out the tome and began to read, shoulder to shoulder. "Poetry, made to measure, on the spot." We took turns to open the book at random and read scraps of sentences with no beginning and no end, changing our voices, changing the rhythm and the meaning, leafing backward and forward, spontaneously, without hesitation and without pause . . . We did not notice the passers-by . . . Zealously we stuck to our task for at least a quarter of an hour.[29]

With George Grosz, the theatre-maker becomes theatre itself. Walter Mehring noted that when he first met Grosz, the man was "dressed in a loud-checked jacket, with face powdered white like a circus clown," posing as "the saddest man in Europe."[30] Grosz had taken upon himself the role of "Propograndada," a walking publicist for the movement's activities. He carried a huge calling card with an artifical eye on one side and the slogan "How do you think tomorrow?" on the other. Instead of a hat, he wore a papier-mâché death's head. What was "real" and what was "role" soon became confused. Grosz,

> adopted the style of the dandy, carrying a cane with a skull on it, pouring his liquor from a bottle with a skull on it, and drinking out of glasses that were made from skulls. Guests to his apartment—especially if they were important personages—were first greeted by a skeleton in the hall and then confronted by a "corpse" in black tights and derby hat, which was draped over the couch. To add to the effect, Grosz would often enlist the support of his friends who, hidden from view, would make bloodcurdling sounds.[31]

The performance activities of Kurt Schwitters and of the Berlin dada group had no direct effect on Paris dada and the surrealist sketch. They do, however, make clear the fact that the developing of a dada performing style was not limited to Zurich alone. Nor were Tzara or Ball the only people who could make dada performance "happen." In this sense, a look at Schwitters, Grosz, Hausmann and Baader is an attempt to demystify the movement by pointing to the proliferation of its traits in other places, and in the work of other people.

A Note on Cocteau's Relationship to the Dada-Surrealists

There was much in Tzara's work that was attractive to Cocteau: the belief in scandal, the use of poetry as an anti-bourgeois weapon. From the start, however he vacillated in his commitment to the Paris-dada group. He did participate in the *Premier vendredi de Littérature,* and had given Tzara three of his poems for publication in *Dada.* They never appeared, for Cocteau retracted them with a letter which read:

> I can even say that Tzara, despite the fact that he works at the opposite extreme from me, is the only poet who moves me so. Ribemont is pure, of that I'm sure. But Dada, Dadaism, affects me with an intolerable discomfort. I liked the fact that they let a bit of air into the cubist room—but the session the other evening was atrocious, sad, timid, far from any audacity, from any inventiveness.[1]

By 1920, there was no love lost between Cocteau and Breton. The first issue of *Littérature* (March 9, 1919), had featured Cocteau's name on the back cover, but no work of his appeared in the journal itself. Breton was "down" on the darling of the literary salons for his "opportunism," and wrote to Tzara in December, 1919:

> My feeling, quite impersonal, I assure you, is that he is the most detestable person now around. Let me repeat, he has done nothing to me, and I assure you that hating is not my strong point.[2]

Aragon, in his "Project d'histoire littéraire contemporaine," included Cocteau with the phrase "Cocteau takes shape," and Ribemont-Dessaignes, at the time of *Parade* (1917), sent a poem under Cocteau's name to Pierre Albert-Birot at *SIC.* The practical joke poem revealed in print the acrostic "PAUVRES BIROT" ("Poor Birot"). Birot's rejoinder was to point out that the squabble was not between himself and Cocteau, but between "the group" that had submitted the poem, and the young poet. Of Cocteau himself, he wrote: "fortunately, the changeabilities of his taste never harmed anyone."[3] Other critics were less sympathetic to Cocteau and shared the dada-surrealists' irritation with him:

M. Cocteau . . . lacks originality. Rostand in vogue, he copies Rostand. The Ballets Russes having superceded Rostand, he copies the Ballets Russes. Cubism overrides the Ballet, he sets about making cubes. Let us just add that there is not the least bit of pre-meditation on his part, not the slightest calculation. It is instinct, without even paying attention, that allows Cocteau to adapt to the taste of the day, the hour, the moment.[4]

Throughout 1920, Cocteau continued his approaches to the dada-surrealist group while at the same time proceeding with his own activities, almost parallel to theirs. A coterie group of young poets surrounded him at the cafe Gaya, not far from the Certa where the surrealists met. When the Paris-dadas threw themselves with fervor into the first manifestations, Cocteau mounted *Le Boeuf sur le toît* with the Fratellini clowns. Refused publication in *Littérature*, he founded his own journal, *Le Coq*. The group's rejection of him, however, was complete. Picabia, in an unprecedented rebuke, ripped up the galley sheets of Cocteau's poems which were to appear in *391*, and in the next edition of the journal, published the poet's angry letter with the following remarks:

> Wanting absolutely to publish a piece by Jean Cocteau, deprived of three poems which he gave me for *391*, and which I couldn't include in the last issue for lack of space, I am happy to be able to provide the public with the following letters, the only manuscript left me under his authorship.[5]

Cocteau responded in *Le Coq* with "Our main reproach to Dada is that it is too timid. Once the rules of the game are broken, why for such meagre results? No dada dares to commit suicide, kill a spectator. One sees plays, listens to music."[6]

Shortly afterward, Philippe Soupault, "the famous illusioniste," at the Salle Gaveau, punctured the balloon labelled "Jean Cocteau," and the split between Cocteau and the Paris dadas was sealed.

Breton's own antipathy for Cocteau was so strong that his name is not mentioned once in Breton's *Entretiens*.

Notes

Chapter I

1. Germain Everling-Picabia. "C'était hier: Dada . . . ," *Les Oeuvres libres,* No. 109 (Paris, juin 1955), p. 137.

2. André Breton, unedited correspondence with Tristan Tzara, in Michel Sanouillet, *Dada à Paris* (Paris, 1965), *passim:* letters Nos. 1, 6, 8, 16, dated: 22 janvier, 4 avril, 12 juin, 29 juillet, 26 décembre, 1919, pp. 440, 444, 447, 453.

3. André Breton, correspondence with Tzara, in Sanouillet, *op. cit.,* letter No. 18, 14 janvier 1920, p. 455.

4. Tristan Tzara, correspondence with Francis Picabia, in Sanouillet, letter No. 71, 19 mars 1919, p. 484.

5. Francis Picabia, correspondence with Tristan Tzara, in Sanouillet, letter No. 72, 28 mars 1919, p. 485.

6. André Breton, *Entretiens (1913-1952) avec André Parinaud* (Paris, 1969), p. 65.

7. Sanouillet substantiates this fear by explaining that so close upon the end of the war, any foreign accent was interpreted by an audience as Germanic; and in fact, when Tzara did read a manifesto out loud at the "Manifestation de la Maison de l'Oeuvre," he was greeted with cries of "A Berlin, A Zurich . . ."

8. Sanouillet, *Dada à Paris,* p. 145.

9. Aragon, reponsible for arranging the readings, had invited Bertin and Herrand among a number of other actors, noted for their sympathy towards the contemporary arts, to participate. Valentine Tessier and Eve Francis refused. Bertin and Herrand agreed on condition that they be allowed to select their own texts and the placement of their selections within the program.

10. The most well-known use of this pun is that at the base of Marcel Duchamp's moustached "Mona Lisa" which was presented to the public for the first time in a sketched reproduction by Picabia printed in the March 1920 edition of the magazine *391* (The pun reads aloud as "Elle a chaud au cul.")

11. Tristan Tzara, "Memoirs of Dadaism," in Edmund Wilson, *Axel's Castle*, p. 304.

12. André Breton, letter to Picabia and Tzara, No. 115, 24 janvier 1920, in Sanouillet, p. 507.

13. Georges Ribemont-Dessaignes, *déjà-jadis* (Paris, 1958), p. 71.

14. Tzara, "Memoirs of Dadaism," in Wilson, p. 304.

15. Hans Richter, *Dada: Art and Anti-Art* (New York: McGraw Hill, n.d.), pp. 77-78.

16. Georges Ribemont-Dessaignes, "History of Dada," in Robert Motherwell, ed. *The Dada Painters and Poets* (New York, 1951), p. 109.

Chapter II

1. Hans Richter, *Dada: Art and Anti-Art* , p. 12.

2. Hugo Ball, *Flight Out of Time, A Dada Diary*, ed., John Elderfield, trans. Ann Raimes (New York: The Viking Press, 1974), entry of 15.X.1915. Further references to *Diary* entries will be listed in the body of the text with the date alone.

3. Tzara, whose real name was Sami Rosenstock, had only lived with this name for a year, having previously tried S. Samyro, Tristan Ruia, and Tristan. "Tristan" was taken from Wagner's opera, and "Tzara" or "tarra" in Rumanian meant "land" or "country."

4. The only other group to bear a name was the *Weissen Blatter* circle which gathered around Renée Schickele's journal of the same name. For a more detailed account of how dada was named, see John Elderfield, "Dada: A Code Word of Saints?" *Artforum,* February, 1974, pp. 42-47.

5. Georges Hugnet, *L'Aventure Dada* (Paris, 1957), p. 23.

6. V.I. Lenin, quoted in Willy Verkauf, *Dada: Monograph of a Movement* (New York, 1917), p. 12.

7. Jan Ephraim was the owner of the Hollandische Meiri cafe at Spiegelgasse 1 in Niendendorf, a slightly disreputable quarter of Zurich. The cafe itself had already served as the base for a cabaret. For several months in 1914, it had housed the Cabaret Pantagruel where Swiss poets met to read their works.

8. Hugo Ball, "Introduction," to the journal *Cabaret Voltaire,* in Robert Motherwell, *The Dada Poets and Painters* (New York: Wittenborn, 1951), p. xix.

9. Richter, *op. cit.,* p.

10. Primary materials, not specifically footnoted, were taken from the clipping files (often unsigned and undated) at the *Fonds Rondel, Bibliothèque de l'Arsenal,* Paris and the *Fonds Doucet,* Bibliothèque St. Genevieve, Paris. See bibliography.

11. Richard Huelsenbeck writes that the name "Cabaret Voltaire" was not accidentally chosen. It was selected ". . . out of veneration for a man who had fought all his life for the liberation of the creative forces from the tutelage of the advocates of power." In Motherwell, *op. cit.*, p. 79.

12. Richard Huelsenbeck, *Memoirs of a Dada Drummer*, ed. Hans J. J. Kleinschmidt, trans. Joachim Neugroschel (New York: Viking Press, 1974), pp. 9-10.

13. Jean Arp, "Arp in New York," in Huelsenbeck, *op. cit.*, p. 99.

14. Huelsenbeck, *op. cit.*, p. 96.

15. For a closer look at the plays see: Eugen Egger, *Hugo Ball. Ein Weg aus dem Chaos*, (Olten: Otto Walter, 1951), and Gerhardt Edward Steinke, *The Life and Work of Hugo Ball, Founder of Dadaism* (The Hague: Mouton, 1967).

16. See Ball's article "Wedekind comedien," in *Obliques*, "L'expressionism allemand," Numéro 6-7. Wedekind was important to Tzara as well, and the young Rumanian included him in a poem of 1913-14: "Pas même la corde ne glisse/Monsieur Wedekind/A côté brule encore la lampe/Mais pas assez même pour cela."

17. Wassily Kandinsky, *The Blaue Reiter Almanac*, ed. Wassily Kandinsky and Franz Marc, New Documentary Edition, ed. Klaus Lankheit, trans. Henning Falkenstein (New York: Viking Press, 1974), p. 17.

18. *Über das Geistige in der Kunst*, Piper and Co., (Munich: January, 1912). Quotations in this essay are from the *Documents of Modern Art* translation (based on Michael Sadleir's authorized translation of 1914 with considerable retranslation by Francis Golffing, Michael Harrison and Ferdinand Ostertag), Vol. 5. *Concerning the Spiritual in Art and Painting in Particular*, 1912. (New York: George Wittenborn, 1947).

19. Three essays on the stage had originally been planned for inclusion, but only Kandinsky's finally appeared in the book.

20. *The Yellow Sound* was written in March, 1909, in German, and originally titled *The Giants*. Four extant versions in Russian and German precede that printed in *The Blaue Reiter*. At about the same time Kandinsky also wrote *The Green Sound* and *Black on White* (both of which exist only in Russian versions and in their French translations). A fourth play, *Violet Sound* (ca. 1911) exists in its original German and in a 1914 Russian manuscript. With the exception of *Violet*, the plays are non-naturalistic, operatic, and await musical compositions for which they basically serve as libretti. The plays are available at the Nina Kandinsky archives in Paris and the Kandinsky archives in Munich. There is some evidence of the existence of earlier stage compositions based on fairy tales: *The Garden of Paradise*, and *The Magic Wings*, begun about 1908. There was also a film comedy and a ballet version of *Daphnis and Chloe*, 1909; scored by von Hartmann to be danced by Sacharoff. When it was learned that Fokine was about to perform his *Daphnis and Chloe*, this project was set aside.

21. Hugo Ball, "Kandinsky," *Flight Out of Time*, p. 227.

22. Thomas von Hartmann, "The Indecipherable Kandinsky," unpublished essay written in 1913 for Herwarth Walden.

23. Wassily Kandinsky, letter to A. Schoenberg, 16.XI.1911, in J. Rufer, *Das Werk A. Schoenbergs*, p. 179.

24. Wassily Kandinsky, "On Stage Composition," *The Blaue Reiter*, p. 20.

25. Wassily Kandinsky, *Kandinsky 1901-1913* (Berlin, 1913), "Ruckblicke," p. ix.

26. Wassily Kandinsky, "Lecture on Painting," in *Vestnik rabotnikov iskusstv*, no. 4-5, Moscow, 1921, pp. 74-75. Quoted in Troels Anderson, "Some unpublished letters by Kandinsky," *Artes III*, Copenhagen, 1966, pp. 106-7. In an unpublished lecture delivered by von Hartmann in New York on the occasion of Kandinsky's death, the composer suggests that this exercise was a prelude to work on *The Yellow Sound*.

27. *Ibid., loc. cit.*

28. Plato in *The Republic* wrote, "Painting is controlled by the same laws as musical rhythm"; by about 1900 the idea of such a relationship was common talk among painters and musicians.

29. Thomas von Hartmann, unpublished lecture.

30. The score was left incomplete and unorchestrated, awaiting information on just what would be the limitations imposed by the theatre producing the piece.

31. Quotations are from Kandinsky, *The Yellow Sound, A Stage Composition*, in *The Blaue Reiter Almanac, op. cit.*, pp. 207-25.

32. W. Kandinsky, "On Stage Composition," *loc. cit.*, p. 206.

33. See: *Aujourd'hui: art et architecture*, numero 17, 3eme année, mai 1958, p. 34.

34. W. Kandinsky, *The Yellow Sound, loc. cit.*, p. 224.

35. W. Ritter, *Chronique des Arts*, Paris, May 20, 1908, quoted in George Fuchs, *Die Revolution des Theaters* (written in 1908), p. 244, trans.

36. L. Sabeneiv, "Scriabin's *Prometheus*," *The Blaue Reiter*, pp. 127-40.

37. Dalcroze's name appears in a Kandinsky notebook of about 1908, and in M. Sadleir's account of his visit to Kandinsky at Murnau in 1912 (see: *Michael Ernest Sadler 1861-1943, A Memoir by his Son*, London, 1949), he recalled that he and his father travelled on from there to Dresden to see the Dalcroze school. The inference is inescapable that they took the detour on Kandinsky's recommendation.

38. W. Kandinsky, *Concerning the Spiritual*, p. 71.

39. Kandinsky was completely ignorant of the fact that Diaghilev and Fokine had chosen the same subject for the Diaghilev ballet (June 8, 1912, Théâtre du Chatelet, Paris).

Plans for the ballet were abandoned as soon as Kandinsky got wind of the Diaghilev project despite the fact that his version of the ballet shared nothing in common with Fokine's.

40. Sergei Eisenstein, in his chapter "Color and Meaning," in *The Film Sense*, (Faber, p. 96), quotes from the play and concludes, "We cannot deny that compositions of this kind evoke obscurely disturbing sensations—but no more than this." For more contemporary criticism, see: R.W. Sheppard, "Kandinsky's Abstract Drama *Der Gelbe Klang:* An Interpretation," *Forum for Modern Language Studies*, April, 1975, 11:165-76. This article lists in footnotes the contemporary German critical sources. An extract by Horst Denkler appears in French as "Kandinsky et le théâtre," *Obliques*, numéro spéciale 6-7, pp. 95-99. As to the performances of the play, von Hartmann himself had, during his Moscow stay of 1917, proposed to Stanislavsky to do the piece at the Moscow Art Theatre with his music and set designs by Kandinsky "but they could not understand it and did not accept it. The designs and my music—everything was lost during the Revolution." A second project failed in Berlin in 1922 where it was supposed to have been produced by the Berliner Volksbuhne. But von Hartmann was in Russia at the time and the plans fell through. *The Yellow Sound* did not receive a full stage production until May 12, 1972, when it was presented at the Guggenheim Museum as part of a Kandinsky retrospective, performed by a group called ZONE under the direction of Harris and Ros Barron. The first full scale European production was on April 6, 1975 as part of the Fêtes Musicales III, at St. Beaume in Provence. It was directed by Jacques Polière and later moved to the Théâtre des Champs Elysées in Paris, March 4, 1976.

41. Arnold Schoenberg, letter to V. Kandinsky, August 19, 1912, Kandinsky Archives, Munich.

42. Ludwig Grote, "Bühnenkompositionen von Kandinsky," *10 Internationale Revue*, Amsterdam, 1928, 2.Jg.n.13, quoted in Henning Rischbieter, *Art and the Stage in The Twentieth Century: Painters and Sculptors Work for the Theatre*, trans. Michael Bullock (Greenwich, Connecticut: New York Graphic Society, Ltd, 1968).

43. W. Kandinsky, *Concerning the Spiritual*, p. 24. Kandinsky's work on vibrations was influenced by the work of the French occultist Colonel Albert de Rochas d'Aiglon whose book *Les sentiments, la musique et la geste* (Grenoble, 1900), he had read. De Rochas attempted to reduce the expressive movements of the human body to the influence of vibration and experimented with an artist's model "with the necessary mediumistic sensibility." Exposing her to words, verses and music, he watched and photographed her reactions. See also: Sixten Ringbom, *The Sounding Cosmos: A Study in the Spiritualism of Kandinsky and the Genesis of Abstract Painting* (Helsingfors: Abo Akademi, 1970), pp. 120ff.

44. W. Kandinsky, "Ruckblicke," *loc. cit.*, p. vi.

45. For more on Kandinsky's relation to theosophy see: Ringbom, *op. cit.*, pp. 57ff.

46. Hartmann later became a follower of the mystic Gurdjiev.

47. See: Johannes Eichner, *Kandinsky und Gabriele Munter, von Ursprungen moderner Kunst* (Munich: Verlag Bruckmann, 1957), pp. 19ff.

48. Hugo Ball, *Briefe 1911-1927* (Einsiedeln, 1957), pp. 29ff.

49. Will Grohmann in his definitive biography of Kandinsky (*Wassily Kandinsky—Life and Work*, trans. Norbert Guterman, New York: Harry Abrams, 1958) points out that "the spiritual in art" was taken for granted by the Chinese as in the *Book of Changes* (I Ching): "Feeling is identical with force, force is identical with spirit, the spirit is identical with the beyond," and that Kandinsky's works as a whole point more to Chinese affinities than to Western European influences (p. 246). For more on Oriental influences on Kandinsky, See: Sihare Laxmi, *Oriental Influences on Wassily Kandinsky and Piet Mondrian 1909-1917*, unpublished dissertation, New York University, 1967.

50. Ravien Siurlai, "Die Aktion," June 5, 1912.

51. Hennings married Ball seven years before his death.

52. It is interesting that Ball, in his description of the "group of five," completely bypasses Emmy Hennings' place in the constellation. Though only sparse documentation exists on Hennings' performances, still she emerges as an active participant in the cabaret. In addition to her appearance in Janco's painting "Cabaret Voltaire," Ball records in his diary a review from the *Züricher Post:* "The star of the cabaret, however, is Mrs. Emmy Hennings. Star of many nights of cabarets and poems . . . today too she presents the same bold front and performs the same songs with a body that has since then been only slightly ravaged by grief." Huelsenbeck, recalling Hennings, wrote: "The light of our dim cabaret lamps shone through her thin dress, revealing her boyish figure. She wasn't merely a child, she knew how to play the child," and he credited her with being the only real "professional" in the group and someone on "whose success or failure as a singer the existence of the cabaret hinged." Despite a voice so "meager" and "boyish" that one feared it would break at any moment, still "She sang Hugo Ball's aggressive songs with an anger we had to credit her with, although we scarcely thought her capable of it." The material on Sophie Taeuber's (later Arp's wife) participation is similarly paltry. She was the only native Swiss among the dada expatriates, taught drawing at the Zurich Institute of Technology, danced with Laban, and performed many dances at the Cabaret. Arp, who met her in Zurich in 1915 wrote that at that time she "had already liberated herself from traditional art." Her dada puppets are documented in photographs and were used at dada performances. What is sorely lacking, however, are the driving personal recollections of these women (those of Hennings are largely concerned with Ball) to help us reconstruct their work in Zurich.

53. Marcel Janco, in Verkauf, *op. cit.,* p. 32.

54. Tristan Tzara, "Zurich Chronicle," *passim,* in Motherwell, pp. 235ff.

55. Jean Arp, *On My Way* (New York: 1948).

56. "Lettre de M. Hennings," quoted in Robert Maguire, *Le hors théâtre: Essai sur la signification du théâtre de notre temps.* Doctorat d'État à la Sorbonne, 1963, p. 68.

57. Georges Burnad, *Les Masques,* (Paris, 1948), p. 85.

58. Futurist experiments in simultaneity were known to Ball and Tzara as well.

59. The last two words he took from Chevreul's treatise on the optics of color.

60. Kandinsky and Delaunay were among the few who found the analogy to music a fruitful gloss to painting: the musicality of the rhythms of colour, the colour value of musical notes, the chromatic rhythms of poetry.

61. Guillaume Apollinaire, *Méditations esthétiques: Les Peintres Cubists*, (Paris: Hermann, 1965).

62. In June 1917, *Théâtre Art et Action* presented an evening of simultaneous poetry including works by Barzun, Divoire and Voirol.

63. Blaise Cendrars, in Jacques Damase, *Sonia Delaunay: Rhythms and Colours* (Greenwich: New York Graphic Society, 1972), p. 51.

64. Guillaume Apollinaire, "La Femme Assisse," *Mercure de France*, Jan. 1, 1914, in Arthur A. Cohen, *Sonia Delaunay* (New York: Harry N. Abrams, 1975), p. 64.

65. Blaise Cendrars, in Damase, *op. cit.*, p. 47. Here Cendrars uses the word "surrealistically" which Apollinaire would later take to indicate a whole new language of art in his 1917 "Introduction" to *Parade*.

66. Roger Shattuck, *The Banquet Years: The Origins of the Avant-Garde in France 1885- to World War I*, (New York: 1968), p. 310.

67. Hugo Ball, in Richter, *op. cit.*, p. 30.

68. Richard Huelsenbeck, "En Avant Dada: A History of Dadaism," trans. Ralph Manheim, in Motherwell, pp. 35, 36.

69. Laszlo Moholy-Nagy, *Vision in Motion* (Chicago: Paul Theobold, 1961), p. 315.

70. Sergei Eistenstein, in Manuel Grossman, *Dada: Paradox, Mystification and Ambiguity in European Literature* (New York, Pegasus) 1971. pp. 122-23.

71. Huelsenbeck, *Memoirs*, p. 23.

72. Hugo Ball, in Richter, p. 121.

73. *Ibid.*, p. 30. The dadas were not the first to write "phonetic poetry." Abstract poetry using sound and nonsense words goes back to the medieval period where in the "comptines" of French folk poetry one can find such lines as "Am-stram-gram pic et pic et colegram," which is vaguely equivalent to "eeny-meeny-miney-mo," or the German "eene, meene, ming-mang, ping-pang, eia weia packe dich, eia weia weg." Raoul Hausmann in his *Courrier Dada* points to the "inner language" of *The Prophetess of Prevost*, a book published by Justinus Kerner in 1840. This included a sentence like "Clemor oona in diu aswinor." Jonathan Swift in the third and fourth books of *Gulliver's Travels* transcribes the speech of the Lilliputians and the horses in the land of the Yahoos. Paul Scheerbart in 1897 wrote a sound poem entitled "I love you," that starts

"Kikakoku! Ekoralaps! Wiao Kollipanda opolasa . . . " and Christian Morgenstern, a turn-of-the-century writer of "metaphysical nonsense," in 1905 invented his own form of nonsense language based on the idea of phonetic poetry.

74. G.B. Cutter, *Speaking with Tongues,* (New York: 1927), p. 121.

75. *Ibid.,* p. 74ff.

76. Ball had read Barzun as well as *La vie des Lettres* of Nicolas Beauduin. In his diary (30.III.1916), he writes of "the simultaneous poem according to Henri Barzun and Ferdinand Divoire. He was also familiar both as a pianist and through the Kandinsky circle with the "sprechgesang," with "Gurre Lieder" or "Pierrot lunaire." Tzara, in "a note for the bourgeois" appended to the simultaneous poem "l'amiral cherche une maison à louer, and published in *Cabaret Voltaire,* credits Barzun with first developing the genre in his theoretical book, *Voix, Rhythmes et chants Simultanés,* while at the same time making clear that his aims in creating a simultaneous poem differ greatly from Barzun's and Divoire's. "Messrs. Barzun and Divoire," he wrote, "are purely formal. They aim for a musical effect which one could achieve by affecting the same abstractions in a partitura for orchestra. I want to create a poem based on other principles, which would consist of the opportunity which I would offer to each listener to select the associations appropriate for him."

77. See: Raoul Hausmann, "Note sur le poème phonétique: Kandinsky et Ball," *German Life and Letters,* 21, n.1, 1967, pp. 58-59.

78. Wassily Kandinsky, *Concerning the Spiritual in Art,* p. 34.

79. Wassily Kandinsky, *Klänge* (Munich: Piper & Co., 1913).

80. See: Jean Arp, "Kandinsky poète," (text of 1954), in Jean Arp, *Jours éfeuilles* (Paris: Gallimard, 1966).

81. First pointed out by Raoul Hausmann, "Introduction à une histoire du poème phonetique," *German Life and Letters,* 19 (1965-66), pp. 19ff. and further discussed in the appendix to the article by Christopher Middleton.

82. V. Markov. *The Longer Poems of V. Khlebnikov* (Berkeley: University of California Publications in Modern Philology, 62, 1962), p. 7.

83. For Roumanian poets who experimented with language and were possibly early influences on Tzara, see the works of Alexandru Macedonsky (who collaborated with Marinetti on his journal *Poesia*), *Opere* (Scriitori Romani, 1969); Urmuz (pseudonym of Demetru Demetrescu-Buzau), *Pagini bizare* (Editura Minerva, 1970). Urmuz was "a Roumanian Jarry" who as early as 1907-8 wrote in a surrealist language. See also: Eugene Ionesco, "Precurseurs roumains du surréalisme," *Les Lettres Nouvelles* (jan.-fev., 1965).

84. See: Arp, Huelsenbeck, Tzara, *Die Geburt des Dada: Dichtung und Chronik der Grunder,* ed. Peter Schifferli (Zurich, 1957), p. 95.

85. For further discussion of the dadas' relationship to phonetic poetry, see Leonard Forster's essay *Poetry of Significant Nonsense*, (Cambridge University Press, 1962), pp. 26-32, as well as portions of his de Carle Lectures (University of Otago, 1968) *The Poet's Tongues: Multilingualism in Literature* (Cambridge University Press with the University of Otago Press, New Zealand, 1970), esp. pp. 79ff.

86. Hugo Ball, in Richter, p. 31.

87. Huelsenbeck in Richter, p. 21.

88. See his "poèmes nègres," in *Dada* 2, 1917; also "notes sur l'art nègre," *SIC*, septembre-octobre, 1917.

89. Hans Richter, *op. cit.*, p. 20.

90. Georges Ribemont-Dessaignes, *déjà jadis* (Paris: René Juillard, 1958).

91. Richard Huelsenbeck, "En Avant Dada," in Motherwell, p. 23.

92. Marcel Janco, "Creative Dada," in Verkauf, p. 28.

Chapter III

1. Luigi Russolo, "The Art of Noise," in Michael Kirby, *Futurist Performance* (New York, 1971), p. 168.

2. Russolo, in Kirby, p. 172.

3. *London Times*, June 16, 1914.

4. Filippo Tommaso Marinetti, "The Variety Theatre," in Kirby, *Futurist Performance*, p. 184.

5. *London Times*, quoted in Kirby, p. 16.

6. *Ibid.*

7. Richter, *op. cit.*, p. 33.

8. Filippo Tommaso Marinetti, quoted in Noemi Blumenkranz-Onimus, "Du Futurisme Italien Aux Mouvements Dada et Surréaliste," *Europe* (novembre-décembre, 1968), p. 206.

9. Tristan Tzara, "Proclamations sans prétention," in *Sept Manifestes Dada*, p. 10.

10. André Breton, "Two Dada Manifestoes," in Motherwell, *op. cit.*, p. 203.

11. Luciano Folgore, quoted in Herbert Gershman, "Futurism and the origins of Surrealism," *Italica* XXXIX (June 1962), p. 118. Gershman in his article takes the Futurist-French literary/artistic connection one epoch farther back to suggest that Marinetti may have in fact been heir to Mallarmé in the area of liberated typography and to Rimbaud

in his anti-passéiste tendencies; then one step forward to show the relationship of futurism to the Paris dada-surrealists.

12. Richard Huelsenbeck, "History of Dada," in Motherwell, pp. 24-25.

13. Hugo Ball, "O Gadji Beri Bimba," in Richter, p. 42.

14. Giacomo Balla, "Discussion of Futurism by Two Sudanese Critics," in Kirby, p. 61.

15. Bruno Corra and Emilio Settimelli, "Negative Act," in Kirby, p. 268.

16. Tristan Tzara, "An Introduction to Dada," in Motherwell, p. 397.

17. Mario Carli, "States of Mind," in Kirby, p. 256.

18. Tristan Tzara, *La Première Aventure céleste de M. Antipyrine* (Zurich, 1916).

19. Filippo Tommaso Marinetti, Emilio Settimelli, and Bruno Corra, "The Futurist Synthetic Theatre," in Kirby, p. 201.

20. Tristan Tzara, *Première Aventure céleste* . . .

21. Francesco Flora, "Dal romanticismo al futurismo" (Florence, 1924) quoted in Joseph Cary, "Futurism and the French Théâtre d'Avant-Garde," in *Modern Philology* (November, 1959), p. 113.

22. George Ribemont-Dessaignes, *déjà-jadis,* p. 39.

23. Marinetti et al., "The Futurist Synthetic Theatre," in Kirby, p. 196.

24. Tristan Tzara, *La Première Aventure céleste* . . .

25. Marinetti, "Manifeste technique de la littérature futuriste," in Blumenkranz-Onimus, p. 207.

26. Marinetti et al., "The Futurist Synthetic Theatre," p. 196.

27. Tzara, in Motherwell, p. 77.

28. Ribemont-Dessaignes, *déjà-jadis,* p. 99.

Chapter IV

1. Jean Arp, "Dada au grand-air," *Dada* (Tarenz-bei Imst, 1921), in Motherwell, p. 102.

2. Tristan Tzara, "Manifesto of Mr. Antipyrine," in Motherwell, p. 78.

3. *Ibid.,* p. 77.

4. Tristan Tzara, quoted in William Rubin, *Dada and Surrealist Art* (New York, 1968), p. 14.

5. Tristan Tzara, "Unpretentious Proclamation," in *Tristan Tzara: Seven Dada Manifestos and Lampisteries,* trans. Barbara Wright, (London: John Calder, 1977), p. 15.

6. Richard Huelsenbeck, "En Avant Dada," in Motherwell, p. 28.

7. Tristan Tzara, *Seven Dada Manifestos,* passim.

8. Rubin, *Dada and Surrealist Art,* p. 16.

9. Marcel Janco, in Elmer Peterson, *Tristan Tzara: Dada and Surrational Theorist* (New Brunswick, New Jersey, 1971), p. 9.

10. Michael Kirby, *Happenings.* (New York: E.P. Dutton, 1971.)

11. Hans Richter, *op. cit.,* p. 77.

12. Albert Einstein, "On the Method of Theoretical Physics," in P.B. Medawar, *Induction and Intuition in Scientific Thought,* (London, 1969), p. 10.

13. Jean Arp, "On My Way," in Motherwell, xx.

14. Hugo Ball, in Motherwell, p. 52.

15. Tristan Tzara, "Dada Manifesto on Feeble Love and Bitter Love," IV, in *Seven Dada Manifestos,* p. 35.

16. Little is known of the dada work with puppets. Georges Hugnet in *L'Aventure Dada* mentions ". . . Ball's satirical couplets against German imperialism and his 'Krippen Spiele', performed by Emmy Hennings' puppets . . ." Ball himself records that at the opening soirée of the Dada Gallery, "Shickele and Grumback improvised a political puppet show with Emmy's 'Czar' and 'Czarina' in the doorway between two pillars." (29.III.1917). Hans Richter recalls "The puppets Arp and Taeuber made were the first abstract puppets ever used at puppet shows. . . . They moved with a grace not of this earth and would have out-circused even Calder's circus in their purity. (They were lost later on. . . .)" (Motherwell, p. 288). Sophie Taeuber Arp's puppets were featured in the Gozzi play "Le Roi Cerf" presented in the summer of 1918 at the Zurich exposition "Werkbund Suisse."

17. Waldemar Jollos, *Werk* no. 8, August, 1918.

18. Hugo Ball, in Motherwell, p. 52.

19. *Ibid.*

20. Tristan Tzara, "Zurich Chronicle," in Motherwell, p. 237.

21. Guillaume Apollinaire, "Cortège," in Shattuck, *op. cit.,* p. 316.

22. Tristan Tzara, "Dada Manifesto 1918," in *Dada Manifestos,* p. 10.

23. Hans Richter, *op. cit.*, p. 27.

24. William G. Seitz, *The Art of Assemblage,* (New York, 1961), p. 37.

25. Jean Arp, "Dada Was Not A Farce," (1949), trans. Ralph Manheim, in Motherwell, p. 294.

26. Hans Richter, p. 51.

27. Jean Arp, *On My Way: Poetry and Essays, 1912-1947,* ed. Robert Motherwell, (New York, 1948), p. 40.

28. *Ibid.,* p. 52.

29. Tristan Tzara, "Lecture on Dada (1922)," in Motherwell, p. 248.

30. The creative use of "chance" is by no means an invention of the contemporary artist. Pliny the Elder tells that Protogenes of Rhodes, upset at his attempts to draw the lather around a horse's mouth, hurled a sponge at the picture. "The sponge deposited the colours with which it was charged in the very manner in which he had sought in vain, and thus chance constructed nature in a painting," quoted in Marcel Jean, *The History of Surrealist Painting,* trans. Simon Watson Taylor, (New York: Grove Press, 1960), p. 23.

31. Guillaume Apollinaire, *Les Peintres cubistes. Méditations esthétiques* (Paris: Figuière) 1913

32. Tristan Tzara, "Zurich Chronicle," in Motherwell, p. 236.

33. Georges Hugnet, *L'Aventure Dada,* p. 22.

34. The text is available in *Revue d'Histoire du théâtre,* no. 3, 1971, p. 288-93, and in Tristan Tzara, *Oeuvres Complètes,* tome I Flamarion, 1975).

35. Tristan Tzara in Edmund Wilson, *Axel's Castle,* p. 317.

36. Georges Charensol, in *Commoedia,* 29 March 1920, quoted in Michel Sanouillet, *Dada à Paris,* (Paris: Jean-Jacques Pauvert, 1965), p. 167.

37. Tristan Tzara, in Wilson, *loc. cit.,* p. 307.

38. Hugo Ball, "Dada Manifesto," in *Flight Out of Time,* Appendix, pp. 219-221.

Chapter V

1. Richard Huelsenbeck, "En Avant Dada," in Motherwell, pp. 32-34.

2. Tristan Tzara, "Zurich Chronicle," in Motherwell, p. 237.

3. Gabrielle Buffet-Picabia, "Some Memories of Pre-Dada: Picabia and Duchamp (1949)," in Motherwell, p. 265.

4. Though the psychoanalytic method was well-established by 1916, the dadas had very little involvement with it. Though Huelsenbeck underwent a few abortive analytic sessions with the Adlerian Dr. Nadia Strasser-Applebaum—his own attitude at the time was rather succinctly summed up as "Sexual, shmexual, who cares?" He himself later became an analyst, which practice he followed until shortly before his death. Neither Arp, Ball nor Janco was interested in psychoanalysis at the time and Tzara only discovered Freud after having joined André Breton in Paris.

5. Hugo Ball, "Occultism and other things beautiful," excerpted in Jean Arp, "Dadaland," in *On My Way.*

6. *Der Sturm,* was a periodical edited by Herwarth Walden and published in Berlin (1910-1933). It promoted a pure abstractionism in painting and literature and counted among its contributors expressionists, futurists, and dadaists.

7. The full program read:

   I Tristan Tzara: introduction; Hans Heusser: "Prelude," "Moon Over the Water" (played by the composer): F.T. Marinetti: "Futurist Literature" W. Kandinsky: "Bassoon," "Cage," "Look and Flash"; G. Apollinaire: "Rotsoge," "The Douanier's Back"; Blaise Cendrars: "Crackling"; Negro Music and dance, performed by five persons with the help of Mlles. Jeanne Rigaud and Maria Cantarelli (masks by M. Janco).

   II H.S. Sulzberger: "Procession and Festival" (performed by the author); Jacob van Hoddis: Poems, recited by Emmy Hennings: Herwarth Walden: August Macke, Franz Marc, August Stramm: Hans Heusser: "Turkish Burlesques," "Festival on Capri" (played by the composer); Albert Ehrenstein: Poems. On Kokoschka.

   III: *Sphinx and Strawman.* A curiosity by Oskar Kokoschka (Masks and production: Marcel Janco).

8. Oskar Kokoschka, *Sphinx and Strawman,* first published in *Oskar Kokoschka, Dramen und Bilder* (Leipzig, 1913), trans. Victor H. Miesel, in *Voices of German Expressionism,* ed. Victor H. Miesel (Englewood Cliffs, N.J.: Prentice Hall, Inc., 1970), pp. 119-25.

9. Tristan Tzara, "Zurich Chronicle," in Motherwell, p. 238.

10. Oskar Kokoschka, quoted in Edith Hoffmann, *Kokoschka: Life and Work* (London, 1947), p. 150.

11. Tristan Tzara, "Zurich Chronicle," in Motherwell, p. 238.

12. After listing the program, Ball records some important members of the audience. Among those present that evening, Ball chose to record a heavy preponderance of Laban dancers: A. Sacharoff, Mary Wigman, Clothide v. Derp and Elisabeth Bergner. He also lists the artists Alexei von Jawlensky and Marianne von Werefkin who had just returned from Lugano where they helped Sacharoff with the staging of his dances.

13. Richard Huelsenbeck, "En Avant Dada" in Motherwell, p. 26. The extent of Huelsenbeck's rage is evidenced by its undiminished intensity over the years. In his "Dada Manifesto

1949" he wrote "For reasons of historical accuracy, the undersigned consider it necessary to state that Dadaism was not founded by Tristan Tzara at the Cabaret Voltaire in Zurich. It is self-evident that Dadaism could not be invented by one man and that all assertions to this effect are therefore false." (in Motherwell, p. xxx).

14. Tzara, "Zurich Chronicle," in Motherwell, p. 236.

15. Ball's break with Tzara in 1917 anticipated Breton's later rupture with the dada leader in Paris in 1921. Both Ball and Breton eventually came to reject dada's emphasis on raucous provocation and Tzara's cult of anti-art and negative values.

16. Tristan Tzara, "Zurich Chronicle," in Motherwell, p. 238.

17. During this time, Tzara continued with false news reports to provoke the public: an announcement that the dadas had imprisoned Marinetti in a public urinal, or the report of an imaginary duel between Arp and Tzara.

18. Viking Eggling was a Swedish painter whose methods of work were in sympathy with those of the dadas and who had been received into the dada group as a "guest member."

19. Hans Richter, *op. cit.*, pp. 77-78.

20. *Ibid.*, pp. 78-79.

21. Tristan Tzara, "Zurich Chronicle," in Motherwell, p. 242.

Chapter VI

1. Richard Huelsenbeck, *Memoirs of a Dada Drummer*, p. 11.

2. Laban's full name was Rudolf Laban de Varaljas.

3. Rudolf von Laban, *A Life for the Dance: Reminiscences* (with drawings by the author) trans. Lisa Ullmann (London: Macdonald & Evans, Ltd. 1975), p. 51.

4. Critics have consistently attacked Laban's seeming inability, in his descriptions of the process of creation in the dance, to achieve a verbal clarity, to strive for "literal statements" to support his awareness. In their rejection of his consistent use of word-chains, however (such groupings as his "Tanz-ton-wort" experiments or his use of "spirit-soul-form" to describe the deepest source of expression for his earth-dances), they fail to respect Laban's fear that a choice of literal terms might calcify the fluidity of an expressive search in movement, might freeze forms before their full potential had been explored.

5. Laban, *A Life for the Dance*, p. 82.

6. André Levinson, "The Modern Dance in Germany," *Theatre Arts*, February, 1929, p. 144.

7. Among those in attendance were the poet Else Lasker-Schuler, and the painter Marianne Werefkin, members of Kandinsky's Munich circle.

8. Laban, *op. cit.,* pp. 85-86.

9. Mary Wigman, *The Mary Wigman Book:* her writings edited and translated by Walter Sorrel (Middletown, Connecticut, Wesleyan University Press, 1973), p. 35.

10. Mary Wigman, *op. cit.,* p. 26. Nolde had met Wigman in Munich in 1912 at the same time that he created his "Candle Dancers," perhaps inspired by dances he had seen her perform. Wigman in turn was exposed to the masks Nolde had begun to paint in 1911. In later years, Nolde would always reserve three seats for Wigman's concerts: one for himself, one for his tubes and pots of paint, and one for his wife who stood guard lest he be disturbed.

11. Alfred Schlee, "La Musique de danse en Allemagne," *Archives Internationales de la Danse,* No. 4, October 15, 1933, p. 158.

12. Rudolf von Laban, *Die Welt des Taenzers* (Stuttgart: Walter Seifert, 1921), p. 55.

13. Laban, *A Life for the Dance,* p. 89.

14. Quoted in C. Madeline Dixon, "Mary Wigman," Wigman negative file Dance Collection, Lincoln Center, Library, New York.

15. Among the three Weisenthal sisters (Grete, Berthe, Else) who played an important part in establishing "free dance" in Vienna, Grete achieved the greatest success. During the years around 1912, she was the favorite of a select coterie of poets, painters and writers, among them Hugo von Hoffmansthal (who wrote *Amor & Psyche* for her), Max Reinhardt (who starred her in his *Sumurum*), Maurice Maeterlinck, and the Austrian painter Erwin Lang, who became her husband. In that formative period just after Isadora Duncan had hurled her challenge in the face of traditional dance, Grete Weisenthal, then a young dancer in the Vienna Opera ballet, was approached by Franz Liszt who advised her: "Stay in the ballet until you learn all you can; then leave and forget all about it; . . . dance as your own heart tells you to dance, not on your toes, not according to any school or teaching, dance from your own soul, express yourself and you will win fame and glory with an art all of your own." (in Colgate Baker "Grete Weisenthal the Dancer and her Art," *New York Review,* April 27, 1912). Leaving the ballet for the concert stage, she and her sisters toured Europe and America in programs that were neither ballet nor Duncan. Of her dancing in New York in 1912, a critic of the New York Times wrote: "Clad in a short frock, with her limbs bare, for the most part her dancing is done on the flat of the foot." Weisenthal was also influential in advancing the cult of dancing in the nude as a means to most completely display the expressive possibilities of the body.

16. The first efforts towards a dance notation system were found recorded in Egyptian hieroglyphics. After that one had to wait until the sixteenth century for the publication of a number of books on the dance which used literal abbreviations as a notation system: such examples are found in a manuscript entitled *Livre sur la dance* by Marguerite d'Autriche,; in a book published in Lyon in 1553, *Bassas dansas* by one Antonius Arena. In Paris in 1558 there appeared a small brochure with drawings and written explanation by Thoinot Arbeau, *Orchesographie.* Arbeau whose real name was Johan Tabourot from Langres, was a Jesuit abbé yet all the dances he recorded were secular. This was the

first serious attempt at a notation system, despite the fact that it employed some use of word abbreviations as well. But as movement in dance became more complicated, this system no longer sufficed. In 1605 there was the attempt of the Italian author M. Fabr. Caroso in his *Il ballarino*. In 1700, M. Lefeuillet in his *Choreographie* took off from the idea of line in space on which all contemporary notation systems are based. From here one moves to the nineteenth century choreographers Saint-Leon and Zorn who amplified the already existing systems and then to the twentieth century German Joachim Vischer whose work chronologically parallels Laban's. Laban's own system, known in Europe as "Kinetography," can be used to record a broad movement intention as well as a precisely detailed action. For more on contemporary notation forms see: "Performance: The Art of Notation," by Roselee Goldberg. *Studio International,* July/August 1976.

17. Wigman, *op. cit.,* p.39.

18. In the eventual growing apart between Laban and Wigman, Laban remained in the camp of dance based on reason, while Wigman moved toward intuition. Laban, who considered the dance as basically a "spatial art," set out to study its configurations—basically a classic attitude which he attached to an as yet ungelled mold. Laban the pedagogue wanted rules. His work in the art of dance would convince by reason, and *Green Clowns,* the piece he presented at Essen, tended toward a severe form which often descended into anecdote. This pantomime imitation of a film clip in slow motion concluded with the eight "mimes," identically masked and executing different gestures, serving to tackle a formal problem: how to confer a unity of sorts on a set of bizarre simultaneous movements. Wigman, the demagogue, saw dance as a vocation. In her fanaticism, she would fascinate by the appeal to instinct. These eventual differences, however, were only beginning to emerge in the period of the early 1920s which follows our discussion.

19. Though such a "revealing costume" on a dancer would today not merit mention, audiences in 1914 stared aghast at the exposed limbs of the performers, and a young French girl who had offered to accompany Wigman left abruptly, explaining "I have not seen either Our Lord or the Virgin Mary dressed in such a fashion."

20. Laban, *A Life for the Dance,* p. 30.

21. *Ibid.,* p. 87.

22. The term is that of Artur Michel in "The Development of the New German Dance," in Virginia Stewart, ed. *The Moden Dance* (New York: Dance Horizons) 1970. Originally published, 1935.

23. Maria Theresa, "What dancers think about the modern German dance," *The Dance Magazine,* May, 1931, p. 14. The rapid advances in science and technology at the end of the nineteenth century had very much encouraged the myth of the machine. In creating his "space crystal," Laban was joining those avant-garde artists who had found, in the imagined workings of a machine, a way to prod a real movement of the mind: Duchamp's "bachelor machine," Roussel's "bed-sky" and "diamond aquarium," Jarry's "supermâle" in his electric chair, Lautréamont's *amoureuse* sewing machine.

24. Wigman, quoted in Lucille Marsh, "The Shadow of Wigman in the Light of Duncan," *The Dance Magazine,* May 1931, vol. 16, no. 1, p. 62.

25. Hugo Ball, letter to his sister, May 27, 1914, in Ball, *Briefe 1911-1927* (Einsiedeln, 1957), pp. 29ff.

26. Mary Wigman, ". . . excerpts from the final lecture addressed to the dancers in the Zurich School, . . . summer 1949," *Dance Magazine*, August, 1950, pp. 15, 29.

27. Huelsenbeck, *op. cit.*, p. 11.

28. Ould Hermon, "The Art of Mary Wigman: Some notes on a new dance form," *The Dancing Times*, London, April, 1926, pp. 37-41.

29. Hugo Ball, *Diary*, p. 102.

30. Hanya Holm, quoted in Walter Sorrel, *Hanya Holm: The Biography of an Artist*, p. 18. In 1923, Wigman choreographed the group dances "circle" and "triangle," which Kandinsky lectured on at the Bauhaus, and her strong belief in any great work of art as growing out of a necessity seems to echo Kandinsky as well.

31. To further this group work Wigman founded her school in Dresden, Ball lived and worked within the dada circle and Duncan, Laban, Dalcroze, even Loie Fuller either lived within a group or built a school around themselves.

32. Wigman, quoted in Sorrel, *Hanya Holm*, p. 17.

33. Wigman, quoted in Walter Sorrel, *The Dance Has Many Faces*, (New York: Columbia University Press, 1966), p. 45.

34. Hugo Ball, *Diary*, p. 103.

35. Wassily Kandinsky, *Concerning the Spiritual in Art*, pp. 71-72.

36. Hugo Ball, "Kandinsky," in *Diary*, p. 234.

37. André Levinson, "The Modern Dance in Germany," *Theatre Arts*, February, 1929, p. 147.

38. Hanya Holm suggests that a physical breakdown sent Wigman to this solitary convalescence.

39. Michel Fokine, in "What dancers think about the Modern German Dance," *The Dance Magazine*, May, 1931, p. 14.

40. Years later, André Breton was to write in his *First Surrealist Manifesto* (1924), enjoining the similarly "blocked" writer, to "add the letter 'l,' for example, always the letter 'l.' "

41. Mary Wigman, quoted in Walter Sorrel, *The Dance Has Many Faces*, p. 43.

Chapter VII

1. Published in *l'Echo de Paris-Mensuel Illustré*, April 23, 1893.

2. Lugné-Poe, Aurelian, *Acrobaties* (Paris: Gallimard), p. 160.

3. *Ibid., loc. cit.*

4. Alfred Jarry, "A Letter to Lugné-Poe," in Roger Shattuck and Simon Watson Taylor, eds., *Selected Works of Alfred Jarry*, trans. S.W. Taylor, (New York: Grove Press, 1965), pp. 67-68.

5. Lugné-Poe, *Acrobaties*, p. 160.

6. Jarry himself gradually phased *Les Polyhèdres* out of the running when he realized that Lugné-Poe would not produce both plays.

7. Alfred Jarry, Letter to Lugné-Poe, August 1, 1896.

8. Lugné-Poe, *Acrobaties*, p. 170-71.

9. *Ibid.*, pp. 174-75.

10. There seems to be some confusion as to the exact date of the *Ubu* scandal. We know that there were two performances, but scholars differ as to the dates of these two performances, and more exactly, on which of the two evenings did the scandal take place. Jacques Robichez in *Le Symbolisme au théâtre* quite clearly pinpoints the premiere on December 10 and the dress rehearsal on December 9 (p. 530). Yet Roger Shattuck in *The Banquet Years* writes, "December 11, 1896, the opening night is worth describing in detail," (p. 206). Gertrude Jasper in *Lugné-Poe and the Théâtre de l'Oeuvre*, describes the same scandalous events as occurring on December 10. Shattuck mentions a dress rehearsal (the first of the two performances), but says: "The dress rehearsal had been fairly quiet." Jasper doesn't mention a dress rehearsal at all. Lugné-Poe himself in *Acrobaties* writes: "The hall, filled to bursting, has been described many times (10 December 1896)." and later adds, "Since this rehearsal *Ubu* has gone down in the annals of the theatre." (pp. 177, 178).

In an attempt to clarify the situation I present information gleaned from an interview with Fermin Gémier (*Commoedia*, November 4, 1921). Gémier, who played Ubu in the original production, is unambiguous about the facts he presents: "The première took place on December 10, 1896. The dress rehearsal was the night before. At that time there were only these two performances." The two performances then took place on December 9 and 10. On which evening did the scandal take place? Gémier makes it clear that the scandal occurred on December 9, at the dress rehearsal. After describing the events of that evening, he writes: "After such a dress rehearsal we expected to have at the première an audience in the mood for anything. I was armed with a tramway-horn, a loud instrument which has disappeared, and I said to myself: "If things get hot I'll blow into it like Roland at Roncevaux." I didn't have to use it but two brief times. The audience at the premiere, as always, was less passionate than that at the dress rehearsal."

Well into the 1920s, a dress rehearsal was announced to the public, sometimes a few days in advance of the "première." The announcement of Cocteau's *Le Boeuf sur le toît*, for example, reads, "Saturday, the 21st, Monday the 23rd—Dress Rehearsal A and B—; Wednesday the 25th and Saturday, February 28th—Box Offices Open." One critic of the "Spectacle d'avant-garde," (21.2.1920) also makes it clear that reviewers were invited to the dress rehearsals rather than to the première. "This afternoon a dress rehearsal of an avant-garde production which will open for the public on the 25th and 28th of February at the Comedie des Champs Elysées, will be presented for the press."

11. Both of Jarry's articles on the theatre appear in English translation in *Selected Works*, pp. 69-75 and 82-85.

12. *Ibid.*, p. 72.

13. *Ibid.*

14. Unless otherwise indicated, details of the original *Ubu* performance were culled from contemporary newspaper articles gathered in the file: Alfred Jarry, Fonds Rondel, Rf 62.878, Bibliothèque de l'Arsenal, Paris.

15. Quoted in Roger Shattuck, *The Banquet Years* (New York, 1968), p. 220.

16. Alfred Jarry, "Preliminary Address at the first performance of *Ubu Roi*," in *Selected Works*, pp. 76-78.

17. Arthur Symons, quoted in Shattuck, *op. cit.*, p. 207.

18. *Commoedia*, November 4, 1921.

19. *La Nouvelle Littéraire*, November 26, 1922.

20. Max Maurey quoted in Gertrude Jasper, *Adventure in the Theatre: Lugné-Poe and the Théâtre de l'Oeuvre* (New Brunswick, New Jersey, 1947), p. 227.

21. *Commoedia*, November 4, 1921.

22. Bauer and the other four: Silvestre, Mendes, Scholl, and Lorrain had all been mentioned by Jarry in his introductory remarks.

23. In Shattuck, *op. cit.*, pp. 211-12.

24. *Ibid.*, p. 214.

25. *Ibid.*

26. "Notes sur la seconde représentation d'*Ubu Roi*," *Cahiers du Collège de 'Pataphysique*, No. 2, p. 51.

27. As Joseph Cary points out in his article "Futurism and the French Théâtre d'Avant-Garde," the name is a light gloss on Rimbaud's piece by that name in *Les Illuminations:* "J'ai seul la clef de cette parade sauvage."

28. Cocteau, in Douglas Cooper, *Picasso Théâtre* (New York: 1968), p. 21.

29. *Ibid.*, p. 21.

30. Rondel Collection RO 12535, Ballets Russes, 10ème Saison, mai, 1917. Bibliothèque de l'Arsenal, Paris.

31. Guillaume Apollinaire, "Parade and the New Spirit," (1917), quoted in Henning Rischbeiter, *Art and the Stage in the Twentieth Century*, (Greenwich, Connecticut: 1968), p. 83.

32. André Gide, *Journals*, p. 688.

33. Apollinaire's other works for the theatre include: a ballet, *L'homme sans yeux et sans oreilles*; a comic opera, *Casanova*; two unpublished comedies, *Le Marchand d'anchois* and *La Temperature*; and the drama *Couleur du Temps*. He also wrote a scenario for a motion picture (in collaboration with André Billy), *La Brehantine*.

34. The performance had originally been announced for 2:30, was at the last moment changed to 4:00 and the doors didn't actually open until 5:00 p.m.

35. Although the term "surrealism" has become accepted in English, the proper translation of the French "surréalisme" would be "superrealism," just as "surnaturalisme" is translated "supernaturalism."

36. Translated by Susan Suleiman, in Guillaume Apollinaire, *Apollinaire on Art: Essays and Reviews 1902-1918,* ed. Leroy C. Breunig, (New York, 1972), p. 452.

37. The review, hand printed by Albert-Birot himself, was founded in January, 1916, and sent, gratis, to soldiers on the Western front. *SIC* (Sounds-Ideas-Colors), was futurist in leaning, tending to invoke movement, speed, simultaneity, and dynamism.

38. Quotations from the play are taken from the translation by Louis Simpson in Michael Benedikt and George E. Wellwarth, eds. *Modern French Theatre: The avant-garde, dada, and surrealism,* (New York, 1966).

39. Guillaume Apollinaire, "Les Tendences nouvelles," *SIC* I (Nos. 8-9-10, August, September, October, 1916), n.p.

40. Apollinaire, in his "Preface" to the play, notes that it was actually written in large part in 1903, the year in which Apollinaire and Jarry first met, when the author was 23. The prologue and the last scene of the second act, he states, were added in 1916.

41. In Arlette Albert-Birot, "Pierre Albert-Birot et le surréalisme," *Europe*, November/December, 1968, p. 101.

42. "Preface," *The breasts of Tirésias, loc. cit.*

43. Pierre Albert-Birot, "*Couleur du temps*, drame de Guillaume Apollinaire," *SIC*, III (No. 36, December, 1918), n.p. In the same article, Albert-Birot deplores the training

of contemporary actors, whose penchant for realism does not allow them to act in the manner appropriate to Apollinaire's work.

44. The repartee loses entirely in translation as the verbal jousting was based on a play of words: "Passez lui les mamelles, Tirésias . . . l'enfant veut du lait." "Du laid, et bien! il est servi . . ."

45. Herrand, because of the recent death of his father, played under the pseudonym of Jean Thillois.

46. Just four years before, Luigi Russolo had published his Futurist manifesto on "The art of noise."

47. In his choice of the name Tirésias, Apollinaire profits from the allusions to the Tiresias of legend who mediates between Zeus and Hera in their imbroglio as to which sex derives more pleasure from the sexual act. In this hermaphrodite Tirésias is a thematic strengthening of simultaneism.

48. The whole aspect of Tirésias' production-line birthing of 40,049 children in a day is quite in line with a renewed interest in the myth of the mechanical and its association with the erotic, as in such works as Jarry's "modern novel," *Le Surmâle* (1902), where the human being is transformed into a love-making machine, Raymond Roussell's photographic bed for Fogar in *Impressions of Africa* (1910) —the dramatization of which Apollinaire had seen with the Picabias and Duchamp, and, of course, Duchamp's own *The Bride Stripped Bare by her Bachelors, Even*, which was in the works when Apollinaire voyaged with the painter in the Jura mountains in 1912.

49. Michel Sanouillet in his study *Dada à Paris* (p. 81) claims that this incident, which did not appear in the newspaper and magazine accounts of the production, was much exaggerated by Breton. Vaché, however, was undoubtedly a catalyst for Breton and interestingly, both Ball and Tzara had such young-dying catalysts in their backgrounds as well. For Ball, it was the expressionist writer Hans Leybold with whom he'd written sarcastic poems under the pseudonym Ha Hu Baley. Leybold died in a military hospital. For Tzara, the figure was the Roumanian symbolist Urmuz (the pseudonym of Demetru Demetrescu-Bazau) whose "pages bizarres" were written in 1907-8 in a unique surrealist language. Urmuz, in 1923, placed a bullet through his head.

50. From the sheet music for the play, reproduced in *SIC*.

51. *Art et Liberté*, the avant-garde theatre group which would become *Art et Action*, had just produced an evening of "drames simultanées," which had also been called cubist.

52. André Breton, *Entretiens 1913-1952*, ed. André Parinaud, (Paris, 1969), p. 27.

53. Guillaume Apollinaire, letter of 28 June 1917 to Pierre Reverdy, facsimile reproduction in *Album Apollinaire, iconographie réunie et commentée* par Pierre-Marcel Adema and Michel Decaudin, (Gallimard, 1971), p. 263.

54. The text of this lecture didn't appear in print until December, 1918, in *Mercure de France*.

55. As recounted by Jacqueline Apollinaire, the poet's wife, in Francis Steegmuller, *Apollinaire, Poet among the Painters,* (New York, 1963), p. 328.

Chapter VIII

1. The title had been suggested by Paul Valéry as an ironic play on Verlaine's famous "tout le reste est littérature."

2. André Breton, *Entretiens,* p. 50.

3. Philippe Soupault, in *Les Lettres francaises,* quoted in Elmer Peterson, *Tristan Tzara: Dada and Surrational Theorist* (New Brunswick, New Jersey, 1971), p. xxi.

4. *Art et Action* sponsored the lecture "From symbolism to Dadaism" on February 27. The lecture was accompanied by readings of symbolist and dada poetry by actors of the *Comédie Française,* the *Odéon,* and the *Vieux Colombier.*

5. Quoted in Sanouillet, *op. cit.,* p. 154.

6. Tzara, in Wilson, *op. cit.,* p. 305.

7. Quoted in Albert Schinz, "Dadaism," *Smith College Studies in Modern Languages,* vol. V (October 1923), pp. 55-56.

8. Quoted in Sanouillet, p. 158.

9. Details of the major Paris dada manifestations were culled from newspaper articles and reviews gathered in the files: *Dada,* Rj2211, Ro2224, Fonds Rondel, Bibliothèque de l'Arsenal.

10. Cousin of Gabrielle Buffet, wife of Picabia.

11. Ribemont-Dessaignes, *déjà-jadis,* pp. 70-71.

12. Quoted in Marcel Jean, *The History of Surrealist Painting,* trans. Simon Watson Taylor, (New York: Grove Press, 1960), p. 82.

13. Georges Ribemont-Dessaignes was the only taker, submitting a text entitled *Zizi de Dada,* the script of which has since been lost and, claims the author, so has his ability to recall the work. What little remains is an image of the Pope, enclosed in a circle of chalk from which he tries unsuccessfully to escape. Lugné-Poe gently refused the play for production and the playwright quite agrees with him though he makes it clear that *Zizi* was no more eccentric than *Le Sérin Muet* had been.

14. For a review of the relationships between Cocteau and the dadas, see Appendix II.

15. The hall, also outfitted with two grand pianos, was generally used for serious concert music.

16. *La Nouvelle Revue Française,* May 27, 1920.

17. Quoted by Tzara, in Wilson, *op. cit.*, p. 308.

18. Ribemont-Dessaignes, *déjà-jadis*, pp. 89, 86.

19. Germaine Everling-Picabia, *C'était hier: Dada*, p. 148.

20. Breton, *Entretiens*, p. 59.

21. Picabia, quoted in Motherwell, p. 183.

22. Picabia, quoted in Georges Ribemont-Dessaignes, "History of Dada," in Motherwell, p. 117.

23. Breton, in Sanouillet, p. 445.

24. Breton, in Motherwell, p. 190.

25. Breton, in *Entretiens*, p. 66.

26. Quoted from "Proceedings of the Barrès trial," in Maurice Nadeau, *The History of Surrealism*, trans. Richard Howard (New York Macmillan, 1965), p. 66.

27. Tzara, stage directions to Act I of *The Gas Heart*, in Michael Benedikt and George E. Wellwarth, eds. *Modern French Theatre: The Avant-Garde, Dada, and Surrealism* (New York: Dutton, 1966), p. 133.

28. Tzara, quoted in Sanouillet, p. 323.

29. André Breton, "Lâchez tout," in Nadeau, p. 67.

30. In 1912, Roussel's *Impressions d'Afrique* was played at the *Théâtre Antoine*.

31. It took Breton many years to forgive Tzara for what he felt was a clear instance of that poet's having handed him and his compatriots into the hands of the police.

32. Jacqueline Chaumont of the *Odéon*, MOUTH; Marcel Herrand, EYEBROW; Saint-Jean of the *Odéon*, EAR; Jacques Baron, NECK; René Crevel, EYE; Pierre de Massot, NOSE.

33. Germaine Everling-Picabia in *C'était hier: Dada*, p. 168.

Chapter IX

1. André Breton, "Entrée des mediums," quoted in Rubin, *Dada, Surrealism and their Heritage*, pp. 62-63.

2. André Breton, "Manifesto of Surrealism," in *Manifestos of Surrealism*, trans. by Richard Seaver and Helen R. Lane (Ann Arbor, Michigan, 1969), p. 26.

3. "Interrupters appeared in every corner. One voice proclaims: 'We will not let you speak. Signed: the surrealists.' Then things grew nastier . . . the police intervened . . . Philippe Soupault leaped onto the stage and stood there, arms folded, defying anyone to remove

him save at bayonet-point. . . Robert Desnos violently harangued the crowd, striding up and down the stage . . . Meanwhile the gentle poet Eluard had been punched; Vitrac dashed forward to defend him . . . the whole house was standing, and threats and insults flew through the air." Quoted in Maurice Nadeau, *The History of Surrealism*, p. 112.

4. Ludwig Wittgenstein, *Philosophical Investigation* (New York: The Macmillan Company), 1958, p. 31[e].

5. I choose the looser term "sketch," rather than "play," in order to include such diverse works as the Breton-Desnos-Peret one-scene "happening" with animals and objects (*Comme il fait beau*, 1923), and Albert-Birot's vaudeville *Le Bon Dieu*, 1920, under one heading. The dada-surrealists themselves were prone to classify their works for the stage under headings which would provide the public with a yardstick for measuring the distance separating their theatre from familiar dramatic forms. Tzara's *La première aventure céleste de M. Antipyrine* (performed in Paris on March 27, 1920), was termed a "double quatrologue"; Ribemont-Dessaignes' *Le Sérin Muet*, on the same bill, was subtitled a one-act play, while Breton and Soupault's *S'il vous plaît* was called a comedy.

6. Bertin was a popular French actor who continually acted in the dada-surrealist performances.

7. Louise Lara was, with her husband Claude Autant, head of the experimental theatre group *Art et Action*.

8. Louis Aragon, "Projet d'histoire littéraire contemporaine," *Littérature* (nouvelle série) no. 4: 3-6, September, 1922.

9. André Breton, "Seconde Manifeste de Surréalisme," (Paris: Jean-Jacques Pauvert, 1962), p. 183.

10. J.H. Matthews, *Theatre in Dada and Surrealism* (Syracuse University Press, 1974), p. 278.

11. What is especially interesting here is that the surrealists, who in the fields of poetry and painting chanted hosanas to a list of admired precursors whom they named, never bothered to make such a list of theatre predecessors, and although Jarry ranked high among their favorites, it was at least as much for his novel, *le Surmâle*, as for *Ubu Roi*. Similarly, it was Raymond Roussel of the novels as much as of the plays who was lauded by the surrealists.

12. Michel Sanouillet, *Dada à Paris*, (Jean-Jacques Pauvert, 1965), p. 423.

13. André Breton, *Entretiens*, p. 56.

14. Roger Shattuck, "The D-S Expedition," *The New York Review of Books*, Part I (May 18, 1972), p. 24.

15. "Entrée des mediums," *Littérature*, nouvelle série, No. 6, November 1, 1922 in *Les Pas perdus*, p. 125.

16. André Breton, "Manifeste du surréalisme" (1924), *loc. cit.*, pp. 44-45.

17. Though not before Breton had been exposed to some of the poet's writing through the journal *Dada,* sampled *chez* Apollinaire in 1917.

18. Sanouillet, *Dada à Paris,* p. 125.

19. Anna Balakian, *André Breton: Magus of Surrealism,* (Oxford University Press, 1971).

20. Pierre Janet, *L'Automatisme psychologique,* (Paris, 1921), p. 464.

21. Balakian notes that Janet's definition of automatic writing helps to point up the distinction between surrealist automatic writing and the writing of the dadaists and later avantgarde writers of the language of the absurd—that is "where the language itself is irrational in structure and content and is offered as symptomatic of man's abject condition as an automaton deprived of his autonomy in a world reduced to automation," p. 30.

22. Louis Aragon, "Une Vague de rêves," *Commerce* (Autumn, 1924).

23. *Ibid.*

24. André Breton, *Les pas perdus,* (Gallimard, 1924), p. 149.

25. This problem is highlighted by Breton in a letter of September 24, 1920, to Simone Kahn, soon to be his wife. There he writes that though both texts were signed jointly by Soupault and himself, he was practically the sole author.

26. Personal interview, Paris, June, 1971.

27. Two scenes of *Vous m'oublierez* were published in the first issue of the magazine *Cannibale* (April 25, 1920). The complete text, dated May, 1920, appeared in *Littérature* (nouvelle série, no. 4, September 1, 1922).

28. Many questions remain to be asked about both the practice and the results of automatic writing, questions such as: "Are talent, sensitivity, and training irrelevant to the operation of automatic processes?"

29. Louis Aragon, *Traité du Style,* (Paris, 1928), pp. 187, 192. Breton, for his part, is said to have explained that when Théodore Fraenkel drew words from a hat, the technique produced no interesting results ("ça ne donne rien") because Fraenkel was not a writer.

30. Anna Balakian, *André Breton: Magus of Surrealism,* p. 63.

31. *Ibid.,* p. 64.

32. See her introduction to Gloria Orenstein's *The Theatre of the Marvellous* where she writes: "Some years ago, upon being asked to do an article on surrealist theatre for an encyclopedia, I reread the fragmental plays that the surrealists had created in the early phase of their cenacle and came to the conclusion that surrealism produced nothing more than a blueprint for theatre. That was before Gloria Orenstein launched on her

global and exhaustive investigation of the flowering of the terrain, vaguely delimited but fertile, which the surrealists had seeded and their followers cultivated" (p. xiii).

33. André Breton, *Point du jour* (Paris, 1934), p. 7.

34. André Breton, *Nadja,* trans. Richard Howard (New York: Grove Press, 1960), p. 40.

35. *Ibid.,* p. 38.

36. André Breton, *Manifesto of Surrealism,* loc. cit., p. 50-51.

37. *Ibid.,* p. 50.

38. André Breton and Philippe Soupault, *If You Please,* Michael Benedikt and Geoge E. Wellwarth, *Modern French Theatre: The Avant-Garde, Dada and Surrealism,* (New York: E.P. Dutton & Co., 1966), p. 170.

39. André Gide, a journal entry of January 3, 1924, in *The Counterfeiters: with Journal of "The Counterfeiters,"* (New York, 1959), p. 406. Parts of the *Pages du Journal de Lafcadio* were originally published in *Littérature,* no. 11, January, 1920.

40. Quoted in Matthews, *The Theatre in Dada and Surrealism,* p. 6.

41. The play was completed by January 14, 1920 (see letter to Tristan Tzara, in Sanouillet, *Dada à Paris,* p. 455). The second Act was performed at the Manifestation Dada-Théâtre de l'Oeuvre, March 27, 1920, and the first three acts were published in *Littérature,* no. 16, September-October, 1920. The fourth act, which completed the play, remained unpublished until the 1967 Gallimard edition of *Les Champs Magnétiques.*

42. Two scenes were published in *Cannibale,* no. 1, April 25, 1920. The play was presented at the Festival de la Salle Gaveau, May 26, 1920.

43. Personal interview with Philippe Soupault, Paris, summer, 1971.

44. Quoted in Sanouillet, *op. cit.,* p. 454.

45. *Ibid.,* p. 455.

46. In a letter of August 25, 1920 (quoted in Marguerite Bonnet, *André Breton: naissance de l'aventure surréaliste* (José Corti, 1975), p. 246) to Simone Kahn, soon to become Breton's wife, Breton makes it clear that both plays were intended to be part of what he called "a sort of love cycle." A third play, consecrated to pleasure, was to have followed. It was never written.

47. Roger Shattuck, "The D-S Expedition," *loc.cit.*

48. Quoted in Rubin, *Dada and Surrealist Art,* pp. 177-78.

49. *Ibid.*

50. Although this information is given by Soupault himself (see personal interview), and supported by Béhar (p. 338) in his listing of only the acting cast for the second act, Tzara in *Le Surréalisme et l'Après Guerre* (Nagel, 1948, p. 20), reports that it was only the first act that was performed, and goes on to give a wildly inaccurate account of Act II.

51. Michael Benedikt, *Modern French Theatre, op. cit.,* p. xxiv.

52. Sanouillet, *Dada à Paris,* p. 166-67.

53. Esslin, Martin, *The Theatre of the Absurd* (Anchor Books, 1961), p. 264.

54. Benedikt, Michael, *op. cit.,* p. xxiv.

55. Matthews, J.H., *Theatre in Dada and Surrealism,* p. 91.

56. In his *Entretiens,* Breton recalls: "Soupault and I . . . we received only small satisfaction except for a sketch which we wrote entitled *Vous m'oublierez,* which we acted ourselves at the Salle Gaveau, notwithstanding a bombardment of eggs, tomatoes, steaks which the spectators had gone to collect during the intermission. What the public thought of us, we repayed them with a hundredfold" (p. 58).

57. Information gleaned from Soupault interview.

58. Matthews does a careful job of showing that Breton, alongside the great stock he placed in Tzara before the latter's arrival in Paris, had serious reservations as well both about the man and the movement even before the leader of Zurich dada set foot in the French capital. The evidence he brings to bear (pp. 85-87), supports his contention that Breton, from early on, found it essential to evade the limitations that dada imposed.

59. Quoted in Rubin, *Dada and Surrealist Art,* p. 263.

60. Breton, in the *Entretiens,* reproduces a statement of Soupault's which he says he would have gladly countersigned: "One does not judge M. de Lautréamont. One acknowledges him in passing and bows to the ground. I will give my life to the he or she who will make me forget him forever" (p. 42).

61. I cannot, within the scope of this essay, commit myself to an analysis in depth of the purely language-games which fill the plays. The tracing of the rejection of clarity and of an orderly pattern in the poetry of dada and surrealism is subject enough for an essay of its own. Where poetic and theatrical considerations join is on the level of an increasingly bold experimentation with spatial form, and the new acknowledgment of an external reality, subject to endless transmutations. What one might say of the shift to the irrational and the fantastic, the increasingly personal and the private, the breaking of rhythm and syntax, I will attempt to discuss in theatrical rather than poetic terms. The new elements of speed, instantaneity, sexual configurations, shock, obfuscations and willful disorganization, the lack of any *fil conducteur,* all identifiable in the pure text, are traceable on the performance level as well. For a solid analysis of the salient characteristics of the experimental poetry of the 1920s see Jean Epstein, *La Poésie d'aujourd'hui* (Paris, 1921). For an in depth study of the poetry of dada and surrealism

see Mary Ann Caws, *The Poetry of Dada and Surrealism; Aragon, Breton, Tzara, Eluard and Desnos* (Princeton University Press, 1970).

62. André Breton, "Les mot sans rides," *Les pas perdus*, p. 167.

63. Members of the audience who frequented the avant-garde theatre could already have seen such huge head-masks at the Théâtre Art et Action production of "le dit des Jeux du Monde."

64. Jean Cocteau, "Avant *Le Boeuf sur le toît* de M. Jean Cocteau, un préambule de l'auteur," in *Commoedia*, 21 fevrier 1920.

65. Jean Cocteau, Preface to *The Wedding on the Eiffel Tower*, in Benedikt and Wellwarth, eds. *Modern French Theatre*, p. 99.

66. Douglas Cooper, *Picasso Theatre*, p. 56.

67. In 1926, the surrealist group repeated the theatrical scandal they had caused at *Mercure*. Again a ballet was the setting; this time, Diaghilev's *Romeo and Juliet* designed in part by Max Ernst. Ernst had asked Breton's advice before taking on the project and Breton had raised no objection. Picasso, now playing Breton's game, attacked the surrealist leader with "If someone gives the revolutionaries a sign, they're ready to work for the White Russians." Breton, raging, issued (with Aragon) a statement in Ernst's absence: "The participation of the painters Max Ernst and Joan Miró in the performances of the Ballets Russes is not capable of devaluing the surrealist idea—a fundamentally subversive idea that cannot go along with such undertakings, whose goal has always been to domesticize the dreams and revolts of physical and intellectual hunger for the profit of the international aristocracy" (quoted in Rischbieter, *Art and the Stage*, p. 127). Surrealism was by this time in its revolutionary phase.

68. In Cooper, *Picasso Theatre*, p. 60.

69. Unless otherwise indicated, details of the *Relâche* performance were culled from contemporary newspaper reviews gathered in the file *Ballets Suédois, 1921, Fonds Rondel*, Ro 12796, *Bibliothèque de l'Arsenal*.

70. In 1920, Satie had written what he called "musique d'ameublement," furniture music, to fill the entr'acte between two parts of a concert. The intermission, he felt, provided too great a break in the general atmosphere, and should be filled in by a kind of music which would be played in the foyer, and to which people would pay no more attention than to the furniture or carpeting. The players were to be put in different parts of the room and the short pieces would be played over and over again while the audience would talk, move about and order drinks. The moment the placard "musique d'ameublement" was put up, however, the audience stopped talking and listened solemnly through thirty repetitions of one of the pieces. By this point, Satie, exasperated beyond reason, dashed around the room shouting, "Talk! Talk!"

71. Rolf de Maré, in Rischbieter, *Art and the Stage*, p. 170.

72. Fernand Léger, "Vive *Relâche*," *Ibid.*, p. 169.

73. For a full analysis of Aragon's play see Annabelle Henkin Melzer, "Aragon's *L'armoire à glace un beau soire;* a play of the surrealists. "Epoque de sommeil," *Comparative Drama,* Vol. II, no. 1, Spring, 1977, pp. 45-62.

74. As in Feydeau's *Une puce à l'oreille* and Sardou's *Divorçons.*

75. All quotations from Aragon's play are from Michael Benedikt's translation in Benedikt and Wellwarth, eds. *Modern French Theatre.*

76. Maurice Nadeau, *The History of Surrealism,* p. 97.

77. Matthew Josephson, *Life Among the Surrealists: A Memoir,* (New York: Holt, Rinehart, and Winston, 1962), p. 124.

78. Tristan Tzara, "Le Secret de *Mouchoir de Nuages,"* *Intégral,* No. 2 (April 1, 1925), p. 7.

79. Tristan Tzara, *Handkerchief of Clouds,* trans. Aileen Robbins, *The Drama Review,* T-56, December, 1972, p. 112.

80. Tristan Tzara, "Le secret de *Mouchoir de Nuages,"* p. 30.

81. These names were attributed by Tzara to his colleagues (quoted in Edmund Wilson's *Axel's Castle,* p. 306).

82. Quoted in Josephson, p. 103.

83. William Seitz, *The Art of Assemblage.* (New York: The Museum of Modern Art, 1961), p. 37.

84. André Gide, quoted in Motherwell, p. xxv.

Appendix I

1. Breton mentions the "Merzbau" in his essay "Genèse et perspective artistique du Surréalisme," (1941), *Le Surréalisme et la peinture* (Paris, 1965).

2. Kurt Schwitters in Motherwell, *op. cit.,* pp. 62-63.

3. Kurt Schwitters and Franz Rolan, "Über die Merzbühne," *Der Strum,* Vol. XIV, nos. 4-6, 1923.

4. Kurt Schwitters, in Motherwell, *op. cit.,* p. 62.

5. Kurt Schwitters, in Rubin, *Dada, Surrealism and their Heritage,* pp. 57, 60.

6. Kurt Schwitters, "Normalbühne Merz," mimeographed handwritten manuscript dated "Gohren, Juli 1925," in the Schwitters papers, quoted in Werner Schmalenbach, *Kurt Schwitters* (New York: Harry N. Abrams, Inc., 1967), p. 191.

7. Huelsenbeck later wrote: "It matters to me that my conflict with Schwitters in those days should be expounded fairly and accurately. . . . At that time I regard Schwitters as

a German Romantic . . . My whole resistance to Germany, then as now, was a resistance to Romanticism, to futile daydreaming, to fear of reality, and to the irresponsibility bound up with the latter . . . . Schwitters as I saw him was a man who ran away from reality." Letter of September 9, 1958 to Schmalenbach, quoted in Schmalenbach, *op. cit.*, p. 247.

8. Richter, *op. cit.*, p. 145.

9. Kurt Schwitters, "Dadaizm," *Blok*, 1924/1925.

10. Kurt Schwitters, in Motherwell, *op. cit.*, p. 59.

11. Quoted in Schmalenbach, p. 243 n. 35.

12. Raoul Hausmann, "29 Jahre Freundschaft mit Kurt Schwitters," in Schmalenbach, p. 253 n. 43.

13. Kurt Schwitters, "Anna Blume," in Richter, p. 141.

14. *Ibid.*, p. 149.

15. Hans Arp, "Franz Muller's Drahftfrüling," *Quadrum*, 1956.

16. Moholy-Nagy, Laszlo. *Vision in Motion.* (Chicago: Paul Theobald, 1961), p. 325.

17. Hans Richter, *op. cit.*

18. *Merz 20*-Katalog, 1927, quoted in Schmalenbach, p. 240.

19. Richter, p. 142.

20. *Ibid.*, p. 143.

21. Kurt Schwitters, "Theo van Doesburg and Dada," in Motherwell, p. 275.

22. Kurt Schwitters, in Richter, pp. 146-7.

23. Schwitters in Motherwell, passim., pp. 57-65.

24. George Grosz and Wieland Herzfelde, "Dadaism," in Lucy Lippard, *Dadas on Art*, p. 86.

25. Richard O. Boyer, "George Grosz, The saddest man in the world," Profile, *The New Yorker*, II (December 4, 1943), p. 46.

26. Grosz and Herzfelde, *op. cit.*, in Lippard, p. 86.

27. Huelsenbeck, in Motherwell, p. 28.

28. Walter Mehring, in Richter, pp. 110-11.

29. Raoul Hausmann, in Richter, p. 124.

30. Walter Mehring, in Manuel Grossman, *Dada: Paradox, Mystification, and Ambiguity in European Literature,* (New York: Pegasus, 1971), p. 77.

31. Grossman, p. 78.

Appendix II

1. *Cannibale,* April 25, 1920.

2. In Sanouillet, p. 105.

3. Albert-Birot, quoted in Sanouillet, p. 105.

4. Lector, in Sanouillet, p. 105.

5. Francis Picabia, in Sanouillet, p. 192.

6. Jean Cocteau, in Sanouillet, p. 193.

Bibliography

I   Bibliographies and Research Aids

Gershman, Herbert. *A Bibliography of the Surrealist Revolution in France.* Ann Arbor: University of Michigan Press, 1969.
Hardré, Jacques. "Present State of Studies on Literary Surrealism," *Yearbook of Comparative and General Literature,* IX (1960): 43-66.
Le Sage, Laurent. "The Direction of Studies on Surrealism." *L'Esprit créateur,* VIII (1968): 230-39.
Matthews, J.H. "Forty Years of Surrealism (1924-1964): A Preliminary Bibliography." *Comparative Literature Studies,* III, No. 3 (1966): 309-50.
Shattuck, Roger. "The Dada-Surrealist Expedition." *The New York Review of Books,* Part I (May 18, 1972), Part II (June 1, 1972).

II   Archival and Unpublished Document Collections

General

Ballets Russes, 10ème saison, 1917. Press clippings. Fonds Rondel, Ro 12535. Bibliothèque de l'Arsenal. Paris.
Ballets Suédois, 1921. Press clippings. Fonds Rondel, Ro 12796. Bibliothèque de l'Arsenal. Paris.
Dada. Press clippings. Fonds Rondel, Rj 2211, Ro2224. Bibliothèque de l'Arsenal. Paris.
Dada Bulletins. Fonds Doucet Ad-III 47. Bibliothèque St. Geneviève. Paris.
Dada Documents. Fonds Doucet, B-IV, 9955, 57, 59. Bibliothèque St. Geneviève, Paris.
Futurism and Dada. Fonds Doucet, DP 6 Bibliothèque St. Geneviève. Paris.
Surrealism. Press clippings. Fonds Rondel, Rj 2233. Bibliothèque de l'Arsenal, Paris.

For archival materials concerning specific persons, see Section Vb.

III   Dada/Surrealism: The Plays, Sketches, Scenarios

Albert-Birot, Pierre. *Matoum et Tevibar.* Serialized in *SIC* (octobre 1918-mars 1919).
_____. *Larountala.* Paris: Editions Sic, 1919.
_____. *L'Homme coupé en morceaux. La vie des lettres.* (janvier, avril, juillet, 1921).
_____. *Le Bondieu.* Paris: Editions Sic, 1922.
_____. *Les Femmes Pliantes.* Paris: Editions Sic, 1923.
Apollinaire, Guillaume. *Les Mamelles de Tirésias.* Paris: Gallimard, 1924.
Aragon, Louis. *Au pied du mur. Le libertinage.* Paris: Gallimard, 1924.
_____. *L'Armoire à glace un beau soir. Le Libertinage.* Paris: Gallimard, 1924.
_____, and André Breton. *Trésor des Jesuites. Variétes,* No. hors série: *Le Surréalisme en 1929,* 47-61.
Artaud, Antonin. *Le Jet de sang. L'umbilic des limbes.* Paris: Gallimard, 1964.

———— . *Les Cenci. Oeuvres complètes.* IV. Paris: Gallimard, 1964.

Ball, Hugo. *Der Henker von Brescia. Die neue kunst,* III (March, 1914).

———— . *Die Nase des Michelangelo.* Leipzig: Ronoholt, 1911.

Baron, Jacques. *Les Voyageurs debout.* Ms. Bibliothèque littéraire Jacques Doucet. Côte 1039-7.

Breton, André, and Philippe Soupault. *S'il vous plaît. Littérature,* première série, No. 16 (septembre-octobre 1920): 10-32.

———— , and Philippe Soupault. *Vous m'oublierez.* scenes i, ii, with variations; *Cannibale,* No. 1 (25 avril 1920); complete text: *Littérature,* nouvelle serie, No. 4 (ler septembre 1922): 25-32.

———— . Robert Desnos and Benjamin Peret. *Comme il fait beau! Littérature,* nouvelle série, No. 9 (ler février, ler mars 1923): 6-13.

Cocteau, Jean. *Parade.* Paris: Rouart-Lerolle, 1919.

———— . *Le Bôeuf sur le toît or the Nothing Doing Bar.* Paris: La Sirene, 1920.

———— . *Les Mariées de la Tour Eiffel.* Paris: Gallimard, 1923.

———— , Raymond Radiguet, and Francis Poulenc. *Le Gendarme Incompris.* Paris: Editions de la Galerie Simon, n.d.

Desnos, Robert. *La Place de l'Étoile.* Serialized in *Le Soir* (28 aout 1928+), revised ed. Paris: Rodez, 1945.

Daumal, Rene. *En Gggarrrrde! Petit Théâtre.* Paris: Collège de Pataphysique, 1957.

Gilbert-Lecomte, Roger. *L'Odyssee d'Ulyssé le Palmipede. Petit Théâtre.* Paris: Collège de Pataphysique, 1957.

Goll, Yvan. *Mathusalem.* Paris: Editions de la Sirène, 1923.

———— . *Assurance contre le suicide. Le Théâtre d'Yvan Goll.* Paris: Editions de l'Arche, 1963.

———— . *Celui qui ne meurt pas. Le Théâtre d'Yvan Goll.* Paris: Editions de l'Arche, 1963.

Jarry, Alfred. *Ubu Roi.* Paris: Editions Mercure de France, 1896.

———— . *Ubu Cocu. Ubu Enchaîné. Ubu Sur la Butte.* in *Tout Ubu.* Paris: Le livre de Poche, 1962.

Kandinsky, Wassily, *Sonorité jaune, Der Blaue Reiter,* Munich: May, 1912.

———— . *Sonorité verte* (1909), *Noir et blanc* (1909), *Violet* (1911), *Écrits Complets.* Paris: Denoie-Gonthier, 1975.

Kokoschka, Oskar, *Hoffnung der Frauen.* Berlin: Der Sturm Verlag, 1909.

———— . *Sphinx and Strohmann: Ein Curiosum. Schriften 1907-1955.* Munich: Albert Langen, 1956.

Marinetti, Filippo Tommaso. *Teatro.* 3 Vols. Rome: Vito Bianco, 1960.

Radiguet, Raymond. *Les Pélican. Oeuvres Complètes.* Paris: Editions Bernard Grasset, 1952.

Ribemont-Dessaignes, Georges. *L'Empereur de Chine.* Paris: Au Sans Pareil, 1921.

———— . *Le Sérin muet.* Paris: Au Sans Pareil, 1921.

———— . *Zizi de Dada. Dada,* No. 16 (novembre 1921), 109.

———— . *Le Bourreau du Perou.* Paris: Au Sans Pareil, 1928.

———— . *Partage des os. Variétés* (15 décembre 1929), 545-64.

———— . *Larmes de couteau. Cahiers de l'Association internationale pour l'étude de dada et du surréalisme,* No. 1 (octobre 1966).

———— . *Sanatorium,* ms. Bibliothèque de l'Arsenal, coll. Art et Action.

Roussel, Raymond. *Impressions d'Afrique.* Paris: Lemerre, 1910.

———— . *Locus Solus.* Paris: Lemerre, 1914.

———— . *L'Étoile au front.* Paris: Lemerre, 1925.

———— . *La Poussière de soleils.* Paris: Lemerre, 1926.

Salacrou, Armand. *L'Histoire du Cirque. Les Idées de la Nuit.* Paris: Librarie Arthème Fayard, 1960.

Satie, Erik. *Le Piège de Meduse.* Paris: Galerie Simon, 1921.

Tzara, Tristan. *La Première Aventure céleste de M. Antipyrine.* Zurich: Collection Dada, chez J. Heuberger, 1916.

———— . *La Deuxième Aventure céleste de M. Antipyrine.* Paris: Les classiques des éditions des Reverbères, 1938. Originally published in two parts: a. *Littérature,* première série,

No. 14 (juin 1920). b. *391*, No. 14 (november 1920).
_____. *Le Coeur à gaz. Der Sturm*, No. 3 (March 1922). Reprinted. Paris: G.L.M., 1946.
_____. *Mouchoir de Nuages.* Paris: Galerie Simon, 1925.
_____. *La Fuite.* Paris: Gallimard, 1947.
Vitrac, Roger. *Les Mystères de l'Amour.* Paris: N.R.F., 1924.
_____. *Victor ou Les Enfants au pouvoir. Roger Vitrac: Théâtre.* Paris: Gallimard, 1946.
_____. *Le Peintre. Roger Vitrac: Théâtre, I.* Paris: Gallimard, 1964.
_____. *Entrée Libre. Roger Vitrac, Théâtre, III.* Paris: Gallimard, 1964.

Dada-Surrealism: the Plays, Sketches, Scenarios

Plays appearing in English:

Anouilh and Aurenche. *Humulus the Mute.*
Apollinaire. *The Breasts of Tirésias.*
Aragon. *The Mirror-Wardrobe One Fine Evening.*
Artaud. *Jet of Blood.*
Breton and Soupault. *If You Please* (Acts I-III).
Cocteau. *The Wedding on the Eiffel Tower.*
Desnos. *La Place de l'Étoile.*
Daumal. *En Gggarrrde!*
Gilbert-Lecomte, *The Odyssey of Ulysses the Palmiped.*
Jarry. *King Ubu.*
Radiguet. *The Pelicans.*
Salacrou. *A Circus Story.*
Tzara. *The Gas Heart.*
Vitrac. *The Mysteries of Love.*
    All of the above in:
        Benedikt, Michael and George E. Wellworth, editor and translator. *Modern French Theatre: The Avant-Garde, Dada, and Surrealism.* New York: Dutton, 1966.

Aragon, Louis. *Backs to the Wall. The Drama Review,* T-64, (December 1964): 88-107.
Artaud, Antonin. *Les Cenci. The Drama Review,* T-54 (June, 1972): 90-145.
Cocteau, Jean. *Le Boeuf sur le Toît. The Drama Review,* T-55: 27-45.
Kandinsky, Wassily. *The Yellow Sound, A Stage Composition.* In *The Blaue Reiter Almanac,* ed. Wassily Kandinsky and Franz Marc, New Documentary Edition, ed. Klaus Lankheit, trans. Henning Falkenstein, pp. 207-25 (New York: Viking Press, 1974).
Kokoschka, Oskar. *Sphinx and Strawman: A Curiosity. Voices of German Expressionism.* ed. Victor H. Miesel. (Prentice-Hall, Inc.), 1970.
Marinetti, Filippo Tommaso. Selected Playscripts. In Michael Kirby, *Futurist Performance.* New York: E.P. Dutton & Co., Inc., 1971.
Ribemont-Dessaignes, Georges. *The Mute Canary. The Drama Review,* T-53 (March 1972), 110-16.
Roussel, Raymond. *Locus Solus* (large sections of the play) in *Locus Solus* (review). New York, No. 5, 1962.
Schawinsky, Xanti. *Play, Life, Illusion. The Drama Review.* T-51 (Summer, 1971): 31-44.
Schwitters, Kurt. *Collision.* In Steinitz, Kate, *Kurt Schwitters; A Portrait from Life.* University of California Press, 1968.
Tzara, Tristan. *Handkerchief of Clouds. The Drama Review,* T-56.

IV Primary Materials

Anthologies

Arp, Hans, Richard Huelsenbeck, and Tristan Tzara. *Dada: Dichtung und Chronik der Grunder.* Zurich: die Arche, 1957.

Huelsenbeck, Richard ed. *Dada Almanac*, Berlin: Reiss, 1920. In English: New York: Something Else Press, 1966.

————. ed. *Dada: eine literarische Dokumentation*. Hamburg: Rowolt, 1964.

Kandinsky, Wassily and Franz Marc, eds. *The Blaue Reiter Alamanc*, New Documentary edition ed., and with an introduction by Klaus Lankheit. New York: The Viking Press, 1974.

Lippard, Lucy, ed. *Dadas on Art*. Englewood Cliffs, New Jersey: Prentice-Hall, Inc., 1971.

————. ed. *Surrealists on Art*. Englewood Cliffs, New Jersey: Prentice-Hall, Inc. 1970.

Lista, Giovanni, ed. *Futurisme: Manifèstes, Proclamations, Documents*. Lausanne: L'Age d'Homme, 1973.

Motherwell, Robert, ed. *The Dada Painters and Poets*. New York: Wittenborn, 1951.

Neumann, Eckhard, ed. *bauhaus and bauhaus people: personal opinions and recollections of former bauhaus members and their contemporaries*. Trans. by Eva Richter and Alba Lorman. New York: Van Nostrand Reinhold Co., 1970.

Schifferli, Peter, ed. *Das War Dada*. Munich: Deutscher Taschenbuch Verlag, 1963.

————. ed. *Als Dada Begann: Die Geburt das Dada. Bildchronik und Erinnerungen der Grunder*. Zurich: Im Verlag der Arche, 1957.

Portner, Paul, ed. *Literaturevolution 1910-1925: Dokumente, Manifèste, Programme*. Darmstadt: Luchterhand, 1960.

Verkauf, Willy. *Dada: Monograph of a Movement*. New York: George Wittenborn, 1957.

Bowit, John E., ed. *Russian Art of the Avant-Garde: Theory and Criticism 1902-1934*. New York: Viking, 1976.

Selected Manifestos, Memoirs and Other Primary Materials (by Author)

Albert-Birot, Pierre. "Théâtre futuriste." *SIC III*, No. 27 (mars 1918).

Apollinaire, Guillaume. *Apollinaire on Art: Essays and Reviews 1902-1918*. Ed. Leroy C. Brunig, trans. Susan Suleiman, New York: The Viking Press, 1972.

Aragon, Louis. "Projet d'histoire littéraire contemporaine." *Littérature* (septembre 1922).

————. *Le Paysan de Paris*. Paris: Gallimard, 1945.

————. *Traité du style*. Paris: Gallimard, 1928.

————. *Le Libertinage*. Paris: Gallimard, 1924.

————. *"Une Vague de reves." Commerce* (automne 1924).

————. "Lettre Ouverte à André Breton sur "Le Regard su Sourd," et l'art, la science et la liberté." *Les Lettres Françaises* (juin 12, 1971).

Artaud, Antonin. *Lettres à Genica Athanasiou*. Paris: Gallimard, 1969.

————. *Oeuvres Complètes*, Vols. I-XIII. Paris: Gallimard, 1964-1974.

————. *A la Grande nuit ou le bluff surréaliste*. Chez l'auteur, June, 1927. Reprinted in Maurice Nadeau. *Documents Surréalistes*. Paris: Editions du Seuil, 1948.

————. "Lettres d'Antonin Artaud à Roger Vitrac." *Nouvelle Revue Française* (1er avril 1964).

————. "L'evolution du décor." *Commoedia*, 19 avril, 1924.

————. "L'Activité du Bureau de Recherches Surréalistes." *La Revolution Surréaliste*, No. 3, 15 avril, 1925.

————. "L'Atelier de Charles Dullin." *Action*, No. 6 bis, hors-série, 1921.

————. "Le théâtre de l'Atelier." *la Criée*, Marseille, No. 17, 1922.

In English:

————. *Antonin Artaud-Selected Writings*. Ed. and with an introduction by Susan Sontag, trans. Helen Weaver, notes by Susan Sontag and Don Eric Levine. New York: Farrar, Straus and Giroux, 1976.

————. *Antonin Artaud-Collected Works*. Ed. Victor Corti, London: Calder & Boyars, 1968. To date vols. I-VI.

————. *The Theatre and its Double*. Trans. Mary Caroline Richards. New York: Grove Press, 1958.

Ball, Emmy Hennings. *Hugo Ball's Weg zu Gott*. Munich: Kosel und Pustet, 1931.
_____. *Ruf und Echo*. Einsiedeln: Benziger Verlag, 1952.
Ball, Hugo. *Die Flucht aus der Zeit*. Munich and Leipzig, 1927. In English, *Flight out of Time: A Dada Diary*, ed. John Elderfield, New York: Viking, 1974.
_____. *Breife 1911-1927*. Einsiedeln, 1957.
Bertin,Pierre. *Le Théâtre est Ma Vie*. Paris: Le Bélier, 1971.
Breton, André. *Manifestos of Surrealism*. Translated by Richard Seaver and Helen R. Lane. Ann Arbor: University of Michigan Press, 1969.
_____. *Entretiens, 1913-1952*. ed. André Parinaud. Paris: Gallimard, 1952.
_____, and Philippe Soupault. *Les Champs Magnétiques*. Paris: Gallimard, 1967.
Cocteau, Jean. *Entre Picasso et Radiguet*. Textes réunis et presentés par André Fermigier. Paris: Hermann, 1967.
_____. *Paris Album 1900-1914*. Trans. by Margaret Crosland. London: W.H. Allen, 1956.
_____. *The Journals of Jean Cocteau*. Ed. and trans. with an introduction by Wallace Fowlie. New York: Criterion Books, 1956.
Daumal, René. *Lettres à ses amis, 1916-1932*. Paris: Gallimard, 1958.
Desnos, Robert. *Panorama de l'evolution du movement dada (y compris) jusqu'à 1927*. Ms. 3361-63 Fonds Doucet, Paris.
_____. *Cinéma*. Textes réunis et presentés par André Tchernia.
Duchamp, Marcel. *Dialogues with Marcel Duchamp*, by Pierre Cabanne, trans. by Ron Padgett. New York: The Viking Press, 1971.
Everling-Picabia, Germaine. "C'était hier dada." *Les Oeuvres libres*, No. 109 (juin 1955): 119-78.
Goll, Yvan. "La Chaplinade ou Charlot Poète." *Le Nouvel Orphée*. Paris: Editions de la Sirène, 1923.
Grosz, George. *A Little Yes and a Big No: The Autobiography of George Grosz*. New York: Dial Press, 1946.
Hausman, Raoul. *Courrier Dada*. Paris: Le Terrain Vague, 1958.
Huelsenbeck, Richard. *Memoirs of a Dada Drummer*, ed. with an introduction, notes and bibliography by Hans J. Kleinschmidt. Trans. Joachim Neugroschel. New York: Viking, 1969.
Hugnet, Georges. *L'Aventure Dada*. Paris: Galerie de l'Institut, 1957.
Jarry, Alfred. *Oeuvres complètes*. 8 vols. Monte Carlo: Editions du Livre, 1948.
_____. "Writings on the Theatre." *Selected Works of Alfred Jarry*. ed. Roger Shattuck and Simon Watson Taylor. New York: Grove Press, 1965.
Josephson, Matthew. *Life Among the Surrealists, a Memoir*. New York: Holt, Rinehart & Winston, 1962.
Laban, Rudolf. *A Life for Dance: Reminiscences*. Trans. and annotated by Lisa Ullmann. London: Macdonald and Evans, Ltd., 1975.
Ribemont-Dessaignes, Georges. *déjà jadis, ou du mouvement Dada à l'espace abstrait*. Paris: René Juillard, 1958.
_____. *Dada: Manifèstes, Poèmes, Articles, Projets (1915-1930)*. ed. Jean-Pierre Begot. Paris: Editions Champ Libre, 1974.
_____. "Lettres," ed. M. Corvin. *Cahiers Dada-Surréalisme*, No. 1 (1966).
Riviere, Jacques. "Gratitude to Dada." In B. Price, ed. *The Ideal Reader*. New York: Meridian, 1960.
Richter, Hans. *Dada: Art and Anti-Art*. New York: McGraw-Hill.
_____. *Dada Profile*. Zurich: Verlag der Arche, 1961.
Roussel, Raymond. *Comment j'ai écrit certains de mes livres*. Paris: Hermann, 1935.
Salmon, André. *Souvenirs sans fin- Troisième epoche (1920-1940)*. Paris: Gallimard, 1961.
Schawinsky, Xanti. "From the Bauhaus to Black Mountain." *The Drama Review*, T-51, summer, 1971, 31-44.
Schlemmer, Oskar. *The Letters and Diaries of Oskar Schlemmer*. Ed. Tut Schlemmer. Middletown, Conn: 1972.
SIC. Paris, 1916-1919. Bibliothèque de l'Arsenal, Paris.
Tzara, Tristan. "Faîtes vos jeux." *Les feuilles libres*, No. XXXI (mars-avril, 1923).

————. *Seven Dada Manifestoes and Lampisteries.* Trans. Barbara Wright. London: John Calder, 1977.

————. "Le secret de *Mouchoir de Nuages.*" *Intégral,* No. 2 (ler avril 1925) 7.

————. "Memoirs of Dadaism." In Edmund Wilson, *Axel's Castle.* New York: Charles Scribner's Sons, 1931.

Vitrac, Roger. "Le monologue interieur et le surréalisme." *Commoedia* (17 mars 1925).

————. "Le théâtre de Guillaume Apollinaire." *Commoedia* (3 novembre 1923).

Wigman, Mary. *The Mary Wigman Book.* Her writings ed. and trans. by Walter Sorell. Middletown, Conn: Wesleyan University Press, 1973.

V Secondary Sources

General

Abel, Richard. "American Film and the French Literary Avant-Garde 1914-1924." *Contemporary Literature* 17 (Winter, 1976): 84-109.

Adams, Charles L. *The Search for Form: An Examination of the Literary Theory and Technique of Cubism, Futurism, Dada and Surrealism.* Unpublished dissertation. University of Oregon, 1960.

Anonymous. "Dada or the meaning of chaos." *Studio International,* CLXXXIII, 940, January, 1972.

Alexandrian, Sarane. *Surrealist Art.* Trans. Gordon Clough. New York: Praeger, 1970.

Alquié, Ferdinand. *The Philosophy of Surrealism.* Trans. Bernard Waldrop. Ann Arbor: University of Michigan Press, 1965.

————, ed. "Surréalisme et Théâtrologie," and "Dada et Surréalisme." *Entretiens sur le Surréalisme.* Paris: Mouton, 1968.

Arnold, Paul. "Du rêve eschylien au théâtre surréaliste." *Arts et Lettres,* 3e année, No. 11 (1948): 78-85.

Audouin, Philippe. "Surrealist games." In René Alleau, ed., *Dictionnaire des jeux.* Paris: Réalités de l'Imaginaire, 1964.

Bablet, Denis. *Esthétique générale du décor de théâtre de 1870 à 1914.* Paris: Centre Nationale de la Recherche Scientifique, 1963.

Balakian, Anna. *Literary Origins of Surrealism.* New York: Kings Crown Press, 1947.

————. *Surrealism: The Road to the Absolute.* New York: Noonday, 1959.

Barr, Alfred H. Jr., *de stijl 1917-1928.* New York: The Museum of Modern Art, 1961.

————, ed. *Fantastic Art, Dada, Surrealism.* New York: The Museum of Modern Art, 1936.

Bataille, Georges. "Le surréalisme et sa différence avec l'existentialisme." *Critique,* 1ère année, No. 2 (juillet 1946).

Béhar, Henri. *Étude sur le théâtre dada et surréaliste.* Paris: Gallimard, 1967.

————. "La Question du Théâtre Surréaliste ou le Théâtre en Question." *Europe,* No. 475-76 (nov.-dec. 1968).

Block, Haskell, M. "Surrealism and Modern Poetry: The Outline of An Approach." *Journal of Aesthetics and Art Criticism,* 18:2 (December 1959): 174-82.

Blumenkranz-Onimus, Noemi. "Du Futurisme Italien aux mouvements Dada et Surréalistes." *Europe,* No. 475-76 (nov.-dec. 1968).

Cahiers de l'association internationale pour l'étude de Dada et du surréalisme. Paris: Lettres modernes.

Calvesi, Maurizio. "Il Futurismo e l'Avanguardia europea." *La Biennale de Venezia.* anno 9/n 36-7, luglio-decembre, 1959.

Cardinal, Roger and Robert Stuart Short. *Surrealism: permanent revelation.* London: Dutton, 1970.

Carnes, E.H. *A descriptive study of form and purpose in the surrealist stage setting.* Unpublished dissertation. University of California, 1966.

Cary, Joseph. "Futurism and the French Théâtre d'avant-garde." *Modern Philology* (November 1959): 113-21.

Caws, Mary Ann. *The Poetry of Dada and Surrealism: Aragon, Breton, Tzara, Eluard and Desnos.* Princeton, New Jersey: Princeton University Press, 1970.

Cesare, G. de Michelis. *Il Futurismo Italiano in Russia 1909-1929.* De Donato editore, 1973.

Change, special issue on *Les Champs Magnétiques*, No. 7 (1970).

Clair, Jean and Harald Szeemann, eds. *The Bachelor Machines.* New York: Rizzoli, 1975.

Cohen, Ruby. "Surrealism and Today's French Theatre." *Yale French Studies*, No. 31 (May 1964).

_____ . *The Cubist Epoch.* New York: E.P. Dutton, 1970.

Corvin, Michel. "Le théâtre dada existe-t-il?: Tzara et Ribemont-Dessaignes ou la problematique d'un théâtre dada." *Révue d'histoire du théâtre*, entire issue, 1971.

_____ . *Le théâtre de recherche entre les deux guerres: Le laboratoire Art et Action.* Paris: Lacite, 1973.

Coutts-Smith, Kenneth. *Dada.* New York: Dutton, 1970.

Clough, Rosa T. *Futurism: The Story of a Modern Art Movement: A New Appraisal.* New York: Greenwood Press, 1961.

Damase, Jacques. *A History of the Music Hall in Paris.* Paris: Editions "Spectacles," 1960.

Déak, František. "The Influence of Italian Futurism in Russia," *The Drama Review*, T-68 (December, 1975): 88-112.

Delpit, Louise. *Paris—Théâtre Contemporain: Deuxième Partie: Tableau du Mouvement Dramatique en France de 1925 a 1938.* Northampton, Massachusetts: Smith College Studies in Modern Language.

Epstein, Jean. *La Poésie d'Aujourd'hui.* Paris: Editions "La Sirène," 1921.

Esslin, Martin. *The Theatre of the Absurd.* Garden City, New York: Doubleday and Company, Inc., 1961.

Fauchereau, Serge. *Expressionisme, Dada, Surréalisme et autre ismes.* Paris: Editions Denoel, 1976.

Faye, Paul-Louis. "Dada and the Temper of 1917." University of Colorado Studies, Series B, Studies in the Humanities, I, 4 (October 1941): 309-41.

Forster, Leonard, *Poetry of Significant Nonsense.* London: Cambridge University Press, 1962.

_____ . *The poets' tongues; multilingualism in literature.* 1970.

Fowlie, Wallace. *Age of Surrealism.* Bloomington, Indiana: Indiana University Press, 1962.

Fuchs, Georg. *Revolution in the Theatre. Conclusions Concerning the Munich Artists Theatre.* Condensed and adapted by Constance Conner, Kuhn. Ithaca, New York: Cornell University Press, 1959.

Franciscono, Marcel. *Walter Gropius and the Creation of the Bauhaus in Weimar: The ideals and artistic theories of its founding years.* Urbana: University of Illinois press, 1971.

Gershman, Herbert S. "Futurism and the Origins of Surrealism." *Italica* XXXIX (June 1962): 114-23.

_____ . "Surrealism: Myth and Reality." in *Myth and Symbol*, Bernice Slote, ed, pp. 51-57. Lincoln, Nebraska, 1963.

_____ . *The Surrealist Revolution in France.* Ann Arbor: University of Michigan Press, 1969.

_____ . "Toward Defining the Surrealist Aesthetics." *Papers on Language and Literature*, II, 1 (Winter 1966): 47-56.

Golding, John. *Cubism: A History and an Analysis 1907-1914.* New York: Harper and Row, 1968.

Goldwater, Robert J. *Primitivism in Modern Painting.* New York: Harper, 1938.

Gordon, Mel. "Dada Berlin: A History of Performance 1918-1920." *The Drama Review*, T-62 (June, 1974): 114-133.

Got, Maurice. *Théâtre et Symbolisme.* Paris: Le Cercle du Livre, 1955.

Gould, Michael. *Surrealism and the Cinema.* New York: A.S. Barnes and Co., 1976.

Gray, Camilla. *The Great Experiment: Russian Art 1863-1922.* New York: Abrams, 1962.

Greenberg, Allan C. *Artists and the Weimar Republic: Dada and the Bauhaus 1917-1925.* Published in Book form by UMI Research Press, Ann Arbor, 1980.

Greer, Thomas H. *Music and its Relation to Futurism: Cubism, Dadaism and Surrealism, 1905-1950.* Unpublished dissertation, North Texas State University, 1969.

Grossman, Manual L. *Dada: Paradox, Mystification, and Ambiguity in European Literature.* New York: Pegasus, 1971.

Guth, Paul. "Le Dadaisme–Une Bombe Littéraire au temps des années folles." *Les Annales* (1962).

Hoog, Armand. "The Surrealist Novel." *Yale French Studies,* No. 8 (1951): 17-25.

Horn-Monvale, Madelaine. "La Revolution théâtrale de 1910-1913." *Intermede,* No. 1 (1946): 34-35.

Huizinga, Johan. *Homo Ludens.* New York: Harper and Row, 1970.

Hausmann, Raoul. "Introduction à une historie du poème phonetique 1910-1913" (with Christopher Middleton's appendix). *German Life and Letters,* Vol. 18-19 (1965): 19-25.

Janis, Harriet and Rudi Blesh. *Collage.* Philadelphia and New York: Chilton Co., 1962.

Jasper, Gertrude Rathbone. *Adventure in the Theatre: Lugné-Poe and the Théâtre de l'Oeuvre to 1899.* New Brunswick, New Jersey: Rutgers University Press, 1947.

Jean, Marcel. *The History of Surrealist Painting.* Trans. Simon Watson Taylor. New York: Grove Press, 1960.

————. and Arpad Mezei. *Genèse de la Pensée Moderne dans la littérature francaise.* Paris: Correa, 1950.

Jolas, Eugene. "From Jabberwocky to 'lettrism.' " *Transition Forty-Eight* No. 1 (January 1948): 104-20.

Kiehl, Jean. *Les Ennemis du théâtre: Essai sur les rapports du théâtre avec le cinéma et la littérature (1918-1939).* Neuchatel, Suisse: Editions de la Baconniere, 1951.

Kirby, Michael. *Futurist Performance.* New York: Dutton Paperback, 1971.

————. *Happenings.* New York: EP Dutton and Co., Inc. , 1964.

Kleinschmidt, Hans J. "The Angry Act: The Role of Aggression in Creativity." *American Imago,* Vol. 24, Nos. 1 and 2 (1967): 105-6.

Klossowicz, Jan. "Avant-garde Drama in the Twenty Year Inter-War Period." *Le théâtre en Pologne,* No. 7-8 (1965): 33-38.

Knowles, Dorothy. *Le réaction idéaliste au théâtre depuis 1890.* Paris: Droz, 1934.

————. *French Drama of the Inter-War Years: 1918-1939.* London: Harrap, 1967.

Kourilsky, Francoise. "Dada and Circus: Peter Schumann's Bread and Puppet Theatre." *The Drama Review,* T-61, (March 1974): 104-9.

Kyrou, Ado. *Le Surréalisme au Cinéma.* Paris: Le Terrain Vague, 1963.

Lang, Lothar. *Das Bauhaus 1919-1933: Idee und wirklichkeit.* Berlin: Teatralinstitut fur Formgestaltung, *1965.*

Maguire, Robert. *Le hors théâtre: Essai sur la signification du théâtre de notre temps.* Doctorat d'État à la Sorbonne,1963.

Malin, Jane Wofford. *Surrealism in the French Theatre between Two Wars.* Unpublished dissertation. University of Texas, 1961.

Markov, Vladimir. *Russian Futurisms: A History.* University of California Press, 1968.

Middleton, J. Christopher. "Dada versus Expressionism, or the Red King's Dream." *German Life and Letters,* Vol. 15, No. 1 (October, 1961): 37-51.

Martin, Marianne W. *Futurist Art and Theory, 1909-1915.* Oxford: Clarendon Press, 1968.

Matthews, J.H. *An Introduction to Surrealism.* University Park: Pennsylvania State University Press, 1965.

————. *Surrealist Poetry in France.* Syracuse: Syracuse University Press, 1969.

————. *Surrealism and Film.* Ann Arbor: University of Michigan Press, 1971.

————. *Surrealism and the Novel.* Ann Arbor: University of Michigan Press, 1966.

————. *Theatre in Dada and Surrealism.* Syracuse University Press, 1974.

————. *The Imagery of Surrealism.* Syracuse University Press, 1978.

Mehring, Walter. *Berlin Dada.* Zurich: Verlag der Arche, 1969.

Middleton, J.S. "Bolshevism in Art: Dada and Politics." *Texas Studies in Literature and Language,* Vol. IV (1962): 408-30.

Moussinac, Leon. *Tendences Nouvelles du Théâtre.* Paris: A. Levy, 1931.

Munsterburg, Hugo. "Fantasy and Surrealism." *Twentieth Century Painting.* New York:

Philosophical Society, 1951.

Nadeau, Maurice. *The History of Surrealism*. Trans. Richard Howard. New York: Macmillan, 1965.

New Directions 1940, an anthology with essays by Kenneth Burke, Nicolas Calas, Herbert J. Muller.

Noziere. "Propos de théâtre: Futurisme, Surréalisme et autres." *Le Temps* (25 juin 1918).

Orenstein, Gloria. *The Theatre of the Marvelous: Surrealism and the Contemporary Stage*. New York: New York University Press, 1975.

Paris/Berlin 1900-1933. Catalogue of Exhibition, Paris: Centre Georges Pompidou. 12 juillet-6 novembre, 1978.

Pierre, Jose. *Le Futurisme et le Dadaisme*. Lausanne: Editions Rencontre, 1966.

Poggoli, Renato. *The Theory of the Avant-Garde*. Trans. Gerald Fitzgerald. New York: Icon Editions, Harper & Row, 1968.

Poupeye, Camille. *La mise en scène théâtrale d'aujourd'hui*. Bruxelles: L'Equerre, 1927.

Prosenc, Miklavz. *Die Dadaisten in Zurich*. Bonn: Bonvier, 1967.

Rageot, Gaston. "Le Surréalisme au théâtre." *La Revue Bleue* (4 juillet 1925).

Read, Herbert. "Surrealism and the Romantic Principle." *Philosophy of Modern Art*, pp. 105-41. London: Faber & Faber, 1952.

Riese-Hubert, Renée. "Le Language de la Peinture dans le poème en prose contemporain." *Revue des Sciences Modernes*, 1962.

Rischbieter, Henning. *Art and the Stage in the Twentieth Century: Painters and Sculptors Work for the Theatre*. Trans. Michael Bullock. Greenwich, Connecticut: New York Graphic Society, Ltd, 1968.

Robert, Guy. "Surréalisme et automatisme." *La Revue Dominicaine*, 65:1 (mai 1959): 208-17.

Robuchez, Jacques. *Le symbolisme au théâtre. Lugné-Poe et les débuts de l'Oeuvre*. Paris: L'Arche, 1957.

Rubin, William S. *Dada and Surrealist Art*. New York: Harry N. Abrams, 1968.

_____. *Dada, Surrealism and Their Heritage*. New York: The Museum of Modern Art, 1968.

Sandrow, Nahma. *Surrealism: Theatre, Arts, Ideas*. New York: Harper & Row, 1972.

Sanouillet, Michel. *Dada à Paris*. Paris: Jean-Jacques Pauvert, 1965.

Sartre, Jean-Paul. "Qu'est-ce que la littérature." *Situations*, II. Paris: Gallimard, 1948.

Schinz, Albert. "Dadaism," Smith College Studies in Modern Languages, Vol. V (October 1923) 51-79.

Schlemmer, Oskar, Moholy-Nagy, Laszlo and Molnar-Farkes. *The Theatre of the Bauhaus*, ed. and with an introduction by Walter Gropius. Middleton, Connecticut: Wesleyan University Press, 1961.

Seitz, William C. *The Art of Assemblage*. New York: The Museum of Modern Art, 1961.

Sellin, Eric. "Surrealist Aesthetics and the Theatrical Event." *Books Abroad*, Vol. 43, No. 2 (Spring 1969): 167-93.

_____. "Simultaneity: Driving Force of the Surrealist Aesthetic." *Twentieth Century Literature* (February 1975, issue devoted to Dada-Surrealism): 10-23.

Sewell, Elizabeth. *The Field of Nonsense*. London: Chatto & Windus, 1952.

Shapiro, Theda. *Painters and Politics: The European Avant-Garde Society, 1900-1925*. Elsevier N. Holland, 1976.

Shattuck, Roger. *The Banquet Years*. New York: Vintage Books, 1968.

Slonimsky, Nicolas. "Music and Surrealism." *ARTFORUM* (September 1966): 80-85.

Sullivan, Marcia Maureen. *Disruptive Techniques in French and German Avant-Garde Drama from 1910-1930*. Unpublished dissertation. Indiana University, 1973.

Tashjian, Dickran. *Skyscraper Primitives: Dada and the American Avant-Garde 1910-1925*. Middletown, Connecticut: Wesleyan University Press, 1975.

Taylor, Joshua A. *Futurism*. New York: The Museum of Modern Art, 1961.

Thalmann, Marianne. *The Romantic Fairy Tale: Seeds of Surrealism*. Ann Arbor: University of Michigan Press, 1964.

Veinstein, André. *Le théâtre experimental*. Bruxelles: La Renaissance du Livre, 1968.

————. *Du Théâtre Libre au Théâtre Louis Jouvet: Les théâtres d'art à travers leurs periodiques.* Paris: Editions Billandot, 1955.

Virmaux, Alain et Odettel. *Les Surréalistes et le Cinéma.* Paris: Seghers, 1976.

Wingler, H.M. *The Bauhaus: Weimar, Dessau, Berlin, Chicago.* Trans. Wolfgang Jabs and Basil Gilbert. Cambridge, Mass, 1968.

Yale French Studies, No. 50. Entire issue on "Intoxication and Literature" (articles on Breton, Desnos, Artaud).

Zyla, Wolodymyr T. *From Surrealism to the Absurd.* Proceedings of the Comparative Literature Symposium, Vol. III. Lubbock, Texas: The Texas Technical Press, 1970.

The People Within and Related to the Movements:

Pierre Albert-Birot

Albert-Birot, Arlette. "Pierre Albert-Birot et le Surréalisme." *Europe* (Nov.-Dec. 1968).

Follain, Jean. *Pierre Albert-Birot.* Paris: Seghers, 1967.

Jourdan, Bernard. "Approche de Pierre Albert-Birot ou le poète et son double." *Critique,* No. 177.

Marottoli, Vincent J. *Futurism and its Influences on the French Poet Pierre Albert-Birot.* Unpublished dissertation. The University of Connecticut, 1974.

Perez, Jorba. *Pierre Albert-Birot.* Paris: Bibliothèque de l'Institut.

Guillaume Apollinaire

Aegerter, Emmanuel and Pierre Labrachérie. *Au Temps de Guillaume Apollinaire.* Paris: Julliard, 1945.

Adema, Marcel. *Guillaume Apollinaire le mal-aimé.* Paris: Plon, 1952.

Aragon, Louis. "Le 24 juin 1917." *SIC,* No. 27 (mars 1918).

Albert-Birot, Pierre. "À propos du drame surréaliste d'Apollinaire." *Marginales,* Nos. 62-63 (décembre 1958).

Bonnet, Marguerite. "Aux sources du surréalisme: la place d'Apollinaire." *La Revue des Lettres Modernes,* No. 104-107, 1964.

Cardine-Petit, R. "Guillaume Apollinaire: La première de *Mamelles de Tirésias.*" *Artaban* (18 octobre 1957).

Carmody, Francis J. *The Evolution of Apollinaire's Poetics 1901-1914.* Berkeley and Los Angeles: The University of California Press, 1963.

Dubreuil, Eugenie. "Apollinaire et les Futuristes." *L'Information d'Histoire de l'Art.* (mai-juin, 1965).

Decoudin, P. "Autour des *Mamelles de Tirésias, Etudes et Informations.*" *Revue des Lettres Modernes,*" No. 123-26 IV, 1965.

Les Mamelles de Tirésias. Press clippings. Fonds Rondel. Rf50164. Bibliothèque de l'Arsenal.

Les Mamelles de Tirésias. Compte rendu. *SIC,* No. 18 (juin 1917), No. 19-20 (juillet-août 1917).

Mackworth, Cecily. *Guillaume Apollinaire and the Cubist Life.* London: John Murray, 1961.

Matthews, J.H. "Apollinaire devant les surréalistes." *La Revue des Lettres Modernes,* No. 3, 1964.

Melzer, Annabelle Henkin, "The première of Apollinaire's *The Breasts of Tirésias* in Paris." *Theatre Quarterly,* Fall, 1977.

Moulin, Jeanine. "Apollinaire et le Futurisme." *Revue de Suisse,* No. 7 (30 avril 1952).

Severini, Gino. "Apollinaire et le futurisme." *XXe Siecle,* No. 3 (juin 1952).

Steegmuller, Francis. *Apollinaire: Poet Among the Painters.* New York: Doubleday and Company, 1963.

Vitrac, Roger. "Le Théâtre d'Apollinaire." *Commoedia* (3 novembre 1923).

Louis Aragon

Beaujour, Michael. "The surrealist map of love; Aragon, le paysan de Paris, 1926." *Yale French Studies*, No. 32 (October, 1964): 124-32.

Becker, Lucille F. *Louis Aragon.* New York: Twayne, 1971.

Gabillet, André. *La littérature au défi: Aragon surréaliste.* Fribourg, Suisse: Galley and Cie., 1957.

Gindine, Yvette. *Aragon, prosateur surréaliste.* Genève: Librarie Drosz, 1966.

Melzer, Annabelle Henkin. "Louis Aragon's *L'armoire à glace un beau soir:* a play of the surrealist *époque de sommeil.*" *Comparative Drama*, Vol. II, No. 1 (Spring 1977).

Antonin Artaud

Antonin Artaud. *Théâtre Alfred Jarry.* Recueil factice: articles de presse. Fonds Rondel Rt 3800. Bibliotheque de l'Arsenal.

Antonin Artaud, Documents. *Théâtre Alfred Jarry.* Collection Doucet. Bibliothèque St. Geneviève. CIV.

Antonin Artaud: The Drama Review (Tulane), XXII (Winter 1963), XXVII (Spring 1965). Complete issues.

Antonin Artaud et le théâtre de notre temps. Cahiers de la Compagnie Madelaine Renaud, Jean-Louis Barrault (mai 1958). Complete issue.

Antonin Artaud. Théâtre (formerly yale/theatre) Vol. 9, No. 3 (Summer 1978). Complete issue.

Antonin Artaud. La Tour de Feu. No. 112 (December 1971). Complete issue.

Artaud. K: Revue de la Poèsie. Nos. 1-2 (juin 1948). Complete issue.

Artaud. Obliques. Numéro 10-11, 1977. Complete issue.

Bermel, Albert. "Artaud as Playwright: The Fountain of Blood." *Boston University Journal,* 1972, (Autumn).

———. *Artaud's Théâtre of Cruelty.* New York: Taplinger, 1977.

Brau, Jean-Louis. *Antonin Artaud.* Paris: Librarie Bonaparte, 1971.

Brook, Peter. "Artaud for Artaud's sake." *Encore,* May-June, 1964.

Caws, Mary Ann. "Artaud's Myth of Motion."*French Review,* February, 1968.

Charbonnier, Georges. *Essai sur Antonin Artaud.* Paris: Seghers, 1959.

Chiaromonte, Nicola. "Antonin Artaud." *Encounter* (August 1967).

Derrida, Jacques. "La Parole soufflée," and "Le théâtre de la cruanté et la clôture de la représentation," in his *L'Ecriture et la différence,* pp. 253-92, 341-68. Paris: Seuil, 1967.

Esslin, Martin. *Antonin Artaud.* London: Penguin, 1976.

Goodman, Paul. "Obsessed by Theatre." *The Nation* (November 29, 1958).

Gouhier, Henri. *Antonin Artaud et l'essence du théâtre.* Paris: Librarie philosophique J. Vrin, 1974.

Greene, Naomi. *Antonin Artaud: Poet Without Words.* New York: Simon & Schuster, 1970.

Grotowski, Jerzy. "Il n'était pas entièrement lui-même." *Les Temps Modernes,* No. 251 (avril 1967), 1887-88.

Hahn, Otto. *Portrait d'Antonin Artaud.* Paris: Le Soleil Noir, 1968.

Hayman, Ronald. *Artaud and After.* New York: Oxford University Press, 1977.

Hort, Jean. *Antonin Artaud; le suicide de la societié.* Genève: Editions connaître, 1960.

Joski, Daniel. *Antonin Artaud.* Paris: Editions Universitaires, 1970.

Kitchin, Laurence. "The Theatre of Cruelty." *The Listener,* (September 19, 1963).

Knapp, Bettina. *Antonin Artaud: Man of Vision.* New York: David Lewis, 1969.

Koch, Stephen, "On Artaud," *Tri Quarterly,* No. 6 (Spring 1966): 29-37.

Lieber, Gerard. *Antonin Artaud, homme de théâtre.* Memoire de D.E.S. Faculté des Lettres et Sciences Humains de Paris, (mai 1967).

Maguire, Robert. *Le 'Hors-théâtre': recherches sur la signification du théâtre en dehors de notre tradition.* Thèse: Université Lettres, Paris: 1960. Sorbonne library: côte W. Univ. 1960 (33), 40.

Mallaussena, Marie-Ange (Artaud's sister). "Antonin Artaud." *La Revue Théâtrale*, 1953.
Marowitz, Charles. *Artaud at Rodez*, a play with appendices. London: Marion Boyars, 1977.
––––. "Notes on the Theatre of Cruelty." *The Drama Review*, T-34 (Winter 1966).
Melzer, Annabelle Henkin. "Hommage to Robert Aron 1898-1975." *Theatre Research International* (February 1977): 131-39.
Nash, John Richard. *Jarry, Reverdy and Artaud: the abrupt path.* Unpublished dissertation. Stanford University, 1967.
Nordmann, Jean-Gabriel. "Antonin Artaud et le surréalisme." *Europe* (novembre-décembre 1968): 153-61.
Novarina, Valere. *Antonin Artaud-theoricien du théâtre.* Memoire de D.E.S. Faculté des Lettres et Sciences Humaines de Paris, 1964.
Polieri, Jacques. "Scenographie nouvelle: les promoteurs de la scenographie moderne– Autant Lara . . . A. Artaud . . . ." *Aujourd'hui*, No. 42-43, 1963.
Prevel, Jacques. "En companie d'Artaud." *La Nouvelle Revue Française,* (mars 1962).
Roy, Claude. "Le théâtre de la cruauté en Europe." *La Nouvelle Revue Française* (mai 1965).
Saillet, Maurice. "Close to Antonin Artaud," *Evergreen Review* (May-June 1960).
Scarpetta, Guy. "Brecht et Artaud," *La Nouvelle Critique,* nouvelle série. No. 25 (juin 1969): 60-68.
Sellin, Eric. *The Dramatic Concepts of Antonin Artaud.* Chicago: The University of Chicago Press, 1968.
Seymour, Alan. "Artaud's Cruelty," *London Magazine* (March 1964).
Sollers, Philippe. "La Pensée emet des signes." *Logiques . . .,* pp. 133-49. Paris: Seuil, 1968.
––––, ed. *Artaud.* Paris: Union Generale d'Editions 10/18, 1973. (Lectures and discussions from a conference held in 1972 at Cerisy-la-salle).
Tembeck, Robert Edward. *Antonin Artaud and the Theatre of Cruelty.* Unpublished dissertation. University of Minnesota, 1965.
Thevenin, Paule. "Entendre/Voir/Lire." *Tel Quel,* No. 39 (automne 1969): 31-63; No. 40 (hiver 1969-70): 67-99.
Tonelli, Franco. *Une étude des théories théâtrales d'Artaud.* Unpublished dissertation. Louisiana State University, 1966.
Virmaux, Alain. *Antonin Artaud et le théâtre.* Paris: Seghers, 1970.
––––. "Artaud and Film," "Artaud: scenarios and arguments." *The Drama Review,* T-33 (Fall 1966): 154-65, 166-85.
Weingarten, Romain. "Relire Artaud." *Théâtre Populaire,* No. 18 (mai 1956): 9-20.
Wellwarth, George E. "Antonin Artaud: Prophet of the Avant-Garde Drama." *Drama Survey,* Vol. 2, No. 3 (1963): 276-87.
Zorilla-Velasquez, Oscar. *Antonin Artaud: Théoricien et Technicien de l'Art Dramatique.* Doctorat d'Étude à L'Université de Montpellier, 1966.

Hugo Ball

Egger, Eugen. *Hugo Ball. Ein Weg aus dem chaos.* Olten: 1951.
Hausmann, Raoul. "Note sur le poème phonétique: Kandinsky et Ball." *German Life and Letters* 21, 11 (1967): 58-59.
Sheppard, Richard. "Sixteen Forgotten Items by Hugo Ball from the Pre-Dada Years." *German Life and Letters,* Vol. 29, 1965, 362-69.
Steinke, G.E. *The Life and Work of Hugo Ball, Founder of Dadaism.* The Hague: Mouton, 1963.

André Breton

Audouin, Philippe. *André Breton.* Paris: Gallimard, 1970.
Balakian, Anna. *André Breton: Magus of Surrealism.* New York: Oxford University Press, 1971.

Bonnet, Marguerite. *André Breton: naissance de l'aventure surréaliste.* José Corti, 1975.
Browder, Clifford H. *André Breton, Arbiter of Surrealism.* Genève: Droz, 1967.
Caws, Mary Ann. *André Breton.* New York: Twayne, 197.
Matthews, J.H. *André Breton.* New York: Columbia University Press, 1967.

Blaise Cendrars

Horrex, S.P. "Blaise Cendrars and the Aesthetic of Simultaneity." *Dada/Surrealism,* No. 6 (1976): 46-57.

Jean Cocteau

Jean Cocteau. Press clippings. Fonds Rondel Rj2200. Bibliothèque de l'Arsenal.
Parade. Press clippings. Fonds Rondel Ro2535; Receuil factice Rj 2224.
Le Boeuf sur le toît. Documents in *The Drama Review,* T-55 (September 1972): 27-45.
Axsom, Richard H. *Parade: Cubism as Theatre.* Unpublished dissertation. University of Michigan, 1974.
Croseland, Margaret. *Jean Cocteau.* London: Peter Nevill, Ltd., 1955.
Fowlie, Wallace. *Jean Cocteau: The History of a Poet's Age.* Bloomington: Indiana University Press, 1966.
Jacob, Max. *Lettres à Jean Cocteau: 1919-1944.* Paris: Morihien, 1950.
Oxenhandler, Neal. *Scandal and Parade: The Theatre of Jean Cocteau.* New Brunswick: Rutgers University Press, 1957.
Raval, Maurice. "Jean Cocteau, homme de théâtre." *Nouvelles Littéraires* (24 juillet 1926).
Steegmuller, Francis. *Cocteau.* Boston: Atlantic, Little, Brown & Co., 1970.

Emile Jacques-Dalcroze

Sadler, Michael T.H. *The Eurythmics of Jacques Dalcroze.* London: Constable & Co., Ltd. 1912.
Martin, Frank, ed. *Emile Jacques-Dalcroze.* Neuchatel: Editions de la Baconnière, 1965.

Sonia Delaunay

Clay, Jean. "The Golden Years of Visual Jazz: Sonia Delaunay's Life and Times." *Réalités* (English language edition), 1965: 42-47.
Cohen, Arthur A. *Sonia Delaunay.* New York: Harry N. Abrams, 1975.
Damase, Jacques. *Sonia Delaunay: Rhythms and Colours.* Greenwich: New York Graphic Society, 1972.

Robert Desnos

Berger, Pierre. *Robert Desnos; une étude.* Paris: Seghers, 1960.
Buchole, Rosa. *L'Evolution poètique de Robert Desnos.* Bruxelles: Palais des Académies, 1956.
Dumas, Marie-Claire. *Robert Desnos. L'homme et l'oeuvre.* Doctorat de l'État à la Sorbonne. Paris, 1961.
Greene, Tatiana. "le merveilleux surréaliste de Robert Desnos." *French Review,* Vol. 40 (November 1966): 193-203.
Desnos. Simoun, Vol. V, No. 22-23 (1956). Complete issue.

Yvan Goll

Yvan Goll et le Théâtre Surrealiste, Press clippings. Fonds Rondel, Rj2234. Bibliothèque de l'Arsenal.
Carmody, Francis J. *The Poetry of Yvan Goll: A Biographical Study.* Paris: Caractères, 1956.

258   Bibliography

Goll, Claire. "Goll et Breton." *Europe* (Nov.-Dec. 1968).
Romains, Jules. *Yvan Goll*. Paris: Seghers, 1956.

George Grosz

Boyer, Richard O. "George Grosz, The Saddest Man in the World." Profile: *The New Yorker*, I (November 27, 1943), II (December 4, 1943), III (December 11, 1943).
Lewis, Beth Irwin. *George Grosz: Art and Politics in the Weimar Republic*. Madison: University of Wisconsin Press, 1971.

Max Jacob

Green, Tatiana. "Max Jacob et le Surréalisme." *French Forum*, Vol. I, No. 3 (September 1976).
Kamber, Gerald. *Max Jacob and the Poetics of Cubism*. Baltimore: Johns Hopkins Press, 1971.

Alfred Jarry

Alfred Jarry. Press clippings. Fonds Rondel, Rf62.878. Bibliothèque de l'Arsenal.
Apollinaire, Guillaume. "Feu Alfred Jarry." *Contemporains pittoresques*, pp. 19-36. Paris: Editions de la belle page, 1929.
Beaumont, K.S. "The Making of Ubu: Jarry as Producer and Theorist." *Theatre Research*, Vol. XII, No. 2 (1972): 139-54.
Church, Dan M. "Père Ubu: The Creation of a Literary Type." *Drama Survey* IV: 233-43.
Chassé, Charles. "Comment est né Ubu Roi." *Les Cahiers d'histoire et de folklore*, No. 1 (octobre-décembre 1955).
_____. *Dans les coulisses de la gloire: d'Ubu Roi au Douanier Rousseau*. Paris: N.R.C., 1947.
_____. "Le vocabulaire de Jarry dans Ubu Roi." *Cahiers de l'Association internationale des études françaises*, No. 11 (mai 1959).
"Declaration sur l'Affaire Ubu." *Littérature*, nouvelle série, No. 1 (1er mars 1922), signe: La Rédaction.
Druart, René. "Notes sur la seconde représentation d'*Ubu Roi*." *Cahiers du Collège de 'Pataphysique*, No. 20 (1955).
_____. "Un témoignage sur la générale d'*Ubu Roi* (celui de Jahan Ades)." *Cahiers du Collège de 'Pataphysique*, No. 20 (1955).
Fitzgerald, P.M. "The Strange Case of Père Ubu," *World Review*, No. 23, (January 1951): 27-32.
Gens-d'Armes, Gandillon. "Alfred Jarry au lycée Henri IV," *Les Marges* (janvier 1922).
Grossman, Manual L. "Alfred Jarry and the Theatre of the Absurd." *American Educational Theatre Association Journal*, December, 1967.
Grubbs, H.A. "Alfred Jarry's Theories of Dramatic Technique." *Romantic Review*, XXVI (October, 1936).
Hertz, Henri. "Jarry collegien et la naissance d'Ubu Roi." *Ecrits Nouveaux* (novembre 1921).
Jacopin, Paul. "L'originalité du language théâtral dans Ubu Roi d'Alfred Jarry." Mémoire de D.E.S. Faculté des Lettres et Sciences Humains de Paris, 1967.
Lefrancois, Philipe. "*Ubu Roi* ou l'heure espagnole." *Miroir de l'histoire* (août 1959).
Quillard, Pierre. "De l'imagination et de l'expression chez Jarry." *La Revue Blanche* (janvier 1902).
Robillot, M., ed. "La presse d'Ubu." (dossier). *Cahiers du collège de 'Pataphysique*, No. 3-4.
Saillet, Maurice. "XII arguments d'Alfred Jarry sur le théâtre." *Cahiers du collège de 'Pataphysique*, No. 5 (1959).
Rachilde. *Alfred Jarry ou le surmâle de lettres*. Paris: Grasset, 1928.
Salmon, André. "Alfred Jarry ou le Père Ubu en liberté." *Ami du lettre*, (1924).

Shattuck, Roger and Samuel Watson Taylor, eds. " 'Pataphysics is the Science." *Evergreen Review*, 4:13 (May-June, 1960).

Soupault, Philippe. "Confrontations: Alfred Jarry." *Cahiers de la Compagnie Renaud-Barrault* (mai 1958).

Therive, André. "Desaveu de paternité (sur l'affaire *Ubu*)." *Les Temps Modernes* (juin 1958).

York, Ruth. "*Ubu* revisited: the reprise of 1922." *The French Review* (February 1962): 408-11.

Wassily Kandinsky

Denkler, Horst. "Kandinsky et le théâtre." *Obliques*, numero-speciale 6-7.

Grohmann, Walter. *Wassily Kandinsky—Life and Work*, trans. Norbert Guterman. New York: Harry N. Abrams, 1958.

Grote, Ludwig. "Buhnenkompositionen von Kandinsky." *i 10; international revue*, jrg 2, No. 13, 1928.

Hahl-Koch, Jelena. "Kandinsky et le théâtre—quelques aperçus." *Wassily Kandinsky à Munich*, Munich: Collection Stadtische Galerie im Lenbachhaus, 1976.

Laxmi, Sihare. *Orriental Influences in Wassily Kandinsky and Piet Mondrian 1909-1917.* Unpublished dissertation. New York University, 1967.

Ringbom, Sixten. *The Sounding Cosmos: A Study in the Spiritualism of Kandinsky and the Genesis of Abstract Painting.* Helsingfors: Abo Akademi, 1970.

Sheppard, R.W. "Kandinsky's Abstract Drama *der Gelbe Klang*: An Interpretation." *Forum for Modern Language Studies.* (April 1975) 11:165-76.

Weiss, Peg. *Kandinsky in Munich; The Formative Jugendstil Years.* Princeton, New Jersey: Princeton University Press, 1979.

Oskar Kokoschka

Hines, J.T. "Collaboration of Forms in a One-Man Show: The Total Performance of *Morder, Hoffnung der Frauen.*" *Dada/Surrealism* No. 4 (1974): 89-99.

Hodin, J.P. *Oskar Kokoschka: The Artist and His Time.* New York, 1966.

Hoffman, Edith. *Kokoschka: Life and Work.* London: Faber and Faber, Ltd. 1947.

Kamm, Otto. *Oskar Kokoschka und das theatre.* Unpublished dissertation. University of Vienna, 1958.

Pam, Dorothy. "Murder, The Woman's Hope," *The Drama Review.* T-67 (September 1975): 5-12.

Wingler, Hans Maris. *Oskar Kokoschka: The Work of the Painter.* Salzburg: Galerie Welz, 1958.

Benjamin Peret

Mayoux, Jehan. "Benjamin Peret, la fauchette coupante." *Le surréalisme, même.* 2 (printemps 1957): 150-58; 3 (automne 1957): 53-59.

Francis Picabia

Sanouillet, Michel. *Picabia.* Paris Editions du Temps, 1964.

Pablo Picasso

Breunig, C. "Picasso's Poets." *Yale French Studies*, 21 (1958): 3-9.

Cooper, Douglas. *Picasso Theatre.* New York: Harry N. Abrams, 1968.

Hubert, Renée Riese. "Les Surréalistes et Picasso." *L'Esprit créateur*, (printemps 1966): 45-52.

Marowitz, Charles. "Picasso's *Four Little Girls.*" *The Drama Review*, T-54 (June 1972): 32-48.

Kirstein, Lincoln, ed. *Picasso in the Theatre. Dance Index* (November-December 1946). Entire issue.

Raymond Radiguet

Clerc, Bernard. *L'amour dans l'oeuvre de Raymond Radiguet.* Unpublished dissertation. Universite de Dijon, 1955.

Cocteau, Jean. "Cet élève qui devint mon maître." *Les Nouvelles Littéraires* (5 juin 1952).

Goesch, Keith. *Raymond Radiguet: Étude biographique (Bibliographie).* Plon: Palatine, 1955.

Massis, Henri. *Raymond Radiguet.* Paris: 1927.

Raymond Roussel

Raymond Roussel. Press clippings. Fonds Rondel, Rf 71821, 71823, 71824, 71826, 71827, 71828, 71835. Bibliothèque de l'Arsenal.

Ashberry, John. "Re-establishing Raymond Roussel." *Art News Annual,* No. 6 (Autumn, 1962).

Berger, Pierre. "Avec Raymond Roussel au seuil de surréalisme," *Lettres français* (juin 1963): 6-11.

Bo, Carlo. "Era il momento giusto perascoltare la voce di Roussel." *l'Europeo,* No. 21, 1964.

Breton, André. "Raymond Roussel." *Anthologie de l'Humour Noir.* Paris: Pauvert, 1966.

Butor, Michel. "Sure les procèdes de Raymond Roussel." *Repertoire.* Paris: Editions de Minuit.

Caburet, Bernard. *Raymond Roussel.* Paris: Seghers, 1968.

Cherniack-Tzuriel, Abba. "Roussel's *Impressions of Africa." The Drama Review,* T-70 (June 1976): 108-23.

Cocteau, Jean. "Raymond Roussel." *Poésie Critique,* Vol. I. Paris: Gallimard, 1959.

Dali, Salvador. "Raymond Roussel, *Nouvelles Impressions d'Afrique." Le Surréalisme au service de la révolution,* No. 6, 1933.

Desnos, Robert. "L'étoile au front." *391,* No. 17, 1924.

Ferry, Jean. *Une Etude sur Raymond Roussel.* Paris: Arcanes, 1953.

———. "Une autre étude sur Raymond Roussel." *Editions du Collège de 'Pataphysique,* (réprise in *Bizarre,* No. 34-35.)

———. "Raymond Roussel au paradis." *Le Mecanicien et autres contes.* Paris: Gallimard.

———. *L'Afrique des Impressions: guide pratique à l'usages des voyageurs.* Paris: Editions College de 'Pataphysique.

Foucault, Michel. *Raymond Roussel.* Paris: Gallimard, 1963.

Hahn, Otto. "Le génie à l'état pur: le vrai secret de Raymond Roussel." *L'Express.* 6.VI.63.

Heppenstall, Rayner. *Raymond Roussel: a critical study.* London: Calder and Boyars, 1966.

Mucci, Robert. "Raymond Roussel e la sua opera." *Ausonia,* No. 3 Sienna, 1954.

Queneau, Raymond. "Recensione a *Nouvelles Impressions d'Afrique." La Critique sociale,* No. 7 (1933).

Leiris, Michel. "Documents sur Raymound Roussel." *Nouvelle Revue Français* (avril 1935): 575-95.

———. "Autour des *Nouvelles Impressions d'Afrique," Cahiers GLM,* IX (mars 1939).

———. "Conception et réalité chez Raymond Roussel." *Critique,* No. 89 (octobre 1954), 821-36.

Levitt, Carl. "*Locus-Solus:* Literary Solitaire." *Substance,* No. 10 (1974), 95-109.

Robbe-Grillet, Alain. "Enigmes et transparences chez Raymond Roussel." *Pour un Nouveau Roman.* Paris: Editions de Minuit.

Plottel, Jeanine Parisier. "Roussel's Mechanisms of Language." *Dada/Surrealism,* No. 2: 23-27.

———. "Structures and Counterstructures in Roussel's *Impressions d'Afrique." Dada/*

Surréalism, No. 5 (1975): 11-19.
Soupault, Philippe. "Raymond Roussel." *Littérature*, (1 avril 1922).
Spada, Marcel. "La Page 33 de *Locus Solus* ou Roussel Porte-clefs."*cahiers dada-surréalisme*, No. 4 (1970): 13-22.
Starobinski, Jean. "Raymond Roussel et le mythe de la défaillance fatale," *Les Lettres Nouvelles*, (octobre 1973).
Vitrac, Roger. "Raymond Roussel." *Nouvelle Revue Française* (1 février 1928): 162-176.

Georges Ribemont-Dessaignes

Georges Ribemont-Dessaignes. Press clippings. Fonds Rondel, Rf 70.505, 70.509, Rj2211, 2212. Bibliothèque de L'Arsenal.
Bidou, Henri. "*L'empereur de chine* de Ribemont-Dessaignes." *Le Journal des débats* (23 mai 1921).
Jotterand, Franck. *Georges Ribemont-Dessaignes*. Paris: Seghers, 1966.

Oskar Schlemmer

Goldberg, Rose Lee. "Oskar Schlemmer's Performance Art." *ARTFORUM*, (September 1977).
Scheyer, Ernst. *The Shapes of Space: The Art of Mary Wigman and Oskar Schlemmer. Dance Perspectives*, No. 41 (Spring 1970).

Kurt Schwitters

Middleton, J.C. "Pattern without predictability or Pythagoras saved: A comment on Kurt Schwitters." Gedicht 25 in *German Life and Letters*, XXII, No. 4 (1969).
Passuth, Christine. "Kurt Schwitters, Theo Van Doesburg et le 'Bauhaus.' " Budapest: *Bulletin du Musée Hongrois des Beaux Arts*, No. 40 (1973): 69-83.
Retiz, Leonard. "Schwitters and the Literary Tradition." *German Life and Letters*, XXVII, No. 4 (July 1974): 303-15.
Schmalenbach, Werner. *Kurt Schwitters*. London: Thames and Hudson, 1970.
Steinitz, Kate. *Kurt Schwitters: A Portrait from Life*. Trans. Robert Bartlett Haas. Berkeley and Los Angeles: University of California Press, 1968.

Gertrude Stein

McMillan, Samuel H. Jr., *Gertrude Stein, the Cubists and the Futurists*. Unpublished dissertation. The University of Texas, 1964.

Tristan Tzara

Divoire, Fernand. "Compte rendu: *Mouchoir de nuages.*" *L'Esprit nouveau*, No. 28 (janvier 1925): 23.
Béhar, Henri. *Tristan Tzara, L'homme et l'oeuvre*. Doctorat d'État à la Sorbonne. Paris, 1965.
Da Silva, Ramos. *Le langage et la solitude dans la poésie de Tristan Tzara*. Doctorat d'université à la Sorbonne. Paris, 1964.
Dugnet, Nicole. "*La conception poétique du mouvement dada, a partir* des *Sept Manifestes* de Tristan Tzara." Mémoire de maitrise, Paris, Sorbonne, 1968-69.
Lacote, René. *Tristan Tzara*. Paris: Seghers, 1952.
Leiris, Michel. "Présentation de 'La Fuite.' " *Labyrinthe*, II, No. 17 (fevrier 1946).
Peterson, Elmer. *Tristan Tzara: Dada and Surrational Theorist*. New Brunswick, New Jersey: Rutgers University Press, 1971.

Roger Vitrac

Béhar, Henri. *Roger Vitrac, un reprouve du surréalisme*. Paris: Nizet, 1966.

Bibliography, 1979–1993

I begin this updated bibliography from 1979, not merely because that is the year just preceding the publication of the first edition of this book and would therefore be the appropriate seam to join to the book's original extensive bibliography, but because 1979 also saw the founding of the Dada Archive and Research Center at the University of Iowa. Comprising a Fine Arts Archive and a Literary Archive, the Center has become one of the largest repositories of dada materials in the world and is now the first place one would go to research the subject. It is open for use by the public and invites inquiries through its director, Rudolf Kuenzli, at the Dada Archive and Research Center, 425 English Philosophy Building, University of Iowa, Iowa City, Iowa 52242-1408, telephone (319) 335-0330.

The almost fifteen years of research and writing in the field of dada and surrealist studies which have elapsed since the original publication of *Dada and Surrealist Performance* in 1980 have seen a prodigious output of catalogues, articles, and books in the field, confirming that dada and surrealism remain seminal not only to the development of the arts in the twentieth century but also to their study. Interviewing Philippe Soupault in the early 1970s, while participating in Marcel Janco's eightieth birthday-party, I was constantly slipping just under the wire, as these early dada-surrealists shared their last memories of these movements. With their demise the time for the bibliographies and the multivolume "Complete Works," much in evidence in the 1980s, began: bibliographies on Aragon, Arp, and endless works on the movements themselves; the complete works of Tzara; the poems and poetics of Soupault; the articles and projects of Ribemont-Dessaignes; and the five-volume edition of Schwitters' literary works. One is ever grateful for the discovery of new primary sources from an epoch in which one believed one had scoured all the drawers. For example, the publication of Emmy Hennings' *Fruhe Texte*, in Siegen in 1983, was surely spurred by the new emphasis placed by feminist critics on women's words and women's work—an area that will find its expression here as well as in a new section, "Women and Gender in Dada and Surrealism." The most significant changes in the shape of this updated bibliography occur in the subject areas I discovered as I researched the field anew: the work on dada and surrealist film; an astonishing flourishing of writing on Futurism; a quiet but continual inquiry into the area of dada and surrealist performance; and work in two areas that had escaped my focus as I wrote in the 1970s—the significance of World War I and the place of the photographer alongside the avant-garde movements in the early years of the century ("World War I and the Early Twentieth-Century Avant-Garde," and "Dada and Surrealist Photography and Photomontage"). The occasional pre-1979 entry in this list slipped through my fingers in the first edition.

I Bibliographies: General

[*See also* "The People Within and Related to the Movements"]
Kuenzli, Rudolf E. "Dada Bibliography: 1973–1978." *Dada/Surrealism*, nos. 10–11 (1982): 161–201.
―――. "Bibliography on Dada, 1978–1983." *Dada/Surrealism*, no. 13 (1984): 129–64.
Ungar, Steven and Rudolf E. Kuenzli. "Bibliography on Surrealism, 1973–1982." *Dada/Surrealism*, no. 12 (1983): 90–126.

II Primary Sources: General

[See also "The People Within and Related to the Movements"]
"Cabaret Voltaire," "Der Zeltweg," "Dada," "Le Coeur à barbe" [Collection des reimpressions des revues d'avant-garde]. Reprint, Paris: Jean-Michel Place, 1981.
Motherwell, Robert, ed. Dada Painters and Poets: An Anthology. 2d ed. Boston, 1982.

III Exhibition Catalogues: Dada-Surrealism: General

[See also "The People Within and Related to the Movements"]
Anxious Visions. Berkeley: University Art Museum, 1990.
Artists in the Theatre: Expressionism, Dada, Purism on the Stage. Newcastle-upon-Tyne: Hatton Gallery, traveling exhibit, 1986.
Dada and Constructivism: Centre de Arte Reina Sofia, Madrid. traveling exhibit, 1989.
Dada and New York. New York: Whitney Museum of American Art, 1979.
Dada and Surrealist Documents and Events. Cleveland: Mather Gallery, 1979.
The Dada and Surrealist Word-Image. Los Angeles: Los Angeles County Museum of Art; Cambridge: MIT Press, 1989.
Dada: Berlin, Cologne, Hanover. Boston: Institute of Contemporary Art, 1980.
Dada-Constructivism. London: Annely Juda Fine Art, 1984.
Dada Once and for All. New York: Ex Libris, 1983. .
The Dada Period in Cologne: Selections from the Fick-Eggert Collection. Toronto: Art Gallery of Ontario, 1988.
No! Contemporary American Dada. University of Washington: Henry Art Gallery, 1986.
Paris-Berlin: Raports et contrastes France-Allemagne, 1900–1933. Paris: Centre Pompidou, 1978.
"Primitivism" in Twentieth-Century Art: Affinity of the Tribal and the Modern, 2 vols. Ed. William Rubin. New York: Museum of Modern Art, 1984.
The Total Word: A Futurist Tradition, 1909–1986. Modena: Galleria Fonte d'Abisso 1986.
The Twenties in Berlin: Johannes Baader, Raoul Hausmann, George Grosz, Hanna Hoch. London: Annely Juda Fine Art, 1978.

IV Secondary Sources: General

Allen, Roy F. Literary Life in German Expressionism and the Berlin Circles. N.p., 1983.
———. "Zurich Dada, 1916–1919: The Proto-Phase of the Movement." In Dada/Dimensions, ed. Stephen C. Foster, 1–22. Ann Arbor, Mich.: UMI Research Press, 1985.
Amossy, Ruth. "Les tribulations du moi dans le récit dadaiste." Mélusine, no. 11 (1990): 191–206.
Bennet, M. Vincent. "Sounded, Sounding, to Sound." High Performance 8, no. 3 (1985): 34–38.
Berg, Hubert van den. "Dada-Zurich, Anarchismus und Boheme." Neophilologus (Amsterdam) 71, no. 4 (1987): 575–85.
Bergius, Hanne. "The Ambiguous Aesthetic of Dada—Towards a Definition of Its Categories." Journal of European Studies 9 (1979): 26–38.
———. Das Lachen Dadas: Die Berliner Dadaisten und ihre Aktionen. Giessen, 1989.
Buckley, Jonathan. "Dada in England." PN Review (Manchester, England) 6, no. 26 (1982): 27–29.
Busi, Frederick. "Dada and the 'Trial' of Maurice Barrès." Boston University Journal 23, no. 2 (1974): 35–41.
Caws, Mary Ann. The Eye in the Text. Princeton: Princeton University Press, 1981.
———. A Metapoetics of the Passage: Architextures in Surrealism and After. Hanover, N.H.: University Press of New England, 1981.
Chenieux-Gendron, Jacqueline. Le Surréalisme. Paris: Presses Universitaires de France, 1984.
Colvile, Georgiana Mary Morton. Vers un langage des arts autour des années vingt. Paris: Klincksieck, 1977.
Dachy, Marc. The Dada Movement: 1915–1923. Trans. Michael Taylor. New York: Rizzoli, 1990.
Danesi, Silvia, ed. L'Arte nella società. Vol. 5 of Il Dadaismo. Milan: Fabbri, 1977.
De Paz, Alfredo. Dada, surrealismo e dintorni. Bologna: Clueb, 1979.

Elderfield, John. "Dissenting Ideologies and the German Revolution." *Studio International* 180, no. 927 (1970): 180–87.

Erickson, John D. *Dada: Performance, Poetry, and Art.* New York: Twayne Publishers, 1984.

Fachereau, Serge, ed. "Naissance du surréalisme: Aragon, André Breton, Philippe Soupault—Inédits." *Digraphe* 30 (June 1983): 19–73.

Federman, Raymond. "The Language of Dada: Intermedia of Words." *Dada/Surrealism*, no. 2 (1972): 19–22.

Finkelstein, Haim N. *Surrealism and the Crisis of the Object.* Ann Arbor, Mich.: UMI Research Press, 1979.

Foster, Hal. "Amour Fou." *October*, no. 56 (1991): 64–97.

Foster, Stephen C., ed. *Dada/Dimensions.* Ann Arbor, Mich.: UMI Research Press, 1985.

Foster, Stephen C., and Rudolf E. Kuenzli, eds. *Dada spectrum: The Dialectics of Revolt.* Iowa City: University of Iowa Press, 1979.

Fourny, Jean-François. " 'Un Jour ou l'autre on saura': De Dada au Surréalisme." *Revue d'Histoire Littéraire de la France* (Paris) 86, no. 5 (1986) 865–75.

Ghinéa, Vergile. *Dada et néo Dada: Happening, fluxus, body-art, land-art, mail-art, art conceptuel, poèmes, actions.* Luxembourg: Edition Renaissance, 1978.

Glauser, Friedrich: *Dada, Ascona und andere Errinnerungen.* Zurich, 1976.

Gold, Margaret. "Who Are the Dadas of *Travesties?*" *Modern Drama* 21, no. 1 (1978): 59–65.

Golowin, Sergius. *Dada im Mittelalter: Notizen zu einer antiliteratur.* Berlin: Libertad Verlag, 1981.

Guenther, Peter. "Berlin Dada: A Few Remarks." *Visible Language* 21 (summer/autumn 1987): 413–51.

Halpern, Joseph. "Describing the Surreal." *Yale French Studies*, no. 61 (1981): 89–106.

Hedges, Inez. *Languages of Revolt: Dada and Surrealist Literature and Film.* Durham, N.C.: Duke University Press, 1983.

Henderson, Robert Brian. "Radical Poetics: Dada, B.P/ Nichol, and the Horsemen." Ph.D. diss., York University, Ontario, Canada, 1982.

Howard, Seymour. "Duchamp, Dali, Tzara, and Dadaist Coprophilia." *Notes in the History of Art* 10, no. 1 (1990): 26–35.

Hughes, Robert. *The Shock of the New.* New York: Knopf, 1981.

Jean, Marcel, ed. *The Autobiography of Surrealism.* New York: Viking, 1980.

Jouffroy, Alain. *La vie réinventée: l'explosion des années 20 à Paris.* Paris: Laffont, 1982.

Kantarizis, "Dada and the Preparations for Surrealism" *Australian Journal of French Studies* 8 (1971): 44–61.

Kemper, Hans-Georg. *von Expressionismus zum Dadaismus.* Kronberg/Ts, 1974.

Kuenzli, Rudolf E. *New York Dada.* New York: Willis, Locker and Owens, 1986.

Last, Rex W. *German Dadaist Literature: Kurt Schwitters, Hugo Ball, Hans Arp.* New York: Twayne Publishers, 1973.

Leavens, Ileana B. *From "291" to Zurich: The Birth of Dada.* Ann Arbor, Mich.: UMI Research Press, 1983.

Lippard, Lucy. "Dada in Berlin: Unfortunately Still Timely." *Art in America* 66, no. 2 (1978): 107–11.

Literatur und Erfahrung, no. 4 (1980). Special issue on Dada and literature.

MacAdam, Barbara A. "Sex and the Surrealists: Investigating Sex: Surrealist Research 1928–1932." *Art News* 91 (November 1992): 20.

Marcus, Greil. "Liliput at the Cabaret Voltaire." *Triquarterly*, no. 52 (1981): 265–77.

————. "die Dada-Connection." *Rock Session*, no. 6 (1982): 92–101.

————. *Lipstick Traces.* Cambridge: Harvard University Press, 1989.

Matthews, J. H. *Eight Painters: The Surrealist Context.* Syracuse: Syracuse University Press, 1982.

————. *Surrealism, Insanity, and Poetry.* Syracuse: Syracuse University Press, 1982.

————. *Languages of Surrealism.* Columbia: University of Missouri Press, 1986.

Mead, Gerald. "Language and the Unconscious in Surrealism." *Centennial Review* 20 (1976): 278–89.

————. *The Surrealist Image: A Stylistic Study.* Bern: Peter Lang Publishing, 1978.

Meyer, Raimund. "Aspekte von Dada Zurich: Chronologie und Dokumentation." Thesis, Universität Zurich, 1982.

Meyer, Reinhart. *Dada in Zurich und Berlin, 1916–1920: Literatur awischen Revolution und Reaktion.* Kronberg: Scriptor Verlag, 1973.

Milman, Estera. "Historical Precedents, Trans-Historical Strategies, and the Myth of Democratization: Coincidences between the Birth of Dada and the Birth of Fluxus." *Visible Language* 26 (winter/spring 1992): 17–34.

Naumann, F. M. "Janco/Dada: An Interview with Marcel Janco." *Arts Magazine* 57, no. 3 (1982): 80–86.

Nilsson, Nils Ake. "The Sound Poem: Russian Zaum and German Dada." *Russian Literature* 10, no. 4 (1981): 307–18.

Oesterreicher-Mollwo, Marianne. *Surrealism and Dadaism: Provocative Destruction, the Path Within, and the Exacerbation of the Problem of a Reconciliation of Art and Life.* Oxford: Phaidon, 1979.

Paulsen, Wolfgang, and Helmut Hermann, eds. *Sinn aus Unsinn: Dada International.* Bern: Francke, 1982.

Perloff. *Art and the Everyday: Popular Entertainment and the Circle of Erik Satie.* New York: Oxford University Press, 1991.

Philippe, Eckhard. *Dadaismus: Einführung in den literarischen Dadismus und die Wortkunst des 'Sturm'-Kreises.* Munich: Wilhyelm Fink, 1980.

Picon, Gaetan. *Surrealists and Surrealism: 1919–1939.* Geneva: Skira, 1983.

Plottel, Jeanine. "The Mathematics of Surrealism." *Romanic Review* 71 (1980): 319–29.

Riha, Karl, ed. *Da Dada da war, ist Dada da: Aufsatze und Dokumente.* Munich: Hanser, 1980.

———. *113 Dada Gedichte.* Berlin: Agenbach, 1982.

Roters, Eberhard. *Berlin, 1910–1933.* New York: Rizzoli, 1982.

Rothenberg, Jerome. *That Dada Strain.* New York: New Directions, 1982.

Rylko, Zdzislaw. *Le Réception du surréalisme française en Pologne entre les deux guerres: Actes du Seminaire organisé par l'Institute de Philology Polonaise et le Centre de Civilisation Française de l'Univerisité de Varsovie.* Warsaw: Centre de Civilisation Française de l'Université de Varsovie, 1975.

Sanouillet, Michel, and D. Baudouin. *"Dada."* Vol. 2, *Dossier Critique.* Nice: Centre du XXe Siècle, 1983.

Seaman, David W. *Concrete Poetry in France.* Ann Arbor, Mich.: UMI Research Press, 1981.

Schneede, Uwe M., ed. *Die Zwanziger Jahre: Manifeste und dokumente deutscher Kunstler.* Cologne: DuMont, 1979.

Shelton, Marie-Denise. "Le Monde noir dans la littérature dadaiste et surréaliste." *The French Review: Journal of the American Association of Teachers of French* 57, no. 3 (1984): 320–28.

Sheppard, Richard W. "Dada and Expressionism," *PEGS* 49 (1979): 46–83.

———. "Dada and Mysticism." In *Dada Spectrum,* ed. Stephen C. Foster and Rudolf Kuenzli, 92–113. Madison: 1979.

———. "Dada and Politics." *Journal of European Studies,* no. 9 (1979): 39–74.

———. "What Is Dada?" *Orbis Literarum,* no. 34 (1979): 195–200.

———, ed. *Dada: Studies of a Movement.* Buckinghamshire, England: Alpha-Academic, 1980.

———, ed. *New Studies in Dada: Essays and Documents.* Driffield, England: Hutton Press, 1981.

Short, Robert. "Paris, Dada and Surrealism," *Journal of European Studies,* no. 9 (1979): 79–98.

———. *Dada and Surrealism.* New York: Mayflower Books, 1980.

Siegel, J. "The Image of the Eye in Surrealist Art and Its Psychoanalytic Sources." *Arts Magazine* 56, no. 6 (1982): 102–96.

Tison-Braun, Micheline. *Dada et le surréalisme: Textes théoriques sur la poésie.* Paris: Bordas, 1973.

Virmaux, Alain, and Odette Virmaux. *La Constellation surréaliste.* Lyon: La Manufacture, 1987.

Watts, Harriett Ann. *Chance: A Perspective on Dada.* Ann Arbor, Mich.: UMI Research Press, n.d.

Wills, David. *Self De(Con)Struct.* Australia: James Cook University of North Queensland, 1985.

Young, Alan. *Dada and After: Extremist Modernism and English Literature.* Manchester, England: Manchester University Press, 1981.

V   The People Within and Related to the Movements

Guillaume Apollinaire

Apollinaire, Guillaume. A pantomime written by Apollinaire, including Savinio's music and decoration, and a "mise en scene" by Picabia and de Zayas. In Willard E. Bohn Jr. "Apollinaire and the Faceless Man: The Origins of His Surrealism." Ph.D. diss., University of California, Berkeley, 1973.
Bohn, Willard. "From Surrealism to Surrealism: Apollinaire and Breton." *Journal of Aesthetics and Art Criticism* 36, no. 2 (1977): 197–210.
_____. "At the Cross-Roads of Surrealism: Apollinaire and Breton." *Kentucky Romance Quarterly*, no. 27 (1980): 85–96.
_____. *Apollinaire and the Faceless Man: The Creation and Evolution of a Modern Motif.* Rutherford, N.J.: Fairleigh Dickinson University Press, 1991.
Carandini, Silvia. "Suoni, Idee, Colori, Forme: Il linguaggio delle art nella prima rappresentazione di *Les Mamelles de Tirésias* di G. Apollinaire." *Rierche di Storia dell'arte*, no. 25 (1985): 39–49.
Debon, Claude. *Guillaume Apollinaire après "Alcools": Le Poète et la guerre.* Paris: Minard, 1981.
Decaudin, Michel. "Apollinaire et Marinetti." In *Mélanges de littérature française moderne offerts à Garnet Rés par ses collegues et amis,* ed. Cedric E. Pickford, 103–15. Paris: Minard, 1980.
Hubert, Renée Riese. "La Présence du théâtre dans 'Le Poète assassiné.'" *Papers in Romance* 3, no. 1 (1981): 1–10.
Leighten, Patrician. "La Propagande par le rire: Satire and subversion in Apollinaire, Jarry and Picasso's collages." *Gazette des Beaux-Arts*, 6th ser., no. 112 (1988): 163–70.
York, Richard A. "Mallarmé and Apollinaire: The Unpunctuated Text." *Visible Language* 23 (winter 1989): 45–63.

Louis Aragon

Aragon, Louis. *Ecrits sur l'art moderne.* Paris: Flammarion, 1981.
Ablamowicz, Aleksander. "Aragon dramaturge." *Romanica Wratislaviensia* 12 (1977): 58–68.
Babilas, W. "A Propos d'une bibliographie des publications d'Aragon: Addenda et corrections." *Romanische Forschungen* 93 (1981) 1–2, 147–66.
Galey, Mathieu. "Aragon sur scène." *Express*, no. 1194 (1974): 61–62.
Geoghegan, Crispin. *Louis Aragon: Essai de bibliographie.* London: Grant and Cutler, 1979.
Vasseviere, Maryse. "*Aurelien,* roman . . . : Théâtre et poésie ou le mélange des genres." *Roman 20–50: Revue d'Etude du Roman du XXe Siecle* (Lille), no. 7 (1989): 17–30.
Voltz, Pierre. "Aragon et le théâtre dans *Le Libertinage.*" In *Sur Aragon: Le Libertinage,* ed. Suzanne Ravis, 155–81. Aix-en-Provence: Université de Provence, 1986.

Jean Arp

Arp, Jean. *Bibliographie.* Comp. Aimée Bleikasten. London: Grant and Cutler, 1981.
Arp: Collages and Reliefs, 1910–1945. Exhibition Catalogue. London: Annely Juda Fine Art, 1982.
Hans/Jean Arp. Le Temps des papiers déchirés. Exhibition Catalogue. Paris: Centre Pompidou, 1983.
Arp, Hans, and Tristan Tzara. *Cinéma calendrier du coeur abstrait.* Reprint, Ann Arbor, Mich.: Thomas Press, 1983.
Backus, Alfons, and Heribert Brinkmann. "Hans Arp's 'Opus Null': Zur Editionsgeschichte eines Dada-Gedichtes." *Germanisch-Romanische Monatsschrift* (Berlin) 32, no. 1 (1982): 97–103.
Cook, Albert. "Aspects of the Plastic Image: Pound and Arp." *Dada/Surrealism*, no. 12 (1983): 37–47.
Deguy, Michel. "L'oeuvre d'Art." *Revue d'Esthetique* (Paris), no. 16 (1989): 41–49.
Grieve, Alastair. "Arp in Zurich." In *Dada Spectrum: The Dialectics of Revolt*, ed. Stephen C. Foster and Rudolf Kuenzli, 176–205. Iowa City: University of Iowa Press, 1979.
Grubel, Rainer. "Hans/Jean Arp und die russicsche Avantgarde." *Text Kritik: Zeitschrift fur Literatur* (Göttingen), no. 92 (1986): 51–65.

Hancock, J. H. "Jean Arp's 'The Eggboard' Interpreted: The Artist as a Poet in the 20's." *Art Bulletin*, no. 65 (1983): 122–37.

Kern, Alfred. "Du Pluriel a la singularité des langues (Jan Hans Arp, 1886–1986): Actes du XIIe Colloque de l'Association Internationale des Critiques Littéraires (Marseille 16–20 octobre 1986)." In *Poésie et critique de la poésie*, ed. Robert André, 85–90. Marseille: SUD/A.I.C.L., 1987.

Kuenzli, Rudolf E. "Hans Arp's Poetica: The Sense of Dada 'Nonsense.'" In *New Studies on Dada*, ed. Richard Sheppard. Driffield, England: Hutton Press, 1981.

Lach, Friedhelm. "Zur Entstehung von Dada-Texten: Sieben Wege zum Verstandnis der Kunst von Hans Arp und Kurt Schwitters." In *The Turn of the Century: German Literature and Art, 1890–1915*. McMaster Colloquium on German Literature, II, ed. Gerald Chapple and Hans H. Schulte, 395–412. Bonn: Bouvier, 1981.

Last, Rex. "Hans Arp and the Problem of Evil." In *New Studies on Dada*, ed. Richard Sheppard. Driffield, England: Hutton Press, 1981.

Malet, Marian. "Hans Arp and the Aesthetics of the Workshop." In *New Studies on Dada*, ed. Richard Sheppard. Driffield, England: Hutton Press, 1981.

Mann, Philip. "Symmetry, Chance, Biomorphism: A Comparison of the Visual Art and Poetry of Hans Arp's Dada Period (1916–1924)." *Word and Image: A Journal of Verbal/Visual Enquiry* 6, no. 1 (1990): 82–99.

Poley, Stefanie. "Max Ernst und Hans Arp, 1914–1921." In *Max Ernst in Koln*, ed. Wulf Herzogenrath. Cologne: Rheinland, 1980.

Riha, Kar. " 'Zweite Fassungen': Zu Text-Modifikationen in der Lyrk Hans Arps." *Text Kritik: Zeitschrift fur Literatur* (Göttingen), no. 92 (1986): 81–88.

Thuysen, Joachim von der. "Hans Arp: 'Das Fibelmeer': Eine Annaherung." *Text Kritik: Zeitschrift fur Literatur* (Göttingen), no. 92 (1986): 99–106.

Trier, Ediuard. "Hans Arp zum 100 Geburtstag." *Jahresring* (Stuttgart) (1987–88): 224–32.

Triomphe, Robert. "Jean Hans Arp et son ami Hugo Ball: Introduction alsacienne aux avant-gardes du XXe siecle." *Filoloski Pregleg* 11, nos. 1–4 (1973): 41–74.

Watts, Harriett. "The Poetry of Kandinsky and Arp: Transposed Landscapes." In *The Turn of the Century: German Literature and Art 1890–1915*, McMaster Colloquium on German Literature, II, ed. Gerald Chapple and Hans H. Schulte, 377–93. Bonn: Bouvier, 1981.

———. "Periods and Commas: Hans Arp's Seminal Punctuation." In *Dada/Dimensions*, ed. Stephen C. Foster, 83–109. Ann Arbor, Mich.: UMI Research Press, 1985.

Antonin Artaud

Brown, Frederick. "A Thirties Harlequinade: Artaud and Jean-Louis Barrault." *Yale/Theatre* 5, no. 3 (1974): 60–65.

Charbonnier, Georges. *Antonin Artaud*. Paris: Seghers, 1980.

Deak, Frantisek. "Antonin Artaud and Charles Dullin: Artaud's Apprenticeship in Theatre." *Educational Theatre Journal* 29 (1977): 345–53.

Greene, Naomi. "Artaud and Film: A Reconsideration." *Cinema Journal*, no. 23 (1984): 28–40.

Knapp, Bettina. "A Spiritual Heir: Antonin Artaud and the Théâtre Alfred Jarry." *Dada/Surrealism*, no. 4 (1974): 10–16.

———. "Antonin Artaud: 'Cinéma Boulversement complet de l'optique, de la perspective, de la logique'—A Melodrama." *Kentucky Romance Quarterly* 28, no. 3 (1981): 229–36.

Lalande, Jean-Pierre. "Artaud's Theatre of Cruelty and the Fantastic." In *Aspects of Fantasy: Selected Essays From the Second International Conference on the Fantastic in Literature and Film*, ed. William Coyle, 113–20. Westport, Conn.: Greenwood Press, 1986.

Thompsen, Peter S. "The Temptation of Antonin Artaud." *Romance Notes*, no. 21 (1980): 42–47.

Virmaux, Alain, and Odette Virmaux. *Artaud: Un bilan critique*. Paris: Belfond, 1980.

———. *Artaud Vivant*. Paris: Oswald, 1980.

Hugo Ball

Ball, Hugo. *Der Kunstler und die Zeitkrankheit: Ausgewahlte Schriften*. Ed. Hans Burkhard Schlichting. Frankfurt am Main: Suhrkamp, 1984.

Bahr, Hans Joachim. *Die Funktion des Theaters im Leben Hugo Ball: Materialien zur Bestimmung der Jahr 1910–1914.* Frankfurt: Peter Lang Publishing, 1982.
_____. "Hugo Ball und das Theater: Die Jahre 1910–1914." In *Hugo Ball Almanach,* ed. Ernest Teubner, 75–133. Pirmasens, 1982.
Balakian, Anna. "A Triptych of Modernism: Reverdy, Huidobro, and Ball." In *Modernism: Challenges and Perspectives,* ed. Monique Chefdor, Ricardo Quinones, and Albert Wachtel, 111–27. Urbana: University of Illinois Press, 1986.
Dery, Mark. "From Hugo Ball to Hugo Largo: Seventy-five Years of Art and Music." *High Performance* 11 (winter 1988): 54–57.
Dohl, Reinhard. "Unsinn der Kunst gegen Wahnsinn der Zeit: Hans Arp und Hugo Ball zum Hundersten." *Text Kritik: Zeitschrift fur Literature* (Göttingen), no. 92 (1986): 66–80.
Hager, Tamara. "Asthetisch und politisch-weltanschauliche Positionen des Dichters Hugo Ball in der Zeit des ersten Weltkrieges." *Wissenschaftliche Zeitschrift der Karl-Marx-Universitat* (Leipzig) 38, no. 3 (1989): 264–70.
Harris, Brian L. "The Michelangelo Dramas of Friedrich Hebbel and Hugo Ball: From Historicism toward Expressionism." In *From the Bard to Broadway,* ed. Karelisa V. Hartigan, 95–106. Lanham, Md.: University Publishers of America, 1987.
Hugo Ball Almanach. Ed. Ernest Teubner. Pirmasens, 1977.
Kuenzli, Rudolf E. "Hugo Ball: Verse without Words." *Dada/Surrealism,* no. 8 (1978): 30–35.
Legband, Paul. "Zeugnis der Schauspielschule des deutschen Theaters für Hugo Ball." In *Hugo Ball Almanach,* ed. Ernest Teubner, 7–8. Pirmasens, 1979.
Mann, Philip H. "Hugo Ball and the 'Magic Bishop' Episode: A Reconsideration." *New German Studies* 4, no. 1 (1976): 204–23.
_____. "Hugo Ball's Expressionist Theatre." *Literaturwissenschaftliches Jahrbuch,* n.s., no. 24 (1983): 175–208.
Prawer, Siegbert. "Dada Dances: Hugo Ball's 'Tenderenda der Phantast.' In *The Discontinuous Tradition,* ed. Peter F. Ganz, 204–23. Oxford, 1971.
White, Erdmute Wenzel. "Das Wunder der Geisteszwiebel: Hugo Ball: Eine Studie zuer Paradoxologie: Zwolftes Amherster Kolloquium zur deutschen Literatur." In *Sinn aus Unsinn: Dada International,* ed. Wolfgang Paulsen and Helmut G. Hermann, 101–19. Bern: Francke, 1982.

Pierre Albert-Birot

Lista, Giovanni. "Les Caractères du 'futurisme français' à travers l'oeuvre de Pierre Albert-Birot: Actes du Colloque intérnational ténu à l'UNESCO." In *Présence de F. T. Marinetti,* ed. Jean-Claude Marcade, 156–75. Lausanne: L'Age d'Homme, 1982.

André Breton

Balakian, Anna. "André Breton and Psychiatry." In *Medicine and Literature,* ed. Enid Peschel, 160–70. New York: Watson, 1980.
Béhar, Henri. "The Passionate Attraction: Breton and the Theatre." *Dada/Surrealism,* no. 17 (1988): 13–18.
Bruno, Jean. "André Breton et l'expérience de l'illumination." *Mélusine,* no. 2 (1981): 53–69.
Cauvin, Jean-Pierre. "Literary Games of Chance: The André Breton." *Library Chronicle of the University of Texas,* no. 16 (1981): 16–41.
Eigeldinger, Marc. "Poésie et langage alchimique chez André Breton." *Mélusine,* no. 2 (1981): 22–38.
Ladimer, Bethany. "Madness and the Irrational in the Work of André Breton: A Feminist Perspective." *Feminist Studies,* no. 6 (1980): 175–79.
Manu, Emil. "André Breton-Tristan Tzara in culisele congresului avangardei de la Paris." *Manuscriptum: Revista Trimestriala Editata de Muzeul Literaturii Romane* (Bucharest) 9, no. 1 (1978): 133–40.
Matthews, J. H. *André Breton: Sketch for an Early Portrait.* Amsterdam: John Benjamins, 1986.
Pierre, José. *L'Aventure surréaliste autour d'André Breton.* Paris: E.P.I. Filipacchi/Artcurial, 1986.
Plouvier, Paule. *Poétique de l'amour chez André Breton.* Paris: Corti, 1983.
Vielwahr, André. *Sous le signe des contradictions: André Breton de 1913 à 1924.* Paris: Nizet, 1980.

Jean Cocteau

Brown, Frederick. *An Impersonation of Angels*. New York: Viking, 1981.
Peters, Arthur King. *Jean Cocteau and His World: An Illustrated Biography*. New York: Vendôme Press, 1986.

Robert Desnos

Caws, Mary Ann. *The Surrealist Voice of Robert Desnos*. Amherst: University of Massachusetts Press, 1977.
Dumas, Marie-Claire. *Robert Desnos ou l'exploration des limites*. Paris: Klincksieck, 1980.
Leonard, Byron. "A Surrealist Poet at the Movies: Robert Desnos." *Stanford French Review*, no. 2 (1978): 103–13.
Sullerot, François. "Desnos, luth constellé." *Mélusine*, no. 3 (1982): 269–77.
Willis, David. "Sur l'oeuvre surréaliste de Robert Desnos." *Mélusine*, no. 2 (1981): 228–37.

Marcel Duchamp

Cabanne, Pierre. *Entretiens avec Marcel Duchamp*. Paris: Editions Pierre Belfond, 1967.
Caws, Mary Ann, and Rudolf Kuenzli, eds. "Duchamp Centennial." *Dada/Surrealism* 16 (1987). Special issue.
Faust, Wolfgang M. "Marcel Duchamp: Dinge und Worte: Rose Sélavy." *Sprache im Technischen Aeialter*, no. 59. (1976): 215–38.
Jones, Amelia. "Duchamp, Gender, and the Radical Alternative to Modernism." *New Observations*, no. 74 (1990): 14–18.
Morgan, Robert C. "In the Space of Androgyny." *High Performance* 10, no. 3 (1987): 62–63.
Schwartz, A. "Marcel Duchamp Alias Rrose Sélavy Alias Marchand du Sel Alias Belle Haleine." *Data* (Italy) 3, no. 9 (1973): 30–38, 86–91.

Roger Gilbert-Lecomte

Powrie, Phil. "Film-Form-Mind: The Hegelian Follies of Roger Gilbert-Lecomte (with reprint of 'The Alchemy of the Eye; Cinema As a Form of Mind')." *Quarterly Review of Film and Video* 12 (September 1991): 19–32.

Ivan Goll

Valentin, Jean-Marie. " 'Das neue Drama sei enorm!' Surréalité et grotesque dans le théâtre d'Ivan Goll." *Etudes Germaniques* (Paris), no. 169 (1988): 82–96.

Georg Grosz

Grosz, George. *George Grosz: An Autobiography*. Trans. Nora Hodges. New York: Macmillan, 1983.
———. *Grosz/Heartfield: The Artist as Social Critic*. Exhibition Catalogue. Minneapolis: University Gallery, University of Minnesota, 1980.
Deshong, A. *The Theatrical Designs of George Grosz*. Ann Arbor, Mich.: UMI Research Press, 1982.
Herzfelde, Wieland, ed. *Pass auf! Hier kommt Grosz: Bilder, Rhythmen und Gesänge, 1915–1918*. Leipzig: Philipp Reclam, 1981.
Knust, Herert. "Grosz, Piscator, und Brecht: Notizen zum Theater im Exil." In *Deutsches Exildrama und Exiltheater*, ed. Wolfgang Elfe, James Hardin, and Gunteher Holst. Bern: Peter Lang Publishing, 1977.

Raoul Hausmann

Hausmann, Raoul. *Texte bis 1933*. Ed. Michael Erlhoff. 2 vols. Munich, 1982.
Benson, Timothy O. *Raoul Hausmann and Berlin Dada*. Ann Arbor, Mich.: UMI Research Press, 1987.

Emmy Hennings

Hennings, Emmy. *Fruhe Texte*. Ed. Bernhard Merkelback. Siegen, 1983.
Rugh, Thomas F. "Emmy Hennings and the Emergence of Zurich Dada." *Woman's Art Journal* 2, no. 1 (1981): 1–6.
———. "Emmy Hennings and Zurich Dada." *Dada/Surrealism*, no. 10/11 (1982): 5–28.

Richard Huelsenbeck

Huelsenbeck, Richard, ed. *Dada Almanach*. 1920. Reprint, Hamburg: Nautilus, 1980.
———. *Richard Huelsenbeck and His Friends*. Exhibition Catalogue. New York: Goethe House, 1975.
Fullner, Karin. "The Meister-Dada: The Image of Dada Through the Eyes of Richard Huelsenbeck." In *New Studies in Dada: Essays and Documents*, ed. Richard Sheppard, 16–34. Driffield, England: Hutton Press, 1981.
———. *Richard Huelsenbeck: Texte und Aktionen eines Dadaisten*. Heidelberg, 1983.
Sheppard, Richard, Karin Fullner, Rolf Italiaander, and Hans J. Kleinschmid. *Richard Huelsenbeck*. Hamburg: Hans Christians Verlag, 1982.
———. *Zurich, Dadaco, Dadaglobe: The Correspondence between Richard Huelsenbeck, Tristan Tzara, and Kurt Wolff*. Tayport, Scotland: Hutton Press, 1982.

Alfred Jarry

Arnaud, Noel. *Alfred Jarry, d'Ubu roi au Docteur Faustroll*. Paris: La Table Ronde, 1974.
Caws, Mary Ann. *Théorie, tableau, texte de Jarry à Artaud. 20th l'icosatheque: Le siècle eclaté: Dada, Surréalisme et avant-gardes*. Paris: Lettres Modernes, 1978.
Erickson, John. "The Gyres of *Ubu Roi*." *Dada/Surrealism*, no. 4 (1974): 5–9.
Knapp, Bettina. "A Spiritual Heir: Antonin Artaud and the Théâtre Alfred Jarry." *Dada/Surrealism*, no. 4 (1974): 10–16.
LaBelle, Maurice Marc. *Alfred Jarry: Nihilism and the Theater of the Absurd*. New York: New York University Press, 1980.
Lamont, Rosette C. "Ubu Roi: A Collage." *Dada/Surrealism*, no. 4 (1974): 17–26.
Schumacher, Claude. *Alfred Jarry and Guillaume Apollinaire*. London: Macmillan, 1984.
Vazzoler, Franco. "Marinetti et Jarry: Actes du Colloque intérnational ténu à l'UNESCO." In *Presence de F. T. Marinetti*, ed. Jean-Claude Marcade, 134–39. Lausanne: L'Age d'Homme, 1982.

Francis Picabia

Picabia, Francis. *Francis Picabia*. Exhibition Catalogue. New York: Solomon R. Guggenheim Museum, 1970.
———. *Francis Picabia*. Exhibition Catalogue. Paris: Centre Pompidou, 1976.
Boucou, Mihaela, Maryline Leduc, and Florence Palou. "Répertoire des recueils de coupures de presse Picabia-Tzara." *Mélusine*, no. 5 (1983): 313–44.
Camfield, William A. *Francis Picabia: His Art, Life, and Times*. Princeton: Princeton University Press, 1979.
Mueller, J. "Films: 'Relâche' and 'Entr' acte.' " *Dance Magazine*, no. 51 (1977): 102–3.

Georges Ribemont-Dessaignes

Ribemont-Dessaignes, Georges. *Hommage à Georges Ribemont-Dessaignes pour ses quatre-vingt ans*. Exhibition Catalogue. Venice: Galerie Chave, 1965.
Begot, Jean-Pierre. "L'oeuvre de Georges Ribemont-Dessaignes de 1915 à 1930." Thèse 3e cycle. Paris III, 1972.
Corvin, Michel. "Georges Ribemont-Dessaignes et le laboratoire 'Art et Action.' " *Cahiers de l'Association Internationale pour l'Etude de Dada et du Surréalisme* 1 (1966): 160–82.
———. "Georges Ribemont-Dessaignes: *Larmes de couteau*," *CEDS* 1 (1966): 144–59.

Favre, Yves-Alain. "La Création poétique chez Ribemont-Dessaignes." *Mélusine*, no. 3 (1982): 191–204.

Lepage, Jacques, ed. "Hommage à Georges Ribemont-Dessaignes." *Marginales* 28, no. 252 (1973).

Matthews, J. H. "Georges Ribemont-Dessaignes." In *Theatre in Dada and Surrealism*. Syracuse University Press, 1974.

Marginales 28, no. 152 (1973). Special issue on Georges Ribemont-Dessaignes.

Ness-Kirby, Victoria. "Georges Ribemont-Dessaignes." *Drama Review* 16, no. 1 (1972): 104–9.

Raymond Roussel

Plottel, Jeanine Parisier. "Machines de langage: *Impressions d'Afrique* et la Mariée mise a nu par ses celibataires, même." *Le Siecle éclate*, no. 2 (1975).

Kurt Schwitters

Schwitters, Kurt. *Kurt Schwitters: Complete Works*. Ed. Friedhelm Lach. 5 vols. 1973–1982.

———. *Kurt Schwitters: Das Literarische Werk*. Ed. Michael Erlhoff. 5 vols. Munich, 1982.

Elderfield, John. *Kurt Schwitters*. London: Thames and Hudson, 1985.

———. "Schwitters: Performance Notes." In *Dada/Dimensions*, ed. Stephen C. Foster, 39–46. Ann Arbor, Mich.: UMI Research Press, 1985.

Erlhoff, Michael, ed. "Zur Rezeption von 'Anna Blume': Dokumente." *Kurt Schwitters Almanach*, no. 1 (1982): 82–120.

Finke, Ulrich. "Kurt Schwitters' Contribution to Concrete Art and Poetry." In *Literature and the Plastic Arts 1880–1930: Seven Essays*, ed. Ian Higgins. New York: Barnes and Noble, 1973.

Kohrt, Manfred. "Dadaismus, Typographie und Rechtschreibung: Kurt Schwitters als Orthographiereformer." In *Sprache: Formen und Strukturen*, ed. Manfred Kohrt and Jürgen Lenerz. Tübingen: Niemeyer, 1981.

Nill, Annegreth. "Rethinking Kurt Schwitters, Part One: An Interpretation of 'Hansi.' " *Arts* 55, no. 1 (January 1981): 112–17.

———. "Weimar Politics and the Theme of Love in Kurt Schwitters' *Das Baumerbild*." *Dada/Surrealism*, no. 13 (1984): 17–36.

Scholz, Christian. "Quelques remarques sur la 'sonate présyllabique' de Kurt Schwitters." *Bérénice*, no. 2 (1982): 77–83.

Sheppard, Richard. "Kurt Schwitters und Dada." *Kurt Schwitters Almanach*, no. 1 (1982): 56–64.

Philippe Soupault

Soupault, Philippe. *Poèmes et poésies, 1917–1973*. Paris, 1973.

———. *Ecrits de cinéma*. [1918–1931]. Paris: Plon, 1979.

———. *Ecrits sur la peinture*. Paris: Lachenal and Ritter, 1980.

———. *En joue!* [1925]. Paris: Lachenal and Ritter, 1980.

———. *Le Bon Apôtre*. [1923]. Paris: Garnier, 1980.

———. *Le Grand Homme*. [1929]. Paris: Lachenal and Ritter, 1981.

———. *Mémoires de l'oubli*. [1914–1980]. Lyon: Laffont, 1981.

———. *Odes*. [1930–1980]. Lyon: Laffont, 1981.

Biron, Lionel A. "Philippe Soupault's Early Contact with Zurich Dada: A Gracious Butterfly Flirting with Dada in *Les Champs magnétiques*." *Rackham Literary Studies*, no. 6 (1975): 41–49.

Bonis, Bernadette. "Bibliographie de Philippe Soupault." *Action Poétique*, no. 76 (1978): 5–10.

Décaudin, Michel. "Soupault, poète en dépit de tout." *Quinzaine Littéraire*, no. 325 (1980): 19.

Gâteau, Jean-François. "Le'come back' de Philippe Soupault." *Mélusine*, no. 3 (1982): 278–84.

Morlino, Bernard. *Philippe Soupault*. Lyon: Manufacture, 1987.

Tristan Tzara

Tzara, Tristan. *Tzara, Tristan: Oeuvres complètes*. Ed. Henri Béhar. Paris, 1975.

———. *Tzara, Tristan: Sieben dadaitische Manifeste*. Hamburg, 1984.

Béhar, Henri. "Hamlet dans le secret de *Mouchoir de nuages*." *Silex* (Grenoble), no. 3 (1977): 98–102.

_____. "Le Vocabulaire freudiste et marxien de Tzara dan *Grains et issues*." In *Actes du 2e colloque de lixicologie politique*, ed. Danielle Bonnaud-Lamotte et. al, 231–46. Paris: Klincksieck, 1982.

_____. "Tristan Tzara, phare de l'avant-garde roumaine." *Revue de Littérature comparée* (Tours) 58, no. 1,229 (1984): 89–104.

_____. "Tristan Tzara, historiographe de Dada." *Mélusine*, no. 11 (1990): 29–40.

Biron, Lionel A. "The Secret French and German Editions of Tristan Tzara's *Dada 3*, or How to Launch an International Movement at the Height of European Nationalism." *Rackham Literary Studies*, no. 6 (1975): 35–40.

Boffey, Peter. "The Lives of Tristan Tzara." *Third Rail: A Review of International Arts and Literature* 6 (1984): 67.

Brioso, Sandro. "Un nodo dell'avanguardia storica: Tzara e Marinetti." *Il Lettore di Provincia* (Ravenna) 13, no. 49/50 (1982): 35–58.

Corvin, Michel. "*Le Coeur à gaz*, ou la fête de la déstruction du théâtre." *Revue d'Histoire du Théâtre* 3 (1971): 265–83.

Europe 53, nos. 555–556 (1975). Special issue on Tristan Tzara.

Kummerle, Inge. *Tristan Tzara. Dramatische Experimente 1916–1940*. Rheinfelden: Schauble, 1978.

Lehuard, Raoul. "La vente Tristan Tzara: African art collection." *Arts d'Afrique Noire*, no. 68 (winter 1988): 13–17.

Lista, Giovanni. "Tristan Tzara et le Dadaisme Italien." *Europe* 53, nos. 555–556 (1975).

Matthews, J. H. "Tristan Tzara." In *Theatre in Dada and Surrealism*. Syracuse: Syracuse University Press, 1974.

Moore, John R. M. "Tzara et Ribemont-Dessaignes: Un Théâtre du merveilleux." *La Licorne* (Poitiers) 10 (1986): 155–67.

Norman, Dorothy. "Two Conversations: Marcel Duchamp and Tristan Tzara." *Yale University Library Gazette* 60, nos. 1–2 (1985): 77–80.

Pop, Ion. "Tristan Tzara si piezia romaneasca de avangarda." *Manuscriptum: Revista Trimestriala Editata de Muzeul Literaturii Romane* (Bucharest) 14, no. 1 (1983): 172–74.

Robbins, Aileen. "Tristan Tzara's *Handkerchief of Clouds*." *Drama Review* 16, no. 4 (1972): 110–11.

Russo, Adelaide M. "Picking Up the Pieces? Tzara's Explosive Text and the Surrealist Strategy." *Miorita: A Journal of Romanian Studies* 9, no. 1/2 (1985): 1–18.

Whitton, David. "Tristan Tzara's *Mouchoir de nuages*." *Theatre Research International* (Glasgow) 14, no. 3 (1989): 271–87.

Wilson, Ruth. "The Plays of Tristan Tzara." *Yale/Theatre* 4, no. 1 (1973): 129–32.

Roger Vitrac

Antle, Martine. *Théâtre et poésie surréalistes: Vitrac et la scène virtuelle*. Birmingham, Ala.: Summa Publications, 1988.

VI   Subject Areas

Dada and Surrealist Film

"Bibliography: Dada and Surrealist Film." Ed. Rudolf E. Kuenzli. *Dada/Surrealism*, no. 15 (1986): 220–54.

Cinéma dadaiste et surréaliste: Exposition itinérante. Exhibition Catalogue. Paris: Centre Pompidou, 1976.

"Dada and Surrealist Film." *Dada/Surrealism*, no. 15 (1986). Special issue.

Earle, William. "Phenomenology and the Surrealism of Movies." *Journal of Aesthetics and Art Criticism* 38 (1980): 255–60.

Kaes, Anton. "Verfremdung als Verfahren: Film und Dada." In *Sinn aus Unsinn: Dada International*, ed. Wolfgang Paulsen and Helmut Hermann. Bern: Francke, 1982.

Kovacs, Steven. *From Enchantment to Rage: The Story of Surrealist Cinema*. London: Associated University Presses, 1980.

Kuenzli, Rudolf E. *Dada and Surrealist Film*. New York: Willis, Locker and Owens, 1987.
Leonard, Arthur Byron II. "Poetry and Film: Aspects of the Avant-Garde in France (1918–1932)." Ph.D. diss., Stanford University, 1975.
Matthews, J. H. *Surrealism and American Feature Films*. New York: Twayne Publishers, 1979.
Michaelson, Annette. "Anemic Cinema: Reflections on an Emblematic Work." *Artforum* 12, no. 2 (1973): 64–69.
Rabinovitz, L. "Independent Journeyman: Man Ray, Dada and Surrealist Film-maker." *Southwest Review* 64 (1979): 355–76.
Thiher, Allen. "The Surrealist Film: Man Ray and the Limits of Metaphor." *Dada/Surrealism*, no. 6 (1976): 18–26.
White, Mimi. "Two French Dada Films: *Entr' Acte* and *Emak Bakia*." *Dada/Surrealism*, no. 13 (1984): 37–47.

Dada and Surrealist Performance

Baal, Georges. "Hungarian Avant-Garde Theatre in the Twenties and Three Unknown Surrealist Plays by Tibor Dery." *Theatre Research International* (Glasgow) 9, no. 1 (1984): 7–16.
Béhar, Henri. *Le Théâtre dada et surréaliste*. New and enl. ed. Paris: Gallimard, 1979.
———. "Dada-spectacle." In *Vitalité et contradictions de l' "Avant-Garde": Italie-France, 1909–1924*, ed. Sandro Briosi and Henk Hillenaar, 161–70. Paris: Corti, 1988.
Berghaus, Gunter. "Dada Theatre, or The Genesis of Anti-Bourgeois Performance Art." *German Life and Letters* 38, no. 4 (1985): 293–312.
Boeschoten, Cheryl. "Tzara et Marinetti: Une Etude de leur théâtre." *Quaderni d'Italianistica: Official Journal of the Canadian Society for Italian Studies* 7, no. 1 (1986): 33–75.
Brater, Enoch. "Dada, Surrealism, and the Genesis of *Not I*." *Modern Drama*, no. 18 (1975): 49–59.
Corvin, Michel. "*Le Coeur à gaz*, ou la fête de la destruction du théâtre." *Révue d'Histoire du Théâtre* 3 (1971): 265–83.
———. "Le Théâtre dada et surréaliste face à la critique." *Mélusine*, no. 2 (1981): 263–79.
Erickson, John D. "Dada Performance: The Great Spectacle of Disaster, Conflagration and Decomposition." In *Dada: Performance, Poetry, and Art*. New York: Twayne Publishers, 1984.
Freeman, Judi. "Bridging Purism and Surrealism: The Origins and Production of Fernand Leger's 'Ballet Méchanique.' " *Dada/Surrealism*, no. 15 (1986): 28–45.
Goldberg, RoseLee. *Performance: Live Art, 1909 to the Present*. New York: Harry N. Abrams, 1979.
Greenberg, Allan C. "The Dadaists and the Cabaret as Form and Forum." In *Dada/Dimensions*, ed. Stephen C. Foster, 23–38. Ann Arbor, Mich.: UMI Research Press, 1985.
Hoover, Marjorie L. "Dada und das russische Theater: Zwolftes Amherster Kolloquium zur deutschen Literatur." In *Sinn aus Unsinn: Dada International*, ed. Wolfgang Paulsen, and Helmut G. Hermann, 211–28. Bern: Francke, 1982.
Lane, Nancy. "Surrealism and the Theater of Jean Tardieu." *South Atlantic Review* 52, no. 4 (1987): 91–105.
Marleau, Denis. "Dada: Un Théâtre internationale de variétés subversives." *Etudes Littéraires* (Quebec) 19, no. 2 (1986): 13–22.
Martin, Marianne W. "On De Chirico's Theatre," In *De Chirico*, ed. William Rubin. New York: Museum of Modern Art, 1982.
McQuillan, Melissa A. "Painters and the Ballet, 1917–1926: An Aspect of the Relationship between Art and Theatre." Ph.D. diss., New York University, 1979.
Nicholls, Peter. "Anti-Oedipus? Dada and Surrealist Theatre: 1916–1935." *New Theatre Quarterly* 7, no. 28 (1991): 331–47.
Sullivan, Esther Beth. "Reading Dada Performance in Zurich through Nietzsche and Bergson." *Theatre Studies*, no. 35 (1990): 5–17.
Tafuri, Manfredo. "Il teatro come 'citta virtuale': Dal Cabaret Voltaire al Totaltheater." *Bollettino del Centro internazionale di studi di architettura Andrea Palladio* 17 (1975): 361–77.
Troy, Nancy J. "Figures of the Dance in de Stijl." *Art Bulletin* 66, no. 4 (1984): 645–56.
Vormus, Helga. "Collage et Montage dans le théâtre dadaiste de langue allemande." In *Collage et montage au théâtre et dans les autres arts durant les années vingt*, ed. Denis Bablet, 216–30. Lausanne: Théâtre Années Vingt, in association with the Centre National de la Récherche Scientifique, 1978.

Zinder, David G. *The Surrealist Connection: An Approach to a Surrealist Aesthetic of Theatre.* Ann Arbor, Mich.: UMI Research Press, 1980.

Marinetti and Futurist Performance

Blumenkranz, Noemie. "Le Théâtre de Marinetti: La Subversion de l'espace et du temps: Actes du Colloque intérnational ténu a l'UNESCO." In *Presence de F. T. Marinetti,* ed. Jean-Claude Marcade, 93–109. Lausanne: L'Age d'Homme, 1982.
Brioso, Sandro. *Marinetti e il futurismo.* Lecce: Milella, 1986.
De Vivo, Albert. "La simultaneita: Tecnica e invenzione in Marinetti." *Nemla Italian Studies,* no. 10 (1986): 85–101.
Diethe, Carol. "Sex and the Superman: An Analysis of the Pornographic Content of Marinetti's *Mafarka le futuriste.*" In *Perspectives on Pornography: Sexuality in Film and Literature,* ed. Gary Day and Clive Bloom, 159–74. New York: St. Martin's Press, 1988.
Gordon, R. S. "The Italian Futurism Theatre: A Reappraisal." *Modern Language Review* (London) 85, no. 2 (1990): 349–61.
Jannini, P. A., ed. *La fortuna del futurismo in Francia.* Rome: Bulzoni, 1979.
Kovtoune, Eugene. "Les 'Mots en liberté' de Marinetti et la 'transmentalité' (zaoum) des futuristes russes: Actes du Colloque intérnational ténu a l'UNESCO." In *Presence de F. T. Marinetti,* ed. Jean-Claude Marcade, 234–39. Lausanne: L'Age d'Homme, 1982.
Khardjiev, Nicolas. "La tournée de Marinetti en Russie en 1914: Actes du Colloque intérnational ténu a l'UNESCO." In *Presence de F. T. Marinetti,* ed. Jean-Claude Marcade, 198–233. Lausanne: L'Age d'Homme, 1982.
Lawton, Anna. "Futurist Manifestoes As an Element of Performance." *Canadian-American Slavic Studies* 19, no. 4 (1985): 473–91.
Marinelli, Donald. "Origins of Futurist Theatricality: The Early Life and Career of F. T. Marinetti." Abstract in *Dissertation Abstracts International* 48 (1988): 1587A.
Quarta, Daniela. "Il teatro prefuturista de Marinetti: Dramma senza titolo, Roi bombace, Poupées electriques." *Revue Romane* (Copenhagen) 16, nos. 1–2 (1981): 120–46.
Roig, Adrien. "La Rencontre de Balise Cendrars et de Marinetti au Bresil." *Quadrant* (Montpellier-Cedex) 6 (1989): 81–92.
Rombout, A. "Des poupées electriques aux 'fantocci elettrici' ou comment se fabrique une 'sintesi futurista' " In *Vitalité et contradictions de l' "Avant-Garde": Italie-France, 1909–1924,* ed. Sandro Briosi and Henk Hillenaar, 195–204. Paris: Corti, 1988.
Rutter, Frank P. "Vincente Huidobro and Futurism: Convergences and Divergences (1917–1918)." *Bulletin of Hispanic Studies* (Liverpool) 58, no. 1 (1981): 55–72.
Saccone, Antonio. *Marinetti et il futurismo.* Naples: Liguori, 1984.
Spedicato, Paolo. "Futurismo italiano e dadaismo internazionale: Arte e anti-arte." *Nemla Italian Studies* 10 (1986): 103–15.
Verdone, Mario. "Marinetti et le cinéma: Actes du Colloque intérnational ténu a l'UNESCO." In *Presence de F. T. Marinetti,* ed. Jean-Claude Marcade, 110–14. Lausanne: L'Age d'Homme, 1982.
———. "Futurisme et cinéma." In *Vitalité et contradictions de l' "Avant-Garde": Italie-France, 1909–1924,* ed. Sandro Briosi and Henk Hillenaar, 225–29. Paris: Corti, 1988.
de Villers, Jean-Pierre A. *Le Premier manifeste du futurisme.* Ottawa: Edition de l'Université d'Ottawa, 1986.
Webster, Michael. "Words-in-Freedom and the Oral Tradition." *Visible Language* 23 (winter 1989): 65–87.
Zurbrugg, Nicholas. "Marinetti, Boccioni and Electroacoustic Poetry: Futurism and After." *Comparative Criticism: A Yearbook* (Cambridge) 4 (1982): 193–211.

Women and Gender in the Early Twentieth-Century Avant-Garde

Arnold, Elizabeth. "Mina Loy and the Futurists." *Sagetrieb: A Journal Devoted to Poets in the Imagist/Objectivist Tradition* 8, no. 1/2 (1989): 83–117.
Augustine, Jane. "Mina Loy: A Feminist Modernist Americanizes the Language of Futurism." *Mid Hudson Language Studies* 12, no. 1 (1989): 89–101.

Blum, Cinzia. "The Scarred Womb of the Futurist Woman." *Carte Italiane: A Journal of Italian Studies* 8 (1986-1987): 14-30.

———. "Rhetorical Strategies and Gender in Marinetti's Futurist Manifesto." *Italica* 67, no. 2 (1990): 196-211.

———. "Woman in the Futurist Fiction of Power." Abstract in *Dissertation Abstracts International* 50 (1990): 2918A.

Greely, Robin Adele. "Image, Text and the Female Body: Réné Magritte and the Surrealist Publications." *Oxford Art Journal* 15, no. 2 (1992): 48-57.

Laffitte, Maryse. "L'Image de la femme chez Breton: Contradictions et virtualités." *Revue Romane*, no. 11 (1976): 286-305.

Lista, Giovanni. "Les Poupées electriques ou la femme chez Marinetti en 1905." *Etudes sur le Futurisme et les Avant Gardes* 1, no. 1 (1990): 15-20.

Raaberg, Gwen. "Surrealism and Women." *Dada/Surrealism*, no. 18 (1990). Special issue.

Rugh, T. F. "Emmy Hennings and the Emergence of Zurich Dada." *Woman's Art Journal* 2, no. 1 (1981): 1-6.

———. "Emmy Hennings and Zurich Dada." *Dada/Surrealism*, no. 10/11 (1982): 5-28.

Sayegh, Alia. "The Concept and Role of Woman in the Works of André Breton." Diss., University of Pennsylvania, 1975. Abstract in *Dissertation Abstracts International* 36 (1975): 328A.

World War I and the Early Twentieth-Century Avant-Garde

Bergius, Hanne. "Le rire de Dada." *Cahiers du Musée National d'Art Moderne* 19-20 (June 1987): 74-93.

Chadwick, Whitney. "The Great War and the Anxious Vision." *Art History* 15 (December 1992): 553-55.

Fiedler, Leonard M. "Dada und der Weltkrieg: Aspekte der Entstehung einer internationalen Bewegung in Literatur und Kunst." In *Literarischene Avantgarden*, ed. Manfred Hardt, 194-211. Darmstadt, Germany: Wissenschaftliche Buchgesellschaft, 1989. Originally published in *Arcardia* 11, no. 3 (1976): 225-37.

Kuenzli, Rudolf E. "Dada gegen den Ersten Weltkrieg: Die Dadaisten in Zurich: Zwolftes Amherster Kolloquium zur deutschen Literatur." In *Sinn aus Unsinn*, ed. Wolfgang Paulsen and Helmut G. Hermann, 87-100. Bern: Francke, 1982.

Lewis, Helena. "Surrealists, Stalinists, and Trotskyists: Theories of Art and Revolution in France between the Wars." *Art Journal*, no. 52 (1993): 61-68.

Pioli, Richard J. *Stung by Salt and War: Creative Texts of the Italian Avant-Gardist F. T. Marinetti.* New York: Peter Lang Publishing, 1987.

Poli, Francesco. "Due malati nevrastenici a Ferrara, cittametafisica." *Arte* 20, no. 209 (1990): 78-83.

Williams, Virginia Parrott. *Surrealism, Quantum Philosophy, and World War I.* New York: Garland, 1987.

Photography/Photomontage
General

Avant-Garde Photography in Germany, 1919-1939. Exhibition Catalogue. San Francisco: San Francisco Museum of Modern Art, 1980.

Dada Photographie und Photocollage. Ed. Carl-Albrecht Haenlein. Exhibition Catalogue. Hanover, Germany: Kestner-Gesellschaft, 1979.

Photomontage in Germany and Russia Following World War I. Exhibition Catalogue. Bronx, N.Y.: Bronx Museum of the Arts, 1983.

Bellony-Rewald, Alice. "Photography in Surrealist Reviews." *Art International* 5 (winter 1988): 86-96.

Edwards, Steve. "L'amour fou, photography et Surrealism." *Art History* 10 (December 1987): 509-17.

Evans, David, and Sylvia Gohl. *Photomontage: A Political Weapon.* London, 1986.

Jaguer, Edouard. *Les Mysteres de la chambre noire: Le surrealisme et la photographie.* Paris: Flammarion, 1982.

Lasalle, Honor, and Abigail Solomon-Godeau. "Surrealist Confession: Claude Cahun's Photomontages." *Afterimage* 19 (March 1992): 10-13.

Lusk, Irene-Charlotte. *Montagen ins Blaue: Laszlo Moholy-Nagy, Fotomontagen und collagen, 1922–1943*. Giessen: Anabas, 1980.
Sobieszek, R. A. "Composite Imagery and the Origins of Photomontage, Part 1: The Naturalist Strain." *Artforum* 17 (September 1978): 58–65.
––––––. "Composite Imagery and the Origins of Photomontage, Part 2: The Formalist Strain." *Artforum* 17 (October 1978): 40–45.

John Heartfield

Bunütze Foto als Waffe! John Heartfield—Fotomontagen. Exhibition Catalogue. Frankfurt am Main: 1989.
John Heartfield. Ed. Peter Pachnicke and Klaus Honnef. Exhibition Catalogue. New York: Harry N. Abrams, 1992.
Herzfelde, Wieland. *John Heartfield: Leben und Werk*. 3rd ed. Dresden: Verlag der Kunst, 1976.
––––––, et al. *Krieg im Frieden: Fotomontagen Zeit 1930-1938/John Heartfield*. 2nd rev. ed. Munich: Hanser, 1973. Translated as *Photomontages of the Nazi Period/John Heartfield* (New York: Universe Books, 1977).
Hoelterhoff, Manuela. "Heartfield's Contempt." *Artforum* 15 (1976): 58–65.
Kahn, Douglas. *John Heartfield: Art and Mass Media*. New York, 1985.
Naggar, Carole. "John Heartfield, dada-monteur." *Revue d'Esthétique* (Paris), no. 1/2 (1975): 237–43.
Scharf, Aaron. "John Heartfield, Berlin Dada, and the Weapon of Photomontage." *Studio International* 176, no. 904 (1968).
Siepmann, Eckhard. *Montage, John Heartfield: Vom club Dada zur Arbeiter Illustrierten Zeitung: Dokumente, Analysen, Berichte*. 2nd ed. Berlin: Elefanten Press Galerie, 1977.
Toteberg, Michael, ed. *John Heartfield in Selbstzeugnissen und Bilddokumenten*. Reinbek bei Hamburg: Rowoholt, 1978.

Hanna Höch

Höch, Hannah. *Hannah Höch*. Exhibition Catalogue. Berlin: Galerie Neirendorf, 1975.
––––––. *Hannah Höch: Collages, peintures, aquarelles, gouaches, desins*. Exhibition Catalogue. Paris: Musée d'art moderne de la ville de Paris, 1976.
––––––. *Hannah Höch: Fotomontagen und Gemalde*. Exhibition Catalogue. Kunsthalle Bielefeld, 1973.
––––––. *Hanna Höch: E. Leben Mit d. Pflanze*. Exhibition Catalogue. Stadtische Kunstsammlung Gelsenkirchen: Kunstsammlung, 1978.
Adriani, Götz, ed., *Hannah Höch*. Cologne: DuMont, 1980.
Pierre, José. "Hannah Höch et le photomontage des Dadaistes Berlinois." *Apeiros*, no. 69 (1974): 58–61.

Text and Typography

Cohen, Arthur A. "The Typographic Revolution: Antecedents and Legacy of Dada Graphic Design." In *Dada Spectrum: The Dialectics of Revolt*, ed. Stephen C. Foster and Rudolf Kuenzli. Iowa City: University of Iowa Press, 1979.
Drucker, Johanna Ruth. "Experimental Typography, 1909–1924, and the Representation of Language." Abstract in *Dissertation Abstracts International* 47 (1987): 2579A.
––––––. "Typographic Manipulation of the Poetic Text in the Early Twentieth-Century Avant-Garde." *Visible Language* 25 (spring 1991): 231–56.
Hubert, Renée Riese. *Word and Image* (U.K.) 4, pt. 1 (1988): 265–74.
Kafalenos, Emma. "Purification of Language: Dada and Visual Poetry." In *Visual Literature Criticism: A New Collection*, ed. Richard Kostelanetz. Carbondale: Southern Illinois University Press, 1979.
Lapacherie, Jean-Gérard. "Gras, maigre, austere (a propos d''Une nuit d'échecs gras' de Tristan Tzara)." *Mélusine*, no. 11 (1990): 207–11.
Riha, Karl. "Dada visuell: Wilde Typographie, optophonetische Poésie, Bildgedichte." *Bildene Kunst* 37, no. 11 (1989): 36–38.

Index

Library of Congress Cataloging-in-Publication Data

Melzer, Annabelle, 1940–
    Dada and surrealist performance / by Annabelle Henkin Melzer. — Johns Hopkins Paperbacks ed.
    p.   cm. — (PAJ books)
    Previously published: Latest rage the big drum. Ann Arbor, Mich. : UMI Research Press, 1980,
in series: Studies in the fine arts : Avant-garde.
    Includes bibliographical references and index.
    ISBN 0–8018-4845-8 (pbk. : acid-free paper)
    1. Theater—History—20th century. 2. Dadaism. 3. Surrealism. 4. Experimental theater.
I. Melzer, Annabelle, 1940–   Latest rage the big drum. II. Title. III. Series.
PN2189.M37   1994
792'.09'04—dc20
                                                                    94-9231
                                                                        CIP